WEXFORD CASTLES

LANDSCAPE, CONTEXT AND SETTLEMENT

Billy Colfer

CORK **CUP** UNIVERSITY PRESS

Irish Landscapes   Volume IV
Wexford Castles
Landscape, Context and Settlement

General Editors
F. H. A. Aalen
Kevin Whelan
Matthew Stout

Published in 2013
by Cork University Press
Youngline Industrial Estate
Pouladuff Road
Togher
Cork
Ireland

All photographs and illustrations are by the author
unless otherwise indicated.

British Library Cataloguing in Publication Data
A CIP catalogue record for this book is available from the British Library.

ISBN 9 78185918 4936

Printed in Italy by Printer Trento.

CONTENTS

PREFACE AND ACKNOWLEDGEMENTS

This volume reflects a long-term interest in castles of all descriptions, which must have been subliminally instilled at a young age. I grew up on the Hook Peninsula where the flat landscape was dominated by three buildings with medieval origins. The beam of the thirteenth-century Tower of Hook, the iconic symbol of the headland, illuminated my bedroom window at metronomic three-second intervals. Our house was overshadowed by the late medieval Slade Castle, the ground-floor chambers of which were used as storerooms for fishing gear. These rooms were known by names such as Hannah's, Mag Dwyer's etc., recalling former tenants who lived in the sub-divided castle, which was rented out by the Loftus Estate up to the early twentieth century.

In the late 1940s, I watched workmen carrying out conservation work on Slade Castle after the structure was taken over by the O. P. W. I may even have seen the great Harold Leask, who presumably supervised the work, as he published an extensive paper on the castle in the early 1950s. At that time, Loftus Hall, incorporating remains of the thirteenth-century Redmond Hall, was a Rosminian Convent. We went to mass in a room there, converted as a chapel by the nuns and made available to the public. The occasional four mile cycle to Kilcloggan, where we bought apples from an orchard in the shadow of the Hospitaller tower house, was also an influence.

As I broadened my horizons, these early impressions raised my awareness of medieval buildings elsewhere in the county, for example, at Ballyhack, Ferrycarrig and Ferns. This interest acquired a more informed focus when I joined the Wexford Historical Society in the late 1960s, particularly after the work of William Jeffrey on *The castles of county Wexford*, edited by Dr Ned Culleton, was published by the Society in a limited edition. The acquisition of a reproduction of Hore's six-volume *History of Wexford* was also influential.

In the 1980s and 1990s, when I eventually embarked on a structured approach to the research of medieval Anglo-Norman colonisation in the county, it became obvious that the construction castles in the county was directly related to the introduction of feudal land holding and to the eventual delimitation of the colony. The location of the county and the nature of the landscape played a fundamental role in the siting and distribution of castles and particularly of late medieval tower houses. This publication expands on that research to explore political conflict and settlement in county Wexford through the twin lenses of landscape and castle building.

I must record my gratitude for the assistance of many individuals, organisations, friends and family. I am particularly grateful to Professor Terry Barry, Trinity College Dublin, for his encouragement and guidance when I was researching medieval settlement in the county. Inevitably, this volume draws on a wide range of published work in the field of castle studies, particularly Leask's *Irish castles* and Sweetman's *Medieval castles of Ireland*. Other influential publications are acknowledged in the endnotes and bibliography. I must express a particular acknowledgement of Michael Moore's *Archaeological inventory of county Wexford*, an essential resource and an indispensable aid to fieldwork.

I wish to acknowledge the help of staff in the following institutions for assistance in sourcing information and illustrations: Wexford County Library, especially Celestine Rafferty in Local Studies; the National Library of Ireland; the National Museum of Ireland; the National Archives; the Royal Irish Academy; the Royal Society of Antiquaries; the British Library and Westminster Abbey. A special acknowledgement of photographer Con Brogan, and photo-archivist Tony Roche, N. M. S. Photographic Unit. The many individuals who allowed images to be reproduced are acknowledged beside the relevant illustrations. My appreciation is extended to all owners of tower houses who allowed access to their property.

I am fortunate in having a wide circle of friends on whom I can call on for assistance: fellow researcher on county Wexford Ned Culleton, a constant source of encouragement; Bernard Browne, always generous with his knowledge of sources and publications; Hilary Murphy for discussions on various aspects of Wexford's history; with Nicky Furlong, Hilary kept me on the right track in search of elusive tower houses; the late Tom Williams was always generous with his extensive knowledge on his native Taghmon. Thanks also to Eithne Scallan and David Rowe for advice on later houses.

I am fortunate and privileged in having the backing of two good friends in the preparation of this book: as always, the inspirational support and encouragement of Kevin Whelan, director of the Keough-Naughton Notre Dame Centre, has been a constant motivation, and the technological skill of Matthew Stout, history lecturer in my *alma mater*, St Pat's, Drumcondra, is evident in the cartography and design. A special appreciation to Con

Manning for reading an early draft of this work and for his incisive comments. The author remains exclusively responsible for the final version.

I wish also to recognise the support of many individuals: Ray Flynn, for his advice on photographic techniques; Chris Hayes, for his expertise on woodlands; Ben Murtagh, conservation archaeologist, for insights into tower houses; Kenneth Nicholls of U. C. C., for advice on references and placenames; Rory Sherlock of U. C. G., for allowing me access to his work on tower houses; Katharine Simms of T. C .D., for information on Irish castles in the bardic poems; Rolf Loeber, for illustrations including an early Dutch map; Richard Stapleton O. P. W., for plans and sections of castles; John Mannion, M. U .N., for images of Ferryland; Conchuir Ó Crualaoich, for access to his forthcoming book on Wexford placenames; Aidan Ryan, for information on Brownswood Castle; Éamonn de Búrca, for a rare image of Wexford town; Ian Doyle, for sourcing publications and illustrations; Tim O'Neill, for references and information on the Butlers; Neville Dukes, for excellent photographs in demanding conditions.

Inevitably, the work involved in the preparation of this volume demanded many hours of selfish isolation, in spite of which, as with all projects that I have undertaken, I have had the complete support of my family. A sincere thanks to Paul and Helen, Eoin and Jackie, Donal, Eamonn, Niall and Lisa. Our grand-children are acknowledged in the dedication of the volume. A special word of appreciation to my architect son, Donal for preparing castle plans and sections, and to my sons Eamonn and Niall, for photographs. As always, my wife Noreen has given me unstinted backup and encouragement and we have enjoyed many leisurely field-trips together during the preparation of this publication. Noreen has also enhanced my work by researching literary connections and references.

Finally, I wish to thank the general editors of the series, F. H. A. Aalen, Kevin Whelan and Matthew Stout for their stimulating and meticulous attention to my work, the indexer Dominic Carroll, and a special acknowledgement to my supportive publishers, Cork University Press, particularly Mike Collins and Maria O'Donovan.

FROM THE EDITORS OF *IRISH LANDSCAPES*

The original *Atlas of the Irish Rural Landscape* appeared back in 1997 at the onset of the Tiger years, and its emphasis on the vulnerability of the rural landscape struck a chord at a period of momentous transformation in Ireland. The second edition appeared in 2011, and offered an opportunity to reflect seriously on the massive changes that had swept through the landscape in the intervening years. Both editions emphasised that landscapes, history in slow motion, formed a complex reef of the collective experiences of Irish generations across time and space. The *Atlas* team highlighted the cumulative ways in which the Irish landscape had evolved as a shared creation of myriad generations. Czeslaw Milosz says, contemplating the Issa valley in Lithuania, where he grew up:

> For the threads spun by our ancestors do not perish,
> they are preserved; we alone among living creatures
> have a history, we move in a gigantic labyrinth
> where the present and the past are interwoven. That
> labyrinth protects and consoles us.

The *Atlas* sought to create a different way of balancing text, maps and images. Rather than the images and maps being derivative and decorative, the aim was to integrate them as the central organising framework, and then weave the text around them seamlessly. Achieving the appropriate blend required a highly flexible design template. We also sought to provide long captions where necessary, explaining in detail what the images and maps actually show. The *Atlas* aimed at a prose style that was elegant, intelligent and accessible. It also sought to find ways to include the necessary supporting documentation in ways that were unobtrusive to the smooth flow of the pages. All this required a massively intrusive editorial intervention, and exceptionally patient contributors. Cork University Press proved to be generous and tolerant in supporting this process, and in producing a scholarly book with coffee-table standards of colour reproduction and design.

The amazing reception of the original *Atlas* (it sold over 20,000 copies) encouraged the editors to embark on the Irish Landscapes series – inaugurated by Geraldine Stout's *Newgrange and the Bend of the Boyne* (2002), followed by Billy Colfer's *The Hook Peninsula* (2004), and *Wexford: a town and its landscape* (2008). These volumes encapsulated the thematic concerns of both editions of the *Atlas of rural Ireland*: the landscape as a dynamic interchange between nature and culture; the variety of regional landscapes as a reflection of cultural diversity, the challenge to the inherited landscape by pervasive development, and the need for interventions to modulate in sympathy with the inherited landscape.

Billy Colfer's *Wexford Castles* expands the series by taking a thematic approach, while still staying loyal to the central landscape focus. Rather than adapting a narrowly architectural approach, he situates these buildings in a superbly reconstructed historical, social, and cultural milieu. County Wexford has three strikingly different regions – the Anglo-Norman south, the hybridised middle and the Gaelic north – which render it a remarkable version *in parvo* of the wider island. His wide-angle lens takes in so much more than the castles themselves, as he ranges broadly and deeply in reading these striking buildings as texts, revealing the cultural assumptions and historical circumstances which shaped them.

In this most cosmopolitan of counties, we traverse far and wide in search of the wide-spreading roots of its cultural landscape – from the Crusades and the Mani peninsula in Greece to the Bristol Channel, from Crac des Chevaliers to Westminster, from the Viking north and the green Atlantic to the blue Mediterranean south. The book breaks new ground in looking at the long-run cultural shadow cast by the Anglo-Normans and their castles, as this appears in the Gothic Revival, in the poetry of Yeats and in the surprisingly profuse crop of Wexford historians and writers.

While most books on a single architectural form can end up visually monotonous, creativity has been lavished on this volume in terms of keeping the images varied, fresh and constantly appealing. The result is a sympathetic and innovative treatment of the castles, understood not just as a mere architectural form, but as keys to unlocking the *mentalité* of those who lived in them. *Wexford Castles: landscape, context and settlement* is a worthy conclusion to Billy's Colfer's superb trilogy of landscape studies.

F. H. A. Aalen, Matthew Stout, Kevin Whelan

For our grandchildren, Finn, Seán, Grace, Jeremy and Joe

A Warning
to Conquerors

This is the country of the
  Norman tower
The graceless keep, the
  bleak and slitted eye
Where fear drove comfort
  out; straw on the floor
Was price of conquering
  security.

They came and won, and
  then for centuries
Stood to their arms; the face
  grew bleak and
  lengthened
In the night vigil, while
  their foes at ease
Sang of the strangers and
  the towers they
  strengthened.

Ragweed and thistle hold
  the Norman field
And cows the hall where
  Gaelic never rang
Melodiously to harp or
  spinning-wheel.
Their songs are spent now
  with the voice that sang;

And lost their conquest.
  This soft land quietly
Engulfed them like the
  Saxon and the Dane
But kept the jutted brow,
  the slitted eye
Only the faces and the
  names remain.

Donagh MacDonagh

Slade Castle

WEXFORD

LEWIS, TOPOGRAPHICAL DICTIONARY, 1837

CARLOW

WICKLOW

Crosspatrick
Part of Kilpipe
Killinor
Coolgreany
Killahurler Hill
Conna Hill
Inch
Clonegal
Part of Moyacomb
Johnstown
Part of Carnew
Kilmichael Point Floating Light
Kilgorman
Kilnehue
Kilcavan Hill
Slievebawn
Lavnboy
Clonilla
Kilkevan
Tara Hill
NEWTOWN BARRY
Kilrush
Giblit Hill
Slievegower
Rossmanogue
Leskinfere
Ballytrought Hill
Ballyfadogh
Gorey
Killtennel
Courtown Harbour
Mount Leinster
Clohamen Bridge
Slievebuy Hill
Tomb
Camolin
Kilcormic
Ballycannow
Ardamine
Poolshone Head
Black Stairs
Kilthomas Hill
FERNS
River Bann
Kilbride
Carrickrew
Ballenagh
Donaghmore
Glassourrick Point
Templeshanbo
Glanamoin Hill
Clone
Schrawalsh Bridge
WALSH
Kiltrisk
Gahore Point
Ballycarney
Ballydungan
Black Water
Monomolin
River Slaney
Kilcormuck
Kilnemanagh
Monart
Tomahanon
Oulart Hill
Oulart
Kilmuckridge
Killan
Ballyhiland
ENNISCORTHY
Melina
Killancooly
Templescobin
St Johns
Ballyhuskard
Castle Ellis
Ballyvaldon
Rossdroit
Ber Hill
Edermine
Killesk
Blackwater
Killeigney
Clonroche
Chapple
Clonmore
Oyl Gate
Kilmalog
Ballyvaloo
Temple Udigan
Kilcowanmore
Ballyheogue
St Nicholas
Skreen
Killew
Ballyane
Clonleigh
Camorus Hill
Ballagh
Rahconohown
Donowney
Ballymaslaney
Old Ross
Lacken
Adamstown
Crossabeg
Artramont
Castle Bridge
St Margarets
NEW ROSS
Carrickburn Hill
Killarin
Chapel Chason
Tickillin
Ardcolme
Big Erin
Great I.
Raven Point
Corbet Hill
White Church Glyn
Kilpatrick
Ardcavan
Roslare Point
Crutch Hill
Kilscanlan
Kilbride
WEXFORD HAVEN
WEXFORD BAY
Park Hill
Newbawn
Ardcandridge
Carrigg
St Little
Slievekieller
Carnagh
Kilgarven
TAGHMON
John St
WEXFORD
Maudittown
Talloraght
Inch
SHELMALIER
St Peter
St Michael
Killilogue
Sand Hills
White Church
Ballybrazill
Fookesmills
Floretown
Coolstuffe
Forth Mountain
Drinagh
Ballyingly
Kilmokea
Killeck
Clongeen
Ballymitty
Rathaspeck
Killiane
Dunbrody
Kilmannan
Kildavan
Kilmocree
Rathroe
Ballylannan
Ambrosetown
Rathmacknee
SHELBURNE
Clonmines
Kileavan
Ballyconnick
Ballybrennan
St Michael
Killinick
Killiane
Ballyhack
Danes Castle
Baldwinstown
Maglass
Kilscoran
Ramsgrange
Carrick
BARGY
Mulrankin
Ballymore
Ishartmon
Tintern
Duncormuck
Kilcoan
Bridge
Tingoat
St Helen
Greenore Point
St James
Arthurs Town
Kill Mills
Killag
Tombaggard
Ibernus
St Margarets
Carne
Grassienton Point
Tucker Rock Light House
Fetherd
Selskery
Kerce Isles
LOUGH
Kilturk
Tacumshane
Church Town
Lady's Island
Saltoe
Duncannon
Templetown
BALLYTEIGUE BAY
Kilmore
Tacumshan Lough
Carnesore Point
Vinnard Point
Bagenbon Head
Crossfarnogue Point
HOUSELAND BAY
SLADE BAY
Hook
Slade
Hook Tower, Light House
Hook Head
St Patrick's Bridge
Saltee Islands
Coninmore Coningbeg Floating Light

KILKENNY
BANTRY
WATERFORD
WATERFORD HARBOUR
BANNOW BAY

ST GEORGES CHANNEL

SCALE OF IRISH MILES
0   5   10

SCALE OF ENGLISH MILES
0   5   10

7° Longitude West from Greenwich

LOCATION AND LANDSCAPE

This analysis of castle building, and of tower houses in particular, is focused on county Wexford in the south-east of Ireland. In the early medieval period, the county (with parts of counties Wicklow and Carlow) formed the minor Gaelic kingdom of Uí Chennselaig. The boundaries of newly created dioceses, established during the twelfth-century reform movement in the Irish church, corresponded to existing units of secular power.[1] The twelfth-century territorial extent of Uí Chennselaig is best represented by the diocese of Ferns, ratified in 1111 as one of five Leinster dioceses at the Synod of Rathbreasail .[2] Some of the rural deaneries in the diocese corresponded to the internal divisions (trícha cét) in the kingdom.[3] The maps used throughout this work show the county boundary with the pre-reclamation coastline as well as the approximate extent of the Gaelic kingdom. The territory of Uí Chennselaig was advantageously located adjacent to the shipping lanes of the Irish and Celtic Seas and within relatively short sea-crossings of Britain and the continent. This stimulated reciprocal sea borne contacts, particularly with Wales, which inevitably fostered cultural cross-pollination.

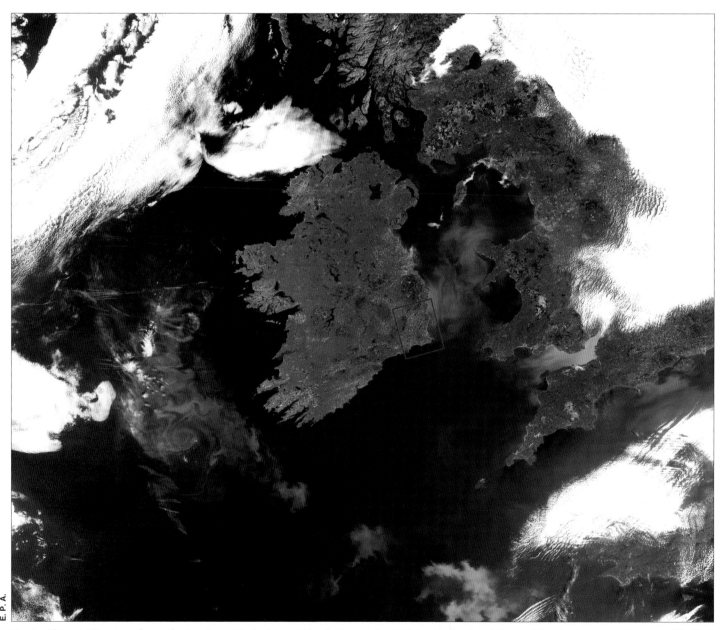

E. P. A.

Fig. 1   This satellite view shows the location of Ireland in relation to the coasts of Wales, England and France. The short sea crossings gave Wexford ports an advantage, particularly when trading with Wales and the Bristol Channel, allowing the south-east to flourish as a hub of trade and commerce.

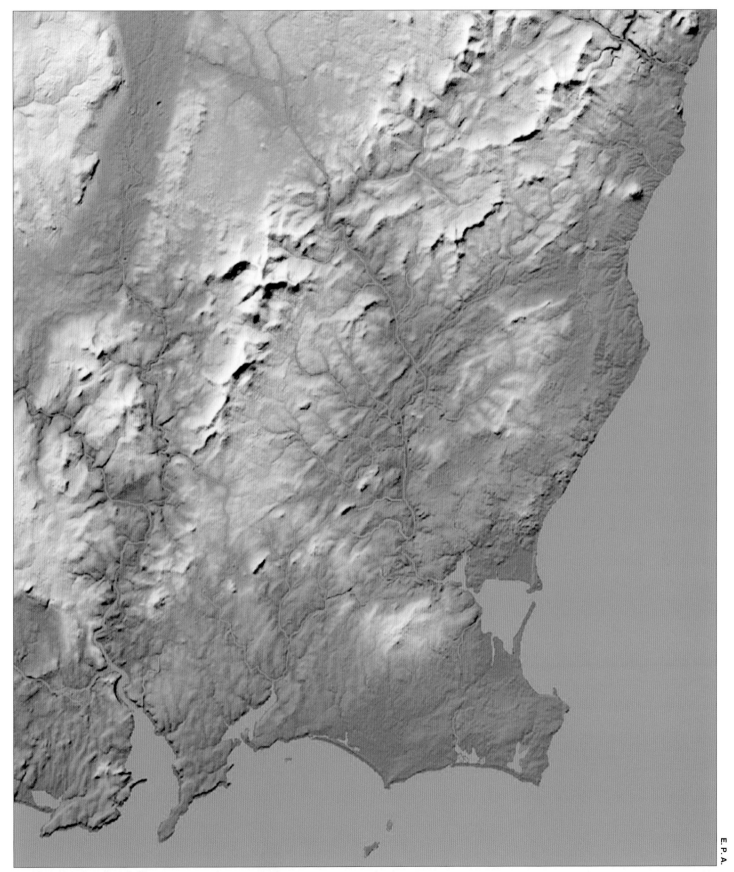

E.P.A.

Fig. 2   This close-up satellite image captures the varied nature of county Wexford's landscape, river valleys and coastline. The uplands of the north and north-west provide a striking contrast to the lowlands of the south and east. The mountains, with the valley and estuary of the Barrow and Nore, form a barrier which effectively isolates the county, creating a distinctive geographical unit, bisected diagonally by the river Slaney.

Fig. 3   The rolling fertile landscape of north Wexford, with the Blackstairs Mountains in the background forming the border between the counties of Wexford and Carlow. The pale grey granite of the Blackstairs was formed by up-flowing molten magma 400 million years ago.

GEOLOGY AND LANDSCAPE

The potential of the maritime location was reduced by the inaccessible nature of the coastline, which consisted mostly of sandy beaches with very few natural harbours, compounded by treacherous offshore rocks and sandbanks. Similarily, the shallow, tortuous estuaries of Loch Garman (later Wexford) and Bannow presented challenges to seafarers. The difficult access to the estuary of Port Lairge (later Waterford) was emphasised by the erection of a thirteenth-century light-tower on the point of Hook. In the ninth and tenth centuries, these navigational problems were overcome by the skilful Scandinavian mariners who established the settlements which became the towns of Wexford and Waterford and who also named many of the county's coastal features. In the late twelfth century, proximity to Wales encouraged the landing of the first groups of Anglo-Normans on the south Wexford coast, an event that would resonate throughout subsequent Irish history. The medieval liberty of Wexford which they created was slightly larger than the modern county and is best represented by the diocese of Ferns.

County Wexford, a well-defined geographical unit, is insulated from the rest of Ireland by natural features. It is bounded on the south and east by the sea; on the west by Waterford Harbour, the river Barrow and the Blackstairs

Mountains, and on the north by the Wicklow Mountains. Routeways through the mountain barrier are confined to gaps along the east coast at Arklow, along the Slaney at Bunclody and along the Barrow valley through the Pollmounty Gap at St Mullins. Secondary routes traverse the Wicklow Mountains at Carnew and the Wicklow Gap, and the Blackstairs through the Scullogue Gap. The landscape of the county, shaped by geological forces and the Ice Ages, includes several distinctive topographical regions.[4] Most of the county consists of a lowland plain,

Fig. 4   Wexford's south and east coasts are comprised primarily of sandy beaches, similar to the one shown here near Lady's Island. The soft shoreline is vulnerable to extensive coastal erosion, particularly along the east coast where there is a deep deposit of glacial drift.

Fig. 5   A view from Slievecoiltia over the lowlands of Forth and Bargy, from Carnsore (left), to Bannow, with the Saltee Islands in the distance.

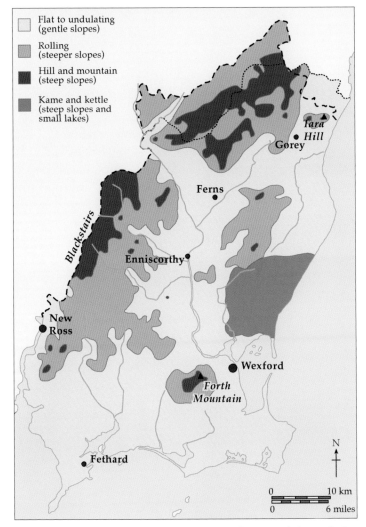

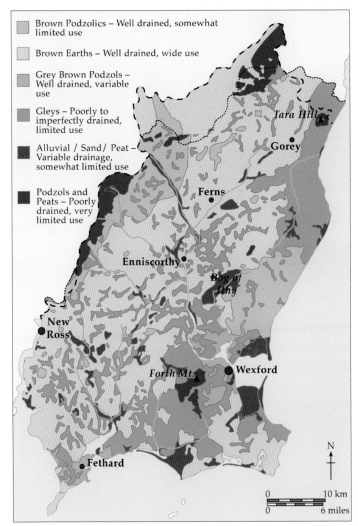

Fig. 6   County Wexford's varying landscapes determined the evolution of settlement in the medieval period. The Anglo-Normans targeted the lowlands of the south and east and the fertile central region, with the Irish initially confined to the wooded uplands of the west and north.

Fig. 7   Soil quality exerted a decisive influence on settlement after the arrival of the Anglo-Normans. Good quality soils were most desirable for arable economy on the manors. The productive land in the northern half of the county was eventually reclaimed by the Irish.

Fig. 8   The Derry river (shown here at Tomnafinnoge Wood near Shillelagh) flows in a south-westerly direction in south County Wicklow and joins the Slaney near Clonegal. The Derry was a natural boundary for the liberty of Wexford, forming part of the northern limits of the parishes of Carnew and Crosspatrick, which were included in the medieval liberty and diocese. Both parishes were divided by the creation of the early seventeenth-century county boundary. The name of the river (from the Irish doire: oak) recalls the oak forest that formerly covered south Wicklow and north Wexford.

Fig. 9 The rock-bound coastline of the Hook presents a sharp contrast to the rest of Wexford's littoral, which consists mostly of clay cliffs and sandy beaches. The underlying limestone rock has resisted the action of the sea for millennia, leading to the formation of the distinctive low-lying peninsula.

under 80m in height. This plain covers the south of the county and occupies a large area in the centre and east, bisected by the Slaney valley. The underlying rocks are mainly shales and slates which are between 400 to 600 million years old, with some limestone and sandstone. The plain is punctuated by a line of volcanic hills running diagonally across the county, the most prominent being Carrigbyrne, Bree, Vinegar Hill and Tara Hill. About 400 million years ago, molten magma formed the granite of the Blackstairs Mountains along the western border of the county; the shale uplands in the north-west date to the same period.

During the Ice Ages, at least two glaciers moved across county Wexford between 150,000 and 15,000 years ago.[5] One came from the midlands, bringing with it large blocks of granite from the Blackstairs, which were deposited across the Wexford landscape. The ice carried with it glacial drift or till, consisting of particles of all sizes, ranging from large boulders to fine clay. This till was deposited over the rocks, in various depths depending on the underlying geology, filling up depressions and levelling the landscape.

The unique 'kame and kettle' landscape on the east coast, just north of Wexford Harbour, is composed of sand and gravel deposited by another ice sheet, which pushed in from the Irish Sea 25,000 years ago. The depressions between the rolling sandhills, or 'kames', contain many small lakes known as 'kettles'. The abundance of sand and gravel was laid down by glacial streams or by melting ice as the temperature rose. Glacial meltwaters cut several spectacular channels in the county, including Mulmontry,

O.S.I.

Fig. 10 The layer of sand and gravel deposited north of Wexford Harbour during the last Ice Age was converted by the action of the ice into low sand hills (kames) and hollows (kettles), many of them flooded. This unique landscape is one of the finest Irish examples of kame and kettle.

north of Taghmon; at Taylorstown at the head of Bannow Bay; on the Slaney at Ferrycarrig and at Pollmounty, north of New Ross. The Mulmontry gorge is of particular relevance, as it defined the northern limit of the Wexford Pale in the late medieval period.

The most crucial legacy of the Ice Age in the county was the nutrient-rich glacial deposits from which a complex pattern of soils was formed. The most fertile soils, with a wide use-range, occur mostly in the band of rolling lowland which extends diagonally across the county from south-west to north-east, with another significant area in the baronies of Forth and Bargy.[6] The nature of the landscape, and particularly soil quality, exerted a decisive influence on the evolution of settlement, as the fertile soils were obviously most desirable. This is demonstrated by the distribution of ringforts, the typical early medieval farmstead, which are concentrated on the well-drained, fertile soils in the west of the county. Similarly, after the arrival of the Anglo-Normans, the best land was reserved for high-status grantees. For example, the demesne manors of Ferns, Ross and Taghmon, all on good quality land, were retained by the lord of Leinster.

In the pre-Norman period, the present county (with parts of counties Wicklow and Carlow) formed the Gaelic kingdom of Uí Chennselaig, which was divided into ten trícha cét (thirty hundreds), each occupied by a distinctive sub-group.[7] The twelfth-century territorial extent of the kingdom of Uí Chennselaig is best represented by the diocese of Ferns,[8] as the present county boundary was not established until 1605.[9] The Mac Murchada dynasty emerged as kings of Uí Chennselaig and Diarmait Mac Murchada succeeded in establishing himself as king of Leinster in the twelfth century. In 1166, his enemies marched on the Mac Murchada power-base at Ferns and Diarmait was defeated. Determined to recover his kingdom, he recruited Anglo-Norman mercenaries from south Wales, lured to Ireland by promises of land.[10]

After their arrival on the south Wexford coast, they quickly reverted to type and exploited the fractured nature of Irish society to seize and occupy territory, resulting in the introduction of feudal landholding and the building of castles. The incomplete nature of the conquest was followed by centuries of conflict in which the landscape played a leading role. The partial colonisation of the lowlands of county Wexford left the native Irish in control of the woods and mountains of the west and north. After a century of relative peace, the Irish emerged under the leadership of the Mac Murchada and, following centuries of struggle, the English settlers were slowly pushed back and confined to a southern enclave defined and protected by topographic features. The distribution of earthwork and stone castles, both offensive and defensive, charted the ebb and flow of the colonists' presence in the landscape over three centuries of conflict, as well as their ultimate retreat to the south.

CONTINENTAL CONNECTIONS

Using county Wexford as a case study, this volume examines the impact of the European feudal model of landscape organisation and political administration, which was imposed by the Anglo-Normans after their initial incursions in 1169–1170. The building of castles as a means of dominating and settling conquered territory was an integral component of the Norman *modus operandi*. The progress of the colony, and the response of the Irish, is examined through the lens of surviving colonial military architecture. These structures, including mottes, stone castles and later tower houses, were derived from the lexicon of European architecture, adapted to suit regional needs and conditions.[1] The Irish tradition of castle building can be placed in a broader context by addressing chronology, typology, distribution and social context.

The introduction of feudalism was by no means the first example of continental influences affecting Ireland, including, in earlier times, the local interpretation of universal fortifications such as hilltop and promontory forts. Although Ireland, 'an island behind an island', might be regarded as remote from the European mainland for neolithic mariners, this was not the case, as the sea facilitated contact rather than preventing it. Seafaring communities undertook long voyages, hugging the shoreline and crossing the open sea only when they had to.

These contacts can be identified as far back as the fourth millennium BC, when the magnificent megalithic passage graves of the Boyne valley were inspired by similar (but older) monuments along the Atlantic coast of Europe, particularly in Portugal and Brittany. The megalithic art at Newgrange was inspired by passage tomb art in Brittany and Iberia.[2] The smaller neolithic portal tombs (known as dolmens) also had a wide continental distribution. In county Wexford, an impressive example survives at Ballybrittas on the slopes of Bree Hill.[3]

R.S.A.I.

Fig. 1   Neolithic portal tombs (also known as dolmens) were originally covered by a mound or cairn. They were extensively used in Ireland, particularly in the north and south-east, but with a wider continental distribution. They consisted of a chamber entered between two portal stones and covered by a massive capstone. The fine monument shown here in a mid nineteenth-century drawing is located at Ballybrittas on the slopes of Bree Hill, the only surviving example in county Wexford. It is now obscured by injudicious planting which should be removed.

Fig. 2 This triple spiral motif from the north-west recess at Newgrange is acknowledged as the finest example of megalithic art in Europe. It has been widely adopted as a national symbol of Irishness.

THE PREHISTORIC ERA

The occurrence of spearheads and swords in the archaeological record show that the late Bronze Age (c. 900–600 BC) was marked by political turbulence. During this era, hilltop forts, found throughout Europe, were built in Ireland, suggesting that an elite class controlled the landscape from their elevated strongholds.[4] An impressive hillfort survives at Rathgall, in south county Wicklow, dating to c. 1000 BC, where evidence has been found for the manufacture of weapons. The 7.5 hectare fort has four circular ramparts. A fifth inner stone enclosure was possibly built in the medieval period, when Rathgall may have been occupied by the Irish of the Wicklow mountains.[5] Smaller univallate examples survive at Ballybuckley and Courthoyle in county Wexford.[6]

From the mid-fifth century BC, a Celtic Iron Age civilisation emerged in central Europe and spread from the Black Sea to the Atlantic, reaching Ireland around the third century BC. On the continent, this La Tène culture, named after a site in Switzerland rich in archaeological deposits, was eventually overrun by the Roman empire but the 'insular Celts' survived in Ireland and parts of the Atlantic fringe for many centuries longer. La Tène sites are concentrated in the northern part of the island while hilltop forts continued in use in the south, where the La Tène impact was less pervasive.[7]

Overseas trade expanded during the first centuries AD, with increased communication on both sides of the

Irish sea. Archaeological finds demonstrate contact with the Roman world. At the end of the first century AD, the Roman historian Tacitus wrote of Ireland: 'the interior parts are little known, but through commercial intercourse and the merchants there is better knowledge of the harbours and approaches'. Coastal promontory forts, also found along other parts of the Atlantic fringe, were constructed by building defensive earthworks across the necks of cliff-bound headlands to provide security at landing places. Five defended coastal fortifications associated with this period are located in county Wexford.[8] The siting of three of them on the shores of Waterford Harbour (originally Port Lairge or Cumar na dTrí nUisce) emphasise the importance of the estuary as a trading centre. Extensive ramparts exist at Nook, just north of Ballyhack, and a minor site on the cliff at

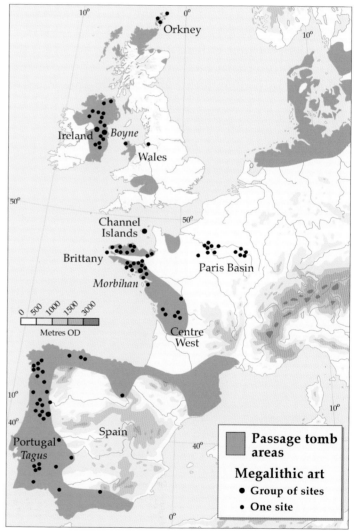

Fig. 3 The locations of fourth-millenium BC passage tombs show that the Irish examples, including Newgrange, Knowth and Dowth, were part of a much wider European phenomenon. The concentrations on the Atlantic fringe, particularly in Ireland, Brittany and Portugal, is a clear indication that the tomb builders had the knowledge and technology to undertake long voyages, bringing their tradition of tomb-building with them.

CON BROGAN, NMSPU

Fig. 4 An impressive hillfort survives at Rathgall in south county Wicklow. Human presence on the hilltop begins as early as the fourth millennium BC. After a long period of abandonment, the site was reoccupied in the Bronze Age between 1300 and 900 BC. The 7.5 hectare fort with its five concentric ramparts has yielded extensive proof for Bronze Age activity. The central stone enclosure was built in the late medieval period, presumably by the Irish of the Wicklow mountains, to be used as a fortress in their constant resistance against the English incursion.

Templetown is also classified as a promontory fort. Although no earthworks survive, the Irish name of the rocky headland of Duncannon (Conan's fort), now occupied by a Tudor military fort, is a strong indication that it was fortified during the Iron Age period. On the east coast of the Hook peninsula, where the headland of Baginbun sheltered an excellent natural harbour, extensive remains of the promontory fort, originally called Dún Domhnaill (Domhnall's fort), can still be seen. The other site in county Wexford is at Pollshone, where a headland is defended by banks and fosses, on the east coast just south of Courtown.[9]

Christianity was by far the most transformative import from the Roman world into Ireland. As well as widespread cultural implications, the architecture associated with the new religion added new elements to the landscape. The adoption of European monasticism promoted numerous monastic foundations, usually defined by circular enclosures. One hundred and fifty-nine Early Medieval ecclesiastical sites have been identified in county Wexford,

including notable examples at Ferns in the north, Taghmon in the south and Kilmokea on Inis Teimle (now known as Greatisland) on the Barrow.[10] Many settlements

CON BROGAN NMSPU

Fig. 5 The surviving hillfort at Courthoyle, on the slopes of Carrigbyrne Hill, a fortification type found throughout Europe, is a good example of a late Bronze Age occupation site, which provided protection for the elite in Irish society and enabled them to dominate the landscape.

Fig. 6 Coastal promontory forts are concentrated in western Europe, suggesting a shared building tradition. Archaeological evidence in Ireland indicates their use as trading centres with the Roman world.

Fig. 7 In the early centuries AD, coastal promontory forts associated with trading activities were constructed around Europe's Atlantic fringe. A fine example at Baginbun, formerly known as Dún Domhnaill, can be seen in south-west Wexford, on the eastern shore of the Hook peninsula.

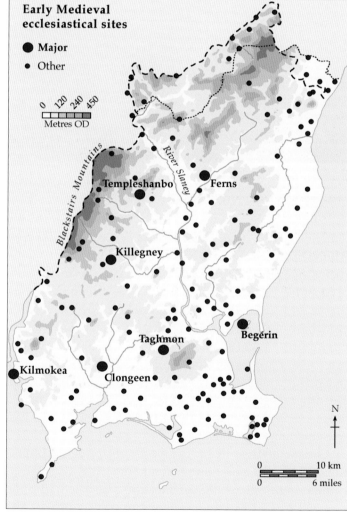

Fig. 8 The arrival of Christianity in Ireland in the fifth century prompted the establishment of numerous monastic foundations, usually defined by circular enclosures. Over 150 have been identified in county Wexford, some identified by the prefix 'Kil', meaning a church (cill). Many of these early churches were adopted as parish centres following the creation of a parochial structure in the medieval period.

associated with these sites became manorial and parochial centres following the feudal colonisation imposed by the Anglo-Normans. This resulted in impressive continuity of occupation, especially in the south of the county where tower houses were built at manorial centres in the fifteenth and sixteenth centuries.

Irish monasteries enjoyed symbiotic links with the continental Christianity from which they had emerged. From the sixth century onwards, monks from Ireland launched pilgrimages throughout Europe and established foundations in England, France, Belgium, Germany, Switzerland, Austria and Italy. Luxeuil in France and Bobbio in Italy were among the most famous.[11] By the seventh century, the principal Irish monasteries were centres of learning and artistic excellence. Skilled craftsmen produced metalwork adorned with intricate Celtic motifs; stonemasons decorated high crosses with biblical scenes, while scribes

GILLIAN BARRETT

Fig. 9   Kilmokea (Cill Machethe) monastic enclosure, defined by the circular enclosure in the foreground, was located on the island of Inis Teimle (now Greatisland and no longer insular due to land reclamation). Strategically situated at the head of Waterford Harbour, and at the confluence of the Barrow, Nore and Suir, the monastery's vulnerable location attracted Viking raids on several occasions. The Island became an important manorial centre in the Anglo-Norman period, with a chartered borough and early stone castle. The diamond-shaped field at left centre marks a moated site from this period.

reproduced copies of the gospels in exquisite manuscripts such as the Book of Kells.[12]

Settlement sites from the Early Medieval period are marked by over 47,000 circular enclosures, the commonest monument in the Irish landscape. These are divided into several categories with variable defensive capabilities. The most common was the ráth or ringfort, usually with earthen banks, the defended farmstead of the period.[13] The designation dún indicates a high-status, fortified site. Stone cashels (from the Latin *castellum*, a fort) and cahers, typically found in the western half of the island, also enjoyed considerable defensive capabilities.[14] The locations of these settlement sites, particularly ráth and dún, are frequently recorded as placename elements.

R. I. A.

Fig. 10   A cross-inscribed boulder and cross-slab from the monastic site of Begerin, located on an island (now reclaimed) in Wexford Harbour. The objects were drawn by G. V. Du Noyer in the mid-nineteenth century.

Fig. 11   A bivallate ringfort in the townland of Monacahee near Ramsgrange, reused as the site for the medieval church of Rathroe. The curvature of the road around the site indicates a contemporary origin.

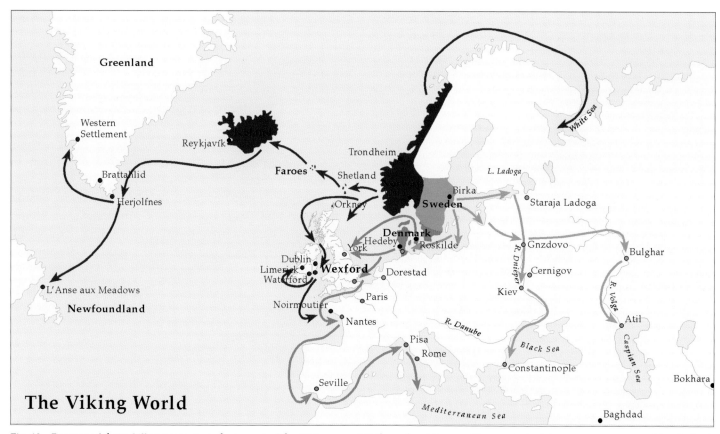

Fig. 12   Because of their skill as navigators, the impact of the Vikings was felt throughout Europe. They undertook long sea voyages, reaching Iceland, Greenland and Newfoundland. Ireland's central location in the Viking world made it a crucial staging point for their expeditions.

Ireland escaped the worst of the 'barbarian' invasions that devastated Europe during the eighth century.[15] However, for three centuries, beginning at the end of the eighth century, western Europe, including Ireland, was subjected to attacks by marauding sea-raiders from Scandinavia in search of plunder.[16] They were known by various names but are now generally described as Vikings (so called from their habit of lurking in the vikr, or inlets) or Norsemen, as those who reached Ireland were mainly from the region now known as Norway.

The background to the Viking raids is obscure but they were facilitated by the innovative design of excellent shallow-draught sailing ships, which brought the rest of Europe within easy reach of Scandinavian sailors. Monastic centres, with their concentrations of people, valuables and food, were tempting targets, especially those situated near the coastline and on navigable rivers.

Viking activity in Loch Garman was first recorded in 819. The monastery on Begerin was attacked,[17] beginning an association with the harbour which persisted for four centuries. This was followed by raids on the monastery of Kilmokea on Inis Teimle on the Barrow about 820.[18] Attacks on Taghmon and St Mullins are recorded for 824–5[19] and at the same period the Norse were defeated

by Cairbre, king of Uí Chennselaig, aided by the community of Taghmon,[20] while further Viking raids targeted Ferns in 835 and 839.[21]

By the middle of the ninth century, the Norsemen were establishing fortified coastal and riparian bases, which the Irish called 'longphort' (ship ports). The first mention of a base in Uí Chennselaig was in 888 when the Norse of Port

ROSKILDE VIKING SHIP MUSEUM

Fig. 13   In 2007, this 30m replica Viking longboat, named the *Sea Stallion from Glendalough*, sailed from Denmark to Dublin to mark the historic link between the two countries. The wreck of the original ship, built in Dublin in the mid-eleventh century, was found in Roskilde fiord.

Lairge (Waterford Harbour), Loch Garman (Wexford Harbour) and St Mullins were defeated by the Irish.[22] The principal settlements, including Weisfiord (Wexford), located on river estuaries, became bustling trading ports protected by town walls.[23] From the mid-tenth century, the Vikings mutated from raiders to traders, and they exerted their greatest impact on Ireland as merchants from their port towns of Dublin, Wexford, Waterford, Cork and Limerick.[24] Strategically placed at the centre of the Viking sphere of activity, Ireland was incorporated into the Viking trading network throughout Europe and the north Atlantic world.

Although Ireland interacted extensively with the continent over the millennia, and continued to engage with Europe in the twelfth century,[25] its remote insularity resulted in a marked divergence from what was regarded as the core European 'norm'. This difference was principally related to what was perceived as a primitive social and political structure in Ireland and the need to align religious observance with orthodox European practice.[26] This view was based on an outdated notion of Ireland, as aspects of its society were already evolving towards the European feudal model by the twelfth century.[27] Discord generated by complex dynastic alliances, described as 'the birth-pangs of a new feudalism', generated endemic violence, with the building of fortresses, the use of war fleets and the employment of Norman mercenaries.[28]

By the twelfth century, in contrast to the previous exalted reputation of Irish Christianity, the Church in Ireland was regarded by Rome as decadent, disobedient and in need of reorganisation. This Roman reform agenda precipitated the papal bull of 1155, known as *Laudabiliter*, which conferred approval for political intervention by Henry II in Ireland.[29] The stereotyping of peoples on the fringes of Europe by commentators at the 'core', who regarded themselves as representing civilised society, resulted in the Irish being categorised as barbarians and pagans.[30] This arrogant attitude of conquering an 'inferior' people for their own good was used to justify the colonial conquest of the Irish by the Anglo-Normans at the end of the twelfth century.[31]

CASTLES IN EUROPE

The castellation of Ireland in the late medieval period represented the expansion of a process that began in Europe several centuries earlier in response to the emergence of feudalism. The disintegration of the Carolingian empire in the ninth century prompted a state of perpetual war, brought about both by internal conflict and invasions from abroad. Vikings from the north, Magyars from the east and Saracens from the south plundered the coasts and raided the heartlands. This harsh and dangerous environment wreaked havoc on political and monastic structures and precipitated the collapse of central authority. Out of this violent dissolution of older political structures, the system now known as feudalism evolved, described as 'the rigorous subjection of a host of humble folk to a few powerful men'. The feudal system, which privatised nearly all aspects of government, consolidated earlier structures to create an unequal, highly efficient society, combining extraction of revenues from the land with the right to exercise authority.[1]

Protection of the rural populace in the fragments of Carolingian Gaul devolved upon regional lords who built castles without official approval and attracted the support of professional fighting men, known as knights, specialising in combat on horseback. The knight as the vassal of his lord was granted a manor or 'fief', held in return for military service.[2] The fortresses constructed by these local lords became centres of population as dependent peasants in need of protection were attracted to live and work in close proximity to them. The creation of a feudal military network was followed by the organisation of the area through rural and urban settlement. Monasteries also offered security and encouraged re-settlement in frontier situations.[3]

Across Europe, a small elite band of aristocrats dominated and exploited the labours of the peasantry; some were laymen trained in warfare, others were clerics and monks, avowedly literate and celibate.[4] Society became unevenly divided into three orders, considered to be the fundamental pillars of civil life: *oratores* (those who prayed), *bellatores* (those who fought) and *laboratores* (those who worked).[5] The building of castles as a focal point by local magnates was a common feature of feudalism, not only for their military capabilities but also as centres of administration and visible authority.[6]

BAYEUX TAPESTRY

Fig. 1   The motte castle became the symbol of the feudal lord. The late eleventh-century Bayeux Tapestry, created to celebrate the Norman invasion of England, depicts several motte-and-bailey castles. This illustration of an attack by the Normans on the castle of Dinan in Brittany shows a typical mound or motte, surrounded by a bank and ditch, with a timber tower on top protected by a stockade. Access to the mound is by a steep ladder crossing the ditch from the bailey. The vulnerability of the wooden fortifications to fire is indicated by the torches carried by two of the attacking group.

Fig. 2 From earliest times, natural strong points on cliff-top and mountain were fortified as places of refuge throughout Europe. The settlements that grew up around them frequently survive as towns in the landscape. The 'perched villages' of Provence, precariously located on cliff-top sites in the south-east of France, provide spectacular examples.

CASTLES

Castles (from the Latin *castrum* or *castellum*; a fortified place), are described as 'large buildings, or group of buildings protected by fortifications'. They have been built in Europe throughout history by people seeking security and protection.[7] In France, fortifications of every kind were called 'castles', including walled towns, ecclesiastical precincts and castellated mansions, descending in scale to temporary earthworks and campaign forts. Even the defensive platform on the bow of a ship was known as the forecastle (now shortened to fo'c's'le), the crew's quarters under the forward deck.[8] Natural strong points were frequently chosen and strengthened with man-made defences. The chaos caused by ninth-century invasions stimulated the construction of unauthorised rural fortresses, which 'enabled their owners, constantly occupied with quarrels and massacres, to protect themselves from their enemies, to triumph over their opponents and to oppress their inferiors'.[9]

Before the construction of feudal castles in medieval Europe, fortresses were already ancient in China, Mesopotamia, Greece and Rome.[10] However, the encastellation of Europe, in the tenth, eleventh and twelfth centuries was of fundamental military and political significance. Compared to earlier strongholds,

Fig. 3 A contemporary illustration of a Saracen on horseback raiding in Europe, with town defences in the background.

these small, high castles, capable of being defended by a few, represented a technical innovation. Height could be gained by building on a natural high point; when this was not available, it was created artificially. The most common early fortresses were the motte-and-bailey castles, wooden towers built on mounds (motte), surrounded by a ditch and often accessed by a bridge, with a fortified stockade (bailey) attached. The building

Fig. 4 This medieval image portrays the three principal orders that were regarded as the fundamental components of feudal life: *oratores* (who prayed), *bellatores* (who fought) and *laboratores* (who worked).

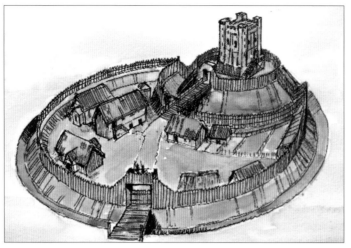

Fig. 5   A reconstruction drawing of a motte-and-bailey castle, showing the lord's tower on the motte with ancillary buildings in the bailey.

Fig. 7   The stone castle at Gisors, in Normandy, associated with the Knights Templars, is constructed on the mound of an earlier motte castle.

of a motte castle in the north of France was described in *c.* 1130.[11] As the residence of the lord, the tower on the motte signified lordship, while the enclosure or 'castle' represented the territory controlled by the castle.[12] The mounds were of three types: natural, artificial or hybrid. Sometimes the motte was added to an existing fortified enclosure known as a ringwork castle. Motte-and-bailey castles were being built in France and the Rhineland in the early eleventh century.[13] Great diversity of form existed within this classification, depending on resources, location and environment.[14]

Because of the speed with which it could be constructed, the earth and timber motte-and-bailey castle continued in use for centuries. It was particularly practical in newly-conquered territory and it was an essential element in the Norman conquest of England in 1066 and of Ireland a century later. However, from the eleventh century, the timber elements of earthwork castles were being replaced by stone, partly because of the vulnerability of timber fortifications to fire but also

because of a growing scarcity of trees and the building of castles in rocky mountainous terrain. As powerful lords aspired to comfort and protection, stone castles emerged as well-designed fortresses and dwelling houses from the end of the tenth century onwards. Many of these replicated in stone the form of the preceding earth and timber motte-and-bailey structures.

The earliest known rectangular stone 'great tower' (later known as a 'keep' or 'donjon') was built at Langeais in Normandy before 995, an architectural form which the Normans brought with them as they spread to other parts of Europe.[15] Over the following centuries, feudal lords built castles of stone, making 'from lime, sand and freestone, gateways and turrets, vaults and spiral staircases'. This building method was slowly adopted by knights of lower rank during the twelfth and thirteenth centuries.[16]

Stone castles represented an entirely new stage in fortification, as they could be successfully defended by the longbow and crossbow. Because they were much more

Fig. 6   The Bayeux Tapestry records Norman knights on horseback in attack mode, galloping past two motte-and-bailey castles.

Description of motte castle *c.* 1130 by Jean de Colmieu

It is the custom of the nobles of that neighbourhood to make a mound of earth as high as they can and dig a ditch about it as deep as possible. The space on top of the mound is enclosed by a palisade of very strong hewn logs, strengthened at intervals by as many towers as their means can provide. Inside the enclosure is a citadel, or keep, which commands the whole circuit of the defences. The entrance to the fortress is by means of a bridge, which, rising from the outside of the moat and supported on posts as it ascends, reaches to the top of the mound.

Fig. 9 A medieval image depicting a moated stone castle and its defenders under attack by a group of knights on horseback.

difficult to take, this required a corresponding escalation in siegecraft technology. A variety of highly effective machines (including mangonels, catapults and trebuchets) were devised for casting stones, darts and firebrands.[17] During the twelfth century, Crusaders returning from the eastern Mediterranean introduced innovative concepts and castle-building techniques, which influenced the construction of castles in Europe. The circular tower originated in the Levant and cylindrical towers and keeps were being built in Europe, especially in France, by the early twelfth century. These towers had the advantage of being easier to defend and more difficult to undermine.

Other transitional keeps, combining both forms, were also being built.[18] The great Crusader castles (such as Crac des Chevaliers) were constructed on rocky spurs defended on three sides by steep cliffs, with the remaining side protected by a ditch and wall.

This choice of site found many parallels in Europe.[19] French and Norman castle builders created the principal

Fig. 8 The remarkable Crusader castle of Crac des Chevaliers in Syria was constructed between the eleventh and twelfth centuries. Situated on a naturally defensive rocky outcrop, it was held by the Knights Hospitallers until it eventually fell to the Muslims in the late thirteenth century. Castle technology developed during the Crusades exercised a considerable influence on castle building, initially in Normandy and then elsewhere in Europe.

FRANCIS CORMON

Fig. 10   The iconic castle of Chateau Gaillard was built by Richard I on a precipice overlooking the Seine, at the end of the twelfth century. Cylindrical towers were in vogue in France at that time, presumably influenced by the architecture of Crusader castles. The castle was taken by the French in 1204.

school of medieval fortification which impacted on castle building throughout Europe. As the powerful lords encased their homes in castles of stone and their bodies in increasingly elaborate armour, the state of perpetual defensiveness was typified by the lookout keeping constant watch from castle towers.[20] As well as acting as the centre of administration for the region under its control, known as the 'castellaria', the castle served as a place of refuge for the rural population and their produce, in return for labour services towards the maintenance of the defences.[21]

NORMANDY

In the north of France, Normandy emerged as an autonomous region. In the late ninth century, a group of Northmen (better known as Vikings) succeeded in establishing a base in the north of France on the channel coast. In the early tenth century, Charles the Simple, king of West Francia, unable to control their raiding, came to an agreement with their leader, Rollo, ceding the region around the mouth of the Seine to the Northmen 'for the defence of the realm'.[22] The Northmen took over as lords

of the manor in the villages of the region, collecting rents and taxes from the French-speaking natives, as well as settlers attracted from a variety of other countries. This ethnically mixed group became French in language and Christian in religion by the end of the tenth century. They regarded themselves as Norman because of their attachment to Normandy. Their identity was reinforced by the adoption of the indigenous placenames, where

Fig. 11   This contemporary illustration captures the divisions in feudal society between master and worker, landowner and serf.

Fig. 12 The Bayeux Tapestry shows the transport of a variety of armour and weapons, including spears, axes, swords and shields. It emphasises the value placed by the Normans on their military equipment.

their land grants were located, as surnames.[23] Though not the first to adopt the structures of feudalism, the Normans quickly recognised its potential and exploited it to the hilt. They were equally quick to appreciate the value of castles and became the masters of castle building in Normandy, Sicily and the near east.[24] Northern and central France and Flanders became the epicentre of feudal society, with extensive clearing of land, foundation of towns and villages, and the establishment of manors. The castle, as the centre of local political power, dominated all of these activities.[25]

The Normans were generous in their church endowments; gifts to the church and the founding of religious orders were prescribed by the church as suitable penances for the expiation of the violence associated with warfare. Endowments to monasteries enabled them to become centres of the arts and civilisation, particularly under Lanfranc and Anselm, transforming Normandy from a land of barbarism to a stable state with a thriving culture. This process encouraged the Normans to see themselves as a distinct people endowed with special qualities.[26]

As a group, they were very conscious and proud of their military heritage and prowess, investing vast amounts in castles and arms. The most essential element in the Norman army was the mounted knight and a fortune was spent on the breeding and training of elite horses,

Fig. 13 Pembroke Castle has close connections with the Anglo-Norman invasion of Ireland. In 1189, William Marshal became Earl of Pembroke and Lord of Leinster through his marriage to Isabella, the daughter of Strongbow and Aoife. Shortly before his first visit to Ireland in 1200, Marshal carried out extensive works at Pembroke, including the construction of the great stone-roofed cylindrical tower. A preference for the cylindrical form is evident in his Irish castles at Kilkenny, Carlow and Ferns. It was also adapted for the construction of the Tower of Hook, the landmark and light-tower built by the Marshal lordship to guide shipping to the new port of Ross, situated on the river Barrow, 30km from the open sea.

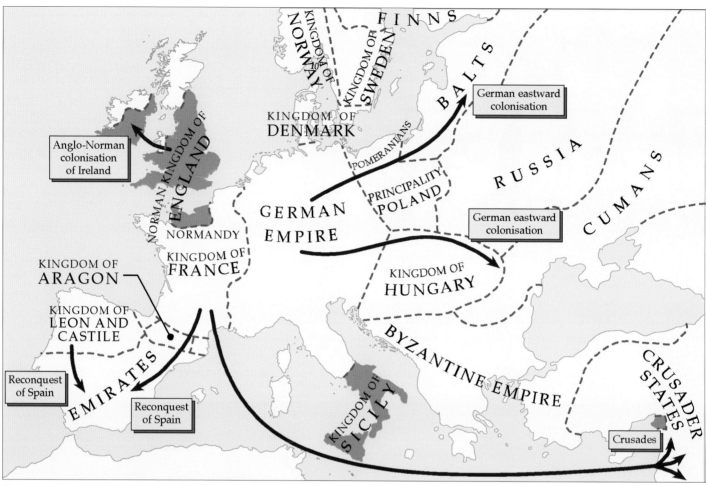

Fig. 14   The aggressive expansion of the Normans out of Normandy to occupy territory and create kingdoms in southern Italy, Sicily, the Holy Land, England, and eventually in Ireland, was part of a pan-European population movement during the twelfth century.

noted for their endurance, speed and strength.[27] By the end of the eleventh century, the mounted knight enjoyed a fearsome reputation; an Arab chronicler of the first Crusade observed that 'a charging Frank would make a hole through the walls of Babylon'.[28] Mercenary service was widespread in twelfth-century Europe and highly-trained Norman knights touted their services as mercenaries to the highest bidder, in the hope of booty and the acquisition of new lands.[29] Out of the Normans' belief in their own military prowess emerged a desire for wider conquest beyond the bounds of their native Normandy.

This rapacity for new lands impelled them to Italy, Sicily and the Holy Land. In 1066, William the Conqueror led a Norman force across the Channel and overwhelmed the English at the Battle of Hastings. This shattering victory allowed William to dispossess almost all of the

English lords and grant their lands to his own men, to be held by military tenure. The imposition of feudal structure and settlement was enforced by numerous castles, initially of the motte-and-bailey variety. The construction of these earth and timber castles is illustrated in the Bayeux Tapestry, produced at the end of the eleventh century to celebrate the Normans' achievement.[30] By the end of the century, the wealth generated by their new estates enabled them to erect numerous stone castles, monasteries and churches throughout England.[31] Because of their failure to subdue the obstinate Welsh, castles were particularly plentiful along the border with England. Norman marcher lords did succeed in occupying the southern coastal strip of Wales and it was from this region that the incursion into Ireland would originate, a century after their arrival in England.[32]

ANGLO-NORMAN COLONISATION

By the early twelfth century, profound economic, social, military and cultural advances had so transformed the English that their Celtic neighbours were regarded as inferior and barbaric. This attitude resulted in an incipient imperialism, four centuries earlier than is generally supposed, providing a convenient moral pretext for the anglicisation of Ireland, Scotland and Wales.[1] Dynastic ambitions and conflict in Ireland facilitated the initiation of this process. In 1166, Diarmait Mac Murchada, deposed king of Leinster and Uí Chennselaig, determined to regain his former power, fled overseas in search of foreign aid.[2] Mac Murchada enlisted the support of a disparate group in south Wales, spearheaded by Anglo-Norman knights who agreed to serve him as mercenaries in return for promises of land.[3] The landing of two small groups in 1169–1170 at Bannow and Baginbun on the south-west coast of Wexford initiated a process that had a catalytic impact on the subsequent evolution of all aspects of Irish life.

The role of the Anglo-Normans mutated aggressively from mercenary to invader and within a relatively short time-span the militaristic expertise of the newcomers enabled them to seize territory in the east and south of Ireland. Colonisation quickly followed, organised according to the feudal system of land occupation implemented by the Normans in Normandy and England. This involved the establishment of a hierarchical society, based on the European model of sophisticated record keeping. As in England a century before, the European concept of castle building was introduced, as centres of military control and civil administration and also as signature statements of status and domination. The locations of feudal manors, based on pre-existing Gaelic land divisions, dictated the siting of early castles. These manors were granted in perpetuity and the manorial framework determined the distribution of the small castles now known as tower houses, in the fifteenth and sixteenth centuries.

Fig. 1   This aerial perspective of Bannow Island, with sandbanks and mudflats exposed at low tide, captures the treacherous nature of the estuary. In later centuries, when the channel was moved to the west by shifting sands, the island where the Anglo-Normans first landed was connected to the mainland by a sand dune. The coastal site of Bannow town can be seen at the right (**A**), identified by the ruins of the medieval parish church of St Mary's.

Fig. 2   The ships that brought the Normans to England in 1066 are portrayed on the Bayeux Tapestry. A century later, similar ships ferried the initial small groups of their descendants to the beaches at Bannow and Baginbun to fight as mercenaries for Diarmait Mac Murchada, deposed king of Leinster.

THE ARRIVAL OF THE ANGLO-NORMANS

Following a meeting with Henry II, king of England and part of France, who granted him permission to hire mercenaries within his kingdom,[4] Mac Murchada directed his recruiting campaign towards the knights of the Pembroke region in south Wales. Diarmait promised money and land in return for military service, but to Richard FitzGilbert de Clare, Earl of Pembroke, better known as Strongbow, he offered his daughter, Aoife, in marriage and (contrary to Irish custom) succession to the kingdom of Leinster after his death.[5] In 1167, Mac Murchada returned with a small band and re-established himself in Uí Chennselaig. In May 1169, a six hundred strong advance party, of mixed origin, including Anglo-Norman, French, English, Welsh and Flemish, landed at Bannow Island on the south Wexford coast, led by Robert FitzStephen and Maurice de Prendergast. They were joined by Diarmait with a force of five hundred men. Their combined army marched on the Viking town of Wexford, which was surrendered by its Hiberno-Norse inhabitants after a short siege.[6]

Diarmait immediately granted the town and all its lands, equivalent to the barony of Forth, to Robert FitzStephen and Maurice FitzGerald, and the baronies of Bargy and Shelburne (two cantreds on the sea between Wexford and Waterford) to Strongbow's uncle, Hervey de Montmorency, the first land grants issued to Anglo-Norman knights in Ireland. The colony subsequently established in the southern baronies of Forth and Bargy survived undisturbed for more than four centuries, making south Wexford one of the most anglicised parts of Ireland. Leaving FitzStephen at Wexford, Mac Murchada marched on Dublin. Possibly fearing a revolt by the Norse of Wexford, FitzStephen constructed a fort on a steep rock on the right bank of the Slaney, two miles up-river from Wexford at a place called Carrig.[7] This first recorded fortification built by the Anglo-Normans in Ireland, classified as a ringwork castle, is now incorporated into the Irish National Heritage Park at Ferrycarrig.

In May 1170, another small force, led by Raymond le Gros, landed at Dún Domhnaill, now called Baginbun, a headland on the south Wexford coast, already the site of an Iron Age promontory fort.[8] They fortified the headland by constructing a second defensive earthwork, described both as 'a somewhat flimsy fortification of branches and sods' and a castle with gates. When the Anglo-Normans were besieged by an army of Norse and Irish from the city of Waterford, they sallied from the gate of their fort and completely routed their attackers.[9] Raymond le Gros occupied the fort at Baginbun for several months, awaiting the arrival of the main force led by Strongbow, which eventually landed at Passage in Waterford Harbour. The combined forces quickly took the city of Waterford. Diarmait brought his daughter, Aoife, to Waterford where she was married to Strongbow, establishing his claim to the kingdom of Leinster.[10] The combined forces then marched on Dublin, which was taken by storm. Three (of five) Viking port towns were now in the hands of the Anglo-Normans, effectively ceding them control of the seas.

In May 1171, Mac Murchada died and the situation changed dramatically for his former mercenaries.[11] Henry II, alarmed at the prospect of an insubordinate Norman kingdom emerging on the neighbouring island, embargoed all shipping to Ireland and ordered his subjects to return.[12] In late 1171, the king intervened personally and landed at Crook in Waterford Harbour, with a large retinue of knights.[13] At Waterford, Henry made a formal grant of Leinster to Strongbow, reserving to himself all seaports and fortresses. After wintering in Dublin, Henry travelled to Wexford, where he spent seven weeks waiting for favourable weather to make the crossing to Wales.[14] In 1172, Henry signed a charter,[15] perhaps while he was still in Wexford, granting extensive estates in Ireland to the Knights Templars, including the manor of Kilcloggan on the Hook peninsula, consisting of the combined medieval parishes of Hook and Templetown, which still bears their name. The Military Orders provided security at strategic locations throughout Europe and the Templars were installed on the eastern (and western) shore of Waterford Harbour for the same purpose.[16]

The Knights Hospitallers were introduced into county Wexford by Strongbow c. 1175 when he granted them lands at Ferns and the church of St Michael in Wexford town. About 1210, William Marshal added to their possessions in Wexford town, notably the church of St John, where they established the Hospital of St John, located just outside the town wall near a town gate which became known as John's Gate. Marshal also granted other unidentified lands to the Hospitallers, described as 'that part of Baliocynan which remained when the land was divided between Brother Maurice, Prior of the Hospitallers, and Geoffrey, son of Robert'.[17] In 1212, several churches in the diocese of Ferns were confirmed to the Hospitallers, including St John's of Balischauc,[18] the first mention of Balischauc which was the principal thirteenth-century Hospitaller manor in county (presumably the Baliocynan of William Marshal's grant). Mistakenly identified for several centuries as Ballyhack on

the Cistercian estate of Dunbrody, Balischauc has recently been identified as the medieval parish now known as Ballyhoge. The strategic location of the Hospitallers at Ballyhoge, on the west bank of the Slaney below Enniscorthy, secured the vital river corridor.[19]

Strongbow died in 1176, leaving a baby daughter, Isabella, as heir, and Leinster was taken into the king's wardship. In 1185, the arrival of Prince John, as lord of Ireland, with a large retinue, signalled a change in emphasis from military domination to colonisation of land. Arriving initially in Ireland as mercenaries, the ambitious Anglo-Norman knights, capitalising on the opportunity to acquire new lands, adroitly seized the initiative and occupied eastern and southern Ireland. Military control was followed by the imposition of a hierarchical landholding system known as feudalism and the introduction of settlers from England and Wales.[20]

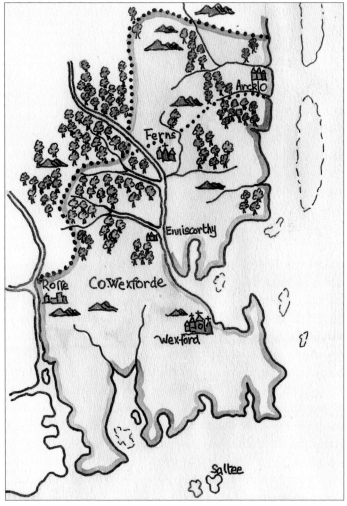

Fig. 3 County Wexford's landscape influenced the establishment and success of the Anglo-Norman colony. The mountainous, heavily-wooded north and west presented a daunting challenge to would-be settlers, as well as providing a safe refuge for the Irish. Boazio's late sixteenth-century map (re-drawn) distinguishes between the northern wooded uplands and the lowlands of the south.

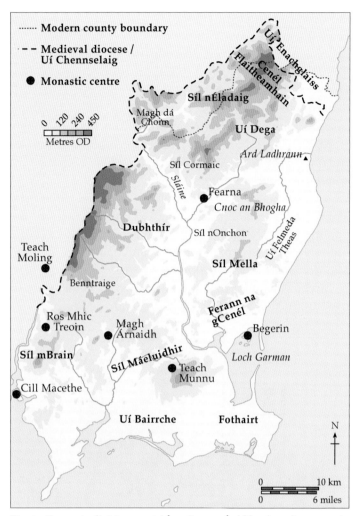

Fig. 4 Ten main divisions, or trícha cét, were held by dynastic groups in the Mac Murchada kingdom of Uí Chennselaig. These were used by Strongbow as convenient units on which to base early land grants.

Fig. 5 The Irish land divisions became the basis for Anglo-Norman grants. The original names were frequently retained but in a mutilated form, as clerks attempted to integrate them into Latin charters.

STRONGBOW'S LAND GRANTS

Following Strongbow's surrender of Leinster to the king and its re-grant by the service of one hundred knights, his main concern was the orderly occupation of the land in accordance with the laws of feudalism. Analysis of these land grants is essential to an understanding of castle building, as the manorial layout determined the location and distribution of all types of earthwork fortifications and stone castles, during the following four and a half centuries. Before allocating land to his principal tenants, the feudal lord reserved demesne manors for his own use, burgage lands for the foundation of towns, and grants intended for the church.

Lacking an intimate knowledge of the landscape, the Anglo-Normans, of necessity, utilised existing Gaelic territorial divisions in the creation of a feudal landholding system.[21] In 1167, there were ten territorial divisions known as trícha cét (thirty hundreds) in the kingdom of Uí Chennselaig.[22] The trícha cét was equated by the Anglo-

Normans with the Welsh cantreds[23] and used as a convenient unit on which to base primary grants. As well as defining the principal manors, the cantreds frequently coincided with diocesan divisions known as rural deaneries.[24] The relationship between civil and ecclesiastical boundaries also applied at a lower level, where the sub-manors of large fiefs underpinned the parochial structure.[25] Parishes were generally created in areas of Anglo-Norman settlement by the tithe-paying tenantry on the manors, following the introduction of a parochial tithing system at the Council of Cashel in 1172.[26] In establishing the locations and boundaries of manors, and the extents of earlier Gaelic territorial units, it is imperative to examine the medieval ecclesiastical structure of diocese, rural deanery and parish, rather than later county and barony boundaries.

Demesne Manors

Strongbow's first concern was the setting aside of lands which would be organised as demesne manors for his

Fig. 6 The manor of Ross was retained by Strongbow as one of his demesne properties. The location of a borough at the manorial centre is marked by a motte (possibly built by Strongbow himself), the site of an early stone castle (**A**), a church site (**B**) and a mill. The winding manorial roads also survive.

personal use. Following a campaign in Normandy in 1173, Strongbow was granted the town of Wexford[27] by the king, which he then made the principal town and seignorial manor of the lordship.[28] He visited Ferns on several occasions; he spent eight days there in early 1172[29] and he returned shortly afterwards to give his daughter in marriage to Robert de Quency.[30] About 1175, Strongbow granted ten carucates (*c.* 1,215ha) and one burgage between the town of Ferns and 'the great water' to the south (presumably the Bann) to the Knights Hospitallers.[31] These associations with Ferns suggest that he had decided to retain the Mac Murchada power base and monastic centre for himself. Ferns became one of the principal demesne manors of his successor.

The manor of Ross, located on the Barrow and associated with the monastic centre of Ros Mhic Treoin, where the surviving motte at Old Ross represents the early earthwork castle,[32] is also linked with Strongbow.[33] The extent of the manor was outlined in a charter of Richard Marshal *c.* 1232, demonstrating that it corresponded substantially to the large parish of Ross.[34] The demesne manor of Taghmon, based on an Early Medieval monastic

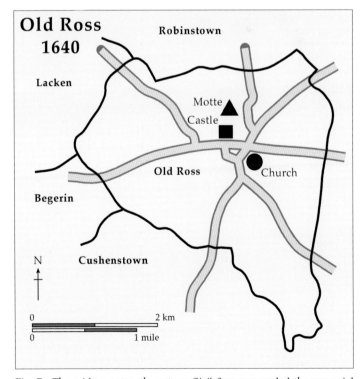

Fig. 7 The mid-seventeenth-century *Civil Survey* recorded the manorial centre of Ross, with its medieval road system, as one townland.

Fig. 8   The region around the Early Medieval monastic centre of Taghmon (Teach Munnu) was retained in the hands of the Lords of Leinster as a demesne manor. The manorial borough was established on the monastic site, as traces of the circular enclosure can be identified in this aerial photograph of the modern village taken in the 1950s. The complex road system may also have monastic origins. The tower house at left centre probably dates to the fifteenth century, when Taghmon was described as 'on the marches' because of the persistent Irish recovery. The possible monastic elements (enclosure, road system, church sites, high cross) are shown on the plan (below) as well as the later tower house.

centre, is described in the same charter, but there is no indication that it was retained by Strongbow. The demesne manors were all based on existing settlement centres. They were presumably selected because of the good quality soil on which they were located.[35]

Primary Land Grants

Strongbow created primary manors by granting large fiefs to knights in his retinue. The amount of land held by the service of one knight varied considerably, depending on land quality and location. The knight's fee in the frontier region in the north of the county was up to four times the size of those in the relatively secure southern region. Not all tenants held by knight's service; some free tenants paid a fixed rent, while settlers were attracted to towns by the offer of burgage status.[36] Following the granting of

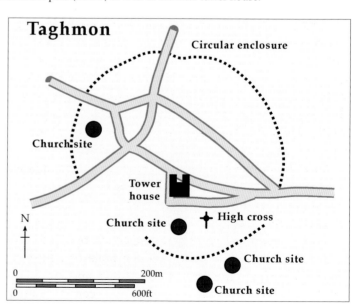

CON BROGAN NMSPU

Fig. 9 Having received a grant of Bargy and most of Shelburne from Diarmait Mac Murchada, later confirmed by Strongbow in 1172, Hervey de Montmorency granted a large estate to the abbey of Buildwas in Shropshire for the establishment of Dunbrody Abbey, the first Anglo-Norman Cistercian foundation in Ireland. Buildwas declined, offering it instead to St Mary's Abbey in Dublin. The offer was accepted in 1182 and eventually, in 1201, the new abbey was consecrated. The ruins, including a fifteenth-century crossing tower, form one of the most impressive Cistercian monuments in Ireland.

primary manors as fiefs to faithful vassals and relatives, the process of sub-infeudation was repeated to create secondary manors.[37] This system of landholding provided a military structure, as a tenant who held land by knight's service was obliged to serve in his lord's army for not more than forty days per fee in any year (or a payment of 40s. per fee). The principal objective of granting land by military tenure was to facilitate a permanent garrison, a vital consideration in stabilising a durable colony in a frontier situation. The construction of castles, initially of earth and timber, was essential to this process.

An examination of civil and ecclesiastical boundaries make it possible to establish the approximate extent of feudal land grants.[38] Security was a priority in the allocation of Strongbow's early grants. He gave the Duffry to his son-in-law, Robert de Quency, by the service of five knights, also making him constable of Leinster.[39] The Duffry (from the Irish words dubh and tír: black country),[40] a heavily wooded district between the Slaney

and the Blackstairs mountains, was an obvious refuge for disaffected Irish and required effective military control. The Duffry had an added significance as it provided access to the Scullogue Gap, a strategic passage through the Blackstairs.[41]

Other routeways through the mountains were also controlled by early land grants. Sometime before 1176, William de Angulo received a large grant, by the service of eight knights, which included modern Moyacomb (Magh dá Chonn: the plain of the two sources – a reference to the Slaney and its tributary, the Derry) and extended to the waters of Mescordin (? Enniscorthy, i.e. the Slaney).[42] This would have effectively guarded the Slaney Gap between the Blackstairs and the Wicklow mountains, as well as the valley of the Derry river. However, it is likely that the grant was never implemented.[43]

When de Quency was killed in 1172 by the Irish of Offaly, Raymond le Gros, his successor as constable, was given Forth and Idrone (in Carlow), as well as Glascarrig

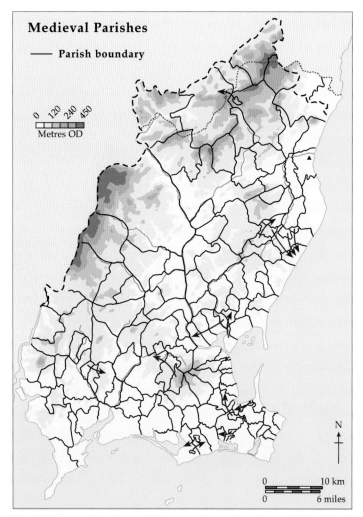

Medieval Parishes

—— Parish boundary

0 120 240 450
Metres OD

N

0   10 km
0   6 miles

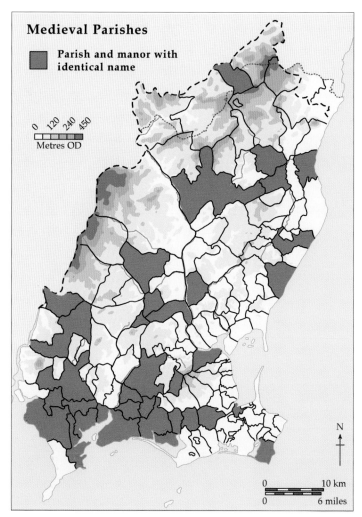

Medieval Parishes

■ Parish and manor with
   identical name

0 120 240 450
Metres OD

N

0   10 km
0   6 miles

Fig. 10   The medieval parochial system (now referred to as civil parishes) evolved in tandem with the feudal landholding pattern imposed by the Anglo-Normans and marked the colony's progress. The difference in size reflects the sprawling, thinly populated grants in the north, contrasting with small, heavily settled manors in the south.

Fig. 11   The sharing of a common name illustrates the affinity between manor and parish, particularly in the south-west of the county.

on the east coast of Uí Chennselaig.[44] His motte-and-bailey castle at St Mullins controlled the Pollmounty Gap and the route along the Barrow valley to Dublin. His motte-and-bailey also survives at Glascarrig, of significance as one of the few landing places on Wexford's east coast.

The confirmation by Strongbow of Diarmait's grant to Hervey de Montmorency[45] had a strategic dimension. The two cantreds on the south coast commanded the land approaches to Bannow Bay and Waterford Harbour, initial Anglo-Norman landing places and vital routeways to England. The determination shown by Montmorency to endow an ecclesiastical foundation on his fief illustrated the priority given within feudal society to the establishment of religious houses. It also represented a strong expression of ownership and a commitment to a permanent presence in Ireland. Having failed in his attempt to attract monks to Bannow,[46] in 1172, he offered a large estate in the manor of the Island in Shelburne to the

monastery of Buildwas in Shropshire, for the foundation of the first Anglo-Norman Cistercian house in Ireland.[47] Following a harsh report on the location and the natives, Buildwas declined the grant, offering it instead to St Mary's Cistercian Abbey in Dublin. The offer was accepted in 1182 and the new monastery, called the Port of St Mary of Dunbrody, was consecrated in 1201 by Herlewyn, bishop of Leighlin, a nephew of the founder. The monastic estate of forty carucates (13,000 statute acres/5000ha) corresponded to the medieval parish of Dunbrody and part of Killesk. Combined with the Templar manor to the south, the Cistercian estate of Dunbrody secured the eastern shore of Waterford Harbour.[48]

Strongbow ensured the security of Wexford Harbour by granting Fernegenel (the Irish Ferann na gCenél) on its northern shore to Maurice de Prendergast by the service of ten knights.[49] Fernegenel, an extensive fee, included the district of Síl Mella to the north, as well as land in Kynelaon (identified as the Gaelic district of Cenél Flaitheamhain located in the cantred/deanery of

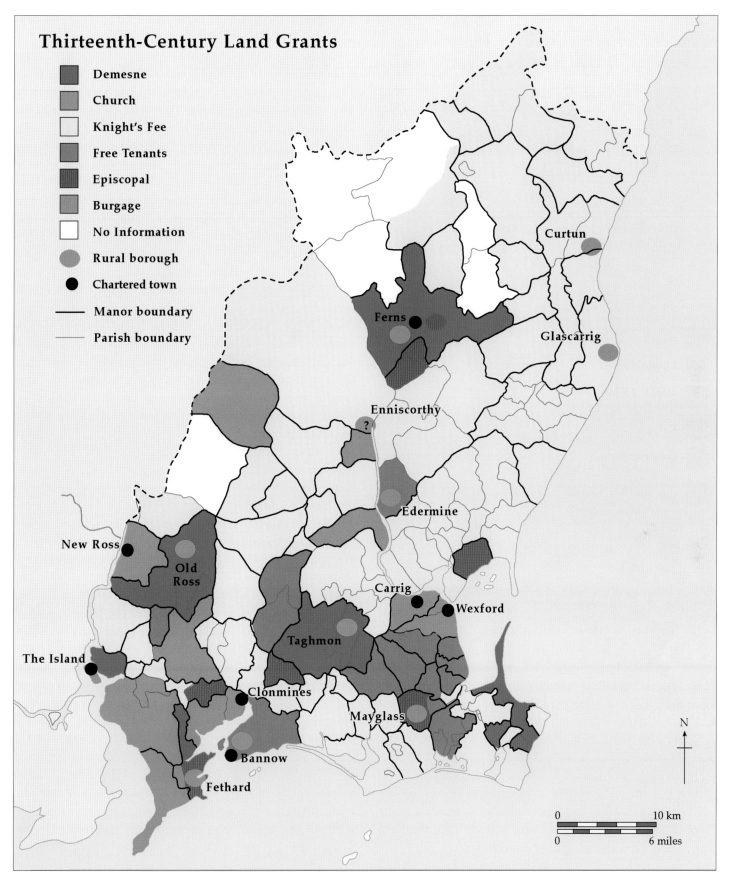

Thirteenth-Century Land Grants

- Demesne
- Church
- Knight's Fee
- Free Tenants
- Episcopal
- Burgage
- No Information
- Rural borough
- Chartered town
- —— Manor boundary
- —— Parish boundary

Curtun

Ferns

Glascarrig

Enniscorthy

?

Edermine

New Ross

Old Ross

Carrig

Wexford

The Island

Taghmon

Clonmines

Mayglass

Bannow

Fethard

N

0   10 km

0   6 miles

Fig. 12   The early thirteenth-century Anglo-Norman settlement created contrasting landholding patterns, which resonate in the landscape to the present day. Apart from the demesne manor of Ferns, the north of the county was parcelled out in sprawling knights' fees, which ultimately proved to be untenable, while the south was divided into a complex of smallholdings of disparate types, which formed the template for a permanent colony.

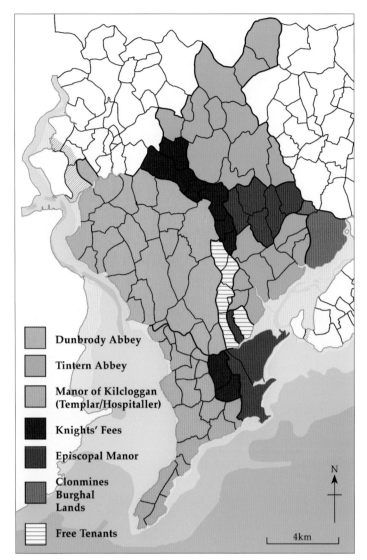

Dunbrody Abbey

Tintern Abbey

Manor of Kilcloggan
(Templar/Hospitaller)

Knights' Fees

Episcopal Manor

Clonmines
Burghal
Lands

Free Tenants

N

4km

Fig. 13 Cistercian abbeys at Dunbrody and Tintern, a Knights Templars preceptory at Kilcloggan and two episcopal manors at Fethard and Kinnagh ensured that the territory in south-west Wexford, bordering Waterford Harbour, remained mostly in the hands of the church.

Oday in the north of the county).[50] The lands of Kynelaon can be identified from land grants that were made there. Sometime before 1229, Philip de Prendergast granted lands to Walter de Barry in Crosspatrick and Kynelaon by the service of one knight.[51] Walter and Raymond de Barry were lords of Ardamine in 1250, presumably in the Kynelaon of the earlier charter.[52] The lands granted to Raymond le Gros by Strongbow descended to his nephews before the end of the twelfth century: the Carews held St Mullins by 1195[53] and the Cauntetons succeeded to Glascarrig.[54] The large Prendergast fief was subdivided. The southern part, the district of Fernegenel, passed into the possession of Robert FitzGodebert (Roche) by the service of five knights.[55] The Roche holding was reduced in the early thirteenth century when Gerald de Rupe sub-

infeudated the south-eastern part of Fernegenel to his kinsmen, the Sinnotts.[56]

To the north of Fernegenel, Gilbert de Boisrohard, who witnessed several of Strongbow's charters, was granted 'Offelimy on the sea',[57] corresponding to the Ó Murchada district of Uí Felmeda on the east coast, still known as the Murroes.[58] At a later date, the coastal routeway to Dublin was protected by the granting (directly from the king) of a manor to Maurice FitzGerald (son of Maurice) by the service of five knights' fees in the district of Uí Enechglaiss south of Arklow. This manor is represented by the parishes of Inch and Kilgorman in the north of county Wexford but in the diocese of Dublin.

These grants were the only ones made by Strongbow for which there is documentary evidence. However, he presumably also made grants to knights who were in Ireland in the early days of the conquest. In Shelmalier, the family of de Heddon acquired the fee of Magh Árnaidhe (later Adamstown) by the service of two knights,[59] while the de Londons were granted the manor of Roscarlon (Rosegarland), at the head of Bannow Bay, by three knights fees.[60] William de Denne received the substantial manor of Kayer, situated on the west bank of the Slaney below Enniscorthy by the service of three knights.[61] Other followers presumably received land grants from him also; from charter evidence, the Brownes, Codds and Russells came with Strongbow, but details of their fiefs only emerge at a later date.

The twelfth-century French poem, *The Song of Dermot and the Earl,* records that, in an effort to appease the Irish, Strongbow granted the kingdom of Uí Chennselaig to Diarmait's nephew, Muirchertach Mac Murchada, and the 'pleas of Leinster' to his son Domhnall Caomhánach.[62] The significance of these grants is obscure. The *Song* states that 'these two were kings of the Irish of the country' and that Strongbow's intention was to 'appease the Irish'.[63] The grants must have been politically motivated, with the intention of keeping the Irish at peace. The strategy was successful as the colony in the liberty of Wexford was allowed to flourish without resistance for almost a century. The newcomers did not allow the rights of the Irish to interfere with their exploitation of newly acquired fiefs. United by ties of race and kinship, they regarded themselves as frontier warriors and superior to those who came after them. In turn, these freebooters were regarded with ill-disguised suspicion by officialdom. This is illustrated by the aphorism attributed to Maurice FitzGerald in Gerald de Barry's 1185 account of the conquest, *Expugnatio Hibernica*: 'Just as we are English to the Irish, so we are Irish to the English.'[64]

Fig. 14 Strongbow's son-in-law, William Marshal, brought a new impetus to the organisation of Leinster and county Wexford. On his first visit to Ireland in 1200, he granted land to Tintern Abbey in Wales, for the foundation of a Cistercian monastery on the shores of Bannow Bay. He completed the settlement of south Wexford by dividing the lands of Forth and Bargy and the manor of the Island into small estates, some held by knight's service, others by free tenants. Following his death in 1219, he was succeeded by his son, William. Their effigies lie side by side in Temple Church, London.

MARSHAL'S LAND GRANTS

Before his death in 1176, Strongbow had allocated much of the land of Uí Chennselaig to his henchmen. William Marshal succeeded as Lord of Leinster by his marriage to Strongbow's daughter Isabella. In danger of shipwreck on the occasion of his first crossing to Ireland in 1200,[65] Marshal vowed to endow a religious foundation wherever his ship reached safe harbour. He evidently arrived at Bannow Bay as it was there that he gave land for the monastery at the head of a small inlet. It was colonised with Cistercian monks from Tintern Abbey in Marshal's manor of Chepstow and named Tintern Minor or *de Voto* (of the vow). Marshal's charter can be dated to 1207–1213 from the names of the witnesses.[66] The land granted to the Cistercians was part of Hervey de Montmorency's fief but it reverted to Marshal after Hervey's death in 1205. The monastic estate, equivalent to the civil parishes of Tintern and Owenduff, consisted of 15,000 acres (6,070ha).[67]

To facilitate the organisation of his lordship, the liberty of Leinster was divided into the four shires or counties of Wexford, Kilkenny, Carlow and Kildare.[68] The medieval county of Wexford included part of modern county Wicklow, being equivalent to the diocese of Ferns. The progress of settlement in medieval Wexford was influenced considerably by changes in ownership of several early grants. The town of Wexford with the cantred of Forth, initially given to FitzStephen and FitzGerald, reverted to Strongbow. It was subsequently subdivided, presumably by Marshal.

Densely colonised and divided into smallholdings, some held by knight service and others by socage tenure (land held by the payment of money rent or other non-military services), the settlement pattern in Forth was noticeably different from the rest of the county. The principal families holding by knight's fee were the Staffords of Ballymacane, the Sinnotts of Ballybrennan, the Codds of Carne, the Lamports [Lamberts] of Ballyhire and the Frenches of Ballytory.[69] Families holding as free tenants included the St Johns of Ballymore, the Butlers of Butlerstown, the Waddings of Ballycogley, the Rossiters of Rathmacknee and the Esmonds of Johnstown.[70] The parishes of Rosslare and Ballymore in the south of the barony were retained as demesne manors. The descendants of the Ostmen (Norse) of Wexford town continued to hold land around Rosslare and maintained their distinct identity for over a century.[71]

Hervey de Montmorency's fief, represented by the modern baronies of Bargy and Shelburne, reverted to the lord of Leinster following Hervey's death in 1205. Much of Shelburne had been alienated to the Cistercians at Dunbrody and Tintern and to the Knights Templars at Kilcloggan. Montmorency established his headquarters on an island (no longer an island due to reclamation) in the Barrow, now known as Greatisland. The island was subsequently known as Hervey's Island and the manor of the Island was later administered with the demesne manor of Ross.[72] Several small sub-manors were held by knight's service: these included the Keating manor of Slievecoiltia,

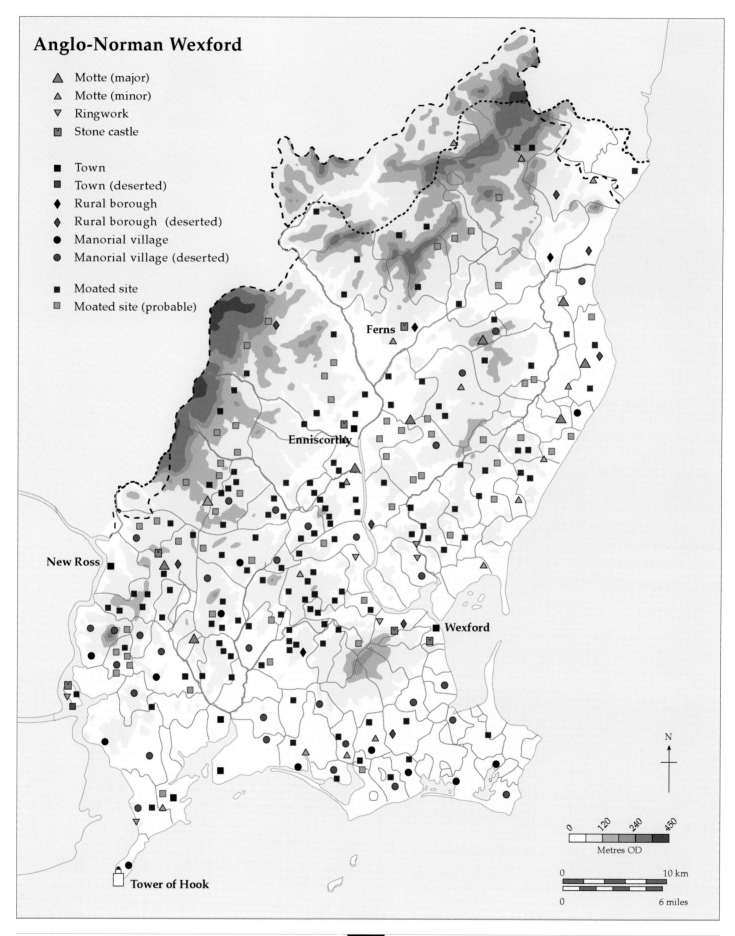

Anglo-Norman Wexford

△ Motte (major)
△ Motte (minor)
▽ Ringwork
⌂ Stone castle

■ Town
■ Town (deserted)
◆ Rural borough
◆ Rural borough (deserted)
● Manorial village
● Manorial village (deserted)

■ Moated site
■ Moated site (probable)

Ferns

Enniscorthy

New Ross

Wexford

N

0   120   240   450
Metres OD

0   10 km

0   6 miles

Tower of Hook

Fig. 16   Founded as a result of Marshal's vow, Tintern *de Voto* (of the vow) was a daughter house of Tintern Major in Wales. Following dissolution in 1541, the abbey and its lands were granted to Anthony Colclough, an English army officer, who converted the crossing tower into a fortified tower house. The church was subsequently adapted as a dwelling in a fortified enclosure, resulting in the destruction of most of the monastic complex.

the de Tullos manor of Tullostown, the Russell (later Sutton) manor of Ballykeerogemore and the de Ponte Chardun manor of Killesk, which later became a FitzGerald fee.[73]

A previously unnoticed charter of de Montmorency, dated to 1177, shows that Hervey had failed to find a tenant for the cantred of Bargy before his retirement to Christ Church, Canterbury *c.* 1180. The charter details the grant of a large fief by Hervey to Osbert FitzRobert, which must have extended over most of Bargy as it was valued at fifteen knights' fees. However, it was offered to FitzRobert for the service of only three knights, obviously an indication of the difficulty experienced by Hervey, and presumably others, in persuading suitable personnel to

Fig. 15 (left)   The distribution of Anglo-Norman settlement features reflect the success of the colony in the county. Sites are scarce in the north, which the Irish had recovered by the end of the thirteenth century. Defensive earthworks are concentrated across the centre of the county, which was the interface between Irish north and English south. Manorial villages are concentrated in the southern 'English baronies' of Forth and Bargy.

occupy manors in Ireland. In this case, even the reduced offer failed, as there is no further mention of FitzRobert as a landholder in Bargy.[74]

Marshal also struggled to attract tenants after the reversion of de Montmorency's manors to him *c.* 1205. As well as installing some new tenants in the cantred of Bargy, Marshal granted much of the land to holders of existing fiefs and in so doing created 'split' manors.[75] The manor of Ballymagir was added to the de Heddon manor of Magh Árnaidhe (later Adamstown).[76] The family of d'Evereux, Marshal's kinsmen from his manor of Strigoil,[77] acquired these manors by marriage *c.* 1250.[78] The Keatings, witnesses to the charters of Dunbrody and Tintern, were granted the manor of Kilcowan in Bargy, establishing their headquarters in the townland of Hooks. Other branches of the family held the manors of Slievecoiltia and Kilcowanmore.[79]

The Boscher (Busher) manor of Ballyanne in Bantry was also increased by the addition of the detached manor of

Fig. 17   The status of the upper echelons of the early settlers, and their confidence in the success of the colony, is evident in the superior quality of the medieval font from St Mary's parish church at Bannow. The highly-decorated font (now in Carrig-on-Bannow parish church), probably imported, may have been donated by a local feudal magnate.

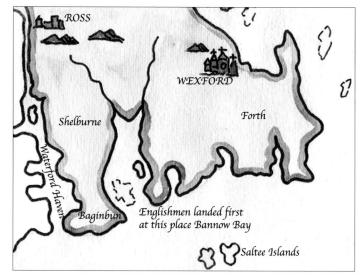

Fig. 18   A note on Boazio's map of 1599 (re-drawn) records that 'Englishmen landed first at this place Bannogh Baie', an indication of an enduring folk memory and the significance of the location among the descendants of the first arrivals, four centuries after the event. The inclusion of Baginbun indicates its importance as a landing place.

Ballyconnick. The de Londons of Rosegarland acquired the manor of Duncormick, where they built a motte castle beside a small estuary, the mound of which still survives. A recent partial excavation beside the motte revealed the ditch of the bailey enclosure. Of particular interest was the discovery of a King John coin, indicating that the site was occupied in the first decade of the thirteenth century, coinciding with Marshal's allocation of the lands in Bargy.[80]

The Ambrose manor of Ambrosetown, the FitzHenry manor of Kilcavan, the Brownes of Mulrankin, the Cheevers of Ballyhealy, the Hores of Tomhaggard and the Whittys of Ballyteige completed the manorial structure of Bargy, where most of the land was held by knight's service.[81] The creation of so many small manors in the three southern baronies created the landscape matrix and the social milieu which facilitated the building of a remarkable number of tower houses in later centuries.

The achievements and reputation of their European Norman forebears imbued the newcomers with tremendous confidence in their own ability as warriors and as conquerors of new lands. The initial beachheads were absorbed into the mythology of the first colonists and their descendants. The status of the landing places

and the 'first comers' resembled the significance attached to the Pilgrim Fathers' arrival in New England in the early seventeenth century. In an act of commemoration, Bannow, although far from being ideally located, became the site of one of the first Anglo-Norman chartered boroughs and ports, established by Hervey de Montmorency, a member of the first group. The memory of the first landing is recorded on Boazio's map of 1599, which refers to Bannow as the place where 'Englishmen first landed'.[82]

The landing at Baginbun,[83] and the defeat of the army from Waterford, was also regarded as significant. Four centuries after the event, the rhyme 'at the creek of Bagganbun, Ireland was lost and won' was recorded by an English historian.[84] This connection with their ancestors demonstrates the colonists' memory of their origins and the value that they placed on attributes inherited from their European forebears, renowned for their military prowess.[85] These qualities underpinned a thriving colony in the southern baronies of Forth and Bargy, symbolised by the building of numerous small castles, known as tower houses, during the endemic civil strife of the fifteenth and sixteenth centuries.

THIRTEENTH-CENTURY CASTLES: CONQUEST AND COLONY

Wherever the Normans went in Europe, the building of castles was integral to their policy for the military and economic domination of newly-acquired lands.[1] This tactic was also implemented in Ireland where the imposition of Anglo-Norman settlement and structures included the establishment of defensive structures at strategic vantage points, as centres of military and administrative control. Initially, these were typically earth and timber castles of the motte-and-bailey type, but defended enclosures, generally referred to as ringwork castles, were also built.[2]

These defensive earthworks created the initial visual expression of Anglo-Norman activity in the Irish landscape. Giraldus Cambrensis recommended that Ireland 'should be secured and protected by the construction of many castles'.[3] The siting of castles was not regarded as a matter of random choice by individual

manorial lords but was to be systematically coordinated for maximum efficiency. This concept was articulated by Giraldus in his advice to the colonists as to how Ireland should be subdued: 'it is far better to begin by gradually connecting up a system of castles built in suitable places and by proceeding cautiously with their construction, than to build large numbers of castles at great distances from each other sited haphazardly in various locations, without forming any coherent system of mutual support or being able to relieve each other in times of crisis'.[4] To implement this systematic approach, castle building was not always left to individual landowners but was supervised by men who had expertise in selecting suitable sites and planning coordinated military defences. In 1180, for example, John the Constable and Richard de Pec were despatched by the king to Ireland, where they built 'a very large number of castles throughout Leinster'.[5]

Fig. 1 The Bayeux Tapestry shows the building of a motte with a wooden palisade on top, shortly after the landing of the Normans at Hastings in 1066. The image illustrates the urgency of the work and the construction method of the campaign fortification. The coloured bands indicate that the mound was built in layers of different materials, presumably to create stability. The workers may have been conscripts from the local population.

Fig. 2   After the fall of Wexford in 1169, Robert FitzStephen built 'a fortress on a crag' at Carrig, on a rock overlooking the Slaney, five kilometres up-river from the town. The cliff has been quarried out to make way for a road but part of the earthwork survives. The first recorded Anglo-Norman fortification in Ireland, the ringwork castle is occupied by a Crimean War memorial in the form of a round tower. The site is overgrown but a modern bridge over the fosse can be seen to the right of the tower. Carrig subsequently became the site of an early stone castle and a chartered borough, of which only the church site remains. The ringwork is now in the townland of Newtown; the townland of Ferrycarrig is on the opposite side of the Slaney.

EARTHWORK CASTLES

The building of castles was a foundational component of the feudal system. They served not only as places of refuge but also as administrative focal points, seats of justice and highly visible centres of authority.[6] Early European castles consisted of an earthen motte (mound), surrounded by a trench or fosse, with a wooden tower, or bretasche, on its summit, protected by a timber palisade. Some mottes had attached enclosures, known as baileys, also defended by a fosse and a timber palisade.[7] The Bayeux Tapestry depicts several motte castles, including one in the process of construction.[8] In a hazardous situation when defence was urgently required, these fortifications could be thrown up quickly using local materials and forced labour. The Normans initially introduced the motte-and-bailey to England to establish control, and then built stone castles to overawe and govern the indigenous population.[9]

A century later, a similar approach was adopted in Ireland. The advance of colonisation in Ireland from 1170 onwards, accompanied by castle building, presents a contrast between relatively 'ordered' English areas and 'waste' (uncultivated regions) controlled by the Irish (as portrayed in English records). In these frontier situations,

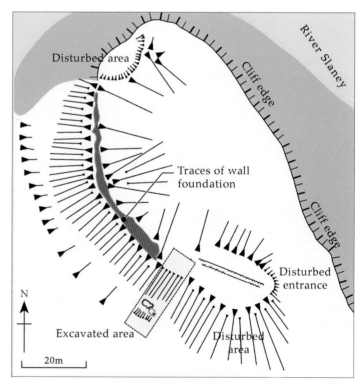

Fig. 3   A plan of the rampart and ditch at Carrig. This authentic earthwork is now included in the Irish National Heritage Park, which otherwise features reconstructions of various habitation sites.

Fig. 4 In May 1170, a second small group of Anglo-Normans, led by Raymond le Gros, landed opposite Bannow Island on the promontory of Baginbun. Baginbun forms a natural harbour with sheltered deep-water anchorage and landing beach. It also had the advantage of being the site of an Iron Age promontory fort which could provide some protection in an emergency. The advantageous nature of the location indicates that Raymond had advance knowledge of the landing place. The new arrivals constructed a second earthwork, which still survives, across the neck of the main headland.

the military functions of castles was at least as significant as their administrative role as centres for the organisation of newly-colonised manors. This intrusion into Ireland was part of the late twelfth- and thirteenth-century movement of people and the exploitation of marginal land in Europe, also based on castles and towns, to meet the 'land-hunger' of an expanding population.[10]

Earthwork castles can only be properly assessed in the context of the manorial framework introduced by the Anglo-Normans. The seignorial lord, who held directly of the king, retained demesne lands for his own use before allocating manors to principal tenants who, in turn, granted secondary manors to tenants of their own. The location and morphology of defensive earthworks was obviously dependent on the status of the holding within the feudal hierarchy. Bigger fiefs offered a wider choice in the selection of a site and better economic support. These factors affected the evolution of the manorial complex as a centre of long-term settlement. For the purposes of this analysis, all mottes of five metres in height and under are treated as minor, and those over five metres as major. Ringworks are not so easily classified as their structures vary, depending on location. The Bayeux Tapestry records the importation of pre-fabricated wooden towers into England, presumably to be erected on mottes, and the same

tactic was used in Ireland. In 1170, two 'wooden castles' and three 'wooden towers' were imported, from Lancaster and Carlisle respectively.[11]

A century ago, the distribution of the motte castle in Ireland was first linked with areas of Anglo-Norman control and identified as their typical fortification, sometimes based on natural features or pre-existing

Fig. 5 The double rampart across the neck of the headland at Baginbun (A–B) represents the fortifications built by Raymond's group, described by Gerald of Wales as a 'fortification of branches and sods'.

Fig. 6 The motte-and-bailey on Raymond le Gros's manor of Glascarrig was strategically located to protect a landing point on the east coast. The manor, the site of a borough and monastic foundation, was recovered at an early stage by the Irish. Originally built at a considerable distance from the sea, eight centuries of coastal erosion (estimated at 30m per century) on the fragile clay cliffs of Wexford's east coast, has caused part of the motte ditch to disappear and the motte itself is now in imminent danger. This significant site is a prime candidate for a rescue excavation.

earthworks.[12] More recently, there has been a growing awareness that other types of defensive earthworks were erected by the Anglo-Normans. Many of these were ringwork castles, defended by a surrounding ditch and palisade with an imposing gate tower.[13] The construction of this type of castle is described in the *Song of Dermot:* 'Then Hugh de Lacy/ Fortified a house at Trim/And threw a trench around it/ And then enclosed it with a stockade'.[14]

However, not all ringworks were of this type; at times, they were built in naturally defended locations, such as riverside promontories. The first Anglo-Norman fortification, erected in 1169 by Robert FitzStephen after the capture of Wexford town, was of this type. FitzStephen's fort, located on a cliff-top overlooking the Slaney at Carrig, three miles up-river from Wexford, could have served as a blueprint for such a structure: 'FitzStephen built a fortress on a steep crag, called Carrig in the vernacular, and improved by artificial means a place naturally well protected'.[15] At a later stage, Gerald dismissed the fortress as 'a most ill-fortified castle which was enclosed by a flimsy wall of branches and sods'.[16] In 1170, Raymond le Gros, following his landing at Baginbun with a small force, constructed earthworks across the neck of the headland, similarly described by the critical Gerald as 'a somewhat flimsy fortification of branches and sods'.[17]

Earthen banks, topped by timber palisades, were presumably erected at both places. The initial defences at Baginbun may have been based on the pre-existing Iron Age fort of Dún Domhnaill. The double-banked earthwork, which still substantially survives across the neck of the headland, may not have been constructed until after the defeat of the Hiberno-Norse force from Waterford.[18] These early fortifications played contrasting roles in the establishment of the colony; Baginbun had no long-term significance but Carrig became the nucleus of a substantial manor with a borough and stone castle.[19]

Twenty-nine defensive earthworks associated with early Anglo-Norman activity in Uí Chennselaig can be identified.[20] Of these, twenty are classed as motte castles and nine as ringworks. Excavations at Carrig and Ferns have produced archaeological evidence to support their ringwork classification. None of the other sites have been excavated, so analysis must, of necessity, remain tentative. The identification of twelve mottes, based on morphology and location within the manorial structure, is certain. Two others, Doonooney and Loggan, although removed from the landscape, were recorded before destruction. Doonooney was described as 'a flat-topped moat' about four metres high.[21] The earthwork at Loggan Lower is depicted as a motte-and-bailey on the 1841 OS map[22] and it

Fig. 7   The motte castle built by Raymond le Gros beside the Early Medieval monastic foundation of St Mullins was strategically located to control traffic on the Barrow and to secure the Pollmounty Gap between the river and the Blackstairs. For several centuries, the Pollmounty Gap was a weak link in the defences of the English colony in Wexford, as it provided access for both English and Irish raiding parties.

was described as such before its destruction.[23] Urn burials were found in association with the mound at Loggan;[24] given that mottes were sometimes based on pre-Norman earthworks,[25] an earlier burial mound was presumably adapted for use as a motte. Walter de Barry, the possible builder, held the manor of Crosspatrick, in which Loggan is situated, by the service of one knight before 1229.[26] The classification of the mound at Castletown (now Monagarrow) is also uncertain.[27] This flat-topped mound, which is four metres above field level, was surrounded by a fosse until the early 1980s, when it was filled in during agricultural activity.[28] This fact, allied with the association of the site with the FitzGerald fee of Maurice Castle, and the placename, provide sufficient justification for its inclusion as a motte castle.

In 1177, the sons of Maurice FitzGerald were given Ferns. They 'immediately built a castle' which was quickly 'razed to the ground' by their enemies.[29] The speed of its construction and destruction indicated that it was built of earth and timber. Excavations at Ferns revealed a rock-cut fosse, to the east of the later stone castle, which has been tentatively associated with the caistéal of Diarmait Mac Murchada mentioned in 1166.[30] A stone-faced earthen rampart discovered underneath the stone castle may represent the ringwork thrown up by the FitzGeralds in 1177.[31]

Three other possible ringwork sites are similarly positioned on river promontories. The initial headquarters of the manor (or barony) of Kayer was presumably a ringwork castle, sited in a naturally defensive cliff-top site

Fig. 8 Dunanore from the south-east showing the rock-cut ditch and bank. A causeway to the entrance crosses the left-hand ditch. The bank ends at the top of a vertical cliff. To the right, the ground falls in a steep incline to the river. The interior, which is almost level with the top of the bank, contains traces of possible house plots. This important site is obscured by forestry planting which has comprised possible archaeological material.

on a double bend in the river Boro.[32] The triangular area, protected on two sides by eighteen metre high cliffs, and defended by an earthen bank and ditch, is similar in morphology to FitzStephen's ringwork, downriver at Carrig.[33] The earthwork on the Boro is known as Dunanore, suggesting that it was based on a Gaelic promontory fort (dún: fort; or: brim/brink; i.e. the fort on the edge; an accurate description). This possible continuity of usage may have given the manor its name, as Kayer is synonymous with the Irish word cathair, a stone fort, although the designation is usually found in the west of Ireland.[34] Alternatively, as frequently happened, the earthwork may have been given its name following the recovery of the region by the Irish.

Two other possible ringworks, at Templetown[35] and Ballyhoge,[36] both located on promontories overlooking streams, can be associated with early foundations of the Knights Templars and Hospitallers, who were prominent in both areas in the late twelfth century,[37] an indication that the military orders had a preference for this type of fortification. The inland promontory at Templetown (now modified) was referred to locally as 'the hill o' the moat'. An earthwork, described as a possible ringwork,[38] on Greatisland could be the *caput* of the manor of the Island. However, an exceptionally large rectangular moated site close to the early medieval site of Kilmokea suggests an alternative manorial headquarters.[39] Moated sites were associated with exclusiveness[40] and, as Strongbow's uncle, Hervey de Montmorency may have

intended the one on his demesne headquarters to reflect his own high status.

After the transfer of Fernegenel to the Roches, the Prendergasts continued to hold Schyrmal and Kynelaon by the service of five knights. The impressive motte at Motabeg[41] on the east bank of the Slaney just below Enniscorthy, marks the *caput* of Schyrmal. The Prendergasts held an extensive fief in Kynelaon by the service of two and a half knights, so presumably they occupied all of the land between Kiltennell and Ardamine

Fig. 9 Not all early fortifications were of the motte-and-bailey type. This diamond-shaped field, located on Greatisland, has been created out of a large moated site with part of the outer bank forming the perimeter. The island gave its name to Hervey de Montmorencey's manor of the Island and the moated site may have been the manorial *caput*.

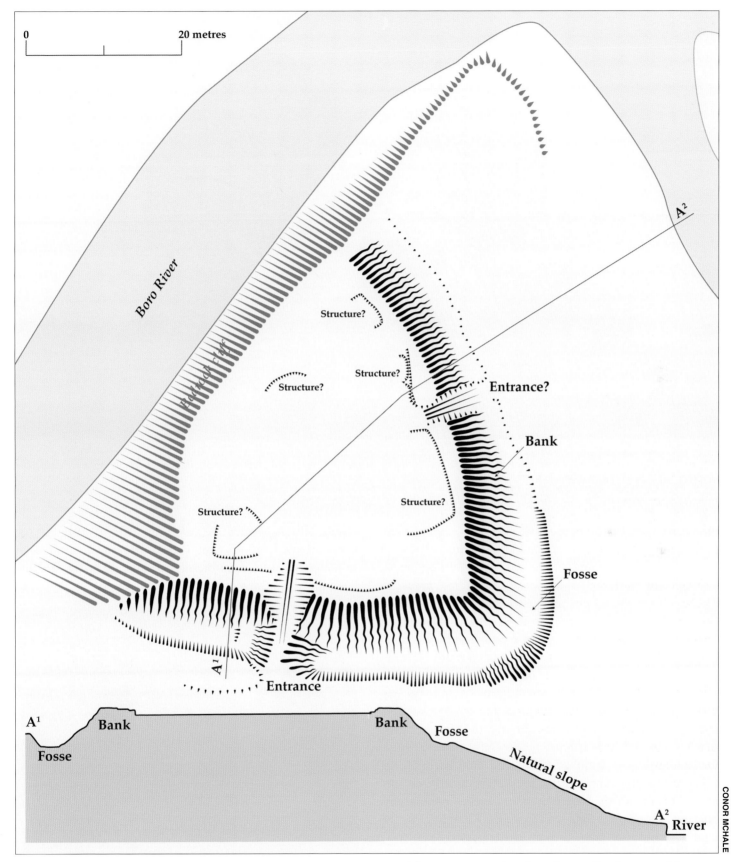

0   20 metres

Boro River

Bedrock cliff

Structure?

Structure?

Structure?

Entrance?

Bank

Structure?

Structure?

A²

A¹

Entrance

Fosse

A¹

Bank

Fosse

Bank

Fosse

Natural slope

A²

River

CONOR MCHALE

Fig. 10   A ringwork, located on a naturally defensive clifftop site on a double bend of the river Boro, may have been the initial headquarters of the manor of Kayer. The triangular site, protected on two sides by eighteen-metre high cliffs, and defended by an earthen bank and rock-cut ditch with evidence for structures in the interior, is similar in morphology to FitzStephen's ringwork, downriver at Ferrycarrig. Dunanore (Dún an Óir, the fort on the edge) is an accurate description of the location. It may have been given this name after the reconquest of north Wexford by the Irish.

Fig. 11   The motte at Old Ross, attributed to Strongbow, marks the manorial centre of the demesne manor and borough. The earthwork fortification was replaced by a thirteenth-century stone castle built on the field in the foreground of the picture, where large stones, presumably from the castle, are sometimes turned up by the plough. Marshal shifted the manorial headquarters to his new town of Ross, more strategically located on the Barrow. In 2012, using Lidar and geophysics, the Old Ross Research Project (ThORRP), funded by the Heritage Council, identified the bailey and what is presumably the site of the thirteenth-century stone castle and ancillary structures, within the bailey.

on the coast and Crosspatrick (an area representing more than half the cantred of Oday). The motte castles at Middletown in Ardamine and possibly at Loggan in Crosspatrick mark the manorial centres on these manors.[42] The motte at Pallis, positioned to control the Wicklow Gap, if not constructed by the Prendergasts themselves, indicates an unrecorded grant of land.[43] The ringwork at Kilpipe, just across the modern county Wicklow border, was also associated with this manor.

About 1190, the Prendergasts doubled their holding when Maurice's son, Philip, succeeded to the five knights' fees of the Duffry, and the constableship of Leinster, by his marriage to Maud de Quency.[44] The Duffry, a descriptive name referring to the heavily wooded land between the Slaney and the Blackstairs, consisted mostly of the sprawling parish of Templeshanbo, but the Prendergast holding was more extensive than this. Killegney, to the south, where a substantial motte survives,[45] was subsequently held by the Prendergast heirs.[46] The remains of an enclosure to the west of the motte presumably originated as the bailey.[47] The existence of a farmstead

within this enclosure indicates impressive continuity of occupation. The *caput* of the Duffry was situated at Enniscorthy, on a rock outcrop overlooking the river at the head of the tidal waters of the Slaney. The site is similar to

CON BROGAN, NMSPU

Fig. 12   The ringwork at Kilpipe in south county Wicklow is similar in siting and form to the earthworks at Dunanore and Ferrycarrig.

JAMES O'GORMAN

Fig. 13 The motte-and-bailey at Killegney, a sub-manor of the Duffry near Clonroche, was at the centre of a settlement which included a medieval church and a moated site. Uniquely, as this mid-twentieth-century photograph shows, the bailey area is still occupied by a farmhouse and outbuildings, indicating many centuries of continuous occupation. As the name implies, Killegney was also the site of an Early Medieval foundation.

Fig. 14 At the present time, like too many other important sites in the county, Killegney motte is almost obscured by a heavy growth of tree cover.

Fig. 15 The classic combination of motte, the medieval church of St Mogue's (still a place of worship) and later fortified house, survives at the former episcopal manor and town of Fethard. A court or castle to the north of the church (where the motte is located) was mentioned in 1200. The early fifteenth-century fortified house incorporates the gatehouse and other fabric of an earlier enclosure castle, possibly associated with the early motte.

Carrig and the late nineteenth-century discovery of a rock-cut trench to the west of the rock[48] indicates that it was the site of the initial earthwork fortification.

Apart from Carrig, Baginbun, Enniscorthy and Ferns, only occasional glimpses of other earthwork castle building activity in county Wexford occur in the historical record. In 1195, Richard de London granted a messuage at his castle to Dunbrody Abbey.[49] The de Londons held the manor of Rosegarland, so the 'castle' must represent the motte-and-bailey at Newcastle. Presumably this was the same Richard de London who was granted the vill of Fethard by Christ Church, Canterbury c. 1200, on condition that he should build a castle there for the defence of the area.[50] This may explain the origin of the low motte beside the early fifteenth-century castle at Fethard.[51] Its site was actually mentioned in the charter from Canterbury, which stipulated that a place for the court should be reserved on the north side of the church, exactly where the motte is situated.[52]

The only other known reference to defensive earthworks occurs in the Marshal deforestation charter of

c. 1234.[53] The description of the boundaries of the forest of Ross mentions the *mota* or fortress which William Ace raised above the water of Bruncuinri (location not known). No trace of a mound survives but the local townland name of Palace may record its existence, as the townland of Pallis (possibly from palisade) in the north of the county does contain a motte.[54]

The motte at Old Ross,[55] the ringwork at Carrig, the large moated site at Greatisland and the possible ringwork at Ferns are the only early earthwork defences associated with seignorial *caputs*. A rectangular motte at Ballymore marks a secondary holding on the demesne manor of Ferns.[56] By the early thirteenth century, the manorial centre at Old Ross had been abandoned in favour of New Ross, positioned on the vital river complex of the Barrow and Nore. Similarly, following their acquisition of the Duffry, the Prendergasts apparently abandoned the motte at Motabeg (the *caput* of Schyrmal), in favour of Enniscorthy, which was more advantageously placed in their fief. The impressive motte at Motabeg suggests that it was intended

CON BROGAN, NMSPU

Fig. 16   Most early castles were of the motte-and-bailey type. The best surviving example is at Newcastle, formerly on the manor of Rosegarland. The circular shape of the bailey, combined with the local name Dungorey (Dún Ghuaire), suggests that the builders re-used an existing ringfort.

to be an important manorial centre, but the absence of other settlement features in the vicinity indicate early abandonment. Similarly, the motte at Ballymoty More and the ringwork at Ballyorley represent secondary manors within the Prendergast holding but lacking nucleated settlement. The Prendergasts may also have been responsible for the initial ringwork marking the *caput* of the Duffry at Enniscorthy, and the motte at Killegney was situated on a secondary manor within the Prendergast fee. The mottes at Loggan and Pallis can also be associated with secondary holdings on the Prendergast fee of Kynelaon in the north of the county, making a total of eight defensive earthworks on the Prendergast lands.

The changes in ownership of Fernegenel, the district to the north of Wexford Harbour, which passed from the Prendergasts to the Roches, who in turn sub-infeudated the Sinnotts, accounts for the complex of defensive earthworks within the region. Defensive earthworks existed at Castlesow and Toberfinnick on a double bend on opposite banks of the river Sow. The Castlesow site has been described as a possible motte[57] and a 'great ringwork';[58] its position on a river promontory, as well as

its name, justifies its inclusion as a ringwork. The minor mottes of Ballinamorragh, Inch and Tinnick can be attributed to secondary settlement on the Roche manor. Continuing northwards along the coast, the major mottes at Kilmuckridge, Glascarrig and Ardamine (Middletown), identify the centres of the de Boisrohard manor of Offelimy, the le Gros/Caunteton manor of Glascarrig and the Barry manor of Ardamine.[59] The possible minor motte of Barnaree suggests a Glascarrig sub-manor.

The motte-and-bailey of Newcastle on the de London manor of Rosegarland is the finest example of its type in the county. Locally, it as known as Dungorey (Dún Ghuaire; Guaire's fort), again indicating that it was based on an existing Gaelic earthwork, possibly a ringfort as the bailey is circular in shape. There is a minor motte at Duncormick on the detached portion of this manor and the de Londons were also responsible for the minor motte at Fethard. Certain families, including the de Londons, were more inclined than others to build mottes. Another 'split' manor, held by the Roches by half a knight's fee, consisting of the parishes of Doonooney in Bantry and Ballyvaldon in Fernegenel, also had a minor motte on each part. Similarly, the mottes at Ardamine and Loggan are linked with the Barrys.

The four demesne manors were chosen within established settlement structures; Ross, Ferns and Taghmon were sites of early medieval monasteries, while Wexford was a fortified Norse town. Unusually, there is no evidence of either an earthwork castle or an early stone castle on the demesne manor of Taghmon, although it had a chartered borough. Of twelve primary land grants, all held by military service, seven were fortified with major mottes, with evidence for baileys at four of them. Three major mottes (Killegney, Ballymoty More, Pallis) were erected on secondary grants in the large Prendergast fief. Five primary grants were fortified with earthworks of the ringwork type. The minor mottes were all either associated with secondary grants or located on the more secure south coast. On the small grant of Kilcowan on the south coast, held by the Keatings by half a fee, part of the circular enclosure of an early medieval church site was adapted as a bailey for a minor motte.[60]

Of the twenty-nine known defensive earthworks, nineteen had adjacent churches, indicating an associated settlement. Twelve of these were at parish centres, with the parish named after the townland in which the earthwork and church were situated: these consisted of three seignorial manors, three church manors, five primary grants and one secondary grant. Nine of the parish names contained the element 'cill', the Irish word for church, suggesting that the earthworks were adjacent to a pre-Norman church and settlement. Six of the earthworks were constructed at medieval borough sites and five of the six thirteenth-century stone castles were preceded by earlier earthworks.

The distribution of the defensive earthworks reveals two distinctive alignments. This may have been a fortuitous pattern resulting from the selection of sites within the manorial framework, in response to strategic, economic and administrative requirements. It could also be interpreted as a co-ordinated approach to selecting their locations within the landholding structure, as recommended by Gerald of Wales. As well as having individual defensive capabilities, the earthworks formed a double defensive line, extending diagonally across the county from south-west to north-east. This line

CON BROGAN, NMSPU

Fig. 17 The motte at Ballymoty More was located on a secondary grant on the Prendergast manor of Schyrmal (Síl Mealla). An adjacent church site suggests that there was an associated manorial village. The tree-covered area in the foreground may have been created by quarrying.

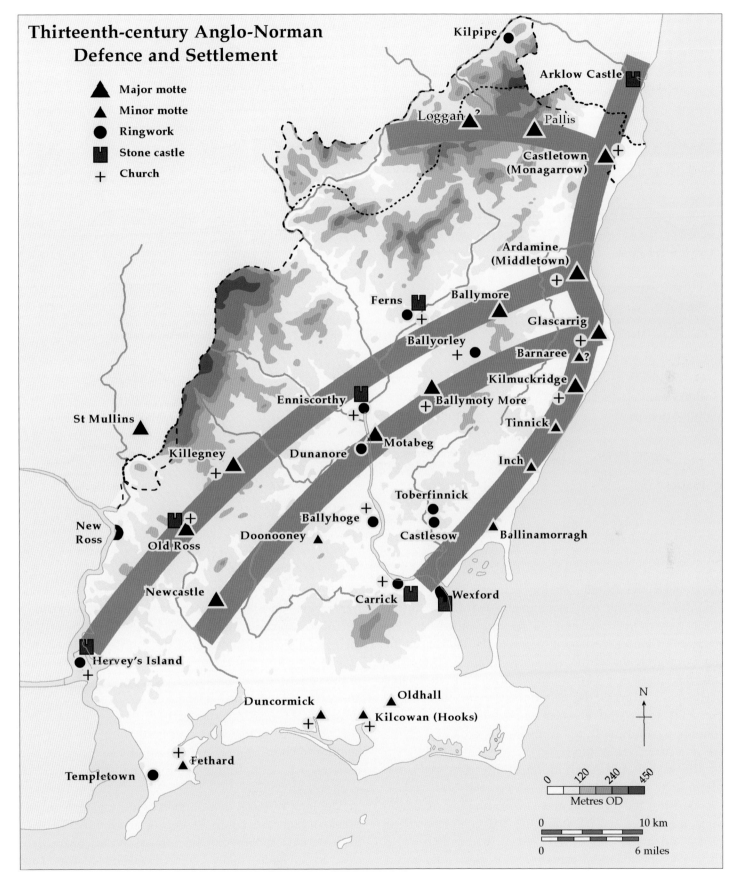

Thirteenth-century Anglo-Norman Defence and Settlement

▲ Major motte
▲ Minor motte
● Ringwork
▮ Stone castle
✛ Church

Kilpipe

Arklow Castle

Loggan ?

Pallis

Castletown (Monagarrow)

Ardamine (Middletown)

Ferns

Ballymore

Ballyorley

Glascarrig

Barnaree ▲?

Kilmuckridge

Enniscorthy

Ballymoty More

St Mullins

Motabeg

Tinnick

Dunanore

Killegney

Inch

Toberfinnick

New Ross

Ballyhoge

Castlesow

Ballinamorragh

Old Ross

Doonooney

Carrick

Wexford

Newcastle

Hervey's Island

Oldhall

Duncormick

Kilcowan (Hooks)

Fethard

Templetown

N

0   120   240   450
Metres OD

0   10 km

0   6 miles

Fig. 18   The presence of three mottes in the far north show that, initially, it was intended to divide almost all of Uí Chennselaig into feudal manors. A system of defensive earthworks and stone castles arranged diagonally from south-east to north-west across the county, indicates an early retraction of the colony and the creation of a frontier zone between the mountainous and wooded Irish north-west and the colonised lowlands of the south and east.

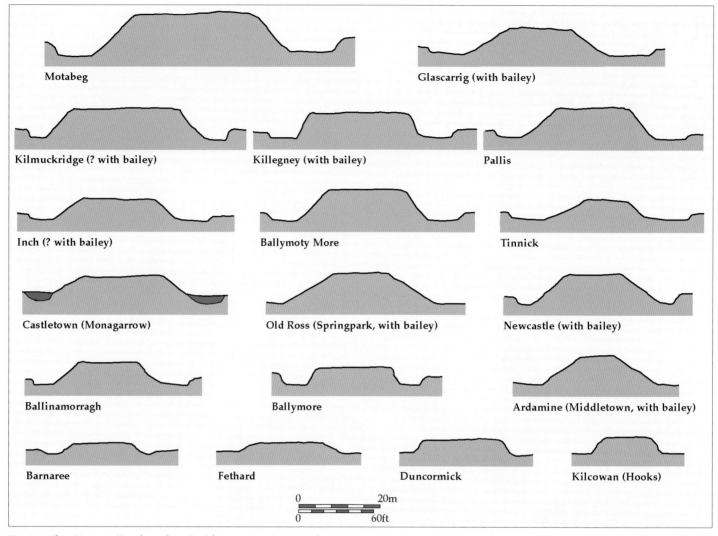

Fig. 19   The above profiles show that all of the mottes included in the double alignment of defensive earthworks and stone castles across the centre of the county were in the major category. Most of the mottes on the east coast were also of a substantial nature. Minor mottes were on the south coast.

demarcated the frontier region between the colonised south and east and the Gaelic dominated district to the north-west. This intermediate region, known as 'the marches', divided 'the land of peace' to the south from the 'land of war' to the north.[61] As well as forming a protective interface between native and settler, the defensive earthworks express the determination of the Anglo-Normans to occupy the best quality land, which also follows a south-west to north-east orientation in the western part of the county.[62]

The second obvious arrangement of earthworks is the alignment of eight mottes along the east coast, emphasising the priority given to controlling access to vital sea routes with Britain and the continent. Their coastal orientation could also reflect the significance of fishing to the manorial economy.[63] Of these, four major mottes are associated with the principal grants of Maurice Castle, Ardamine, Glascarrig and Offelimy, with three

minor mottes on secondary grants in Fernegenel and one minor motte on a possible secondary grant at Glascarrig.

The conspicuous absence of defensive earthworks in the cantreds along the south coast can be explained in a number of ways. The more secure conditions in the south of the county was an obvious factor, possibly resulting in an early colonisation of the region. Apart from the ringwork at Carrig, no other early earthwork defences has been identified in the cantred of Forth. Here the land was held by fractions of knights' fees and by rent-paying free tenants, whose holdings were perhaps too small to support fortification.

The land of Bargy was largely held by tenants whose principal manors were in Shelmalier and Bantry. The two minor mottes in Bargy at Duncormick and Kilcowan were close to navigable inlets before nineteenth-century land reclamation. A mound at Oldhall in Mulrankin, referred to as 'the motte of Oldhall' in the *Civil Survey*, may mark the

C.U.C.A.P.

Fig. 20   The earthworks and cropmarks in this 1950s aerial picture show that a small motte was built within an Early Medieval church site, using part of the circular enclosure as a bailey, on the Keating manor of Kilcowan on the south coast of the county. The motte and part of the enclosure survives. The addition of a moated site and later tower house in close proximity created an unusual continuity of occupation on the site.

original manorial centre, as the name suggests.[64] In two instances, at Ballymagir and Ballycappoge (Mulrankin parish), large moated sites, whose remains can still be traced, may have served as manorial centres.[65] Both, with a similar moated site at Ballymacane (Tacumshin parish) in Forth, were occupied by later tower houses.[66] These sites still contain farm complexes, unlike smaller moated sites of the later thirteenth century, which are typically in more peripheral locations and show no signs of continuity of occupation. The moated site at Ballymagir (later known as Richfield) is of particular interest, as it still contains the remains of a tower house with original hall, now incorporated in a modern restoration.[67]

EARLY STONE CASTLES

There is no historical record to show when initial earthwork defences in county Wexford were replaced by stone castles. Six early thirteenth-century castles (presumably of stone) are recorded at Wexford, Carrig, Ferns, Old Ross, the Island and Enniscorthy. Five of these, including the castle on the manor of the Island, which had reverted to Marshal after Montmorency's death, were built on seignorial manors. The exception was the castle of Enniscorthy, erected by the Prendergasts, holders of the largest fief in the county. Ferns and Old Ross, and probably Enniscorthy and the Island, were on, or near, early earthwork frontier defences. All, with the possible exception of Enniscorthy, had associated boroughs. With stone castles can be included the town walls built to protect the towns of Wexford and New Ross. Like castles, town walls with mural towers served a dual purpose, providing economic and administrative, as well as defensive functions.[68]

Henry II may have commissioned a castle at Wexford before his departure in 1172.[69] The castle was positioned to the south-east of the town, on a natural glacial mound just outside the town wall.[70] William Marshal presumably initiated a programme of stone castle building before his death in 1219. His son, William II, was similiarly engaged, as in 1222 and 1225, the service which he owed to the king was cancelled to enable him 'to fortify a castle in Ireland'.[71]

Castles (presumably of stone) existed on demesne land in the county by 1232; following the younger Marshal's death in that year, the castles of Wexford, Old Ross, Carrig and the Island were taken into the king's hands[72] and the castle of Ferns was given in dower to Marshal's widow, the countess of Pembroke.[73] In 1233, William Marshal's second son, Richard (d. 1234) signed charters to Dunbrody Abbey at his castle of Ross, while the castles of Carrig and Old Ross were again referenced in the deforestation charter of 1234.[74] The castle of Enniscorthy, built by the Prendergasts on a rock at the head of the tidal waters of the Slaney, does not appear in thirteenth-century records. It was first mentioned in the early 1370s, when it was taken into the king's hands.[75] After being destroyed by fire in 1569, it was 'repaired' in 1586 when it assumed its present shape.[76] It is unlikely that the present castle at Enniscorthy resembles the original. Some consider it to be a re-building on the lines of a similar towered keep[77] and others regard it as a sixteenth-century structure.[78] A recent survey of the fabric identified no medieval remains.[79]

Ferns Castle, the only survivor of the six, is one of several castles which are considered unique to south-east

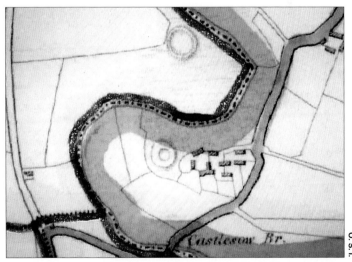

O.S.I.

Fig. 21   Two atypical earthworks on promontories overlooking double bends on the river Sow are associated with the Anglo-Norman period. Castlesow, near the centre of the map, has been described as both a ringwork and a motte; Toberfinnick is a possible ringwork. The fortifications may be related to the sub-division of the Roche manor of Fernegenel, north of Wexford Harbour. *Griffith's Valuation* records that the farm cluster beside the motte was occupied by four families in the 1840s, indicating continuity of occupation on the medieval site.

PRIVATE COLLECTION

Fig. 22   The Anglo-Normans brought the concept of the chartered walled town to Ireland as a centre of defence, economic activity and administration. In county Wexford, two boroughs were protected by town walls. The existing Viking defences of Wexford were strengthened and extended and New Ross was enclosed by a wall in the 1260s. Described as the 'north entrance to Wexford', this sketch captures the defensive capabilities of Wexford's town wall, mural towers and gates. It shows a length of the wall with partially surviving battlements, with (from the right) Abbey Gate tower (now restored), the tower of Selskar Abbey church inside the wall, and, at the extreme left, a unique illustration of Westgate (formerly known as Cow Gate), leading to the present-day Westgate Street. Two gatetowers protruded into the street with a wooden gate in situ. Following the Rebellion of 1798, the town gates were restored by the Corporation but these had been removed by 1835 to facilitate road-widening. The battlements of Selskar Abbey Church tower (centre right), restored in the late 1820s, are shown in a ruinous state, so the sketch must be earlier. The recently discovered collection to which this sketch belongs also contains a drawing of Wexford courthouse, completed in 1808, so it is likely that the above scene was recorded in the intervening period.

Ireland, classified as towered keeps.[80] They consisted of a strong rectangular tower, two or three storeys in height, with a massive circular turret at each corner. Carlow, where building may have started in the period 1210–1215, is considered the earliest.[81] Other possible examples include Lea and Terryglass. A recent study of Ferns Castle has examined the validity of this categorisation.[82] Wexford Castle may have been of this type also, as it is depicted on a seventeenth-century map as having four towers with conical roofs.[83] A description from 1323 supports this view:

> There is one stone castle in which there are four towers roofed with shingles whereof the easements extend to no price, because there is nothing to be received thereof in leasing the building, nor in profits, but it needs much repair. There is also one hall roofed with shingles, and two other houses, thatched, the value of which is nought for the reason stated.[84]

Wexford Castle was in bad repair in 1323, indicating that it may have been built early in the previous century. The castle at Carrig was described as being in ruins at the same period.[85] There is similar evidence for the dilapidated state of the castles of Ross and the Island at the end of the thirteenth century. The manorial accounts contain details of repairs to the Castle of the Island in 1286. An expenditure of £9 4s. 9d., mostly on the roof, represented a considerable investment at the time.[86] However, its effectiveness was short-lived; in 1307, the castle on Hervey's Island was unroofed and worthless.[87] In the same

year, the castle at Old Ross, described as 'an old hall, surrounded with stone walls, unroofed', was in a similar decrepit condition.[88]

By the beginning of the fourteenth century, the castles of Carrig, Ross and the Island were already abandoned and derelict. This may have been precipitated by the partition of Leinster in 1247, when the manors of Ross and the Island became part of the Bigod lordship of Carlow.[89] Subsequently they became outlying manors, administered by officials and visited only occasionally by the absentee owners. The castles may have been used as hunting lodges, as there are several references to hunting dogs in

Fig. 23   This late eighteenth-century illustration of Ferns Castle from *Grose's Antiquities* shows that the structure was already in a dilapidated state with the survival of fabric very similar to its present condition.

Fig. 24   Wexford's thirteenth-century castle was constructed just outside the town wall, on a natural mound near the water's edge to the south-east of the town. A fourteenth-century account described it as having 'four towers roofed with shingles'. This mid-seventeenth-century map also depicts the castle as having four towers with conical roofs. The castle acted as a gaol and a centre of administration for several centuries.

both places.[90] By the end of the thirteenth century, the boroughs of Old Ross and the Island were also in decline, overshadowed by the burgeoning economic power of New Ross. Similarly, the borough of Carrig, with its castle, had to compete with the long-established town of Wexford, situated just five kilometres down river. By 1307, Wexford itself, with 127 waste burgages, was in decline,[91] one of the reasons for the ruinous state of its castle.

Although not strictly speaking castles, two other thirteenth-century stone buildings, both with Marshal connections, can be included. The circular turret known as the Tower of Hook belongs to the same period as the other Marshal castles. It was constructed using the same technology, and presumably personnel, as part of the infrastructure of the lordship of Leinster.[92] Realising the vital nature of Waterford Harbour and its river system for trade and shipping, Marshal established the port of New Ross on the Barrow, 30km from the open sea. Other towns in his lordship were also located on the Barrow and Nore, principally Carlow and Kilkenny. Perhaps influenced by his own narrow escape from shipwreck on his first crossing to Ireland in 1200, Marshal recognised that shipping needed to be guided safely into Waterford Harbour, if his new port of Ross was to be successful. As a navigation aid, he had a thirty-six metre high circular tower erected at the tip of the peninsula to act as a landmark by day and a fire-tower by night. The monks from the nearby monastery of Rinn Dubháin were involved in the construction of the tower and acted as lightkeepers. In 1247, the custodian and chaplains of St

Saviour's of Rinn Dubháin 'who there built a tower as a beacon for ships' were granted maintenance in 'money and otherwise' from the Marshal Lordship, with 'all arrears due to them'.[93] The payment of arrears indicates that the tower had been in operation for some time. As completion would have taken a considerable timespan, it was presumably initiated in the early decades of the century. The use of the monks as custodians was not unusual; in medieval times, religious establishments were often responsible for the display of warning lights.[94]

Marshal's idea for a light-tower may have been inspired by Mediterranean examples, such as the Crusader lighthouse at Acre or the Pharos lighthouse in Alexandria, which he presumably saw when on crusade to the Holy Land.[95] The Tower of Hook was based on the cylindrical castles (known as keeps) which were popular in France, where Marshal spent many years. Marshal castles at Chepstow, Pembroke, Ferns, Carlow and Kilkenny had circular towers.[96] The monks lived in the tower, which served as a monastery as well as a lighthouse. For four centuries, the Tower of Hook remained in the control of the town of Ross. In 1411, the sovereign and community of Ross held the Tower of Hook, with twelve acres of adjoining land.[97] On a 1591 map of Waterford Harbour, the tower is shown with battlements. Seven years later, it was included in a list of the principal castles in the county.[98] With the addition of modern technology, the sturdy thirteenth-century tower survives intact, still serving its original function.

Marshal's grant for the foundation of the Cistercian abbey of Tintern *de Voto* in 1200 emanated from a vow made when in danger of shipwreck. The monastic estate was in two detached parcels, several miles apart, one, on which the abbey was built, beside Bannow Bay, with the isolated section to the north-west.[99] Because of the distance from the abbey, Rathumney Hall, located in the townland of Rathumney (mentioned in the foundation charter), may have served as a headquarters for the lay brothers who

Fig. 25   Gargoyles from Old Ross Castle, found near the adjacent motte, now housed in the Royal Society of Antiquaries.

Fig. 26 **A** The late seventeenth-century view of the Tower of Hook shows that the structure was originally battlemented, emphasising the use of castle architecture in its construction. The annex at the base, which may have been a chapel for the use of the early lightkeeper monks, had an external stairway to a mural chamber in the tower wall. It also shows the first glass lantern, installed during restoration work carried out in the 1670s, to protect the warning beacon from the elements. **B** The rib vaulting, identical on each level, contains the imprint of plank centering, a typical feature of thirteenth-century castle building. **C** The isometric projection shows the internal arrangement of the structure, including the three vaulted chambers, mural stairway, mural chambers and garderobe. The narrower section on top carried the fire beacon.

The Tower of Hook

 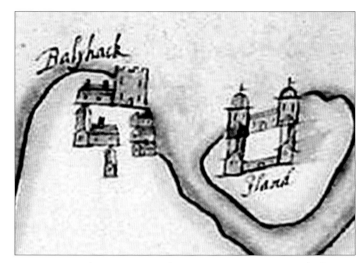

Fig. 27   Two representations of the Castle of the Island, on late sixteenth and early seventeenth-century maps, have features in common. Both show an enclosure with possibly a keep and perimeter towers. Ballyhack Castle is quite accurately depicted in the right-hand image, giving credibility to the Island drawing. These images may suggest the design of the other removed castles, at Old Ross, Carrig, Wexford and Enniscorthy.

worked on the detached portion of the estate. Emphasis was on residential requirements rather than defence in the rectangular hall house (25m x 9m), dated to the thirteenth

Repairs to the Castle of the Island 1296

For one wagon and ten stone of lead bought for the castle of the Island to be newly roofed, together with the carriage of the same from Wales, 60s.

Paid a certain plumber for melting and applying the said lead, 7s. 4d.

For breaking slates for newly roofing the said castle [no cost given],

For 16 quarters of lime for the castle, together with the carriage, 4s. 10d.

For roofing anew the castle by taskwork, 26s. 8d.

For mortar made beside the lead, as by agreement, 2s.

For timber bought for the repairs to the said castle, and for turf and combustible materials obtained for melting the lead, 11s. 10d.

For 200 boards bought for the same castle with their carriage, 7s. 6d.

For sundry nails bought for the same, 11s. 11d.

For 250 laths bought, 1s. $^{1}/_{2}$d.

For tin bought, for tallow for the waggon fetching stones, for digging the land and for porterage, as appears by particular items, 11s. 8d.

For crest tiles bought for the same, 2s.

For a certain carpenter hired by the day, 27s. 6d.

For a certain man employed in repairing the slates on the castle of the Island, at taskwork, 18d.

For the moat, for lime, and for nails bought for the castle of the Island, 8s. 11d.

century.[100] Ruggedly constructed, the two-storey structure had ground-floor entrances and generous windows, some with typical thirteenth-century plank centering. A ground-floor hall in the centre rose to the full height of the building with two storeys at each end. There are fireplaces on the ground and first floors, with garderobes at the south-east and north-east angles. The internal features no longer exist and the walls are damaged but even in its dilapidated state it is obvious that this unique building was intended to be a comfortable residence rather than a defensive structure. This would indicate an early thirteenth-century date, before the colony in south county Wexford came under threat from the resurgent Irish.

MOATED SITES

Castles were invariably connected with the upper echelons of Anglo-Norman society, who were the recipients of extensive land grants. As lands without tenants were of little value, settlers were lured from Britain to become farmers on the manors and to act as 'hewers of wood and drawers of water'. Little is known about the many people of disparate ethnic origins who were prepared to live in a hostile environment in pursuit of an improved status and lifestyle. Frequently allocated land in the most exposed areas on the periphery of manors, they protected themselves and their stock by constructing moated defences around their farmsteads.[101] These rectangular moated sites were enclosed by an earthen bank topped by a wooden stockade and surrounded by a ditch or moat, sometimes fed by a stream. In some cases at least, the entrance was protected by a strong wooden gate and drawbridge.

The distribution of the settlers' moated farmsteads suggests that the withdrawal to the south was gradual. The

Fig. 28 Rathumney Hall, a unique thirteenth-century residental building, was part of the infrastructure on the estate of Tintern *de Voto*, the lack of defensive features reflecting its ecclesiastical environment. The horizontal building had a central hall from ground floor to roof level, with a second storey at each end. **A** The exterior. **B** Collapsed garderobe. **C** Doorways on west wall and corbels for supporting the first floor. **D** Chimney flue and corbels for fireplaces on ground and first floor. **E** Window with plank centering. **F** Conjectural reconstruction of ground floor plan.

DONAL COLFER

Fig. 29 Manorial farmsteads, now referred to as medieval moated sites, were protected by rectangular stockaded banks with an external moat, sometimes fed by an adjacent stream. This reconstruction drawing of a late thirteenth-century site is based on a description of one built on the manor of Ross in 1280. The material for the wooden stockade, massive gate and roof shingles was cut in the adjacent forest.

densely wooded north of the county, never heavily settled, had few moated sites, indicating early desertion. In contrast, moated farmsteads were clustered in a broad band running south-west to north-east across the centre of the county, suggesting that the colony survived in some form here over a considerable period.

The resources needed to create such a sophisticated complex indicates that the sites were occupied by relatively prosperous farm families. Although many have been levelled, the eroded remains of the earthwork elements of these sites, described as the 'architecture of fortified farms',[102] still dot the landscape. Although at the bottom end of the scale of medieval fortifications, moated sites contribute to an understanding of manorial settlement. The sites are also relevant as possible forerunners of some tower houses. The relationship

between several moated sites in county Wexford and later tower houses suggests the abandonment of the moated sites in favour of a more secure defended stone residence.

In south-east Ireland, sites vary considerably in area and width of moat, but 76% have areas of between 500 and 2,500 square metres, with moat widths of between two and seven metres.[103] A site at Carrowreagh, near Taghmon, enclosed an area of 900 square metres with a five-metre moat fed by a stream.[104] These sites, regarded as being outside the first phase of manorial settlement, are associated with a later, unrecorded, generation of settlers, who were often allocated previously unoccupied lands in more peripheral locations.[105]

A map of the moated sites supports this theory, particularly on the larger manors. It is also corroborated by archaeological evidence, which attributes the emergence of moated sites to the second half of the thirteenth century.[106] The recent excavation of a medieval moated site at Coolamurry, county Wexford, shows how these sites functioned. As well as uncovering proof for an internal building, the discovery of worked timbers in the ditch suggest that the entrance was protected by a drawbridge. The generally accepted time-span was confirmed by the dating of pottery to the later thirteenth-early fourteenth century.[107]

Fig. 30 A moated site at Rochestown, one of several defended farmsteads on the manor of Old Ross. The stream which fed the moat continues to do so. Adam Roche held two carucates here in 1307.

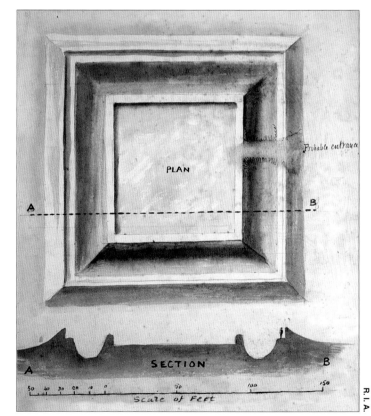

Fig. 31 A plan and section of a still surviving moated site in the townland of Craane, west of Enniscorthy, drawn by Du Noyer c. 1850.

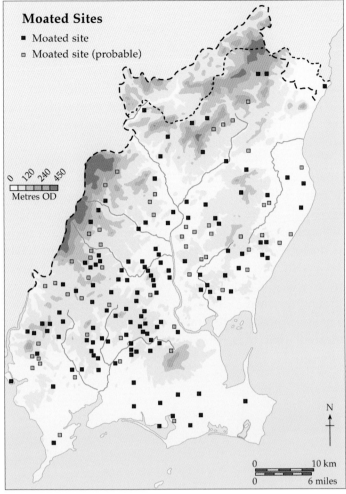

Moated Sites

■ Moated site

□ Moated site (probable)

0 120 240 450

Metres OD

N

0　　　　　　　　　10 km

0　　　　　　　　　6 miles

Fig. 32 Moated sites are concentrated in a broad band running diagonally across the county. This was the interface region between Irish north and English south where the beleaguered colonists, in an effort to survive, erected moated defences around their farmsteads.

Construction of the moated site at Ballyconnor on the manor of Old Ross 1283–84.

The trench at Ballyconnor

53 perches recently dug around the haggard at Ballyconnor: 22s. 3d.

660 stakes or saplings cut in the wood to make a fence upon the same trench: 19d.

For sharpening the said stakes: 3s.

For the wages of Thomas the ditcher, enclosing the fence upon the said trench for 21 days: 5s. 3d.

For the wages of Robert Passer, helping the said Thomas during the same time: 2s. 7d.

For the carriage of the barricading gate for the said fence: 5s. 3d.

For a man hired to help William Brown to make the gate of the haggard there: 12d.

Expenses for the barricade at Ballyconnor

68 planks made in the wood by Gregory, the son of the carpenter: 2s. 10d.

Wages of Gregory O'Murrough, the carpenter, for fashioning timber for 41 days: 13s. 8d.

Wages of William de Stokes and Raymond his brother, for making a palisade around the haggard, for 18 days: 15s.

Wages of Matthew, the carpenter, and Ric. Stokes, for the same, for 18 days: 12s.

For Gregory O'Murrough, for the same time for the aforesaid work: 4s. 6d.

For 2 hired workmen making trenches before the palisade for 18 days: 4s. 6d.

Total: £4 10s. 0d.

This secondary phase of land clearance and colonisation was under way in Wexford in the 1230s. The charter of deforestation issued by Richard Marshal *c.* 1233 permitted his free tenants to 'clear, enclose and cultivate' their lands within 'the metes and bounds of the forests of Ross and Taghmon'.[108] A unique account of the building of a moated site on the grange of Ballyconnor on the demesne manor of Old Ross is contained in the Bigod ministers' accounts for the year 1284.[109] While the exact location of Ballyconnor is not known, it may be identified as the surviving site of Mylerspark, peripherally located in hilly terrain.[110] The creation of the site, referred to as the haggard (hay garth), required a considerable economic input by the demesne manor officials as it was much bigger than usual. Individual farmers needed to have significant resources, in money, time and labour, to build much smaller sites. Of 135 moated sites identified in county Wexford, fifty-five have been destroyed, with a further tentatively identified forty-eight sites. A total of 183 moated sites provides eloquent proof of the extent of Anglo-Norman settlement in the county.[111] It is also possible that more moated sites lie unrecognised under modern farmsteads, many with a rectangular courtyard layout.

There were contrasting reasons for the low density of sites in the south and north of the county. Defence was not a primary consideration in the more secure south, where a high level of initial settlement ruled out the need for the second wave, with which moated sites are usually associated. The light density in the north reflects the speculative nature of initial settlement and subsequent withdrawal from the region. The high concentration of moated sites across the centre of the county mirrors the earlier alignment of mottes and ringworks. The colonisation of this fertile hybrid area, the interface between the native Irish and the colonists, demanded determination, ambition and an unremitting focus on defensive requirements.

FERNS CASTLE

Ferns enjoyed symbolic status as the centre of monastic, episcopal and temporal power in the kingdom of Uí Chennselaig.[1] Strongbow had close associations with Ferns after his arrival in Ireland, selecting it as one of his demesne manors. His wife, Aoife, formerly resided in the Mac Murchada caistéal and teach (house), possibly destroyed by her father when he burned Ferns in 1166 to prevent his enemies from seizing it.[2] A borough had been established at Ferns before Strong-bow's death in 1176, a strong indication of its demesne status.[3] In the following year, the manor of Ferns, equivalent to the medieval parish, was assigned to the services of Wexford.[4]

The bishop retained the episcopal lands at Ferns and later incumbents played a prominent role in the history of the castle. The bishop's landholding is recorded in the townland name of Bolinaspick to the north-east of the village (Baile an Easpaig: Bishops-town). In 1177, when Ferns was in the king's hands after Strongbow's death, William FitzAldelin, the governor of Leinster, assigned the manor to the sons of Maurice FitzGerald. They 'immediately built a castle' which was quickly 'razed to the ground' by their enemies;[5] The speed of its construction and destruction indicated that it consisted of earth and timber. The remains of a stone-faced earthen rampart discovered underneath the stone castle represent either the remains of Mac Murchada's caistéal or the FitzGerald earthwork.[6]

It has not been established who initiated the erection of the present castle. Stone castles on demesne land in the county had all been built by 1230: following William Marshal II's death in that year, the castles of Wexford, Old Ross, Carrig and the Island were resumed into the king's hands[7] while the castle of Ferns was given in dower to a Marshal widow, the Countess of Pembroke.[8] Ferns, valued at £82 in

Fig. 1 Ferns Castle was built on the site of an earlier earthwork fortification. Consisting of an impressive rectangular keep, with a cylindrical tower at each corner, initial work on the castle is attributed to the Marshals, with further additions by William de Valence, who succeeded to the liberty of Wexford by his marriage to a Marshal heiress. Located in the frontier region between Irish north and English south, the castle played a fluctuating role in the struggle for supremacy between English colonists and native Irish. It was taken by the Irish and held by them for considerable periods of time.

Fig. 2 The nature of the castle's internal arrangements has not been established. There may have been a range of wooden domestic buildings against the walls around a central courtyard. The entrance doorway was on the first floor with access to the ground floor from above.

1247, became the most lucrative demesne in the county for Strongbow's successors. In order to protect this valuable asset, located in the vulnerable north of the county, Marshal, in customary fashion, would have built a fortification at Ferns and on other demesne manors in the county. Marshal was engaged in building stone castles; in 1210–1215, construction started on Carlow Castle, designed to control traffic on the Barrow.[9] The

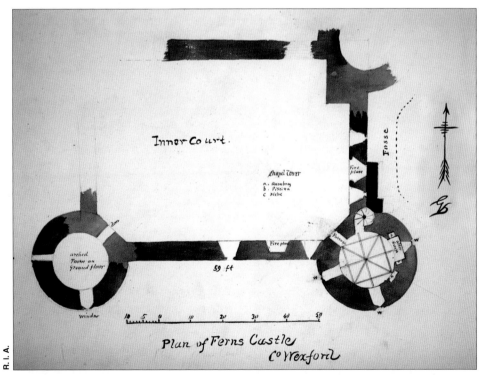

Fig. 3 This mid-nineteenth-century plan by Du Noyer indicates that the castle was in much the same condition as at the present time, apart from possibly depicting elements of the south wall and the north-east tower that no longer exist. Traces of the moat are shown to the east of the castle.

Fig. 4 Mid-nineteenth-century drawings by Du Noyer of two windows, one cusped ogee-headed, and a cross-loop from Ferns Castle.

Fig. 5   A mid-nineteenth-century pencil drawing of Ferns Castle by Du Noyer shows that the survival of the fabric was essentially the same as at present.

castle recorded at Ferns in 1232 can be attributed to Marshal senior or junior, or perhaps a combination of both. Ferns has been classified as a peculiarly Leinster type, referred to as 'towered keeps', including Carlow, Lea (county Laois), Terryglass (county Tipperary), and the former thirteenth-century castle at Wexford. These Marshal-inspired castles consisted of large rectangular keeps with circular towers at the angles.[10] The design features common to the 'towered keeps' suggest a shared knowledge of a specific plan. The concept of the circular tower was brought back from the Crusades and became popular in Normandy, from where it spread to England and Wales.[11] In the late twelfth century, Marshal added circular towers to his castles at Chepstow and Pembroke. The usage of circular towers in the lordship of Leinster was the logical continuation of an established design policy.

The surviving ruins at Ferns cannot be completely attributed to the structure recorded in 1232, as architectural details of windows and chapel date to the mid thirteenth century. Opinion is divided as to whether the later windows and chapel were inserted in the existing castle or if the earlier edifice was completely replaced.[12] The fabric of many medieval structures was altered at a later date. Building in stages was common, as at the castles of Lea and Carlow, where the mid-thirteenth-century upper level windows mark a second building phase.[13]

Later work on Ferns can be attributed to William de Valence, the king's cousin, who succeeded to the lordship of Wexford at the partition of Leinster in 1247 by his marriage to a Marshal heiress.[14] From 1250 onwards, there were persistent rumbles of discontent among the Leinster Irish and de Valence may have upgraded the existing castle to protect his own assets, and the Wexford colony, from the resurgent Irish.[15] Apart from its military capabilities, the high quality of the castle's architecture and craftsmanship, still evident even in its present dilapidated condition, declared the power and social status of the owner.

DESIGN AND ARCHITECTURE

Ferns Castle consisted of a strong, almost rectangular keep, 20m x 18m, three storeys in height, with a massive circular tower at each angle. Most of the east wall and part of the south remain standing. The south-east tower is complete but without battlements, while half of the south-west tower, with battlements, survives. The ground floor has long cross-loops, with larger trefoil windows on the upper floors. The layout of the interior is conjectural, as no internal features are extant; domestic accommodation was possibly provided by a complex of wooden buildings keyed into the external stone walls, as at Lea and

Fig. 6   The south-east tower and east wall, with a chimney, restored windows and cross-loops.

Fig. 7 North elevation of Ferns Castle. The original crenellations survive on the south-west tower.

Carlow.[16] If the interior was of timber rather than stone, it might explain reports that the castle was burned and repaired on several occasions. Excavations revealed an entrance on the south wall, accessed by a drawbridge over a rock-cut fosse (presumably the bridge over the river mentioned in 1536), protected by a barbican (gatehouse).[17] A possible entrance on the east wall had been blocked up.[18] As at

Lea and Carlow, Ferns had a first-floor entrance with access to the ground floor from above. The main hall was on the first floor where a fine fireplace (restored) and garderobes survive. The ground floor chamber in the south-west tower, presumably used as a prison, was only accessible through a trap-door from above, a feature shared with the castles of Terryglass and Carlow. A projecting

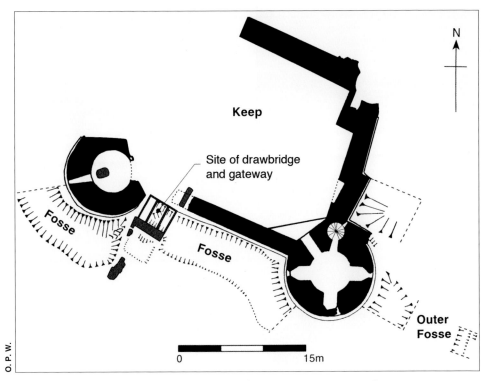

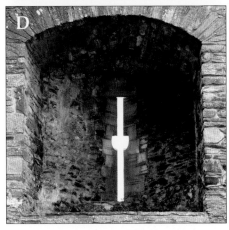

Fig. 8 Plan of Ferns Castle based on extensive archaeological excavations in the 1970s.

Fig. 9 Architectural details from Ferns Castle: **A** Gargoyle on south-west tower **B** Restored first-floor fireplace **C** Loop from the south-west tower **D** Cross-loop in an embrasure.

NEVILLE DUKES

Fig. 10 A section through the south-west tower showing four floors. A vaulted, partially underground chamber, accessible through a trapdoor from above, served as a prison.

wall on the east side indicates the existence of outer defences.

The most impressive existing architectural feature is the 'remarkable' circular chapel on the second floor of the south-east tower.[19] Lit by three single-light windows, it is covered by a vaulted roof with moulded ribs, incorporating six carved heads, springing from corbels in the form of capitals. The altar niche in the east wall has two small aumbries for the storage of the sacred vessels. The most perfect example of a castle chapel in Ireland, it is regarded as a superb example of thirteenth-century architecture.

HISTORY OF THE CASTLE

Ferns Castle, built in a frontier location, was in 'the land of war' for the three and a half centuries that it functioned as a military stronghold. Frequently taken and re-taken, the castle's martial function always took precedence over domestic needs and Ferns probably saw more 'active service' than any other Irish fortress. The history of the castle can be divided into four phases.

Phase 1 The Valence period 1250–1330
During the second half of the thirteenth century, the castle at Ferns was central to the struggle for supremacy over north county Wexford, as it was essential to the retention of lands held by the English colonists.[20] The effectiveness of the castle was diminished by the absentee de Valences, who appointed constables in their place. The castle was targeted by the Irish because of its strategic location and military significance, but also because Ferns had been the ancestral powerbase of the Mac Murchada dynasty. By 1275, the Mac Murchada had emerged as leaders of a loose coalition of the Leinster Irish, including the O'Byrnes, the O'Tooles

Chapel

R. STAPLETON, O.P.W.

Fig. 11 A cross-section through the south-east tower, showing the chapel on the second floor.

Fig. 12 The circular chapel on the second floor of the south-east tower is the most impressive architectural feature of Ferns Castle. Covered by a vaulted roof with moulded ribs, incorporating six carved heads, it has two small aumbries for the storage of sacred vessels.

Fig. 13 Details from the chapel. A One of six stone heads B An aumbry for the storage of sacred vessels C A decorated capital.

and the O'Nolans. Due to an acute lack of resources, the government used a mixture of threat and reward in an effort to maintain the peace. Establishing a tactic that would continue for centuries, the Mac Murchada were paid a retainer to keep the Irish under control, skilfully oscillating between rebellion and acting as peacekeepers.

As the fourteenth century progressed, an already chaotic situation deteriorated dramatically due to the Bruce wars, famine and the plague known as the Black Death. The Irish tactic of clearing land of settlers and claiming it back for themselves was obviously successful. This process can be observed in the decline of the manor of Ferns, in spite of the protection provided by the castle. Worth £82 in 1247, land and burgages were being abandoned by

1299;[21] it was valued at only £39 in 1307[22] and by 1324 the manor was considered worthless, as it was 'totally wasted by Irish felons'. At that stage, the castle 'standing on the borders of the Irish' was badly in need of repair and maintenance.[23]

Phase 2 In the king's hands 1330–70
In 1331, the Leinster Irish raided the county and burned Ferns Castle. They were then defeated by the English, many of them drowning in the Slaney while trying to escape.[24] Shortly afterwards, the castle and manor were taken over by the crown through the Statute of Absentees. Under this decree, people with lands in Ireland, 'in the march or elsewhere', were obliged to live on their property and make provisions for the preservation of the peace; otherwise their possessions were

Fig. 14   The vaulted roof of the chapel has six moulded ribs springing from corbels in the shape of ornamented capitals. Decoration is added to the vaulting in the shape of six stone heads.

resumed into the king's hands and managed by the state. For several years, the crown appointed constables to organise the defence of the castle. These were members of well-known Anglo-Norman families, with names such as Whitty, St John, Meyler, Rochford and Roche, whose ancestors had received grants of land in the early days of the colony. This did not prevent the Irish from again seizing the castle in 1346, but it was quickly recovered and the damage repaired.

In 1349, the castle was the scene of a bizarre incident involving Bishop Esmond of Ferns who, for some unknown reason, was deposed by the Pope. The bishop, a popular member of an esteemed Anglo Norman family, refused to accept the ruling and barricaded himself into Ferns Castle, with his relations and members of other prominent Wexford families. The newly appointed Bishop Charnells appealed to the authorities for help but the sheriff declined to assist him because of staunch support for Esmond. Eventually, one of Charnell's followers gained access to the castle and opened the gate; Esmond was arrested and bound to the peace. In the late 1350s, the castle was again taken by the Irish, the walls were 'levelled' and the bridge (drawbridge) over the river broken, but Bishop Charnell recovered the castle and repaired the damage. Apparently as a reward, he was subsequently appointed joint custodian of the castle and manor.

Phase 3 Controlled by the Mac Murchada 1370–1536

By the late fourteenth century, the Mac Murchada and their allies were gaining the upper hand, presumably helped by the adverse impact of the Bruce wars and the Black Death on the colonists. In 1370, the Mac Murchada again seized

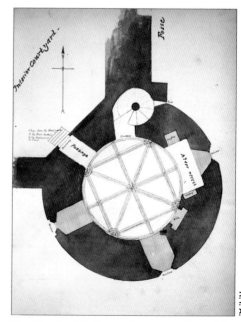

Fig. 16   A mid-nineteenth-century plan of the circular chapel, showing access from the ground floor and from the tower's spiral stairway.

Fig. 15   A mid-nineteenth-century sketch by Du Noyer of the impressive chapel.

Fig. 17 Archaeological excavation exposed part of the castle's dry, rock-cut fosse to the south, showing the entrance to the castle accessed by a drawbridge with a possible gatehouse.

Mac Murchada (at this stage increasingly referred to as the Kavanaghs) control over much of the county. Various schemes aimed at improving the situation of the colonists were proposed by the Irish Privy Council, including the planting of north Wexford with new settlers and the repatriation of thousands of Irish living in England to occupy the south-east of Ireland.[27] Demands escalated for more decisive action and in 1536, when the Mac Murchada were once more in rebellion, the Lord Deputy led a force to lay siege to Ferns. The attackers were equipped with cannon and firearms (possibly their first recorded use in county Wexford) and the Irish occupants of the castle surrendered. However, in an effort to placate the Irish, the Mac Murchada were left in charge of the castle, although at a vastly increased fee.[28]

This event was a turning point in the history of the castle. It was the first time in a century that a force of this size had been led into Wexford by the Lord Deputy and the authorities must have been encouraged by its success. The growing availability and deployment of cannon and firearms had rendered the castle more vulnerable and this development must have influenced the thinking of both the Mac Murchada and the government.

the castle at Ferns and it remained in their control until 1536. The castle was practically uninhabited after the middle of the fourteenth century until the seventeenth century, indicating that the Mac Murchada may not have maintained a continuous presence during this period.[25] The emergence of Art Mac Murchada Caomhánach (McMurrough Kavanagh) as leader signalled the emergence of a new potent force in Leinster. By 1378, he was claiming to be 'chief of the Irish of Leinster' and 'king of Leinster'. During the 1380s, he was granted a fee of eighty marks by the authorities as an inducement to keep the peace. He also extracted a 'Black Rent' from the English settlers, paid in the (vain) hope that they would not be molested. His activities instigated two unsuccessful Irish expeditions by Richard II, after which the resourceful Art continued to straddle the two cultures.[26]

During the fifteenth century, possession of Ferns Castle gave the

Fig. 18 The south-east fosse showing the location of the drawbridge and entrance.

Taking of Ferns Castle by the Lord Deputy, Leonard Grey 1536

The Lord Deputy prepared the army with all celerity to repair to Ferns castle. My Lord rode all that night and was there early in the morning and viewed it. The same was warded [garrisoned]. My Lord demanded whether they would surrender, and deliver the same to him, or not. They made plain answer that they would not leave the same, using very spiteful language. And so passed the day in preparing ginnes [machines], instruments and other necessities for the obtaining thereof; bringing them nigh to the castle, to the intent they might see my Lord would not leave the same, as he promised them, till he had attained it; bestowing his men in the ditches and fastness of that ground, to watch the gate, lest they should evade; and caused some of them to go to the castle, and break the outer gate, entering to the drawbridge. I, perambulating about the same, espied one of the ward often to resort to one place, desired a servant of my brothers, a gunner, to resort privately to a secret place by the castle, and to bestow [hide] himself, which he accomplished, and so killed him; and as it fortuned, the same person was he which was governor and gunner of the castle. Wherefore shortly after they desired to speak with my Lord; who showed them that in case they would not deliver the castle unto him before his Lordship had bestowed his ordnance, which was coming within a mile, that afterwards if they would have delivered the same, it should not be accepted of them, but man, woman and child should suffer for the same. Which all together, with the death of their captain, discomfited them; and they surrendered and yielded the same to my Lord, who for that night put a captain and men in the same, and the next day put a ward of MacMurroughs in the same. And MacMurrough himself came in hostage with my Lord Deputy to Dublin, to agree with his Lordship and Mr. Treasurer for the taking of the same, which was let very lately for 5 marks Irish or thereabouts. Albeit the same MacMurrough hath delivered good hostages to surrender the same castle at the king's pleasure, or his deputies, and to pay yearly 80 marks Irish. For he that had possession thereof before was such a malefactor, that he robbed and wasted about the same. And there[upon] all the nations and principals of the Kavanaghs contented themselves to receive such order and laws as the Deputy and Council shall prescribe unto them and none other. Assuring your honorable good Mastership that the said castle is one of the ancientest and strongest castles within this land, and of the earl of Shrewsbury's, or the duke of Norfolk's, old inheritance, being worth sometime 500 marks by the year; situated nobly within 10 miles to Wexford and 12 miles to Arklow. So as there dwelling a good captain may quiet, order, and rule all those parties. We departed hence along the coast to Dublin, camping in the fields nightly, which way no English Deputy has come this hundred years, within which time no such enterprise has been achieved with so little time and cost. I have seen three weeks' victuals not so well spent with the rising out of the whole English Pale.

Phase 4 English Constables 1536–1600
As the impact of the Reformation exacerbated the religious and political rift between the English and Irish, the Tudor administration sought to establish their law-and-order in Ireland. In 1540, the Lord Deputy demanded that a Great Master would be appointed by the crown with a force of twenty horsemen as well as six gunners on horseback, to be based in Ferns Castle (described as being 'in sore decay') with jurisdiction over the surrounding countryside.[29] This resulted in the appointment of a new type of English official, mostly Protestant, who regarded the appointment as a licence to acquire property and wealth by any means possible. Principal among them were Anthony Colclough, Nicholas Heron, Thomas Stukely, Henry Wallop and Thomas Masterson, who, with their descendants, played a considerable role in the subsequent history of the county. Ambitious, ruthless and violent men, they watched each other jealously and were quick to report perceived wrongdoing in the hope of self-aggrandisement. These men instigated an orchestrated opposition to the Leinster Irish, especially Masterson, who was appointed constable of Ferns Castle in 1569. However, the Irish were by no means pacified. In 1577, the Kavanaghs, allied with Fiach McHugh O'Byrne, burned the castle at Ferns, and in 1580 they were again in rebellion. At that time, the situation in the north of the county was so desperate from the colonists' point of view that a proposal was made to create a new shire of north Wexford to be called 'Ferns'. This apparently only failed due to the lack of suitable office-holders.

In 1583, the Queen granted Thomas Masterson a sixty-year lease of the castle and manor in recognition of his service 'in bringing the Kavanaghs under control'. He was required to repair the structure and maintain a garrison. During the Nine Years' War, the Kavanaghs were again in rebellion in support of the northern leaders, O'Neill and O'Donnell, but this was their 'last hurrah', as defeat of the Irish at Kinsale in 1601 is conventionally regarded as the ultimate death-knell of Gaelic Ireland.[30]

In 1610, the plantation of north Wexford implemented a 'surrender and re-grant' scheme in which the Gaelic landowners participated. Most of the land, however, was granted to new English owners, who fortified their estates with plantation castles.[31] Ferns Castle featured briefly once more as a military fortification in 1649, when the Confederate garrison surrendered to Cromwellian soldiers. It was subsequently allowed to moulder and it had already deteriorated to its present state by the end of the eighteenth century. For a period in the twentieth century, part of the front wall was used as a handball alley. During the 1970s, a major archaeological dig focused attention on the castle and it became accessible to the public as a national monument. The O. P. W. has erected an impressive reception centre from which guides operate tours during the summer season.

Ferns Castle is regarded as one of the finest examples of a medieval Irish castle. It is paradoxical that a building of this quality with such fine architectural details may seldom have been occupied by its builders, if at all. There is also a strange irony in the fact that it was an asset rather than a hindrance to the native Irish for more than a quarter of its useful existence, the very people that it was meant to exclude and dominate.

THE SHIFTING FRONTIER

Following the establishment of a feudal landholding structure, the colony in county Wexford prospered in stable conditions for more than half a century. The leadership of the Mac Murchada had been devastated in the aftermath of the Anglo-Norman arrival and their successors disappeared from the record for almost a century.[1] During the first half of the thirteenth century, the area in Ireland under Norman control was expanded and consolidated.[2] But from 1250, the settlers experienced a reversal, due to more efficient opposition from a reinvigorated generation of Irish leaders. The Irish recovery was aided by a complicated partition of Leinster in 1247, with an ensuing long-term damaging effect on the stability of the colony.[3] Factional conflict amongst the settlers accelerated a gradual decline and an increase in lawlessness.

The landscape initially facilitated a natural segregation between native and colonist. The Irish, whose pastoral economy required only flimsy dwellings, were forced to occupy the wooded uplands of the Blackstairs and Wicklow mountains, leaving the English settlers to establish an arable economy in the coastal lowlands and river valleys.[4] The loss of much of their best land and the disruption of their traditional lifestyle, combined with the implementation by the colonists of a system of legal apartheid, inevitably generated resentment among the native Irish and an unquenchable desire to recover their lost status. By the end of the century, the Leinster Irish, led by the Mac Murchada, were in general revolt. During the fourteenth century, the colony was undermined by the Bruce invasion (1315–1318) and the Black Death, which appeared in 1348 and continued to devastate the population, particularly the colonists in the towns, for the rest of the century.[5]

The Irish recovery had a dramatic impact on the English occupation of county Wexford. By the end of the fourteenth century, the north of the county was controlled by the Irish. The settlers of English extraction were largely restricted to the southern 'English' baronies of Forth and Bargy, with parts of Shelmalier and Shelburne, protected by the natural barriers of Forth Mountain and the Corock and Owenduff rivers. The difference between the Irish north and English south of the county is reflected in the divergent cultural landscape of both regions.[6]

Fig. 1   The rocky eminence of Forth Mountain (235m), extending south-west from Wexford town, formed part of the natural defences of the English Pale, which extended over the southern lowlands. The Aughnagroagh river, rising on the north slope of the mountain, flows south-west to join the Corock, which flows into Bannow Bay. Another stream flows east to join the Slaney. These water-courses defined the limits of the Wexford Pale.

BRITISH LIBRARY

Fig. 2 Jean Creton, a French artist who accompanied Richard II's 1394 expedition to Ireland, depicted the meeting of Art Mac Murchada and the earl of Gloucester. He used contrasting landscapes, dress, equipment and military techniques to represent a stereotypical clash of the two cultures.

THE IRISH REVIVAL

From the mid-thirteenth century onwards, the colony experienced a reversal. This was related to a more concerted opposition from an energised generation of Gaelic leaders, which led to a gradual recovery of lands and assimilation or expulsion of settlers.[7] The Irish recovery was aided by the complicated partition of Leinster in 1247, which had a long-term debilitating effect on the lordship.[8] The colony in Ireland was further sapped by baronial rebellion and reform in England during the 1260s, and simultaneous, but apparently unrelated disturbances in Ireland, caused by factional conflict between the Geraldines and de Burgos.[9] These, combined with the failure of the Irish administration to handle the problems related to the fragmentation of Leinster and a growing problem with absentee landlords, prompted a gradual decline in the colony and an eruption of lawlessness.[10]

By the 1270s, the Leinster Irish were in general revolt. This may have been motivated by the need for subsistence,

JB

Fig. 3 A reconstruction of a thirteenth-century settler's farmhouse which was recently found at Moneycross, in the north of the county near Gorey. The associated finds indicate a short period of occupation, confirming the historical record of early abandonment.

Fig. 4   This view looking north from Slievecoiltia shows the Blackstairs Mountains, which form the western boundary of county Wexford. The formerly heavily wooded Duffry to the east remained in the hands of the Irish for centuries. The piedmont region to the south was known as the Fassagh (wilderness) of Bantry. Duffry is an anglicised form of the Irish 'Dubhthír' (Black country) which is also echoed in the name of the mountains.

due to a famine caused by the severe weather of 1271.[11] The annals for that year recorded 'very bad weather' and 'a great famine and pestilence', so that 'multitudes of poor people died of cold and hunger and the rich suffered hardship'.[12] The Mac Murchada emerged as the leaders of the Leinster mountain Irish, including the O'Nolans, O'Tooles and O'Byrnes, who were devastating the manors of the colonists. Military expeditions against the Irish ended in disaster before the Dublin authorities eventually managed to impose short-term control.[13] The government's ability to respond militarily to the Gaelic revival was limited by an acute lack of resources, due to the demands for men, provisions and finance for the king's war in Wales, Scotland and Flanders. The situation of the colonists in Ireland was undermined by the removal of large numbers of men to fight abroad.[14] This facilitated lawlessness, including attacks by both Irish and English on poorly defended manors. The deteriorating situation at the end of the century was reflected in the liberty of Wexford by a fall in revenue and a decline in the colony.[15]

By the beginning of the fourteenth century, war was endemic in Ireland. The Mac Murchada and their followers were in rebellion. In 1305 Gilbert de Sutton, the seneschal of the liberty of Wexford, was killed by the Irish. The confrontation took place near the town (villam) of Haymund (Old French Aymon) de Grace, who also fought in the battle but survived.[16] The village of Clohamon (Cloch Aymon: Aymon's castle), on the Slaney in the north-west of the county, presumably represents the site of his 'town'.[17] The situation was exacerbated by the problem of rebel English, sometimes allied with the native

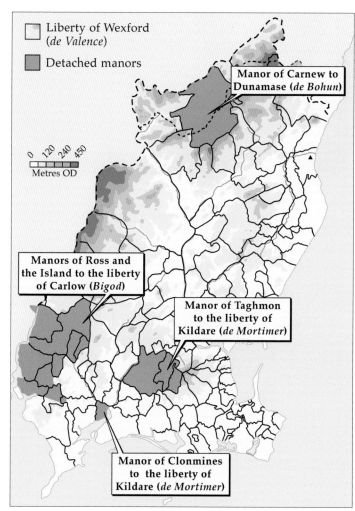

Fig. 5   In 1247, following the death of William Marshal's five sons without male heir, the lordship of Leinster was divided among his five daughters. The need to create equal shares fragmented county Wexford, with a consequential adverse impact on the future of the English colony.

NEVILLE DUKES

Fig. 6   The oak woods of north Wexford, the Duffry and the Fassagh of Bantry, played a determining role in the history and settlement of the county. The dense forest impeded the development of the colony in the west and north and facilitated the Irish resurgence by providing an impenetrable refuge from which to pressurise the colonists. The clearing of the woods, for security as well as economic considerations, was initiated by Elizabethan officials in the late sixteenth century. The timber industry, centred on Enniscorthy, resulted in the obliteration of Wexford's woodlands within a century.

Fig. 7 This view looking north-east from Slievecoiltia, towards the Wicklow Mountains in the distance and the Blackstairs on the left, shows the fertile land across the centre of the county. For several centuries, this region was the interface between the Irish in the north and the English colonists in the south. The majority of thirteenth-century motte castles, stone castles and moated sites were concentrated along the same orientation. In this interface region, there was inevitable contact between the two groups, resulting in considerable acculturation. By the sixteenth century, the frontier area had migrated further south, confining the colonists to the southern Pale of Forth and Bargy, with part of Shelmalier.

Irish.[18] For example, the de Caunteton family of the manor of Glascarrig, allied with the O'Byrnes, ravaged the countryside in 1306, until they were suppressed by a force of horse and foot dispatched by the justiciar.[19] Subsequent to the defeat of the de Cauntetons, the devastation of the manor of Glascarrig by the Mac Murchada serves as an illustration of the destruction and desertion of the rest of the march lands in the north of the county. It also demonstrates the effectiveness of the Irish tactics in ridding the land of settlers and reclaiming it for themselves. The lands of Glascarrig were 'in the march and sterile', because no one dared to 'put hands on them' for fear of the Mac Murchada. The houses were ruinous and beyond habitation. Most significantly, many tenants fled the manor, possibly to the more secure south of the county or even across the Irish Sea to Wales or England.[20] The recent discovery of an undefended Anglo-Norman farmstead at Moneycross, near Gorey, provides a valuable insight into the abandonment of the north of the county by the colonists. The site, comprising a medieval long-

house with an associated enclosure, was occupied for a short period only. Pottery finds indicate occupation between the late twelfth to the fourteenth century, followed by abandonment, a timescale which tallies well with the historical record.[21]

During the first decade of the calamitous fourteenth century, the resurgent Irish of the Leinster mountains were in a state of almost continuous war. The authorities, establishing a precedent that would persist for centuries, used a mixture of threat and bribe in an effort to maintain the peace. The Mac Murchada, for example, were frequently given a retainer for their efforts in maintaining the peace, and alternated between open rebellion and acting as paid peacekeepers for the authorities.[22]

Because of the aggravated security situation, the king's council ordered that a special meeting, presided over by Edmond le Botiller [Butler], should be held at Ross in 1312 to organise the suppression of the rebels. Three custodians were appointed, each to be provided with twenty horsemen, thirty hobelars (lightly armed archers mounted on ponies) and twenty-six foot, to be stationed at Clonmore (county Carlow), Arklow and Wicklow.[23] The seneschal of the liberty of Wexford and Adam Roche were to raise a force to be based at Ferns. Muiris Mac Murchada, who undertook to wage war against the Irish rebels, was employed to travel about to trouble spots with a force of one horseman, thirty hobelars and twenty-four foot-soldiers.[24] In 1314, he was paid £76 for fighting the

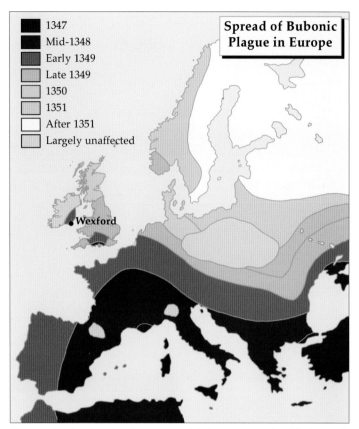

Fig. 8 Originating in the eastern Mediterranean, the Black Death spread aggressively along shipping routes, arriving in Ireland in early 1349. The Anglo-Irish inhabitants of the heavily populated ports suffered to a greater extent than the more dispersed rural Irish. In county Wexford, the plague hastened the eventual abandonment of the port towns of Bannow, Carrig, Clonmines and the town of the Island.

O'Byrnes and guarding the marches of Wexford and he was granted the manor of Curtun (Courtown) in the north of the county.[25]

In 1315, in a dramatic escalation of the war in Scotland, Edward Bruce invaded Ireland with an army of 6,000 men.[26] Bruce had himself crowned king of Ireland and sought to unite the Irish in an attempt to expel the English. His plan was unsuccessful. Bruce was killed at Faughart in county Louth in 1318 after a bitterly fought campaign.[27] The campaign, which coincided with the worst famine of the middle ages, caused widespread hardship.[28] County Wexford, perhaps because of its natural defences of mountain and river, was not directly involved in the war,[29] although the neighbouring liberty of Carlow was devastated.[30] The ferocity of the Bruce campaign, combined with famine, had a debilitating effect on the economy and population of Ireland. This led to a general breakdown in the rule of law and accelerated the gathering momentum of the Gaelic revival.[31]

The crisis in county Wexford was further deepened by the partition of the liberty between the families of the two sisters of Aymer de Valence, lord of Wexford, who died

without heir in 1324. The castle of Ferns was subsequently taken into the king's hands because of neglect by its absentee owners.[32] Following Valence's death, a survey of his possessions detailed lands that were 'waste because of the war'. Abandoned lands included the manor and borough of Ferns, and 221 burgages in Wexford town. Most deserted lands were in the north of the county but even in the manor of Carrig, just north of Wexford town, the tenants were 'destroyed by war'.[33]

In the chaotic aftermath of the Bruce invasion, the Mac Murchada made a decisive move to recover their former position as kings of Leinster. In 1327, in an event which symbolised the extent and scope of the revival:

> The Irish of Leinster came together and made a certain king, that is Domhnall, son of Art MacMurrough, who, when he had been made king, ordered that his banner should be placed within two miles of Dublin and afterwards to travel throughout all the lands of Ireland.

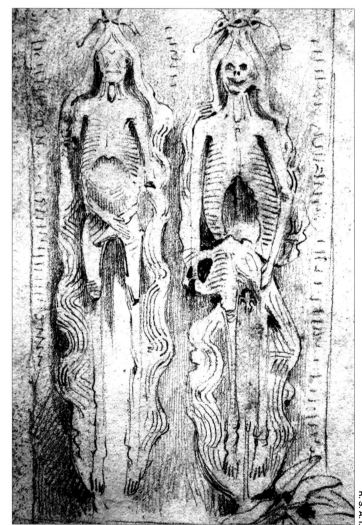

R.S.A.I.

Fig. 9 This cadaver grave slab in Drogheda reflected a European-wide obsession with death and human frailty induced by the Black Death.

Fig. 10   The abandonment of the port of Clonmines at the head of Bannow Bay may have been accelerated due to the devastation wrought by the Black Death. Founded by William Marshal, the town's early significance is indicated by the nature of the surviving stone buildings. **A** Fortified parish church. **B** A unique fortified building combining a chapel and meeting house. **C** Augustinian priory. **D** Two tower houses, one integrated in a modern farmhouse with a farmyard that may represent the original bawn (bottom left). **E** A remnant of an early seventeenth-century Jacobean house.

Even though Domhnall was subsequently captured and imprisoned in Dublin Castle, the ambitious nature of the event signalled a more menacing and persistent challenge to the government by the Leinster Irish.[34] His escape in 1331 precipitated a rising, during which the castle of Ferns was taken and county Wexford ravaged. The English of the county attacked and defeated the Irish, many of whom drowned in the river Slaney while attempting to escape. Those who had taken part in the rebellion were subsequently excommunicated.[35]

The disruption and suffering fomented by the disturbed political situation in Ireland escalated dramatically with the arrival of the plague known as the Black Death. Appearing in Europe in 1347, the plague spread stealthily along the trade routes and arrived in Dublin and Drogheda in 1348. The terror provoked by the outbreak resulted in the convergence of pilgrims, from all over Ireland and from all levels of society, at the monastic site of St Mullins to pray for deliverance from the pestilence.[36] The Black Death of 1349, combined with the sporadic outbreaks which continued into the next century,

ravaged the population.[37] An initial mortality rate of 25–35% among the colonists may have risen to 40–50% per cent by the end of the century, due to recurring outbreaks.[38] The Anglo-Irish, concentrated in the towns, suffered to a greater extent from this rat-borne disease than the more dispersed Irish population.[39] As one of the most heavily settled counties, with as many as seven ports trading with Britain and the continent, Wexford must have been traumatised by the epidemic. The plague hastened the eventual abandonment of four of the port towns: the Island, Bannow, Clonmines and Carrig. One of the few mentions of the plague in the county refers to the town of Ross. An account in 1349 described it as being:

> on the borders of the enemy, divers persons killed, as often by frequent hostile invasions as by warlike conflicts for the defence of the town, as by mortality from pestilence, impoverishment, and even total destruction … the community are in such an unaccustomed state of misery, poverty and helplessness … a great part of the men of the said town are ready to leave and fly to foreign parts.

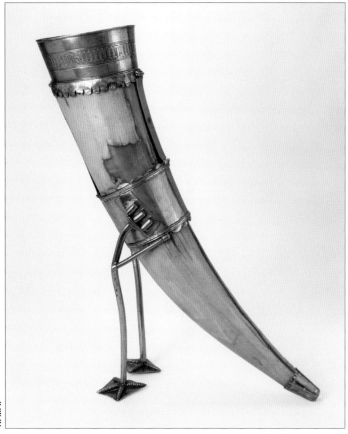

Fig. 11 This exotic artifact, known as the Kavanagh Charter Horn, survives as a symbol of kingship between the thirteenth and fifteenth centuries. The ivory horn, dating to the thirteenth century, may have been a hunting horn. During Art Mac Murchada's reign, in the late fourteenth/early fifteenth century, a detachable brass mount was added, standing on clawed birds feet. The maker's name, Tigernan Ó Lavan, is inscribed on the mount. The horn may then have been used as a ceremonial drinking vessel, possibly during inauguration ceremonies. The Down Survey recorded that the Garryhill branch 'had a vessel or cup to drink out of called Corne-cam-more' [presumably corn cam mór – the great crooked cup – an apt description of the object].

Because of the state of emergency in Ross, a debt to the king of £100 was reduced by 50 marks (3 marks = £2), the money to be spent on the defence of the town and adjacent countryside.[40] The only other known mention of the Black Death in county Wexford refers to Ferns, where Bishop Groseld died of the plague in 1348.[41] The insidious effects of the plague eventually expanded Mac Murchada influence, with a resultant deterioration in the security of Leinster. Branches of the Mac Murchada established clan territories in minor lordships in what is now northern county Wexford. The various branches of the lineage adopted different surnames. The surname Mac Murchada (MacMurrough) was not used by any of these groups but was reserved as the title of the king of Leinster. All the Kavanaghs descended from Art Caomhánach (Kavanagh), the son of Diarmait Mac Murchada; the Kinsellas, descended from his nephew, held a large territory in the Macamores, between Ferns and the sea. Descendants of

Raymond Mac Murchada, known as the Clan Raymond (later changed to Redmond), ruled along the sea coast down to the early seventeenth century. The MacWaddicks, descendants of Uadóg (Walter Mac Murrough), established an independent lordship between Ferns and Gorey. Other Mac Muchada septs included the Mac-Hendricks and the Mernaghs, both with territory in the north of the county.[42]

From the mid-fourteenth century onwards, the English colony in Ireland retracted steadily as the settler population was reduced and manors fell derelict. Lordships were abandoned, while castles were neglected and fell into disrepair. By the 1320s, for example, the castles of Wexford and Carrig were both in a poor condition.[43] Officialdom blamed 'the wars of the Irish rebels' but the situation was aggravated by internal dissent among the settlers and the diversion of English attention to France by the start of the Hundred Years War.[44] During the 1350s, the government used a combination of war and diplomacy to maintain law and order, aided by money and troops from England, a trend that persisted for the rest of the century.[45]

North Wexford was under continuous pressure during this period: Ferns Castle was repeatedly taken and 'destroyed' by the Irish in 1358. It was retaken and

Fig. 12 The seal of Dómhnall Riach Mac Murchada Caomhánach, grandson of Art and king of Leinster 1432–76. The Mac Murrough lion forms part of the motif. It continued in use until the sixteenth century.

Fig. 13   The manor and borough of Taghmon were held in demesne by the Lords of the Liberty. By the 1380s, Taghmon was 'on the marches of the county' and played a strategic part in resisting the advancing Irish. Taghmon Castle was presumably built by the Palatine lords in the fifteenth century as part of the defences of the Wexford Pale. The fortress-like structure, one of the largest tower houses in the county, consists of four storeys with a loft under the ground floor vault. The round-headed doorway was protected by a machicolation, portcullis and murder-hole. The military function was emphasised by two corner machicolations on the north-west and south-east angles. As at the Cistercian tower house at Ballyhack, which Taghmon resembles in size and design, a stone head on the north-facing wall of Taghmon Castle kept perpetual watch over the march lands to the north.

BRITISH LIBRARY

Fig. 14 Jean Creton depicted the late fourteenth-century fleet of ships that transported the king's army to Waterford Harbour in 1394, a valuable maritime image from that era. Note the fore and aft castles, a feature of shipping of the period, which were manned by archers when attacking enemy shipping. The abbreviated form of fo'c's'le (forecastle) is still used to describe the crew's quarters beneath the forward deck of a ship.

repaired by the bishop at a cost of £100.[46] During the same period, John Meyler, the sheriff of the county, was allowed £20 for horses and equipment lost in conflict with the Breens of the Duffry.[47] At a parliament summoned in Kilkenny in 1366, the laws known as the Statutes of Kilkenny were enacted in an effort to stabilise eroding English race, law and culture in 'the land of peace'. Many were re-enactments of earlier laws, mostly related to the defence of the colony, and had little real impact. Prohibited activities included the game called 'hurlings, with great clubs at ball upon the ground', which was to be abandoned in favour of 'gentle noble games which pertain to arms'.[48]

In the mid 1370s, the advent of Art Caomhánach, of Muirchartach's line, as leader of the Mac Murchada, signalled a new force in Leinster. The emergence of a strong leader of the Leinster Irish resulted in repeated directives to the custodians of the peace, including the bishop of Ferns, the abbot of Dunbrody and the preceptor of the Hospitallers at Ballyhoge, to organise the defence of the county and to have regular musters of men-at-arms. They were also authorised to negotiate and make treaties with the Irish enemies.[49]

By 1378, Art was claiming to be 'chief of the Irish of Leinster' and 'king of Leinster', and he was in receipt of a fee of eighty marks during the 1380s.[50] He also extracted a 'tax', or Black Rent, from communities throughout Leinster. Perhaps guided by the experiences of his predecessors, Art adroitly maintained the delicate balance which allowed him to fulfil conflicting roles: he succeeded in ruling as Gaelic king of Leinster while in receipt of a fee from the crown and contributions from the English settlements.[51] By occupying the Barrow valley, Art severed the routes of communication between Dublin and the south-east, dealing a crippling blow to English administration outside the Pale.

The pressure exerted by Art on the colony resulted in a flight from the manors and towns, which the authorities attempted to prevent by allowing no one, except merchants, to travel to foreign parts.[52] In 1389, a sessions held at Taghmon for five weeks with sixteen men-at-arms and horse 'greatly curbed the malice of the Irish'. Taghmon was described as being 'in the marches', an indication that the frontier between English and Irish had retreated further south due to incessant Irish pressure.[53]

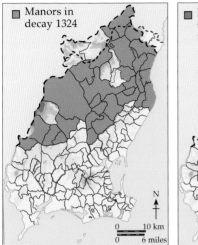

Fig. 15   The lands in the north of the county confiscated by Richard II in 1394 and granted to Beaumont, corresponded largely to the manors, east of the Slaney, that were recorded as being 'in decay' as early as 1324.

The strategic frontier location of Taghmon led to the construction of the fortress-like tower house, which still dominates the village, by the Talbot lords of the Liberty, possibly in the mid-fifteenth century.

The English in Ireland had made repeated appeals to the king to come to Ireland to curb the activities of English and Irish rebels. The situation had unravelled to such an extent, in particular from the activities of Art Mac Murchada and the Irish of the Leinster mountains, that Richard II eventually had no option but to intervene in person. Extensive preparations were made for the recruitment of a large army and all absentee landowners were ordered to return to Ireland under pain of forfeiture. Richard landed at Waterford in October 1394 with the biggest army to be sent to Ireland in the middle ages, 8,000 men accompanied by a naval force.[54] Art Mac Murchada promptly burned New Ross and withdrew deep into the

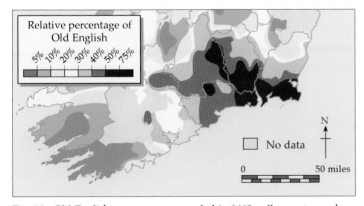

Fig. 16   Old English surnames as recorded in 1660 poll-tax returns show that their heaviest presence corresponded to the original areas of dense Anglo-Norman colonisation in the south-east lowlands. The baronies of Forth and Bargy had the strongest concentration of Anglo-Norman names in the country, with a corresponding density of 'town' placenames. The map illustrates the division of county Wexford into an 'enduring trilogy of regions'; an Irish north, an English south, with a transitional hybrid zone.

woods of the Blackstairs.[55] By placing a ring of garrisons around this district, the king confined Mac Murchada to the woods, while establishing control over the rest of Leinster. On one occasion, Art narrowly escaped capture by the king's forces in the wood of Leverough; among the items taken was a seal describing him as king of Leinster.[56]

The sheer size of Richard's army, and the success of his strategy, intimidated Mac Murchada and the other Gaelic leaders. The terms of their submission show that the king planned to create a new English land in Leinster. Art and his followers were to depart Leinster to make war on rebels elsewhere; any lands which they conquered were to be held of the king. Richard's intention to initiate a new plantation was indicated by the land grants that he made before his departure in May 1395. To his admiral, Sir John de Beaumont, he granted a vast estate in north-east Wexford, consisting of the land between the Slaney and the sea, an area effectively controlled by the Mac Murchada.[57] The placename Clobemon (Cloch Beamainn: Beaumont's castle), indicates that an unsuccessful attempt was made to

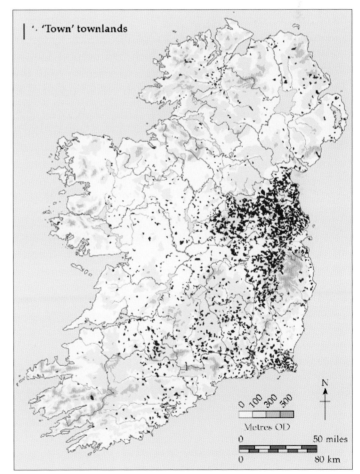

Fig. 17   The extent of Anglo-Norman colonisation in the late medieval period is evident in the distribution of townland names containing the suffix 'town'. There is a cluster in the Dublin Pale and also in the south Wexford 'English' baronies of Forth and Bargy. The prefixes of these townland names frequently record the names of early settlers.

Fig. 18 The traditional culture of Forth and Bargy is manifested in various ways but none more unique than the funeral custom, on the way to the graveyard, of placing a wooden cross under a seach bush. Now confined to Kilmore, the practice was formerly widespread. These pictures illustrate the continuity that persists at Kilmore to the present time. The drawing from 1850 by Du Noyer, showing crosses in a bush beside a stone pier, is replicated by the modern photograph, showing crosses in and under presumably the same bush and beside the same, but dilapidated, traditional round pier.

settle this territory. The long-term significance of the grant was its use, two centuries later, as a pretext for the plantation of the area by the wily James I.[58]

The re-grant by Richard II of extensive lands in north Wexford was a pivotal event in the history of settlement in the county. Predicated on the removal of the Mac Murchada leadership, it was an implicit acceptance of the failure of English settlement in the lands which had been reclaimed by the Irish. Following the king's departure and the withdrawal of the garrisons, the Irish chiefs predictably renounced their submissions and returned to war. The government failed to honour the agreement made with Art Mac Murchada and he resumed his role as king of Leinster. Following the killing of Roger Mortimer, heir to the throne of England, in an engagement with the Irish in county Carlow, Richard led a second, smaller expedition to Ireland in 1399. This time, Mac Murchada was better prepared and decisively defeated the English army. During the king's absence in Ireland, his rival, Henry of Lancaster, claimed the throne and a chastened Richard returned to imprisonment, deposition and death.

Art Mac Murchada, continuing to operate with impunity in both cultures, resumed his former pattern of raids and negotiations. Ironically, the institutions of colonial society had no choice but to permit, and to some extent legalise, his methods. In 1403, the king allowed New Ross, 'situated in the march and surrounded by Irish enemies', to trade with the Irish and to pay an annual tribute of ten marks to Mac Murchada. In 1409, the government authorised the seneschal of Wexford, the sovereigns of Ross and Wexford and four principal men of the county to pay him eighty marks.[59] Art, 'the most dreaded enemy of the English in Leinster', straddled both cultures until his death at Ross in 1418, reputedly by

poisoning. He had succeeded in restoring the Mac Murchada kingship of Leinster while undermining much of the English colony.[60]

The limited extent of the English settlement in county Wexford at the end of the fourteenth century differed substantially from the planned colonisation which had been envisaged two centuries previously. The initial intention was to colonise the region represented by the modern county but the Irish recovery forced the frontier

Fig. 19 This mid-nineteenth-century image by Du Noyer shows that, at Carrig-on-Bannow, the crosses were placed, not in a bush, but beside three stone crosses at a cross-roads, described by the artist as 'a resting place for funerals'. The stone crosses presumably originated in the medieval churchyard and the placing of wooden crosses there may have symbolised the community's enduring association with the medieval site.

steadily southwards, ultimately confining the settlers to the southern baronies. The contrast between the north and south of the county underpinned a characteristic administrative and settlement landscape in both areas. This distinctiveness was expressed in a variety of ways. The granting of much larger estates to attract settlers to the dangerous march lands of the north led to a dramatic difference in the scale of manorial and ecclesiastical divisions. The sprawling parishes of the north and north-west, serving a small, scattered population on large manors, contrasted with the network of diminutive, sometimes fragmented parishes, created by the small, densely populated manors in the south, particularly in the barony of Forth.

The isolation of the 'Wexford Pale' of Forth and Bargy was so complete that it permitted the emergence of a unique dialect known as Yola, based mostly on Chaucerian English, which persisted down to the nineteenth century.[61] A custom, which still survives, of placing a wooden cross in a bush on the way to the graveyard, may have come with the Normans from France, where it was also practised.[62] This cultural exclusiveness found expression in other ways also; one of the greatest concentration of Old English 'town' placenames in Ireland is found in Forth and Bargy and the region had the highest percentage of families of Old English origin in the country in the seventeenth century.[63]

Earthworks, castles, churches, towns, villages, surnames and placenames present an eloquent record of the Anglo-Norman migration into Wexford in the late twelfth and thirteenth centuries. Tower houses, mostly built in the fifteenth and sixteenth centuries by the descendants of the thirteenth-century settlers, provide the most compelling landscape evidence for the contrasting settlement of north and south. The distribution of these distinctive structures, almost completely absent from the Gaelic north, scarce in the central hybrid frontier area, profuse in the English south, illustrates the three enduring cultural divisions in the county Wexford landscape. The concentration is particularly heavy in the south Wexford pale of Forth and Bargy, contained within a river referred to as the Pill.[64] The most remarkable testament to the resilience and endurance of those 'ancientest gentlemen' is provided by their numerous descendants, whose distinctive surnames remain synonymous with county Wexford.

SOCIAL TURMOIL

The ignominious failure of Richard II's expeditions to impose English law on the Irish of the Leinster Mountains at the end of the fourteenth century was followed by two centuries of social disorder and confrontation.[1] The clash between areas of English colonial feudalism and Irish Brehon Law resulted in the emergence of warlords in both cultures. It also created an interface region where acculturation occurred.

From the colonists' perspective, the extreme turmoil in Wexford was intensified by the fact that the county was not subject to the crown, having descended from the Marshals to the earls of Shrewsbury as an independent palatinate. As the Shrewsburys were absentee landlords, their ability to assert their authority was diluted by the delegation of law and order to their officials. This situation persisted until 1536, when the possessions and powers of the absent palatinate lords were resumed by the Crown.[2] The normally resident earls of Ormond in the neighbouring Butler lordship (represented by the modern counties of Kilkenny, Carlow and part of Tipperary) exerted rigorous control over their territory, using a combination of feudal and Gaelic law to administer justice.[3] The Butlers, like other semi-autonomous warlords, maintained a small standing army for defensive and offensive purposes. The considerable expense involved led to the quartering of the soldiers (horsemen, gallowglasses – originally gallóglaigh or foreign warriors – and light infantry known as kerne) on the manorial tenantry.

This coercive system, known as 'coign and livery', inflicted severe hardship and was bitterly resented. It had serious repercussions for county Wexford as the Butlers obviously regarded Wexford as a soft target, accessible from the Ormond lordship through St Mullins and the Pollmounty Gap. In 1455, for example, Edmund MacRichard Butler, his son James and James's father-in-law, MacMurrough, king of Leinster, 'with banners displayed, burnt and destroyed the county of Wexford for four days and four nights'.[4]

During the sixteenth century, the Butlers continued to make frequent forays into the county to extract provisions and fines to pay for their private army.[5] Butler aggression may have been in retaliation for raids into their territory by those MacMurrough Kavanaghs whose lands bordered the Butler lordship.[6] The county officials also used force to extract taxes from the English inhabitants; for example, in 1548, the burgesses of Fethard appealed to the Lord Deputy to prevent the rapacious sheriff, Patrick Meyler of Duncormick, from inflicting coign and livery on the town.[7]

Fig. 1   The Pollmounty Gap, between the Blackstairs (right of picture) and the Barrow (at the foot of Mount Brandon on the left) was a vulnerable point in county Wexford's natural defences. This gap had been occupied by the early medieval monastery of St Mullins, at the tidal limit of the Barrow. The erection of an Anglo-Norman motte-and-bailey castle beside the monastery emphasised the strategic nature of the location. Both the Mac Murchada and the Butlers from the neighbouring Ormond Lordship exploited the gap to dispatch raiding groups to plunder the colonists of south Wexford. Infiltration and escape was facilitated by the Fassagh of Bantry, a heavily wooded area at the southern extremity of the Blackstairs, to the north of New Ross.

Fig. 2 This detail from a 1521 painting by the German artist Albrecht Durer (1471–1528), portrays a Scottish gallóglach (gallowglass) at left, wrapped in a feileadh mór (great cloak) and carrying his claidheamh mór (great sword). He is accompanied by two Irish kern (supporting henchmen) armed with pole axes. One also carries a long battle horn.

RAIDS AND RALLIES

The intrusions by the Butlers accentuated an already polarised situation in county Wexford. As the Irish consolidated and extended their hold on the wooded areas near the mountains of the north and west, the colonists were forced further south to the 'English' baronies of Forth, Bargy and Shelburne. This process was accompanied by incessant plundering and retaliatory expeditions between territory under Irish control and the 'Wexford Pale'. This confrontation created three regions in the county, with the colonists confined to a shrinking 'land of peace' in the south, an expanding Gaelic lordship referred to as the 'land of war' in the north, and a transitional zone dividing them, which moved inexorably southwards. Inevitably, this hybrid district lacked strong political influence, resulting in an intermixing of the social and cultural characteristics of both sides. This unstable compound was by no means specific to county

Wexford, as it was replicated throughout Ireland, Wales and Scotland.[8]

The retreat to the south of the county was epitomised by the bishop's decision to provide an alternative to the Episcopal See in the frontier town of Ferns by establishing a headquarters in the relative security of New Ross. In 1409, Bishop Patrick Barrett was granted permission to build a 'castle of stone crenulated' at Mountgarrett, overlooking the Barrow two kilometres north of Ross. He was permitted to recruit quarrymen and masons from the counties of Wexford, Kilkenny and Waterford to construct the castle. The bishop is also credited with restoring the town gate leading to St Mary's church, which became known as Bishop's Gate.[9]

A castle or 'court' already existed on the episcopal manor of Fethard, constructed when it was temporarily in the hands of Christ Church, Canterbury.[10] The small surviving motte marks the location. A gatehouse equipped with a drawbridge, indicating the presence of a moat, was added to the complex in the second half of the fourteenth century. The later construction of a sophisticated fortified house gave the bishop an alternative safe haven in the southern part of the county. The L-shaped building, incorporating the earlier gatehouse, has a circular tower

Fig. 3 In 1409, the bishop of Ferns was given permission to build a castle at Mountgarrett, to the north of New Ross. The Butlers acquired the property in the sixteenth century and the partially surviving castle, which is fitted with gun-loops, can be attributed to them. It has not been established if the bishop's castle was incorporated in the later structure.

Lordships of Leinster _c._ 1530

·· **Tower Houses**

0   25 km
0   20 miles

N

Fig. 4   This map of political divisions in sixteenth-century Leinster shows the border between Wexford and Kilkenny, which enabled the Butler earls of Ormond to extract fines and goods from the colonists in Wexford. The Butlers acquired considerable property in the county, principally Mountgarrett and the manor of Kayer. The map also illustrates the divisions within county Wexford and the similar distributions of tower houses in the southern parts of Wexford and the Dublin Pale.

with rib-vaulting on the south-west angle. The vaulted ground floor of the tower, accessed from the first floor through a trapdoor, served as a dungeon. Prison cells were widely used in episcopal castles to enforce clerical discipline.[11] The use of Dundry stone in some of the window surrounds of Fethard Castle indicate a construction date in the late fourteenth/early fifteenth century.[12] In 1420, the motivation for the bishop's move was shown by the levying of 19s. on each carucate (ploughland) of diocesan land for the protection of the lands around Ferns.[13]

Some colonists persisted in occupying their holdings in the centre of the county, at least in the fifteenth century. In 1450, John Furlong of Tomhaggard, the sheriff of the county, complained about the numbers of persons:

without any visible means of existence, wandering the country between Enniscorthy and Ferns, camping out in the woods in the summer, and during the harvest, visiting houses and homesteads in small parties of six to a dozen, demanding alms, food and drink, under veiled threats of mischief in case of refusal, terrifying the female occupants and committing robberies and violence on many occasions, those injured fearing to appear against them, in dread of reprisals.[14]

These outlaws may have been a mixture of Irish and English as there were considerable problems with rebel English in the county.[15] The reference to farming is a convincing indication that some settlers were still trying to eke out a living in the vicinity, probably encouraged by the protection of the castles at Ferns and Enniscorthy.

Although situated in the marches, Enniscorthy managed to survive in some form, helped by the security provided by the castle and the communication route along the river to Wexford town. It served as a pragmatic economic interface between the Gaelic Irish and the English colonists in times of relative peace. By the second half of the fifteenth century, the town was under the

The Wexford Pale: Richard Stanihurst 1584

Of all other places, Wexford with the territory bayed, and perclosed within the river called the Pill, was so quite estranged from Irishry, as if a traveller of the Irish (which was rare in those days) had pitched his foot within the pill and spoken Irish, the Wexfordians would command him forthwith to turn the other end of his tongue, and speak English, or else bring his trouchman [interpreter] with him. But in our days they have so acquainted themselves with the Irish, as they have made a mingle mangle, or gallamaulfrey of both the languages, and have in such medley or checkerwise so crabbedly fumbled them both together, as commonly the inhabitants of the meaner sort speak neither good English nor good Irish... There was of late days one of the Peers of England sent to Wexford as Commissioner, to decide the controversies of that county, and hearing in affable wise the rude complaints of the country clowns, he conceived [understood] here and there, sometimes a word, other while a sentence. The noble man being very glad that upon his first coming to Ireland, he understood so many words, told one of his familiar friends, that he stood in very great hope, to become shortly a well spoken man in the Irish, supposing that the blunt people had prattled Irish, all the while they tangled English. Howbeit to this day the dregs of the old ancient Chaucer English, are kept as well there as in Fingall.

Fig. 5   The thirteenth-century gatetower in New Ross known as Bishop's Gate (also Maiden or Fair Gate) was associated with Bishop Barrett early in the fifteenth century, presumably used by him as he commuted between Mountgarrett and St Mary's. The gateway was decorated with elaborate rib-vaulting, of which a few fragments survive. The surviving decorated corbel (below right) hints at the original high architectural quality of the gatetower.

control of the Mac Murchada (at this stage generally known as the MacMurrough Kavanaghs), and the foundation of the Franciscan Friary by them in 1460 indicates that Enniscorthy was still a significant urban settlement, despite two centuries of unrest.[16] The mendicant Franciscans were the monks most sympathetic to Gaelic culture in the late medieval period.

As the influence of the Kavanaghs waxed, the authorities were called on in the 1530s to repair and garrison castles in the south-east, including Ferns and Enniscorthy, in an effort to reclaim lands from the Irish that had been formerly held by English colonists.[17] At that time, the castles were in disrepair. In 1537, it was recommended that 'a castle and town should be builded' [i.e. repaired], at Enniscorthy and that gentlemen from England should be appointed to Enniscorthy, Ferns and other places, each 'to keep soldiers in wages for two or three years' with lands in freehold allotted to them. The reason given was that 'the king's enemies rob and spoil his subjects in the county and then retreat to the fassagh [fásach:wilderness] where they could not be pursued without a force strong enough to withstand the tenants as well as the robbers'.[18]

In spite of the enactment of the Statutes of Kilkenny in 1366, aimed at preserving the English way of life, the shambolic situation resulted in acculturation, as

Fig. 6   The castle on the episcopal manor of Fethard was built in the late fourteenth- early fifteenth century. This date is suggested by the presence of dressed Dundry stone in some of the tower windows, as the use of this imported stone was phased out *c.* 1400. Bishop Thomas Denne, who died at the end of the fourteenth century, and whose graveslab lies in the adjoining churchyard, could have been associated with the construction. Bishop Barrett who succeeded him, and who built a castle at Mountgarrett, is also a likely candidate. The castle, which is really a fortified house, consists of two independent elements forming an L-shaped structure with a vaulted ground floor. The hall was on the first floor of the long wing, presumably the episcopal residence. The annex may have been for the bishop's second-in-command. The round tower, at the angle of the L, acted as a belfry and added a unifying element of architectural style and elegance. The building incorporated a gatehouse with a drawbridge and other fabric of an earlier structure, perhaps an enclosure castle associated with the adjacent small motte. In the 1630s, the manor and castle of Fethard was acquired by the Loftus family.

individuals from both traditions collaborated in exploiting the lawless situation. In 1534, for example, the Prendergasts and MacMurroughs combined in a raid on the Devereux manor of Ballymagir in Bargy; in 1547, the Irish, led by Robert Roche, were preying the county; in 1572, nine people were killed during a raid by the Kavanaghs and Furlongs on the 'barony' of Dunbrody.[19] This inevitable Gaelicisation is also hinted at in the frequent use in the sixteenth century of Irish language elements in some English family names (notably Walsh, Power, Sutton, Furlong and Roche). These hybrid names, concentrated in a band stretching from New Ross to just north of Wexford town, marked the interface between Gaelic north and English south.[20]

In 1526, a tragic family quarrel graphically illustrated the potential for disputes at a family level that this cultural intermingling generated. Edmond Hore of Harperstown Castle, who had married a daughter of Gerald Kavanagh, decided to pass on his estate according to Brehon rather than English law. His uncle, David Hore, broke into the castle and murdered Edmond and his wife, claiming that his nephew had transgressed the Statutes of Kilkenny. In spite of the horrendous nature of this atrocity, David Hore eventually obtained possession of Harperstown Castle and estate, deepening the resentment and tension on both sides.[21]

There is a marked correlation between the distribution of these mixed personal names and the locations of medieval moated sites, the late thirteenth-century farmsteads associated with a secondary colonisation wave. The occurrence of hybrid names in this no-man's-land area indicates that some colonists clung to their farms, despite the dangers of living in a frontier area. In general, the pattern of townland names provides a valuable proxy for settlement in the medieval county.

Fig. 7 Details from Fethard Castle: **A** Vault of the prison with trapdoor at the base of the tower **B** Pivot stone of the drawbridge **C** Cusped ogee window in the tower with Dundry cut stone **D** Running machicolation around top of the tower **E** Fireplace on first-floor hall **F** Restored garderobe **G** Rib-vaulting with plank centering in the tower roof.

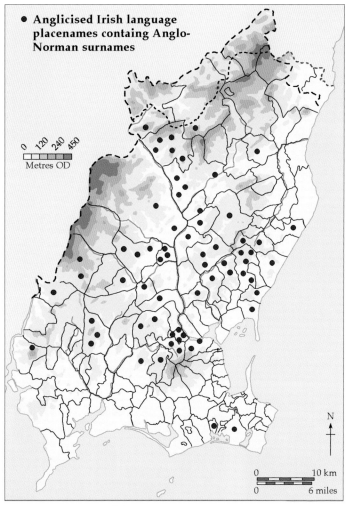

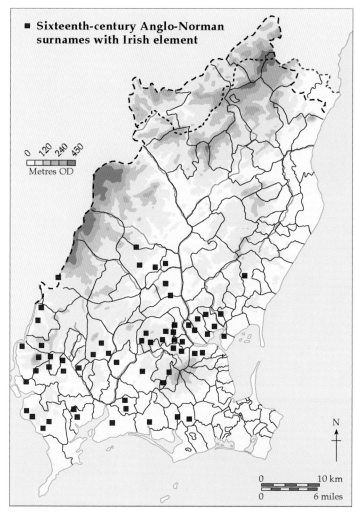

Fig. 8 Anglicised Irish-language townland names containing Anglo-Norman surnames reflect an earlier period of colonisation, when settlers were struggling to retain their holdings in the north of the county, particularly along the Slaney corridor. A concentration across the centre of the county, just south of Enniscorthy, identifies the frontier region at the time when these names were established. Mixed language placenames hint at a hybridised community. Some names may have been Gaelicised after the retreat of the English-speaking colonists.

Fig. 9 The occurrence of Old English personal names with an Irish element is evidence of social interaction between the two groups in the sixteenth century. The hybrid names are grouped in a band across the frontier zone, between the Irish north and English south, where everyday personal contacts leading to acculturation were most likely. The prevalence of these names just to the north of the Wexford Pale suggests that this was the region of greatest contact between the colonists and the Irish. There is a marked concentration to the north-west of Wexford town.

The volatile nature of the frontier is demonstrated by the large number of townland names in the north of the county containing English surnames that became Gaelicised as Irish influence and occupation expanded inexorably southwards.[22] These placenames are concentrated on fertile land along the Slaney, with clusters adjacent to the towns of Wexford and Enniscorthy. There is also a grouping north of Wexford Harbour, in the southern part of the barony of Ballaghkeen. The absence of Gaelicised English names in the northern barony of Gorey and eastern Scarawalsh show that this part of the county was never effectively colonised. A dense band of 'baile' townland names runs along the east coast region, indicating enduring Irish occupation. The absence of these names in the west of the county corresponds to the wooded and mountainous region of the Duffry and the

Fassagh of Bantry, which were never successfully penetrated by the colonists.

The southern baronies of Forth and Bargy (with the Pale area around Dublin) have the heaviest concentration in Ireland of placenames containing the English suffix 'town'; combined with other English townland names, they constitute half of the total. The remainder are Irish names with a profusion of 'baile' prefixes (the Irish equivalent of town). This unique intensity of both 'town' and 'baile' in the same region suggests the presence of a truly mixed community in the medieval period. Elsewhere in Ireland, the 'baile' element is rare in the 'town' zone.[23]

The enclosed nature of the Wexford Pale made it less susceptible to acculturation. This cultural divide was noticed by several commentators. In 1584, Stanihurst observed that formerly only English was used in the

Fig. 10 Fethard Castle from Philips' 1591 map of Waterford Harbour. The architectural representation is quite accurate as it shows the battlemented round tower and the gatehouse, with the hall in between.

Wexford Pale but by the end of the sixteenth century 'a mingle mangle, or gallamaulfrey' of Chaucerian English and Irish was spoken.[24] An account by an English official in the 1590s, the *Dialogue of Silvynne and Peregrynne*, criticised the intermingling of the colonists with the Irish elsewhere in Ireland but extolled the gentlemen of the Wexford Pale, 'the successors of the first English conquerors', who had maintained their old English language by keeping themselves apart from the Kavanaghs and other Irish 'borderers'.[25] In 1626, Thomas Fleming, the Catholic archbishop of Dublin, observed that 'in the diocese of Ferns there are many who do not know a word of English and many who speak English but not a word of Irish'.[26]

The landscape formed an allegorical backdrop to the conflict between native Irish and English settler. The dense forested uplands of the north and west provided the Irish with a secure base from which they frequently emerged on their fast light horses to harass the colonists, ultimately restricting them to the southern lowlands of the 'English Pale'. A late fourteenth-century account of an Irish settlement in the wood of Leverough describes the house of the MacMurrough Kavanagh chieftain, surrounded by fourteen villages and a large herd of cattle.[27]

The forested region known as the Fassagh (wilderness) of Bantry, in the piedmont of the Blackstairs Mountains to the north of New Ross, played a crucial strategic role in staging the raids and rallies of the sixteenth century. Because of Bantry's location south of the Duffry, the heavily wooded terrain provided a continuous corridor for Irish raiding parties to infiltrate the south of the county unnoticed and to retreat unscathed into the woods

before retaliatory action could be taken. Bantry also interfaced with the Ormond Lordship, giving the Butlers access along the Barrow valley and into Wexford through the Pollmounty Gap. As well as being a security risk, the woodlands were essential to the manorial economy as they provided the timber that was vital for building. Items sourced included rods for the manufacture of wattle, boards, beams, laths and shingles. Some wood was exported and waste timber was used for firewood.[28] In contrast to the wooded uplands of the west and north, the southern Wexford Pale consisted of flat lowlands defined by topographical features; the northern limits were protected by the Mullmontry Gorge, the marshy valley of the Corock and its tributary the Aughnagroagh, the rocky eminence of Forth Mountain and a tributary of the river Slaney.

Because of its location adjacent to the Fassagh, the barony of Shelburne to the south, particularly the lands of Dunbrody Abbey, was frequently raided. In 1538, the seneschal of Wexford reported that the occupants of the Fassagh of Bantry, leased to Richard Butler but farmed by the MacMurrough Kavanaghs, were supplying provisions to the 'king's enemies', who were 'burning and robbing' the king's subjects and returning to the Fassagh to divide the spoils. Because of insufficient resources, the seneschal was unable to pursue the raiders into Bantry, where he

---

Letter from Fethard to the Lord Deputy 1548

Master Sheriff of the county of Wexford [Patrick Meyler of Duncormick] came to Fethard of the said county this last Saturday past with a number of kerne and horsemen in complete harness well appointed to fight against the king's poor subjects, and then and there rigorously and extortly the aforesaid sheriff, with his naked sword drawn in his hand, in the presence of many, did strike and beat the poor orator, the portreeve of the aforesaid town of Fethard's officer, about the head, that he is not able as yet to repair unto your lordship to complain, and in like manner ran at one of the burgesses there and cut him in the hand, if he had not borne off the stroke with a staff his hand had been cast off quite, one of his fingers is in danger never to recover and another poor man his finger is cast off and never had [healed] since, because he cried out seeing the portreeve so beaten for refusing the sheriff of an Irish custom named coign and livery, it never was paid to no sheriff before, which inconvenience shall be proved by many honest persons if it be your lordship's will. In consideration whereof your poor complainants beseech your lordship for the love of God for a true remedy and they will pray to God daily for your honourable estate in prosperity long to continue.

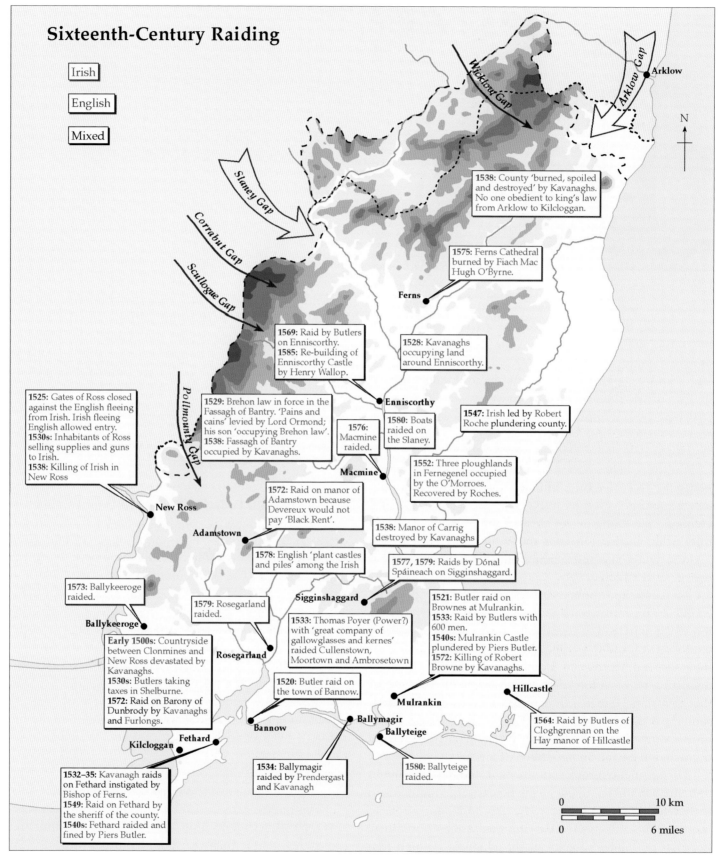

Sixteenth-Century Raiding

Irish

English

Mixed

Arklow

N

Wicklow Gap

Arklow Gap

1538: County 'burned, spoiled and destroyed' by Kavanaghs. No one obedient to king's law from Arklow to Kilcloggan.

Slaney Gap

Corrabut Gap

Scullogue Gap

1575: Ferns Cathedral burned by Fiach Mac Hugh O'Byrne.

Ferns

1528: Kavanaghs occupying land around Enniscorthy.

1569: Raid by Butlers on Enniscorthy.
1585: Re-building of Enniscorthy Castle by Henry Wallop.

1525: Gates of Ross closed against the English fleeing from Irish. Irish fleeing English allowed entry.
1530s: Inhabitants of Ross selling supplies and guns to Irish.
1538: Killing of Irish in New Ross

Pollmounty Gap

1529: Brehon law in force in the Fassagh of Bantry. 'Pains and cains' levied by Lord Ormond; his son 'occupying Brehon law'.
1538: Fassagh of Bantry occupied by Kavanaghs.

1576: Macmine raided.

1580: Boats raided on the Slaney.

Enniscorthy

1547: Irish led by Robert Roche plundering county.

1552: Three ploughlands in Fernegenel occupied by the O'Morroes. Recovered by Roches.

Macmine

1572: Raid on manor of Adamstown because Devereux would not pay 'Black Rent'.

New Ross

Adamstown

1538: Manor of Carrig destroyed by Kavanaghs

1578: English 'plant castles and piles' among the Irish

1577, 1579: Raids by Dónal Spáineach on Sigginshaggard.

1573: Ballykeeroge raided.

1579: Rosegarland raided.

Sigginshaggard

1521: Butler raid on Brownes at Mulrankin.
1533: Raid by Butlers with 600 men.
1540s: Mulrankin Castle plundered by Piers Butler.
1572: Killing of Robert Browne by Kavanaghs.

Ballykeeroge

Early 1500s: Countryside between Clonmines and New Ross devastated by Kavanaghs.
1530s: Butlers taking taxes in Shelburne.
1572: Raid on Barony of Dunbrody by Kavanaghs and Furlongs.

1533: Thomas Poyer (Power?) with 'great company of gallowglasses and kernes' raided Cullenstown, Moortown and Ambrosetown

Rosegarland

1520: Butler raid on the town of Bannow.

Hillcastle

Mulrankin

1564: Raid by Butlers of Cloghgrennan on the Hay manor of Hillcastle

Kilcloggan   **Fethard**

Bannow

Ballymagir
Ballyteige

1532–35: Kavanagh raids on Fethard instigated by Bishop of Ferns.
1549: Raid on Fethard by the sheriff of the county.
1540s: Fethard raided and fined by Piers Butler.

1534: Ballymagir raided by Prendergast and Kavanagh

1580: Ballyteige raided.

0   10 km

0   6 miles

Fig. 11   This map of recorded incidents illustrates the widespread nature of raiding in sixteenth-century Wexford. It also emphasises the complex and fluctuating alliances that existed between the Irish and the English, notably the Butlers of Ormond. Individual families in the southern baronies were frequently targeted, particularly those who led the opposition against the Irish. Concerns about personal security among the Old English community led to a profusion of tower houses in the Wexford Pale and the construction of 'offensive' tower houses to the north of the Pale boundary.

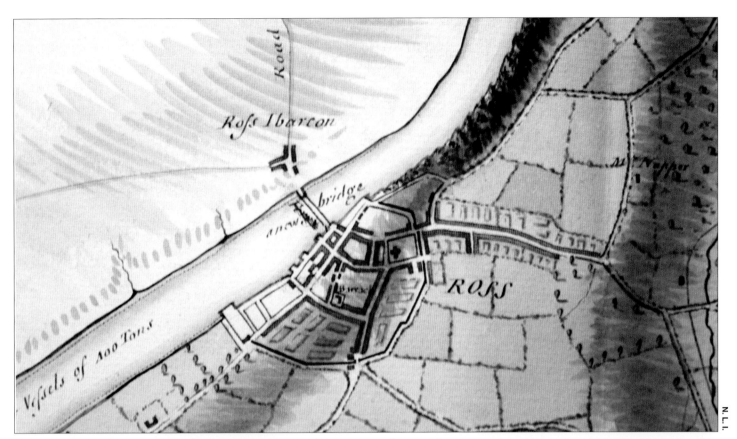

Fig. 12   Vallancey's map of New Ross made in 1776. The line of the town wall is shown by the semi-circular red line and road. Not all of the space within the wall had been fully developed. The straggling suburb of Irishtown extends to the east from Bishop's Gate. A new waterfront is being constructed on reclaimed land to accommodate ships of up to 400 tons burden. 'A new bridge' refers to a proposed bridge, constructed by Lemuel Cox in 1796.

would be faced by the combined force of the 'pretence' tenants and the raiding party. Because of the Butlers' ominous presence, no one was obedient to English law from Arklow to Kilcloggan in the south of Shelburne.[29]

In spite of the construction of a stone town wall in the 1260s,[30] the location of New Ross on the frontier, adjacent to the southern limits of the Fassagh, had a defining impact on the town's fortunes.[31] Although a highly successful port in the late thirteenth century, Ross had sunk to crisis level by the end of the fourteenth century.[32] The killing of twenty-seven townsmen by the Irish in 1333 was an indication of its vulnerability.[33] Following the burning of the town by Art MacMurrough Kavanagh in 1394, conditions reached such a low ebb that the burgesses were given permission to trade with the Irish. They were also permitted to pay an annual tribute (the 'cíos dubh' or black rent) of ten marks protection money to the MacMurrough, a similar amount being paid by the county.[34]

Because of their exposed situation, and a dependence on the Irish for trade, the burgesses of New Ross, unwilling to antagonise the Irish, adopted the high risk strategy of straddling both cultures. Their priority was the appeasement of the Irish. In 1526, for example, the gates of the town were closed against Nicholas FitzHenry and

other English colonists fleeing from the Irish, exposing them to be slain outside the gates. However, Irish 'rebels' pursued by Thomas FitzHenry and other English (presumably seeking revenge) were allowed entry. Ten years later, the inhabitants of Ross were accused of the same offence and of selling not only provisions but also weapons to the Irish. In 1538, the murder of some of Cahir Mac Art's men in the town alarmed the town officials, presumably fearing reprisals. The killings took place at the 'conduit' (water channel), recalled in the current name of Conduit Lane.[35]

The endemic 'incessant plundering warfare' between native Irish and settlers of English descent generated the underlying instability, but it was not the only cause of the turmoil in sixteenth-century county Wexford. The turbulent situation was exploited by renegade English from both inside and outside the county. The raiding forays of the Butlers were augmented by mercenary work and ransom demands. In 1521, for example, the Butler earl of Ormond seized Walter Browne of Mulrankin and imprisoned him for one year until a ransom was paid. On another occasion, Piers Butler, hired by a merchant of Waterford to enforce a debt from the Brownes, plundered Mulrankin Castle, reputedly with a contingent of 600 men.

On his way home, he extracted a fine from the town of Fethard to support his entourage.[36]

The anarchic state of the county was epitomised by the bishop's collaboration with the Irish to exploit the lawless situation to his own advantage. In 1532, and again three years later, Bishop John Purcell, possibly in a dispute over rent, enlisted the aid of the Kavanagh chieftain, Cahir Mac Art, and together they robbed and burned the houses of the episcopal town and manor of Fethard. On the second occasion, they drove away cattle, sheep and swine. The wily bishop arranged to have his own cattle stolen with the rest and subsequently had them retrieved by his servant.[37]

Although raiding on the southern part of the county by the Irish, and by groups of mixed ethnicity, was generally indiscriminate, particular individuals were targeted. The Browne and Devereux families, who were strenuous in opposing the Irish, were singled out. The Browne manor of Mulrankin was plundered by the Butlers in 1521, again in 1533, and by a mixed force in 1572. The killing of Robert Browne on the last occasion elicited a letter from Queen

Killing of Robert Browne: Elizabeth I 1572

That Robert Browne of Mulrankin within our county of Wexford (a young gentleman of great valour, wholly given to our service against the disobedient Irishrie of that county upon whom his father hath valiantly builded a fortress, and he, after his father's death hath so valiantly kept the same to the amplifying of our obedience, being also near of blood to the houses of our right trusted and well-beloved cousins, the earls of Kildare and Ormond) is traitorously murdered by Brene M'Coder Kavanagh and his brethren, Hugh McShane's sons, under the rule of Francis Agard and one Mathew Furlong. We cannot but think the loss of such a subject very hurtful to the state of that our realm. — And that you do further not only look to the safety of the poor young gentlewoman his wife, and her children, but also have good regard to the defence of the said Browne's castle and towns, which are holden to us, against the said murderers and their followers.

R. I. A.

Fig. 13 Mulrankin three-storey tower house in 1840. The later house was apparently stepped back to leave the doorway of the tower, with its machicolation, exposed. The house, with some modifications, is still occupied, complete with the massive chimney stack on the left.

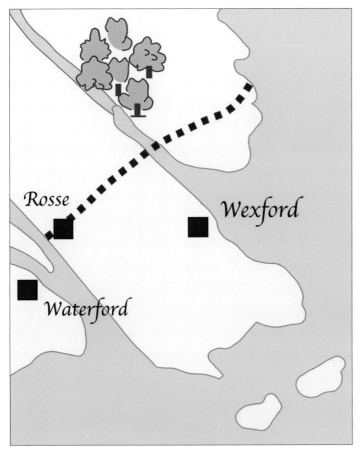

Fig. 14 This detail from an early seventeenth-century map shows a dotted line from New Ross to just above Wexford Harbour, demarcating the ethnic divide between north and south in county Wexford.

Elizabeth, which described Browne as 'wholly given to our service against the disobedient Irish of that county', whose father 'had valiantly built a fortress, which he, after his father's death, had so valiantly kept and defended'.[38]

The Devereux manor of Ballymagir was attacked in 1534 and again in 1547. George Devereux appealed for the appointment of Englishmen to defend the county because 'there were divers Irishmen preparing to prey openly on the county'.[39] The aggressive attitude of the Devereuxes is evident in a letter from Nicholas Devereux of Ballymagir in 1572, complaining that his manor of Adamstown was raided by the Kavanaghs and Furlongs because he refused to pay the 'Black Rent'.[40]

DISSOLUTION OF THE MONASTERIES

From the mid-sixteenth century, external events impinged decisively on Irish affairs. The opening up of the Americas moved Ireland from being a peripheral European island to a strategically central location in the Atlantic world, making it attractive to European powers looking towards the New World. Politically, Ireland's relationship with England became more complex after the Reformation, as the Irish remained Catholic, unlike their political rulers in England who embraced the new religious ethos. This divergence had profound political implications. Ireland was now regarded as a natural ally of France and Spain, England's Catholic adversaries. To prevent Ireland from

Fig. 15 In 1545, the Dunbrody Abbey estate was granted to Sir Osborne Etchingham, the marshal of the king's army in Ireland. The lands remained in the possession of his descendants until the late twentieth century. The Etchinghams lived in a Tudor house incorporating the south transept of the abbey.

Fig. 16   The Cistercian tower house at Ballyhack was one of the residences on the Dunbrody estate occupied by the Etchingham family.

being used as a 'back door' for an invasion by European enemies, Tudor England initiated a determined campaign to impose control over the Irish by whatever means necessary from the mid-sixteenth century onwards.

The advent of the Reformation, with the proclamation of Henry VIII as head of the Irish church in 1536, precipitated transformations in social and political life.[41] The monastic estates were suppressed by the new regime, partly because of a decline in religious life but also because they were regarded as places of refuge for the rebel Irish. This decision had profound implications for county Wexford, as the south-west of the county consisted almost entirely of the

---

Dialogue of Silvynne and Peregrynne 1590s

It was not tolerable amongst us of the English Pale, to permit or suffer, any of the O'Neills, O'Donnells, Maguires, McMahons, O'Reillys or any other Irish borderer to inhabit amongst us: by which means, we are so fast tied in consanguinity, alliance and amity, one to another that it was as hard a matter to snap a sheaf of arrows in pieces, being fast bound together. Look but into the county of Wexford where most part of the gentlemen of that country, and the successors of the first English conquerors, retaining as yet, their old English tongue, which argues their little combination with the Kavanaghs and other the Irish borderers. First by reason of combination with the Irish as aforesaid, in crept their language to be almost general amongst us, and that within a short time scorning our old English speech, which our ancestors brought with them at the first conquest, thinking it too base. By reason whereof we thought our selves mightily well appointed to be armed with two languages, so that being thus furnished, we were able to go into the Irish countries and truck with them, commodity for commodity (which they in former times were driven to bring theirs unto us) and either bought ours again with the money they received for it, or bartered ware for ware, by an interpreter. Now this kind of intercourse with the Irish bred such acquaintance, amity and friendship between them and us, being so furnished with their language, that we cared not contrary to our duties, in balancing our credits, to make fosterage, gossipreds, and marriages, as aforesaid with them, so that now the English Pale, and many other places of the kingdom, that were planted with English at several conquests, are grown to a confusion of septs, most of the port towns, replenished with merchants of that kind.

Fig. 17   In 1543, the Tintern Abbey estate was granted to Anthony Colclough, an officer in the king's army in Ireland, on condition that he would adapt it as a fortress against the king's enemies. This did not take place until the 1570s, when he converted the crossing tower into a tower house and the chancel into an attached three-storey house. His descendants occupied the abbey until the middle of the twentieth century.

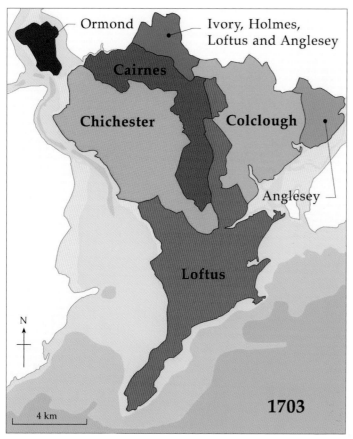

Fig. 18 Following the dissolution of the abbeys, all of the church lands in south-west Wexford were granted to English officials and soldiers who were loyal servants of the crown. After the Confederate war, the Loftus family acquired more land in the Hook and Fethard. The descendants of these families retained the estates into the twentieth century.

two Cistercian estates (Dunbrody and Tintern) and the Hospitaller manor of Kilcloggan. The religious houses in the towns also enjoyed considerable property and land. In the case of Dunbrody, the right of sanctuary written into its charter was an added incentive for its closure. In 1533, a report advised that abbeys should be suppressed because they were 'adjoining the Irish and giving more support to those Irishmen than to the king or his subjects'.[42]

The confiscation of church property, combined with the acquisition of the possessions of absentee owners, gave the crown the opportunity to grant these lands and buildings to loyal, Protestant officials who would fortify them against the 'Irish rebels' and recruit new tenants from England. This attracted a new wave of English fortune-hunters to Wexford, who combined active military service against the Irish with the predatory acquisition of estates and wealth. Significantly, their arrival coincided with the increased use of handguns from the middle of the century, with the replacement of the longbow by the musket ultimately exerting a decisive influence on the 'pacification' of the county.[43]

The confiscated church lands in county Wexford were all granted to ambitious, energetic, newly-arrived English officials. The lands of Tintern Abbey were acquired by Anthony Colclough from Staffordshire in 1543. As Colclough was on active duty with the king's army in Ireland, he did not take possession of his new estate until 1562. In 1566, he applied to the authorities for money to fortify the abbey, as it was 'on the borders,' and he undertook to defend the surrounding countryside from the Queen's enemies. Colclough's title to Tintern was confirmed and he was directed to build 'a sufficient fortress' within three years and to maintain three English horsemen and four archers or arquebusiers (soldiers carrying a portable firearm).[44]

Colclough adapted the Cistercian church at Tintern as a residence, which his descendants occupied and continued to alter for four centuries. The crossing tower was transformed into a six-storey tower house. Trees used in the work were felled in 1570, indicating that this part of the work was carried out in the 1570s. The chancel was converted into a three-storey house or hall, attached to the tower. Fireplaces were inserted in blocked-up arches, Gothic lancet windows were built up and mullioned windows with Tudor hood mouldings were inserted.[45] Stone from the dismantled monastic buildings was later used to build defensive walls and a battlemented bridge. Anthony Colclough's monument survives in the little church near the abbey where successive generations of the family were interred.

Sir Osborne Etchingham from Suffolk, fourth cousin of Queen Anne Boleyn and a high official in the court of Henry VIII, was marshal of the English army in Ireland and a member of the Privy Council.[46] In 1545, he successfully petitioned for a grant of the Dunbrody Abbey estate but it is doubtful if he ever occupied his new property, as he died in the following year. He was

Butler raid on Enniscorthy fair 1569

Sir Edmond Butler, the captain and seneschal of all the earl of Ormond's countries, utterly spoiled a great fair held at Enniscorthy, a house and town of the Queen's in the county of Wexford. I am sure that fair is the greatest of any in Ireland, and held yearly, and usually at a day certain. The horrible rapes, the shameful murders, with the total rapine of all the goods that could be carried away, were too loathsome to be written or read. There were assembled there, beside a multitude of country people, the most of the merchants of the good town of Wexford, either in their own persons, their wives, or their servants, who were ravished, killed, or spoiled, all looking for no such an unheard of harm there, whither peaceably they came by water.

Fig. 19   Kilcloggan Castle. In the 1590s, Dudley Loftus, a member of an influential Elizabethan family, was granted the manor of Kilcloggan and took up residence in the tower house. In the 1630s, the family acquired the episcopal manor of Fethard and occupied the castles of Fethard and Dungulph. The lands of the Hook came into their possession after the Cromwellian confiscations and they occupied Redmond Hall, changing its name to Loftus Hall.

NED CULLETON

Fig. 20   This image from 1780 shows the tower house at Ferrycarrig strategically located on a rock overlooking the Slaney gorge. One of the few tower houses in the county that was built primarily for a military purpose, the presence of gun-loops indicate that it was constructed *c*. 1550 to protect river traffic between Wexford and Enniscorthy, which was vulnerable to attack as it passed through the narrows. The tower was also well placed to control and protect the lucrative ferry crossing. A new road may have been quarried out of the old red sandstone bedrock to create an impregnable vantage point and presumably to supply some of the material for the construction of the tower, which is solidly built of local stone. The new road also serviced the ferry, which is shown loaded with cattle as well as people. A steep, narrow pathway accessed the ferry on the opposite side. For several centuries, a large cot known as the Slaney gabbard (the boat with the sail) carried cargo on the river, until it became obsolete in the mid twentieth century.

succeeded by his son Edward, whose title was confirmed in 1565. Described as 'of dissolute character', Edward compromised the estate by taking out various mortgages and issuing disadvantageous long leases to different people, principally Sir William Drury and Sir Nicholas White. The lands of Dunbrody were finally confirmed to John Etchingham in 1602 and remained in the possession of his descendants until the late twentieth century. The

> ### County Wexford 1578 (Hore and Graves)
> The south part, as the most civil part, is contained within a river called the Pill, where the ancientest gentlemen, descended of the first conquerors, do inhabit; the other also, without the river, is inhabited by the original Irish and the Cavanaghs, Moroghes and Kinselighes, who possess the woody part of the county, and yet are daily more scattered by our English gentlemen, who encroach upon them and plant castles and piles within them.

Etchinghams lived in a Tudor house incorporating the south transept of the abbey and they also occupied the castles at Duncannon and Ballyhack. The construction of an ambitious defended residence known as Dunbrody Castle was initiated in the early seventeenth century but it was never completed.[47]

By 1596, the manor of Kilcloggan had been acquired by Sir Dudley Loftus, a member of an influential English family established in Ireland as part of the Elizabethan plan for imposing law and order.[48] They were heavily involved in military affairs, two of them being killed in action against the Irish.[49] In 1634, the Loftus family also acquired the castle and manor of Fethard from the bishop of Ferns in exchange for other lands, giving £300 to the bishop for the construction of a new episcopal residence in Ferns.[50] Kilcloggan Castle was occupied by Dudley Loftus at the end of the sixteenth century. Following the acquisition of the manor of Fethard, the family lived in the castles of Fethard and Dungulph. In the late seventeenth

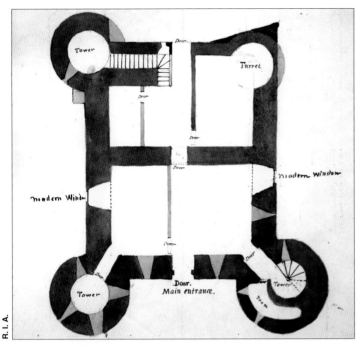

Fig. 21 A mid-nineteenth-century ground-floor plan of Enniscorthy Castle, drawn by Du Noyer, showing internal divisions.

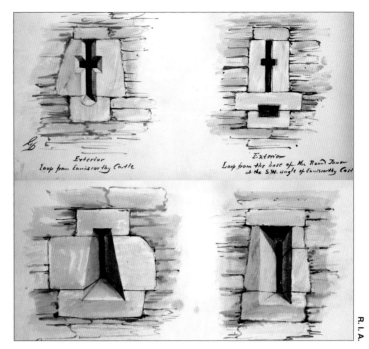

Fig. 23 Four gun-loops from Enniscorthy Castle, of varying design, drawn by Du Noyer in the mid-nineteenth century.

century, Redmond Hall on the Hook was taken over by Henry Loftus. As Loftus Hall, it became the family's principal residence for more than two centuries.

The possessions of the religious orders in the towns were granted to various individuals, some of whom influenced subsequent political and military events in the county. The property of the Friars and Augustinians in New Ross, as well as the episcopal lands and castle of Mountgarrett, were granted to the earl of Ormond, giving the Butlers a foothold in the county, where they eventually held lands with a rental valuation of £10, mostly located in the Fassagh of Bantry.[51] In the 1560s, the manor of Ferns and the manor and Friary lands of Enniscorthy were leased to Nicholas Heron, a tough captain in charge of a garrison in the north of the county. Heron was also

granted lands formerly in the possession of the Irish, with draconian powers to collect taxes and enforce English law. Heron's success was followed by the appointment of Thomas Masterson as constable of Ferns Castle in 1569 and lessee of the abbey lands of Ferns, which he occupied in spite of opposition from the Kavanaghs who then joined in the Butler rebellion of 1569.[52]

The Kavanaghs' involvement may explain one of the worst atrocities of the rebellion. Sir Edmund Butler and his followers raided Enniscorthy on the annual Lady Day fair, the 'greatest of any in Ireland', and committed

Fig. 22 This sepia detail of Enniscorthy Castle shows the doorway protected by a system of gun-loops. The curved top and the hood moulding are replicated at the fortified hall-houses of Bargy and Dungulph in the south of the county, both belonging to the same period.

Fig. 24 A pencil drawing of Enniscorthy Castle by Du Noyer showing Tudor hood moulding over the windows and typical Elizabethan chimneys.

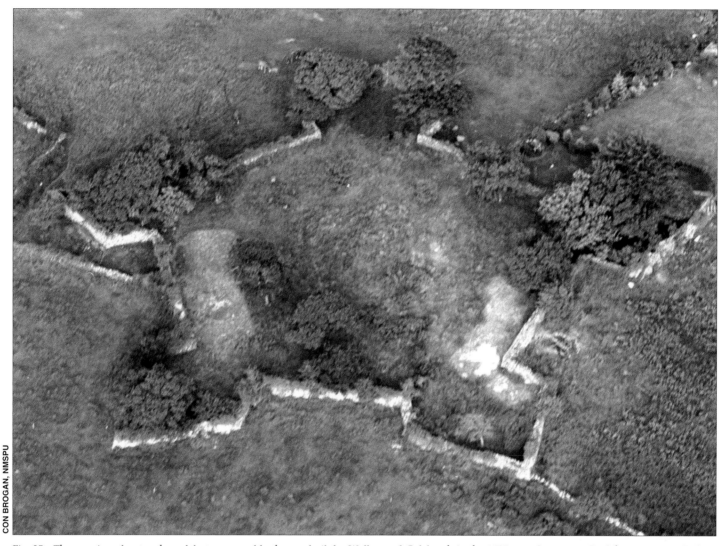

Fig. 25   The remains of a star-shaped fort, presumably the one built by Wallop and Colclough in the 1580s, can be seen at Coolyhune, county Carlow, north of St Mullins. The pentagonal fort has bastions (spear-shaped projections) on each corner from which all sides could be covered by gunfire. It was well positioned to protect traffic on the Barrow and to control the Pollmounty Gap, which allowed raiding parties access to county Wexford between the river and the Blackstairs. The fort fulfilled a similar function as the mottle-and-bailey castle built at St Mullins four centuries earlier.

'horrible atrocities', as well as stealing all that they could carry away.[53] A (possibly exaggerated) account of the incident described a flourishing town, where there was a 'multitude of country people' as well as 'most of the merchants of Wexford and their wives', who had travelled by boat up the Slaney; many of whom were killed. They also 'spoiled' and burned the castle and a 'great store of timber that had been felled and cleft' by Thomas Stukely, who apparently initiated the exploitation of the forests of north Wexford.[54] Stukley's occupation of Enniscorthy was of short duration; in 1581, the poet Edmund Spenser, of *Faerie Queene* fame, held the lease briefly but presumably he did not visit the town as he passed it on to Richard Sinnott after three days.[55] In the same year, elaborate plans were made to build a bridge across the Slaney at Enniscorthy but no bridge was built until one hundred years later.[56]

In 1579, Sir Henry Wallop, who, with his descendants, would exert a key influence on the growth of Enniscorthy, arrived in Ireland as a 'captain in the army'.[57] In the following year, he was in Wexford with Lord Deputy Grey, who reported that 'the rebels were much diminished by the garrisons planted among them', but that 'the Irish were 'so united as they were able to annoy greatly the good subjects both of the Pale and the county of Wexford'.[58] Wallop expressed his own bloody opinion of both the situation and the Irish people, which presumably reflected the official line, when he stated that 'there is no way to daunt these people but by the edge of the sword, and to plant better in their place. H[er] M[ajesty] were better to give them over to their own government and let them cut one another's throats than thus still to consume treasure to no purpose'.

Anthony Colclough was commissioned by Wallop to build a strong fort at St Mullins as a defence against the

PRIVATE COLLECTION

Fig. 26   A late eighteenth-century view of Enniscorthy showing Henry Wallop's castle built in the 1580s and the first bridge built a century later. The friary tower can be seen to the left of the castle. The traffic on the river and the landing of cargo highlights the value of the Slaney to the town.

Kavanaghs, who came through the pass of Pollmounty to raid settlers on the Wexford lowlands. As the fort also protected traffic on the Barrow, it was funded by contributions from Carlow and Waterford as well as County Wexford. Colclough was appointed as the fort's first captain, succeeded by Walter Browne in 1589.[59] The remains of the fort survive at Coolyhune, north of St Mullins in County Carlow, controlling the gap between mountain and river.

Wallop targeted the lucrative opportunities for personal advancement offered by county Wexford and in particular Enniscorthy, which he acquired in 1585 from Richard Sinnott, the lessee since 1581. In a detailed letter, he outlined his plans for the town. He immediately began to 'repair' the castle, in order 'to make a better defence of the border'. It is not clear if he incorporated some remains of the medieval structure, described as 'ruined and defaced', or if a new building, possibly on the same lines as the original, was erected. The work on the castle was described variously as 'fortifying, building and strengthening', 're-edifying' and 'sumptuously building'. Wallop's continuous stress on security was matched by

his relentless ambition for personal economic and social aggrandisement. He recognised the vast economic potential of the 'marvellously great' woods in the north and west of the county, particularly along the Slaney, 'whereof there is as fair and great a store, strong good and sound, as is to be found in any place in the world'. He planned to buy the woods from the Irish and float the timber down the Slaney to Enniscorthy. To achieve this, he improved navigation on the river above the town by breaking rocks that obstructed passage, enabling trees to be floated downstream. Because of his investment, and his success in 'planting the border', he demanded a lucrative monopoly on the export trade in timber.

In 1587, the market, abandoned since the Butler attack, was reinstated. Wallop claimed that the district, where he had 'settled many English men as well as some Irish', was as well inhabited as any part of Ireland and had been reduced to 'obedience and quiet'. His claims must be regarded as boastful exaggeration, as they were invariably accompanied by pleas for extra funding from the authorities. The Crown rewarded Wallop's campaign in 1595 by granting him Enniscorthy, with its castle and lands, to be held by knight's service. Wallop's plans to create a timber industry at Enniscorthy were very successful. He brought over 'a number of timbermen' from England, who organised the converting of the tree trunks into beams, boards, rafters, laths, oars, ship planks, pipe staves and poles. This process created added value and made the timber more manageable. These products were transported down the Slaney to Wexford (probably in the forerunners of the famous Slaney gabbard) and from there exported to England, Wales, France and Spain. The tower house at Ferrycarrig, built in a commanding location on a rock overlooking the Slaney and well provided with musket loops, was presumably constructed in the second half of the sixteenth century to protect river traffic.

The Slaney was the safest and most efficient means of communication between the two towns and, because of the benefits of the timber industry to both communities, steps were taken to ensure the security of this strategic lifeline. The authorities in Wexford built a strong barge, propelled by twelve oars, defended by two cannon and thirty muskets, so that supplies could reach the garrison at Enniscorthy at all times.[60] Enniscorthy also used an armed boat for the same purpose. During the Nine Years War, when Dómhnall Spáineach and his followers prevented traffic on the river, Wallop:

> as well as for his own private as for the public weal [welfare], did cause a small boat to be made, which carried eight tons of victuals besides men, close covered overhead, with fourteen men and

so many muskets, and a falken [small cannon] in the prow, by which they passed the river in spite of the rebels, supplied the garrison of Enniscorthy, and transported as often as was necessary without danger.

During the war, Dómhnall Spáineach defeated an English force near Enniscorthy led by Masterson, Wallop and Colclough, and he remained in rebellion for several years after the war had ended.[61]

In the 1570s, the process known as 'surrender and re-grant', initially tried but suspended in the 1540s, was re-introduced and completed by the early 1590s. This involved the surrender of lands by the Kavanaghs, who then received some of their former estates back to be held from the crown. Following the granting of their former lands to Masterson and Richard Sinnott, the Kavanaghs rose in rebellion but a defeat in the Duffry in 1582, by an English force led by Masterson, greatly weakened their ability to resist further encroachment.[62]

In spite of internal conflict, the Kavanaghs remained a significant force. The State Papers of 1598 commented that 'The Kavanaghs, present in great numbers in the woods of Carlow, are good soldiers, famous horsemen and still breathing the spirit of their ancient nobility, even in their abject poverty'.[63] The surrender and regrant of Gaelic lands was completed in the 1590s, and in 1610 the discovery that the crown allegedly had a 'legal' title to much of north Wexford, based on Richard II's confiscation in 1395, was exploited to legitimise the plantation of the north of the county.[64]

DEFENDING THE COLONY

The inevitable response by the colonists in county Wexford to relentless pressure from the native Irish was to abandon lands in the northern part of the county for the safety of the southern baronies and (in some instances) a return to their homeland across the Irish Sea. This reaction was not universal. The more resolute settlers fought to retain the landholdings which the Irish regarded as rightfully theirs. This was the case in the vicinity of Ferns and Enniscorthy, where the thirteenth-century stone castles offered some security. However, by the 1380s, the frontier had retracted as far south as Taghmon, which was then described as 'on the marches of the county'.[1] As the colony was restricted to the more heavily settled southern baronies, further retreat was no longer an option, resulting in a more determined resistance to incursions by the Irish. The failure of moated sites to provide adequate protection against Irish raiding prompted more substantial fortifications. By the early fourteenth century, alternative defences were being considered in the north of the county. In 1305, David de Caunteton was funded to build a 'fortalice' on his manor of Glascarrig, on the northern coast of the county, 'to resist the malice of the Irish'.[2] It is not known what type of fortification was intended or if it was ever constructed. It was not a conventional moated site (typically the defended residence of a single farm), as the construction was to be funded by the wider settler community.

The meaning of 'fortalice' is elusive. It might refer to fortification in general but it could have the same meaning as 'castle'.[3] In this context, 'fortilages' were recorded in the sixteenth century at Newbay, Carrigmannon, Aughnagan and Cleristown, presumably referring to the tower houses in those places. Similarly, the 'castle or fortilage' on the manor of Kilcloggan must refer to the surviving tower house.[4]

Fig. 1   The low tower house and attached offset hall at the Devereux headquarters of Ballymagir, now integrated in a modern dwelling, can be seen to the right of the tennis court, which is in what was originally the castle bawn. The location of the complex within a large moated site (hidden in trees) epitomises the close association of moated site and tower house that exists in eleven instances around the south of the county.

Fig. 2 This well-preserved, thirteenth-century tower at Haliartos in Greece is one of the best examples of free-standing Crusader fortification. It serves as an exemplar of the European tradition out of which tower houses emerged in Ireland several centuries later.

TOWER-HOUSE ORIGINS

In the turbulent conditions of the fourteenth, fifteenth and sixteenth centuries, when central authority failed to guarantee protection, an effective, compact defence system was required by the colonists to ensure security at a local level against sporadic raiding and low-level hostility.[5] This prompted the emergence of the defended residences, now known as tower houses, which are one of the most characteristic landmarks in the south Wexford landscape. The Denne's castle of Kayer was mentioned as early as 1374, when it was in the King's hands because of the killing of Fulk Furlong. Custody was granted to Stephen Furlong, to hold at the King's pleasure, provided that he 'could provide sufficient ward and provisioning'.[6] Kayer was perilously close to the Duffry and the Fassagh of Bantry and this suggests that the castle, presumably of stone, was regarded as essential to the defence of the colony. However, it cannot be definitively described as a tower house.

The design of these vertical houses, echoing early motte-and-bailey castles and small-scale Norman keeps,

combined height with defensive features to create a refuge for the occupants against hit-and-run raiding, as well as providing a balance between domestic and security requirements. Although built to a similar plan with shared design features, regional and chronological distinctions evolved over several centuries.[7] Now often standing in isolation, the towers were originally part of a complex which included a bawn (enclosure) and a hall, usually attached to the tower. Perpetual vigilance was highlighted by the provision of at least one lookout turret on the summit of each tower, affording commanding views over the surrounding countryside.

On a European level, towers had been built from the earliest times to provide security for their occupants and as aids to communication. Their verticality generated an expression of power and pride, especially in a flat landscape lacking prominent landmarks. From a religious perspective, they were regarded as a spiritual and philosophical link between sky and earth. During the Renaissance, the concept of the tower was re-interpreted, prompted by innovations in architecture, desire for greater personal freedom and the adoption of firearms. A fifteenth-century Italian commentator observed that: 'about two

Fig. 3 The small size and rugged construction of the tower house at Newcastle, on the slopes of Forth mountain, indicates that it might be one of the subsidised fifteenth-century border towers. The attached dwelling house presumably represents a modernised version of an early hall.

Fig. 4 At first sight, the rugged construction of the small tower house at Sigganshaggard indicates an early date, but a closer examination shows that it is later. The pointed doorway is guarded by a machicolation, yett and murder-hole; all windows are narrow slits, and the tower is equipped with twenty-nine gun-loops, indicating a date in the mid-sixteenth century. These defensive capabilities, combined with its location near the Pale border on the slopes of Forth Mountain, suggest that it was built as an 'offensive' tower house c. 1550, when the inhabitants of the Pale were making aggressive moves to protect their property in the north of the Pale and to reclaim land from the Irish outside of the Pale boundary.

ST. PETER'S COLLEGE

Fig. 5 None of the three tower houses recorded in Wexford town survive: Hayes's, in Hayes's Lane, Stafford's at Stonebridge on South Main Street and Wadding's in Peter Street. This image of Stafford's castle is taken from a view of Wexford from Ferrybank, painted in 1820.

hundred years ago there seems to have been a craze for constructing towers, even for the smallest of castles, and so it seemed that no head of family could do without one, and all over one would see a mass of towers'.[8]

The great majority of tower houses in Ireland date to the fifteenth and sixteenth centuries, although some were built in the preceding and succeeding centuries.[9] The emergence of the Irish tower house was unrelated to the use of a similar architectural form in the parts of Europe where low-level conflict was endemic.[10] Even Scotland, which shared a cult of the tower house with Ireland, had no direct influence on this building type in Ireland. The military, architectural and social aspect of Scottish towers differed from the Irish version. Unlike Ireland, the Norman building tradition was absent in Scotland, where the tower houses formed a distinct species both in design and political origin.[11]

The Irish tower house evolved from the tradition of colonial architecture, adapted to suit current exigencies,[12] its emergence linked to the architecture of the earlier hall-houses which were prevalent in the west of the country.[13] In county Wexford, these elegant small castles, combining domestic and defensive requirements, are synonymous with the south of the county, particularly the lowland baronies of Forth and Bargy. As distinctive architectural elements, their distribution defines regional difference and landscape character generated by historical events within the county. At a national level, the building of tower houses spread to areas under Irish control, an indication of the efficiency and flexibility of the design. Their adoption by Gaelic chieftains was not surprising. In the fourteenth century, the Irish were already constructing 'limestone

towers' with 'halls', 'battlements' and 'white-walled ramparts'.[14] Apart from their practical functions, the highly visible towers expressed prestige and lordship in the landscape for colonist and Irish alike.

The relationship between fourteenth-century fortified urban houses and fortified churches has been linked to the emergence of tower houses.[15] In county Wexford, tower houses were built in the boroughs of Wexford, Clonmines, Bannow and Taghmon, as well as episcopal castles at Fethard and at Mountgarrett just outside New Ross. With the exception of Fethard, where the early fifteenth-century castle incorporated earlier elements, none of these can be attributed to the fourteenth century. The location of the fortress-like tower house at Taghmon 'on the marches' suggests an early date. Taghmon was part of the Wexford palatinate and the castle was possibly built by Sir Gilbert Talbot in the fifteenth century, when he was lord of the Liberty.[16] Unusually, all three upper floors of the four-storey tower were similarly designed as living quarters, equipped with fireplaces and garderobes, possibly because it was primarily intended to house a garrison of soldiers.

Churches were regularly 'incastellated' in England in the twelfth century and in France during the Hundred Years' War (1337–1453), as places of refuge for rural dwellers in times of peril.[17] During the fifteenth century, similar fortification of churches took place in and around the Dublin Pale, where towers added to existing churches served as both residences and fortresses.[18] At Kilmurry in

AFTER WAKEMAN R. I. A.

Fig. 6 Taghmon Castle, after an 1840 drawing. It appears much the same as at present, except with more of the corner machicolations surviving.

south-east Kilkenny, a building traditionally regarded as a castle has proved to be a small church with an attached residential tower, dated to the 1430s.[19] Similarly, the fortification of late fourteenth- and fifteenth-century churches in south-west county Wexford coincided with the emergence of the tower house.[20]

The densely colonised region to the south of Taghmon, (Forth, Bargy, and south-west Shelmalier) was partially protected by landscape features. These natural defences consisted of the deep valleys of the Corock and its tributary the Aughnagroagh, flowing into Bannow Bay, the rocky eminence of Forth Mountain and the lower reaches of the Slaney, with a small tributary flowing along a marshy valley into the Slaney at Polehore. The authorities decided to augment these topographical features as a defensive line to protect the English colonists to the south. A custodian and bailiff for the waters between Ross and Wexford was appointed in 1409.[21]

Between 1428 and 1454, various statutes were passed directing the citizens of the counties around Dublin to pay a subsidy of £10 to landowners who built a castle or tower, twenty feet in length, sixteen feet in width and forty feet or more in height, for the protection of the Dublin Pale.[22] Traditionally, these subsidies are considered to have

Fig. 8   The restored Selskar Abbey Gate on Wexford's town wall was in effect a four-storey tower. A gateway through the ground floor connected the precinct of Selskar Abbey, which was divided by the town wall.

Fig. 7   A tower was added to the church of Selskar Abbey, in Wexford town, in the late fourteenth/early fifteenth century, a date indicated by the use of Dundry cut-stone in some window surrounds. The restored crenellations date to the 1820s, when a new church was built to the east.

initiated the tower house era.[23] While the role of the '£10 castles' in the evolution of the Pale tower house is controversial, it may have accelerated a process that was already under way, with origins in the fourteenth century.[24] However, the subsidies exerted a decisive impact on the building of towers along the perimeter of the Dublin Pale, which was dotted with castles by the end of the fifteenth century.[25]

In 1441, in response to a petition from the 'faithful lieges of the Liberties of Wexford and the Cross' [Church lands], the Wexford Pale attained official recognition and the building of tower houses in the county attracted financial support. An Act of Parliament acknowledged the military significance of the defensive line. The Crown allocated £300 out of the

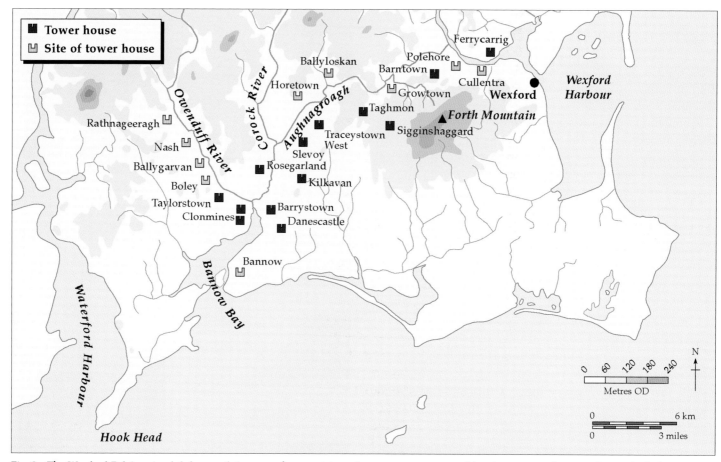

Fig. 9   The Wexford Pale's natural defences of river, marsh, mountain and gorge were augmented by sixteen tower houses, eleven of which survive in various states of repair. Protection was improved by damming the river, ensuring that the water would be maintained at a sufficiently deep level to prevent an easy crossing, of particular significance during drier summer conditions. A similar (if unofficial) defensive line existed along the Owenduff.

profits of the Liberty for the 'building and maintaining of certain towers or castles upon the river called the water [or Pill] of Taghmon, and for the damming up or obstructing of the said water for the expulsion of our enemies'.[26] The damming deepened the water, creating a more effective obstruction.

A further order was issued in 1453 that 'none shall break the fortifications or [re]strainings of Taghmon in county Wexford nor shall make no ways on the same water from the wood of Bannow to the pill [of Polehore] adjoining the river Slaney'. These rivers, with Forth Mountain, insulated the 'English' baronies of Forth and

Fig. 10   Winter flooding along the marshy valley of the Corock shows the effectiveness of the 'water of Taghmon' as a protection for the Wexford Pale.

Fig. 11   North of the village of Taghmon, a glacial feature known as the Mulmontry Gorge snakes across the landscape towards Bannow Bay. The prominent gorge, with the river flowing through it, was an essential component of the natural features which formed the boundary of the Wexford Pale.

Fig. 12 Houseland Castle, overlooking the sea on the Hook peninsula, was drawn by Du Noyer in the mid-nineteenth century. It collapsed early in the 1900s. The illustration shows that it was a typical Wexford tower house with a vaulted ground floor and three upper storeys. The castle was built by the Keatings on the Hospitaller manor of Kilcloggan.

The Tower-House Builders

The recipients of early landgrants in the southern baronies during the first phase of the Anglo-Norman colony in county Wexford established a distinctive community that endured until the mid-seventeenth century. Holding their small estates in perpetuity, their descendants, frequently acquiring more lands elsewhere in the county, enjoyed minor gentry status until the dispossessions following the Confederate War of the 1640s. A comparison between the holders of thirteenth-century manors in the south of the county and occupiers in 1640 shows that twenty-five families remained in possession for four centuries. Although relatively few in number, cohesiveness was maintained by marrying within the peer group. Imbued with hereditary affection to the crown, they were described in the sixteenth century as having retained their 'language, lands and loyalty'.[30]

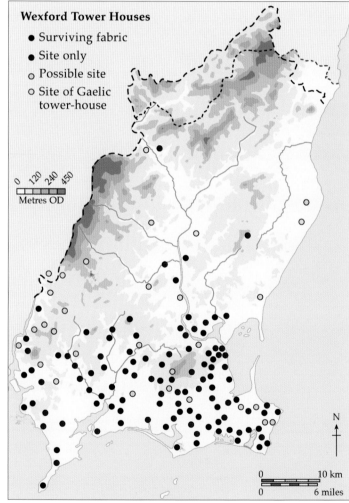

Fig. 13 Existing and removed tower houses are heavily clustered in the southern part of the county and particularly in the Wexford Pale, consisting of the baronies of Forth and Bargy and the southern part of Shelmalier. There is also a distinctive grouping in the northern part of the barony of Shelburne, known as the manor of the Island.

Bargy, and part of Shelmalier West, demarcating the distinctive cultural and social landscape of the Wexford Pale.[27] In 1598, a description of county Wexford noted that 'the south part, as the most civil part, is contained within a river called Pill, where the ancientest gentlemen, descended from the first conquerors, do inhabit'.[28]

Although not part of the Wexford Pale, the frequently raided south-western barony of Shelburne was not penetrated by the Irish. Mostly comprising the Cistercian estates of Dunbrody and Tintern and the Hospitaller manor of Kilcloggan, the north-western part of the barony, known as 'the manor of the Island', continued to be occupied by descendants of the original settlers. An order made by parliament in 1463 for the 'building of a castle at Coole on the borders of Shelburne'[29] indicates official concern for the security of the area, possibly because of its strategic location in relation to Waterford Harbour. There is no indication that this castle was ever built in the townland of Coole on the northern border of the Dunbrody Abbey estate.

R.I.A.

Fig. 14   The four-storey, rectangular tower house at Danescastle, near Bannow, is shown here in a mid-nineteenth-century drawing by Du Noyer. The pronounced batter adds to the graceful profile of the slender tower. A doorway on the shorter wall was protected by a machicolation. Unusually, a second doorway at ground-floor level provided access to a house attached to the longer wall. The tower remains relatively intact but heavily overgrown.

R.I.A.

Fig. 15 The status of the early manorial lords is reflected in the quality of this thirteenth-century sarcophagus cover, one of several in the church of St Mary's at Bannow. A mid-nineteenth-century drawing of the slab by Du Noyer shows an added inscription, in sixteenth-century script, commemorating John Colfer and his wife, Anna Siggin.

An appreciation of the qualities inherited from their Norman ancestors made them natural leaders in politics and the church. This pride in their Norman heritage survived the calamitous confiscations of the seventeenth century, after which the dispossessed families continued to be regarded as the legitimate leadership class.[31] The 'origin story' was kept alive by the descendants of the original colonists, whose names were perpetuated by passing on estates to male heirs. The family memory was reinforced by the naming of many townlands (Sinnottstown, Horetown, Pettitstown, Rochestown, Sigginstown, Butlerstown etc.) after the original grantees.

This awareness of Norman antecedents surface in later centuries. In 1687, Luke Wadding, bishop of Ferns, whose family had lost Ballycogley Castle and estate, reminisced about a relic brought from the Crusades by his ancestor, Gilbert Wadding, in the possession of the Waddings since they first arrived in Ireland.[32] In 1732, the Redmonds of the Hook described themselves as 'among ye best Catholic gentry of the kingdom', an 'ancient and illustrious family ever since the first coming of the

English into Ireland with Strongbow nearly 600 years ago'.[33] As late as the mid-nineteenth century, a member of the Devereux family attributed Wexford's heroic contribution during the Rebellion of 1798 to the legacy of the *invicta Normanorum gens*.[34]

From this tightly-knit group of landowners in the south of the county was drawn the juries to represent the commons of the county of Wexford.[35] They also held office as sheriffs, constables and other officials. Dedicated to their religion, they contributed abbots to Dunbrody and Tintern, commanders to the Hospitallers at Kilcloggan and Ballyhoge, monks to the religious orders in the towns as well as the majority of priests and bishops to the diocese.

They were to the forefront in resisting encroachment by the Irish. They constructed tower houses at their manorial centres to defend themselves and their tenants from retaliatory raids. As well as providing protection, the numerous towers in the south of the county, highly visible in the flat landscape of Forth and Bargy, reflected the confident cultural identity of their owners. The building of

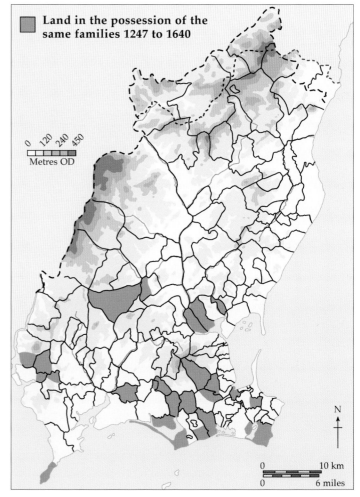

Fig. 16 Continuity of occupation over four centuries by twenty-five families, of Anglo-Norman descent, in the south of the county sustained a society with a distinctive culture and tradition.

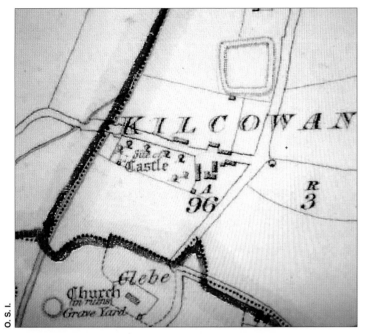

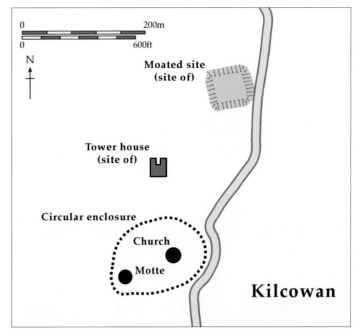

Fig. 17   On the south-coast Keating manor of Kilcowan, a progression of habitation sites provide evidence for impressive continuity. An early medieval church enclosure was occupied by a small Anglo-Norman motte castle, succeeded by a moated site, which was in turn replaced by a tower house.

137 of these distinctive towers is recorded in county Wexford, the majority during the fifteenth and sixteenth centuries, concentrated in the southern baronies (appendix 1). Sixty survive in various states of conservation, ranging from substantially complete structures to fragments incorporated in later buildings, providing the most dramatic visual evidence for the strength of the colony in the south of the county.[36] There is no indication that any of these towers were built as a result of the 1441 subsidy. Some of the tower houses recorded along the perimeter of the Wexford Pale no longer exist and several, equipped with gun-loops, are mid-sixteenth-century. The partially surviving example at Slevoy, although the right size and in the right location, seems to be later, as it has no base-batter. The small tower house at Newcastle, on the slopes of Forth Mountain, ruggedly built and with no evidence of a garderobe, represents the only possibility.

There is scant knowledge of the residences that were occupied by this group of minor gentry before the advent of the tower house. Placenames containing the element 'old' (Oldhall, Oldcourt) almost certainly refer to structures that had been replaced by tower houses, 'court' in this instance meaning a manor house. For example, the Furlong residence at Horetown was described as a 'mansion' in 1416.[37] One of the few early residences for which there is some evidence was occupied by the Anglo-Norman family of Redmond, who built a thirteenth-century hall on the Hook Peninsula, on lands held from the Knights Templars of Kilcloggan.[38] The residence was so distinctive that the family was referred to as the

Fig. 18   Townland names containing elements such as 'court', 'hall' and 'old' suggest the existence of pre-tower house residences.

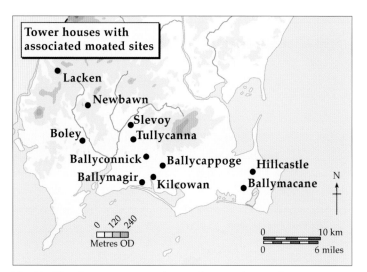

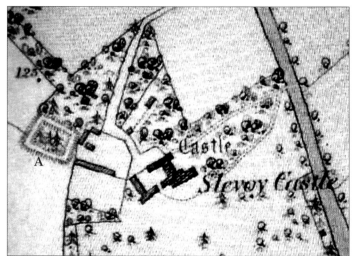

O. S. I.

Fig. 19 The close association of moated site and tower house in eleven instances, particularly in the south of the county, suggest that, in some cases, tower house builders had previously occupied moated sites. Castles were built inside large moated sites at Ballymagir and Ballymacane.

Fig. 20 The O. S. first edition shows Slevoy Castle with a moated site (**A**) in the same farmyard complex. This proximity suggests that the moated site preceded the tower house as the manorial dwelling. The location close to the Pale boundary made protection essential.

Redmonds of the Hall (*de Aula* in Latin). For example, Robert *de Aula* was summoned to attend an inquisition in Clonmel in 1281.[39] The hall became known as Redmond Hall in the townland of Hall (now Loftus Hall). 'Court' (a manor house) placenames, often combined with an Irish element, are concentrated in the north of the county, suggesting early abandonment. Courthoyle (parish of Adamstown) is the site of a tower house, built by the Howell family. Other placenames – Newtown (19 instances), Yoletown (Ye old town) (5), Oldtown (4) Newcastle (4) and Newbawn – also indicate movement to new habitation sites.

In county Wexford, a relationship existed between some medieval moated sites and tower houses. A Stafford tower house was built inside the large moated site at Ballymacane, where traces of the earthworks survive. The castle recorded in the *Civil Survey* at Ballycappoge in Mulrankin parish, presumably a tower house, was also within a moated site (now occupied by a modern farm complex).[40] Substantial remains survive (28m x 45m), with a moat 3m wide. The most impressive site, 6,300m² in area,

is at Ballymagir (Richfield) on the south coast of Bargy, where extensive remains of the fosse and banks exist.[41] This site was the headquarters of the Devereux family and it is of particular interest as its late medieval castle remains occupied down to the present time. A recent survey has established that the castle consisted of a low, double-vaulted tower, with a somewhat later hall offset to the north-west.[42] The medieval fortifications may have been reinstated during the Confederate War of the 1640s, as depositions taken after the war described Ballymagir as being 'fortified with breastwork, moat and drawbridge'.[43]

These large moated sites were occupied over a long timescale because they were spacious enough to contain more ambitious building projects. In other instances, where the remains of smaller moated sites survive in the vicinity of tower houses, the confined space of the early habitation was abandoned in favour of a more suitable, but adjacent, location. This is evident at several tower houses, either recorded or surviving, including Ballyconnick, Kilcowan, Newbawn and Slevoy, where tower houses and moated sites existed in close proximity.

Ballyteige lookout turret

FORTIFIED CHURCHES

Across Europe, when central authority imploded during periods of political turbulence, churches were fortified as places of refuge for the common people. In eastern Europe, for example, from the thirteenth century onwards, 'church castles' were constructed in volatile Transylvania as refuges and to prevent the occupation of territory by invading forces.[1] In Ireland, a similar strategy was adopted in the vicinity of the Dublin Pale during the turbulent fourteenth and fifteenth centuries.[2]

Several fortified churches in county Wexford, mostly in the south-west, belong to the same period. Four of these were located in an urban setting. In Wexford town, the Augustinian Priory of SS Peter and Paul, known as Selskar Abbey, was fortified by the addition of a 15m tower to the east of the nave.[3] The lofted ground floor was covered by a stone vault. A spiral stairway at the south-east angle rose to two upper chambers and stepped parapets with a lookout platform. The upper chambers contained no fireplaces or garderobes. The small windows are dressed with Dundry stone, suggesting a late fourteenth- early fifteenth-century date.[4]

The integration of the tower with a new church in the 1820s led to some alterations, including restoration of the battlements.[5] The precinct of the abbey, bisected by the town wall, was connected by a gate-tower (now restored), with obvious similarities to a tower house, emphasising the need for security. The tower had three floors over the vaulted ground floor gateway, with a mural stairway to first and second storey, both with a fireplace and garderobe. The wall-walk was reached through a doorway on the second floor. A spiral stairs continued to the third floor and parapet, which had lookout platforms on two angles.[6]

The ruins of the parish church of St Nicholas in the deserted medieval town of Clonmines, at the head of Bannow

NED CULETON

Fig. 1   This late eighteenth-century illustration of Selskar Abbey church shows the tower before it was restored in the 1820s, when it was integrated with a new Protestant church built to the east. This intervention involved the removal of the original chancel, shown here to the right of the tower.

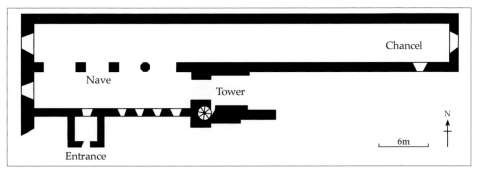

Fig. 2 A late eighteenth-century plan of Selskar Abbey church showing the location of the tower to the east of the south nave. The south wall of the nave and the south and east walls of the chancel no longer exist. The north wall now forms the boundary wall of the church site and graveyard.

Bay, include the remains of a tower attached to the west end, which originally had a vaulted ground floor and at least two upper storeys.[7] The tower was possibly a later addition as it had a separate entrance. The use of Dundry stone in the tower indicates a late fourteenth- early fifteenth-century date.[8] This time-span fits with a recorded 'enlargement' of the church in 1399.[9]

NIALL COLFER

Fig. 3 This building at Clonmines, which resembles a two-storey tower house, is in fact a unique one-storey structure, referred to as a fortified church or a chapter house. The tower house appearance is heightened by the presence of battlements, two lookout towers and a machicolation over the door. The ground floor, two-thirds of which has rib-vaulting, served as a chapel; the rest has plain barrel-vaulting over a loft supported on corbels. The loft is accessed by a spiral stairway.

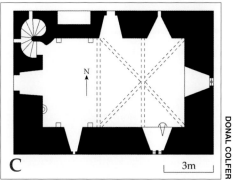

DONAL COLFER

Fig. 4 **A** The east end of the chapel with elaborate rib-vaulting **B** A view towards the west which has plain barrel-vaulting. The door to the stairway and the entrance to the loft is also shown. The holy water stoup inside the door implies religious activity. **C** The ground-floor plan shows the rib-vaulted and barrel-vaulted sections and the corbels for the loft.

Fig. 5   A tower was added to the west end of the parish church of St Nicholas in Clonmines, the use of Dundry stone in the windows indicating a date of *c*. 1400. The tower had a vaulted ground floor and at least two upper chambers. The church and tower had separate entrances.

Another fortified structure at Clonmines, just east of the parish church, is of special interest.[10] This unique and attractive building advances a step further in combining the secular and religious. From the outside, it appears to be a small rectangular castle, complete with stepped battlements and two high lookout turrets, with walls 1.5m in thickness and an external measurement of 11m by 7.5m. However, the interior of the building presents a very different character. The building has two entrance doors, one on the west side protected by a machicolation, and another on the north wall giving direct access to the church section. Details relating to ecclesiastical functions include a stoup, aumbries and a piscina (basin). Unusually, traces of the consecration crosses can still be identified, etched on the plaster.[11]

The eastern two-thirds of the space, rising to the full height of the structure, has a groined vault with chamfered ribs. In sharp contrast, the western portion is covered by a barrel vault, which originally contained a loft or gallery supported on corbels and separated from the church by a partition.[12] A spiral staircase in the north-west angle leads to the gallery and the battlements.

This remarkable building was designed to serve several functions, not least the provision of security in times of danger. It may also have served as a chapter house or meeting place for diocesan clergy. In 1460, for example, an ecclesiastical court of inquiry convened in the parish church of Clonmines was probably conducted in the adjacent chapter house.[13] The fortified multipurpose building may have formed part of the diocesan infrastructure associated with the bishop's move from Ferns to the more secure south.

The medieval parish church of St Mary's is all that remains of the deserted town of Bannow.[14] Of possible late twelfth- early thirteenth-century date, the simple nave and chancel church, with north and south entrances, passed into the possession of Tintern Abbey in 1245. All the surviving windows in the nave are inserted. One of the two-light windows in the south chancel wall was cusped ogee-headed. The east window originally had tracery and hood-moulding. Crenellations and a wall-walk were added to the nave in

Fig. 6   The parish church of St Mary's at Bannow, of late twelfth- early thirteenth-century date, was fortified by adding crenellations and wall-walk to the nave in the fourteenth- fifteenth century.

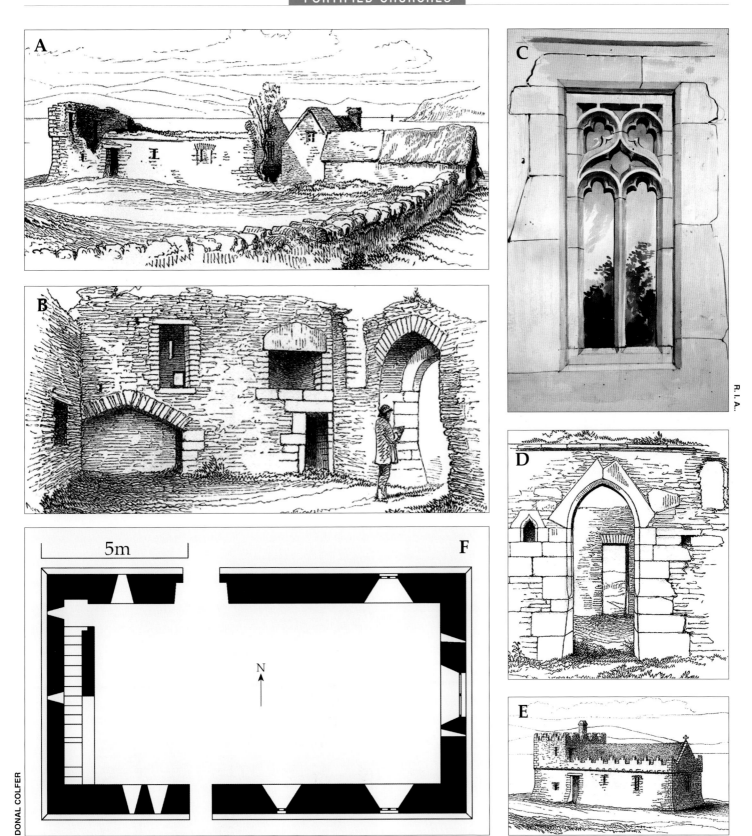

Fig. 7   Mid-nineteenth-century drawings by Du Noyer of St Catherine's church on the Cistercian grange at Nook, located on a clifftop overlooking the estuary. Buttermilk Castle was situated on the shoreline, a short distance away. The farmhouse beside the church has been replaced by a modern dwelling. **A**   View of the ruin showing the remains of the low tower at the west end. **B**   The interior of the building looking west, showing the doorway to the stairs in the tower and the entrance to the first floor. The artist is gazing out the north doorway. **C**   The elegant, two-light east window with cusped-ogee decoration **D**   An exterior view of the pointed north doorway with lintelled south door opposite. The pointed niche beside the doorway may have held a light to guide shipping on the estuary. **E**   A reconstruction drawing from the north showing the church with pronounced base batter and a battlemented tower and wall-walk. **F**   A plan of the church showing the 1.75m thick walls and the arrangement of windows.

Fig. 8 A church was mentioned at Killesk in 1370, presumably referring to the surviving ruin. Traditionally believed to be a castle, the unique structure consists of a tower with base-batter, formerly of three storeys, and a slightly narrower church, built as a unit. The vault of the tower, with its gallery, was included in the church. The arched entrance, located in the tower, was protected by a murder-hole. The church had a wall-walk, accessed through a first-floor doorway in the tower. A mid-nineteenth-century drawing by Du Noyer (below) shows the building in a similar condition as at present, except for the east gable of the church which has since fallen. The priest's residence in the tower had a garderobe but there is no evidence for a fireplace.

the fourteenth/fifteenth century, due to the threat from incursions by the Butlers and Kavanaghs.[15]

Two fortified churches were associated with the estate of Dunbrody Abbey, not surprisingly as the area was exposed to raiding by the Irish from the Fassagh of Bantry. Significant remains of both churches survive. St Catherine's church was built on one of the abbey granges, in a commanding cliff-top location in the townland of Nook, overlooking the estuary a kilometre north of Ballyhack. The grange included the small tower house known as Buttermilk Castle, built at the base of the cliff as a headquarters for fishing activities on the estuary. The small church (12m x 6m) catered for the

Fig. 9   This view from the east end of Killesk church shows the vault under the tower and the entrance to the gallery from the spiral stairway, a similar arrangement to the 'chapter house' at Clonmines. The vault demonstrates the efficiency of the building method. The wall-plates for the gallery were supported on corbels and fitted into wall sockets. Corbels and wall sockets over the church suggest the presence of a loft. The doorway to the wall-walk can be seen at the top left.

NEVILLE DUKES

spiritual needs of the lay brothers and other workers on the grange and for their security when necessary. Ruggedly built of old red sandstone, presumably quarried from the cliff-face at Ballyhack, the building had 1.5m thick walls with a pronounced base batter. The western end was designed as a dwelling for the resident priest. A stairway in the gable rose to a second storey, with fireplace and timber floor, and to the battlemented wall-walk. Many of the architectural features no longer exist but fortunately the church was surveyed and recorded in the mid- nineteenth century.[16] The decorative cut-stone details were of a high quality,

Fig. 10   Details from Killesk church from the top. **A** The pointed doorway with old red sandstone cut-stone. **B** The entrance to the machicolation over the doorway with the door to the gallery on the right. **C** The ogee top of the sole (partially) surviving church window.

Fig. 11 The insertion of crossing towers in religious foundations, such as at Dunbrody Abbey and the Augustinian Priory in Clonmines (above, with another slender tower at the angle of the walled enclosure) fulfilled a similar function to the smaller fortified churches.

particularly the south doorway and the two-light east window with its graceful cusped tracery.

The other fortified church associated with Dunbrody Abbey was in the neighbouring parish of Killesk, held by a branch of the FitzGeralds by knight's fee. In 1370, the abbot of Dunbrody acquired the advowson

(patronage) of several churches, including Killesk.[17] The present building is either the original or an extension of the 1370 structure. The impressive remains at Killesk consist of a tower (8.2m x 5.5m) with base-batter, and a slightly narrower and lower but contemporary church, projecting 7.3m to the east. The

Fig. 13 The Hospitallers added a tower to the Templar church at Templetown. As at Selskar, the tower was restored as a belfry and sacristy for a new Protestant church in the early nineteenth century. The ruins of the Templar church are to the right of the tower.

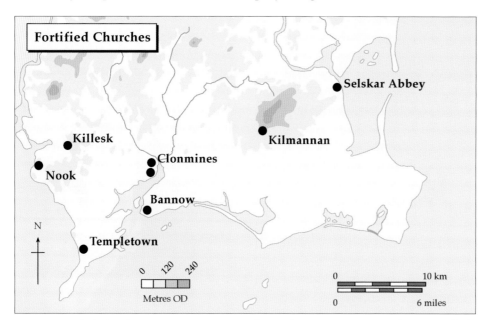

Fig. 12 Fortified churches were concentrated in the south-western barony of Shelburne which, because of easy access from the Fassagh of Bantry, was more exposed to incursions than Forth and Bargy. Kilmannon church, on the western slopes of Forth Mountain, was also vulnerable.

Fig. 14 The tower in Kilmannan graveyard represents the only rural fortified church in the Wexford Pale, presumably because of its vulnerable location. The scar of the church gable can be seen on the wall of the tower.

church incorporated the vaulted ground floor of the tower. It had a tall, narrow window on the north, south and east walls.

The pointed entrance, protected by a murder hole, was in the south wall of the tower. A spiral stairway in the south-west angle of the tower led to a gallery under the vault. A mural stairs in the south wall, continued to the wall-walk (destroyed) of the church and an oubliette off the stairs. A spiral stairs rose to first floor level, which had four narrow lights but no fireplace. The second floor no longer exists but the stairs and garderobe chute can still be seen.[18] The building is robustly constructed of large rubble with cut-stone quoins, mostly of old red sandstone, particularly higher up.

The surrounds of the pointed entrance door and most of the windows are also of old red sandstone.

At Templetown, on the Hook Peninsula, a tower was built to the north of the Templar church by their successors, the Knights Hospitallers.[19] Only a fragment of the church can be seen but the tower survives substantially, albeit in an altered state. The ground floor had two round-headed doorways (now blocked up) and a barrel vault with wicker centering. A spiral stairs at the south-east corner climbed to the first floor. The second floor was partially vaulted. As at Selskar, the tower was altered c. 1820 when it was adapted as a sacristy and belfry for a new Protestant church attached to the

north side. Large openings were inserted and the top was ornamented with modern crenellations.

The isolated medieval parish church at Kilmannan, on the southern slopes of Forth Mountain, was protected by the addition of a tower, presumably due to its exposed location near the border of the Wexford Pale. Only the four-storey tower remains standing, heavily covered with ivy.

As well as providing an architectural template, the building of fortified churches also created a school of tower-building expertise, which facilitated the construction of more elaborate secular tower houses during the political and social turbulence of the fifteenth and sixteenth centuries.

TOWER-HOUSE ECONOMY

The Irish tower house evolved in response to endemic low-level conflict, principally during the fifteenth and sixteenth centuries. While its genesis remains uncertain, it is accepted that the concept had an indigenous origin, evolving from a complex combination of factors.[1] The coherent architectural tradition that emerged was not unique but was based on a particular interpretation of inherited forms adapted to local requirements. Combining domestic essentials and security needs, the vertical towers used height and defensive features to project a sense of impregnability.[2] The county Wexford examples are assigned to the simple, earliest type, found mostly in the east of the country.[3] The landholding system created by the Anglo-Normans in the thirteenth century determined the location of these towers two centuries later. In county Wexford, this was particularly relevant in the southern baronies of Forth and Bargy and in the north-west of the barony of Shelburne, where the patchwork of small feudal holdings encouraged the proliferation of defended residences.

Fig. 1 Sigginstown Castle, near the south coast, is among the most graceful of tower houses. Well constructed of pink granite sourced at nearby Carnsore, good quality cut-stone was utilised for quoins and windows. The angles are fitted with cross-loops for firearms, indicating that it was constructed around the middle of the sixteenth century. A possibly late seventeenth-century brick house is attached to the west side, covering the entrance and rendering the machicolation obsolete. The steep-roofed structure provides a link between late medieval and Georgian architecture.

Fig. 2   An aerial perspective of the lowlands of Bargy looking east towards Forth, with the fishing port of Kilmore Quay and the Forlorn Point in the foreground. This area was the heartland of tower house building in county Wexford and it contains many of the best-preserved examples. The village itself is of relative modern date, having developed following the building of a small pier in the early nineteenth century. Since then a series of bigger piers have created a much larger harbour. Kilmore Quay is renowned for the retention of a large number of thatched houses along the village street.

MANORIAL ECONOMY

The tower house emerged from the economic model introduced into Ireland by the Anglo-Normans. This system consisted of a hierarchical landholding network, based on the granting of land in return for military service, in order to ensure a low-cost permanent martial structure. The seignorial lords established secondary manors in their fiefs by granting lands to their knights and other followers, mostly holding military tenancies, as well as others who were free, rent-paying tenants, both granted in perpetuity. These sub-manors were organised according to the feudal template but on a more modest scale. Because tenants on sub-manors were obliged to pay tithes to the manorial church, the manor became equivalent with the medieval parish (which later survived as the civil parish).

A description of Forth in 1682

The inhabitants [of Forth] were mostly freeholders, but their freeholds very small, and being never forfeited, remained as they were first set out and divided to FitzStephen's soldiers. The soil of this barony is naturally coarse and barren, yet by the industry of the people, together with the contiguity of the sea, from which they bring ouze or oure [woar] seaweed, with which they manure their cultivated lands, it is made the granary of the county and parts adjacent, especially for barley in which it abounds. They breed few or no cattle in this barony.

Manorial income was principally generated by agriculture, rents from tenants, services in kind and income from mills.

The sub-infeudation of south Wexford by William Marshal created a complex of small manors, establishing a unique colonial society that endured for four centuries. The construction of tower houses in the county originated with these hereditary landholders. As descendants of the early colonists, they were familiar with the concept of castle building and the architectural tradition of small

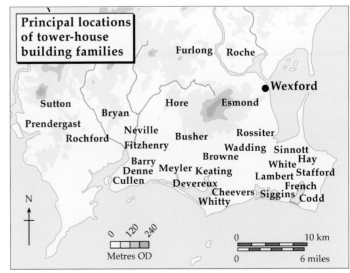

Fig. 3   Tower houses were built by a relatively small but influential group of landowners, concentrated in the baronies of Forth and Bargy.

Fig. 4   The three-storey tower house of Tellarought, located in northern Shelburne, is unusual in several ways, possibly suggesting an early date. It has a system of three murder-holes over the entrance, no evidence for loops on the ground floor and no sign of a garderobe.

keeps. At a wider level, new ideas percolated easily as contact was maintained within the colonist community through kinship connections as well as political and military involvement. Marriage alliances were particularly relevant as the landholding gentry habitually married within their own peer group.

In county Wexford, for example, as well as being connected to many of the principal families in the county, the Redmonds of the Hall found wives in counties Waterford, Kilkenny, Cork and Dublin.[4] In 1572, a letter from Elizabeth I described the Brownes of Mulrankin as being 'near of blood to the houses of our right trusted and well-beloved cousins, the earls of Kildare and Ormond'.[5] Some Wexford manor holders presumably continued to communicate with their 'parent' families in England. This was demonstrated in 1599, almost four centuries after the Anglo-Norman colonisation, when the Lord Deputy, Robert Devereux, earl of Essex, moving through the county with an army, stayed with his kinsman, James Devereux of Ballymagir.[6] However, his arrival may not have been completely welcome, as, according to tradition, Devereux had to sell part of his

estate to finance the elaborate arrangements for the Lord Deputy and his retinue.

As well as providing security for the occupants, the gradual spread of these iconic vertical residences, with their ancillary buildings, projected a potent symbol of lordship in south Wexford. Collectively, the distinctive towers, highly visible in the low landscape, typified a unique cultural environment in a well-defined topographical region, reflecting the character of the inhabitants. They symbolised the society, shaped by historical events, which evolved in the secluded Wexford Pale, a region eulogised by several seventeenth-century commentators because of its unique attributes. These descriptions applied in particular to Forth, presumably because of its proximity to Wexford town, but they have a wider application.

The 1441 allocation of a £300 incentive out of the profits of the Liberty for 'building and maintaining certain towers or castles upon the river called the water [or Pill] of Taghmon' implied that the considerable financial burden placed on potential builders was inhibiting the adequate defence of the colony.[7] As in the case of the Dublin Pale, this subsidy stimulated the building of towers along the borders of the Wexford Pale. This in turn generated a ripple effect in

Fig. 5   The four-storey tower house at Baldwinstown stands complete to battlements but with structural cracks. The loft under the vault has an unusual stirrup-loop. The principal domestic quarters, on the first and second floors, were similarily equipped with fireplaces and garderobes.

A description of Forth *c.* 1680 (H. F. Hore, 1862)

The barony of Forth in all emergencies of public concerns in the county preceedeth and hath pre-eminence. The gentry and inhabitants first in all courts called, and in time of war, expeditions, rising-in-arms in order to the opposing and suppressing of turbulent seditions, factions, or known and celebrated rebels, some prime gentlemen thereof had the conduct and command of forces raised in the county. The said barony in longitude extends from the north-west part of the commons of Wexford inclusive, unto the extremest point of Carne, Kemp's Cross, about ten miles. Its breadth is dilated from the west side of the mountain of Forth, six miles – comprehending by ancient computation 20,000 of arable acres of land – naturally not fertile, but by the solicitously ingenious industry and indefatigable labour of the inhabitants so improved and reduced to that fecundious perfection, that it abounds with all sorts of excellent bread-corne and grain, gardens, orchards, fruits, sweet-herbs, meadows, pasture for all sorts of cattle (wherewith all is plentifully supplied) not much inferior, if not equivalent, to the best in Ireland – though not generally so great in body or structure.

The inhabitants commonly use pacing nags, singularly performeth in travel, and easily kept in good case [condition]. Their farms are so diligently and exactly hedged and fenced, that neighbours seldom trespass one another. They greatly sow furze seed, or plant the same in rows, some few ridges distant, which ordinarily in a few years grow to 8 or 10 feet in height, to that bigness and strength that (better timber being there deficient) dwelling-houses are therewith all roofed. It also in the extremest violence of winter tempests affords their horses, sheep, and goats, both food and shelter; being planted in the hedges, it becomes a singular fence for their cornfields, and afterwards their only fuel for all occasions – being cut or grubbed in March, it makes the clearest fire and flame, the most lasting and hardest coal of any firewood, except juniper, with least quantity of ashes. The whole barony at a distance, viewed at harvest-time, represents a well-cultivated garden with diversified plots.

Fig. 6   Because of the scarcity of trees, furze was cultivated as a multipurpose crop in the barony of Forth (and presumably also in Bargy), creating a flamboyant blaze of colour in late Spring and early Summer. As well as providing impenetrable field-boundaries, it was harvested for use in the construction of houses and as good quality fuel, and also served as fodder and shelter for livestock. This association of the plant with the highly cultivated and prosperous southern baronies presumably gave rise to the expression 'Gold under furze, silver under ferns, famine under heather'.

Fig. 7   Before its demise, the port of Bannow acted as a trading centre for the Wexford Pale, and particularly for Bargy. The site of the town, which may have suffered from the effects of the Black Death, is marked by the ruins of the medieval parish church only (foreground, left of centre). The treacherous sand bars and ever-shifting channels in Bannow Bay had a devastating impact on the port, which may have been focused on the inlet at centre left of the picture before the silting up of the deep water between the mainland and the island of Bannow. Stone artifacts in the church reflect the high status of the early town.

the rest of the region, influenced by fashion and status, leading to a surge in the popularity of the prestigious defended residences. Some of the border towers were built by holders of more secure manors further south. They may have been motivated by the subsidy and a desire to stabilise vulnerable land on the borders of the Pale. For example, the Rossiters of Rathmacknee, a well-known manor south of Wexford town, constructed castles close to the Pale border at Slevoy and Newcastle. Their basic architectural footprint, which is close to the specifications for the towers of the Dublin Pale, suggest a possible early date for the partially surviving towers.

MANORIAL AGRICULTURE

The construction of a tower house, a highly visible emblem of the economic and social status of the lord of the manor, demanded a considerable financial investment. In the early seventeenth century, it was estimated that it would cost £600 or £700 to build even the 'meanest' castle.[8] This was particularly relevant in the Wexford Pale where the extents of holdings were modest and farming was the main source of income. The matrix of unusually small townlands and parishes in Forth and Bargy evolved from the initial patchwork of medieval landgrants.

On the demesne lands held by the lord of the manor, crops were rotated in a three-field system to maximise yield. The village lands were laid out in open fields in which the under-tenants held dispersed strips.[9] Relic remains of this archaic type of landholding survive on the Hook Peninsula.[10] Manors were divided into arable ('under the plough'), pasture and meadow. Woodland was also essential as a source of fuel, timber for building and coppicing for wattle making. Because of the scarcity of woods in south Wexford, furze was cultivated as a multi-

Fig. 8   For centuries seaweed (known as 'woar' in south Wexford) was collected for use as a fertiliser, especially on farms adjacent to the coast. This mid-nineteenth-century painting by Du Noyer of seaweed gathering at Bannow captures the urgency required to beat the incoming tide.

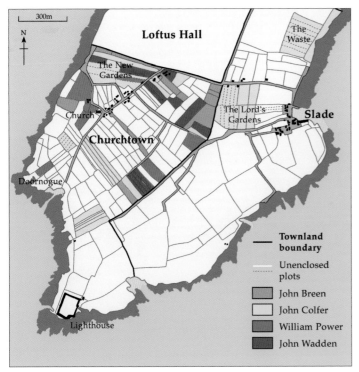

Fig. 9   The Loftus Estate maps of 1872 show that, on the tip of the Hook peninsula, the smaller tenants held dispersed plots in long narrow strips, some in open fields. This archaic system resembled the way in which land was held on medieval manors. The townland of Churchtown contained eighty-eight hectares, shared by twenty-eight tenants. The land held by four of these illustrates the dispersed nature of the holdings. Although much modified, the field pattern survives, and it is emphasised by the large enclosures of the demesne to the north, and the big fields in the townland of Slade, which was held by a principal tenant.

purpose resource.[11] Land was measured in carucates (the unit of land ploughed by a team of oxen in a year), each containing 120 medieval acres, equivalent to 300 statute acres (122ha). Some placenames in Forth and Bargy refer to medieval land usage: Roughmead and Wetmeadows record areas of meadow; Fortyacres, Twentyacre, Twelveacre, Tenacre (2), Sixacre and Threeacre originated as medieval land divisions. They contain two-and-a-half times as many statute acres, the generally accepted ratio between medieval and modern acres.[12] Forth, Bargy and Shelmalier Commons represent the commonage on the heathlands of Forth Mountain.

Manorial economy was based on mixed agriculture, dominated by cereal growing. The maximum expansion of arable was achieved c. 1300 after which the Irish recovery resulted in the widespread abandonment of manors and a resultant drop in corn production.[13] This collapse in arable did not occur in the more secure Dublin Pale, where a 74% arable acreage on demesne land in 1300 was matched 350 years later by a similar figure in the *Civil Survey*. Presumably, there were some dips in yields, particularly during the turbulent fourteenth century.[14] In general, the deterioration in grain growing prompted an increase in

cattle and sheep and a corresponding rise in the export of wool and hides to Britain and the continent.[15]

Originally, the land of Forth and Bargy was of mixed quality. Bog and poorly drained areas are recorded in townland names such as Moortown (4), Moor, Moorfields, Redmoor, Reedstown and Riesk (riasc, a marsh). Centuries of hard work by the colonists and the persistent application of 'woar' (seaweed) and 'ouze' (sand) as manure, transformed the region into 'the granary of the county and beyond'.[16] The improvement of manorial land with seaweed and sand had been ongoing since the thirteenth century.[17] As well as grain, the Wexford Pale 'abounded in gardens, orchards, fruits, herbs, meadows and pasture, not much inferior, if not equivalent, to the best in Ireland, representing a well-cultivated garden with diversified plots at harvest time'.[18] A map of seventeenth-

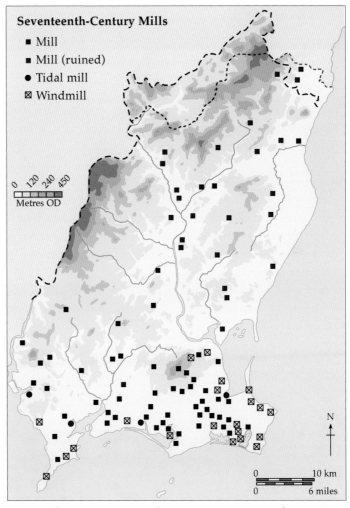

Fig. 10   This map of seventeenth-century mills illustrates the correlation between mills and tower houses. The large number of mills in the tower-house area of the south-east implies that tower house economy depended on intensive grain-growing agriculture. Conversely, the mills in the tower house barren north are almost all shown as being in ruins. There is a profusion of windmills in the southern coastal area, which also had four tidal mills at Ballybrennan, Duncormick and the two Saltmills at Tintern and Dunbrody. Traces of the tidal mill complex at Dunbrody survive.

N. L. I.

Fig. 11   As this late seventeenth-century illustration by Phillips shows, the Cistercian grange of Ballyhack was well placed to control the approach road to the pier and the lucrative ferry-crossing to Passage. The position of the ship shows the presence of deep water close to the shore. The tower house was built to accommodate the lay brothers who supervised the fishing industry. It is surrounded by a scatter of houses, some of them fishermen's cabins but several, possibly owned by merchants, of a substantial nature. The roofless church, dedicated to St James, can be seen on the clifftop.

century mills, essential sources of income for manor holders, reinforces the economic connection between the grain industry and tower-house building. This is most obvious in their complementary coincidence in the baronies of Forth and Bargy.[19] Grain was one of Ireland's principal exports for two centuries (1250–1450), much of it going to feed the English army in France and elsewhere. The deteriorating political situation in Ireland resulted in a collapse of agriculture and a shortage of grain. As in the Dublin Pale, this must have aided the grain producers in the relatively secure Wexford Pale, where it was possible to continue normal farming.

BOOK OF HOURS

Fig. 12   This medieval German illustration shows lay brothers fishing with a seine net. Because of the abbey's proximity to the estuary, fishing also played a significant part in the economic life of Dunbrody Abbey.

The topographical insulation of river, mountain and marsh that provided security for the southern baronies also hindered outward transport of goods. The port of Wexford, located within the Pale, was the natural market for surplus produce, as well as the exit port for the region. In 1345, for example, £11 was paid in custom dues at Wexford on wool and hides, presumably from the hinterland of Forth and Bargy.[20] The port of Bannow would also have featured in the early centuries of the colony, before its demise was sealed by shifting sands, both real and economic.

FISHING

Apart from agriculture, manor holders in south Wexford derived income from a variety of sources. The sea obviously sustained the economy of the region. Fishing was crucial, with Wexford town being one of the principal ports. Bannow was also a fishing centre, at least at local level; in the early fourteenth century, the fishery around the Keeragh Island made a considerable contribution to the town's finances.[21] The sandy nature of the south Wexford coastline, with no natural harbours, prevented any large-scale exploitation of fishing stocks by local boats. In the fifteenth and sixteenth centuries, the Irish fishing grounds were frequented by large fleets of continental and British fishing boats.[22] The teeming fishing grounds off the south Wexford coast were

LUTTEREL PSALTER

Fig. 13   This unique image, dating to the early fourteenth century, illustrates two aspects of the medieval economy. The race above the water-mill contains wicker eel-traps, a technique that was used widely across Europe and presumably also in Ireland.

principally noted for herring, particularly in the fifteenth and sixteenth centuries. In the 1580s, the construction of Duncannon Fort provided protection for 450 foreign fishing vessels operating seasonally in Waterford Harbour, exploiting the rich but pirate-infested waters off south-east Ireland.[23]

On the south-west coast of Ireland, the Gaelic lordships, also based in tower houses, operated a sophisticated system to extract money from the fishing fleet, composed mostly of foreign boats. Each boat had to pay nineteen shillings, a barrel of flour and salt, a hogshead of beer, as well as a dish of fish three times a week, for permission to use the fishing grounds and anchorage. If fish were brought ashore for drying, the crew was charged another eight shillings and six pence. There was also an income from selling provisions to the boats, especially beef,

mutton and pork. This capitalisation of the fishing fleet made the sea the economic mainstay of the area around Bantry Bay in the late medieval period.[24] In like manner, manorial lords and religious houses on the east coast around Dublin exploited the foreshore of their properties by levying payments on fishing boats.[25]

With such an extensive fishing industry off Wexford's south coast, income was similarly generated on coastal estates, as authority over fishing activities was included in the terms of original land grants. In 1611, the services and rents listed in a confirmation of their ancestral estate to the Staffords of Ballymacane included 'wrecks from the sea, prisages [taxes] and fishings'.[26] Some of the finest examples of surviving tower houses are on the southern littoral, their construction possibly supplemented by extracting payments from foreign fishing boats. These

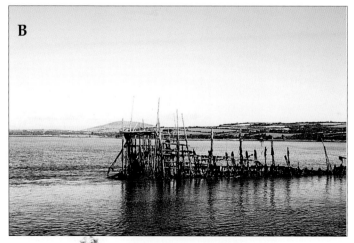

Fig. 14   Buttermilk Castle was built by the Cistercians on the grange of Nook, as a base from which fishing activities on the Barrow could be operated. A mid-nineteenth-century drawing (**A**) shows fishermen tending a weir in front of the castle. In the late twentieth century, a modern weir, using a similar technique, operated on the same site (**B**). The method of construction and fish-catching technique varied little over the centuries.

Fig. 15 **A** The Cistercian tower house at Ballyhack was advantageously situated near the confluence of the Suir with the Barrow and Nore. In 1515, it was claimed that 'the king's commissioners always used to sit at Ballyhack', indicating a fifteenth-century date for the castle's construction. Like other buildings in the area (Kilhile tower house, St Catherine's church), the tower house at Ballyhack was built of local old red sandstone. All windows facing the high ground are mere slits, with larger windows on the west, facing the estuary. The south-east angle was protected by a corner machicolation on the battlements. Before the construction of the nineteenth-century road from Arthurstown around the cliff edge, the castle controlled traffic on the original approach road down the hill. **B** A drawing of the granite entrance doorway which was protected by a machicolation, yett and murder hole. The doorway was above ground level due to the sloping nature of the site, probably reached by stone steps or a wooden ladder, which could be withdrawn if necessary. **C** The altar recess on the second floor, equipped with altar slab, aumbries and candle holders, represents the ecclesiastical aspect of the tower house. **D** The restored loft under the ground-floor vault. **E** High up on the west wall, a stone head keeps perpetual watch over traffic on the river, perhaps suggesting the monks' unceasing vigilance. **F** A slop-stone or laver on the first floor, sometimes indicating a kitchen. **G** Two slit windows drawn by Du Noyer in the mid-nineteenth century. **H** A plan of the second floor showing the altar recess with a mural chamber to the left which may have been used as a sacristy. The extra thickness of the wall on the east side accommodated the spiral stairway, an oubliette, a garderobe and the altar recess.

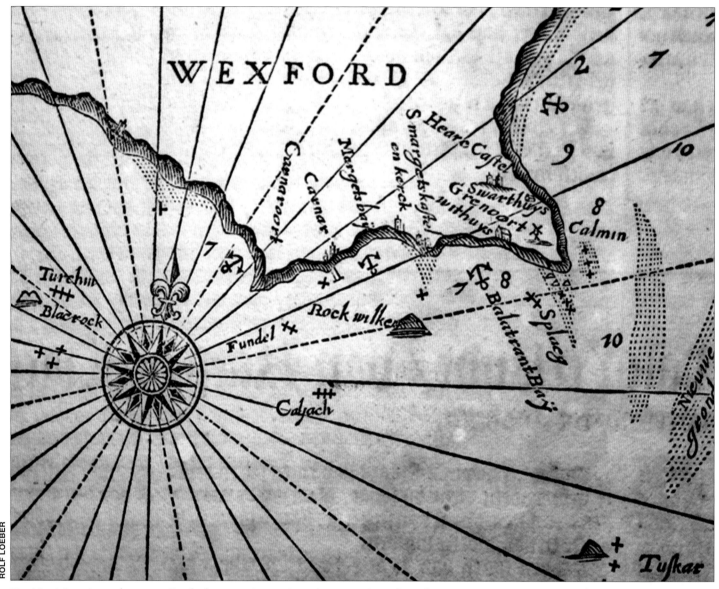

Fig. 16   A late sixteenth-century Dutch chart contains precise information about the inshore waters and coastline of south-east Wexford. Dangerous shoals and sandbanks are shown, with crosses marking the sites of shipwrecks. Placenames (still in use) include Tuskar, Splaugh, Greenore, Ballytrent and Carne. The anchor symbols identify good anchorage and landing beaches. Significantly, adjacent tower houses are shown, presumably to act as navigation aids guiding fishing boats to the beaches, where they could cure their catch before returning to home ports. One beach has what appears to be a jetty. The 'tax' levied for this amenity was a valuable source of income for tower house builders and owners. The quality of the information on the map indicates considerable knowledge about the littoral and coastal waters, reflecting a high volume of foreign shipping and fishing activity.

include Clougheast, Sigginstown, Ballyhealy, Ballyteige and Slade.

A late sixteenth-century Dutch chart displays surprisingly precise information about the inshore waters and coastline of south-east Wexford. Dangerous shoals and sandbanks are indicated, with crosses marking the sites of shipwrecks, while good anchorage and landing beaches are marked by anchor symbols. Significantly, adjacent tower houses are shown, presumably to act as navigation aids to guide fishing boats to the beaches, where they could cure their catch before returning to home ports. The 'tax' collected for this amenity was a potentially valuable source of income for the tower house

owners. The range of the information on the map reveals considerable knowledge among continental mariners about the littoral and coastal waters of south Wexford, reflecting the high volume of foreign shipping and fishing activity. The risk of attack from the sea may have incentivised the building of coastal tower houses. This was illustrated in 1594 by the capture and subsequent ransom of Richard Whitty of Ballyteige Castle,[27] whose name is recorded on the Whitty tomb in Grange cemetery.

There is some evidence for the control of fishing in other parts of the county. The Cistercians at Dunbrody, whose lands bordered Waterford Harbour, erected castles at the granges of Ballyhack and Nook to control the

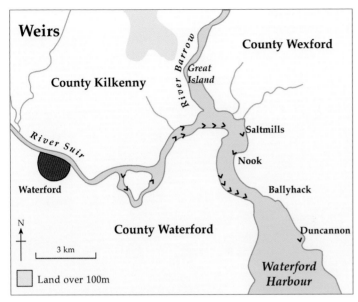

Fig. 17 Fishing weirs still in use in the Waterford estuary in the mid-twentieth century. The weirs at Saltmills, Nook and Duncannon were originally operated by the Cistercians of Dunbrody Abbey.

economic resources of the estuary, particularly the salmon fishery. The importance of the fishing industry was reflected in the large number of weirs positioned along both shores of the estuary.[28] At Nook, a small tower house known as Buttermilk Castle was built just above the high-water mark, overlooking one of the monastic fishing weirs. The site of the tower is now marked by a pile of rubble but the weir is still in operation. The fortified church of St Catherine was built for the use of the monks on the grange. A rental of 48s 4d from three fishing weirs, equivalent to the income from half a ploughland, underlined the value of the estuary to Dunbrody Abbey.

The large fifteenth-century tower house at Ballyhack is strategically placed with a commanding view of the estuary. The investment in a tower house of this size reflects the economic potential of the fishery. The extent drawn up in 1541, following dissolution, divulges the value of the fishing industry to the abbey, particularly the income from foreign boats which needed to land for provisions and to process fish before returning to their home ports. The two fishing boats owned by nine fishermen at Ballyhack, as well as all foreign boats landing at 'le key', were bound to render 'one fish out of a catch of large fish; one hake out of a catch of hake and one fish out of a catch of small fish'. The occupants of the nine tenements and eight cottages also paid a tithe of fish worth 20s.[29]

The Cistercians operated the lucrative ferry between Ballyhack and Passage. It is not possible to calculate a yearly income but it must have been substantial, considering the investment in the tower house, which had a chapel on the second floor, implying that it was intended

to be a permanent residence for the lay brothers managing the fishery and ferry. Material excavated from the garderobe chute proves the widespread continental origins of boats visiting Ballyhack, as the pottery originated in Spain, France, Portugal, Holland and England.[30]

The high level of taxes generated at New Ross by the new custom imposed on wool and hides in 1275 indicates that Dunbrody and Tintern became involved in sheep farming during the thirteenth century, in common with other Cistercian houses.[31] The Irish placename of Rathnageeragh (Rath of the sheep) suggests that the monks depended on Irish tenants to manage the sheep on the northern part of the estate. Apart from farming, the surveys also identify other economic activities. The tidal waters of the inlets near the two Cistercian abbeys were

Fig. 18 An early sixteenth-century ship with a single square-rigged sail, showing the method used to land on a beach by gangplank while keeping the ship afloat. It also provides an illustration of how an early cannon was fitted in a ship. The sailors are collecting what appear to be bones.

Fig. 19 The economic advantages of a sheltered landing beach resulted in the construction of the tower house at Slade, adjacent to the shoreline and the only natural anchorage and landing place on the Hook peninsula. Located on the Hospitaller manor of Kilcloggan, the tower was presumably built by the Knights in order to manage maritime activity at the most suitable location on their estate. The link between the towers at Kilcloggan and Slade is indicated by their size, among the smallest in the county, and the absence of base-batter. Even smaller than the tower house at the manorial centre, the tower at Slade may have been military rather than residential, a function that is suggested by the double lookout turret on its summit. The lack of accommodation, and the value of the location, is indicated by the addition of a later fortified hall-house, attached to the corner of the tower but not interconnected, perhaps emphasising the distinction between the military and domestic functions.

harnessed to operate tidal mills (salt mills) in what became the two townlands of Saltmills.

The small tower house at Slade, on the Hospitaller manor of Kilcloggan, had close associations with the sea.[32] Situated near the tip of the Hook peninsula, the tower was perched on the cliffedge, overlooking the sole sheltered landing beach on the headland.[33] The castle is the only tower house in the county with two surviving vaults; one over the ground floor, the other forming the roof. It was sited on land held by a tenant on the manor but an investment of this nature indicates the involvement of the Hospitaller overlords. Although there is no explicit evidence for this, it is suggested by the potential of the landing beach for fishing and trading activities.

The slender footprint and plain architecture suggest that it was built for commercial rather than domestic purposes, presumably well before the dissolution of the monasteries in 1541. The prominence of the tall, narrow

R.I.A.

Fig. 20 The proximity of Slade Castle to the low cliff-edge is shown in Wakeman's 1840 drawing, before the modern road was built between the castle and the shoreline, as part of a famine relief scheme in 1847.

Fig. 21   A doorway in Artramon tower house with a granite surround with holes for securing a metal yett to protect the entrance, and a decorative double-light, cusped ogee window, of granite and sandstone, in Rathmacknee tower house. As granite was not generally available in the county, the type generally used for features where cut-stone was required may have been sourced in the Leinster or Wicklow Mountains, or even from abroad. The cut-stone may have been produced by skilled masons at the quarries and transported to where it was required.

tower on the low-lying peninsula acted as a navigation aid to guide fishing boats to the landing beach. The financial success of the site is emphasised by the later investment in a fortified house, constructed as an independent entity but connected to the tower on the diagonal. The house is even nearer the sea than the tower, with larger windows on the first floor overlooking the beach. The extensive vaulted ground-floor area could have been used for storage.

The economic advantages of Slade as a small fishing and trading centre is demonstrated by later developments. In the 1680s, following his acquisition of the Hook lands, Henry Loftus immediately built a quay at Slade (still called 'the ould kay'), obviously because he realised that it would be financially viable.[34] He leased the castle and lands of Slade to William Mansell, his wife's brother-in-law, a political refugee from south Wales, who constructed a second pier and set up a saltworks using rock salt imported from Cheshire.[35] This was clearly a response to the thriving fishing industry, as salt was required by foreign fishing boats to preserve their catch for the return voyage to home ports.

MASONS AND MATERIALS

The construction of a tower house depended on a skilled team, including architects, masons, quarrymen and labourers. The permission granted to Bishop Barrett in 1409 to bring 'competent quarrymen and masons' from the counties of Kilkenny, Waterford and Wexford for his castle at Mountgarrett suggests that the erection of tower houses in the county was initially hampered by a lack of skilled local craftsmen. Although the Wexford towers belonged to the simple eastern type,[36] it required expertise to arrange the various domestic and defensive requirements within such a confined vertical space. As work on tower houses gained momentum, with a concurrent enhancement of expertise, a growing number of tower house 'contractors', influenced by the wishes of clients, designed similar towers but with variations in individual features, resulting in some regional differences.

The existence of tower house specialists is shown by the survival of an agreement from 1582 between the Lord Deputy and a craftsman named Paul Finglas for the raising of a three-storey guard tower on a proposed bridge at Enniscorthy (never subsequently built). The specifications

Enniscorthy Bridge Castle 1582

The said Paul [Finglas] doth covenante and promise to and with the said Lord Deputie and Counsell, to build in the middle of the said river and bridge a square castell or Tower of lyme and stone, built upon a new foundation, with two gates to goe through the said Castell of tenne foot in breadth and ten foot in height; the said Castell to have two storeys in it above the vault of the gate, and to contain in breadth on the outside 28 foot the one way, and 22 foot the other way, with battlements, a strong roof, and flower windows [cusped ogee], and murdering holes as many as shall be needful; and at each of the two gates aforesaid to place a drawbridge with crossbarres of iron, great spikes, and chains of iron to draw the said two bridges close to the Castell, and which the said Paul Finglas doth covenante and promise to finish between this and Lady Day next in March come twelve months, which will be the 25th of March, 1583.

Sisley Skerett, payments for work done 1585

Paid to two churls that were felling the scraws of the kitchen   6d

Paid for two men that were felling timber of the kitchen   6d

Paid for the capell [horse] and for the man that was drawing lime   7d

Paid for two capells and for the man that was drawing scraws   14d

Paid for the capell and for the man that was drawing scraws   7d

Paid for timber to Rory O'Flarty [O'Flaherty]   2s. 4d.

Paid for one man that was three days setting scraws on the house   1s.

Paid for one man that was one day setting scraws on the other side of the house and the man that did serve him   14d

resembled those of a typical tower house and the work was to be completed within a year.[37] The wages of skilled builders must have represented a substantial part of the overall cost of a tower house. To combat this, the rapid growth of the tax known as coign in the second half of the fifteenth century led to the billeting of artisans and the provision of carriage duties on tenants.[38] Manorial lords in county Wexford, who wished to finance a tower house, presumably resorted to a similar strategy.

Building stone was a basic requirement and, where possible, this was hewn from the local bedrock. Examples can be seen at Ferrycarrig, Scar and Ballyhack, where the tower houses were built mostly of old red sandstone, sourced in adjacent quarries. In the elegant tower house at Sigginstown, pink granite from nearby Carnsore was mostly used; Ballyteige is built of local shale, while Slade Castle consists of limestone quarried from the cliffs on which it is situated. Many towers contain a mixture of material from different sources, indicating that no suitable quarry was available locally. When required, cut-stone was sourced elsewhere, particularly sandstone and granite.

For reasons of status and security, the south Wexford tower houses were erected by the descendants of settlers who had been granted lands in the early thirteenth century. Although the estates were modest in size, the enduring nature of the colony resulted in the growth of a highly developed system of mixed agriculture, dominated by grain production. The coastal location was of fundamental significance as it facilitated an export trade as well as providing seaweed and sand to improve the soil, which was of mixed quality. The rich fishing grounds off the south coast, frequented by continental boats, provided a secondary income for owners of estates bordering the foreshore, who could exact a 'tax' from foreign vessels. In the fifteenth and sixteenth centuries, revenue from farming, tenants' rents, and in some instances the fishing industry, enabled the proliferation of tower houses in the south of the county.

TOWER-HOUSE LANDSCAPES

The spread of the tower house as an architectural concept, principally during the fifteenth and sixteenth centuries, was intimately related to the confrontation between native Irish and English colonists. Occurring predominantly on lands originally settled by the Anglo-Normans, the distribution of tower houses reflects the extent of the colony, being most prevalent in counties Limerick, Kilkenny and Tipperary, parts of Clare, Galway and Westmeath and in the southern parts of Dublin and Wexford. Although present in all counties, tower houses are densest in areas of Anglo-Norman settlement, including south Dublin, south Wexford, Louth, Kilkenny, Tipperary, west Limerick and Westmeath. In Clare and Galway, many were constructed by Irish overlords.[1]

The description 'tower house' includes a wide range of structures encompassing regional, social, chrono-logical and functional differences, with some crossing of typological boundaries. All shared the common element of a stone tower. Many small towers associated with the Dublin Pale have pronounced angle-turrets housing stairways and garderobes. The large, more elaborate examples in the west, descended from thirteenth-century hall-houses, have halls over a third-floor vault, with smoke from a central fireplace escaping through a vent in the roof, a feature also found elsewhere but not in Wexford.[2] Some towers in Kilkenny, Tipperary and Clare are round, while others in Cork and Tipperary have rounded corners. Towers in all of these counties can have multiple vaults. In all regions, tower houses of the late sixteenth and early seventeenth centuries have thinner walls, no vault, gun-loops and gables flush with the external walls.

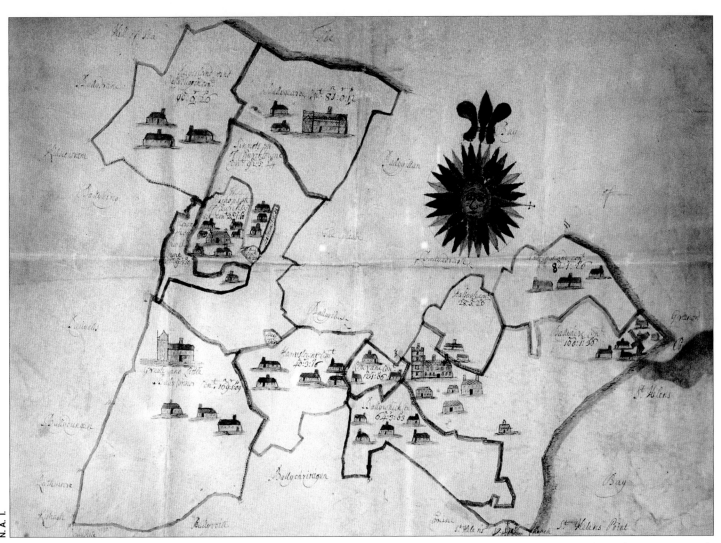

Fig. 1   A 1727 map of the Edwards' estate in the barony of Forth. This records a landscape of tower houses with attached halls, the medieval parish church of Kilrane in the manorial village of Churchtown, a windmill, manorial villages with cabins, and one two-storey house with two chimneys.

Tower Houses

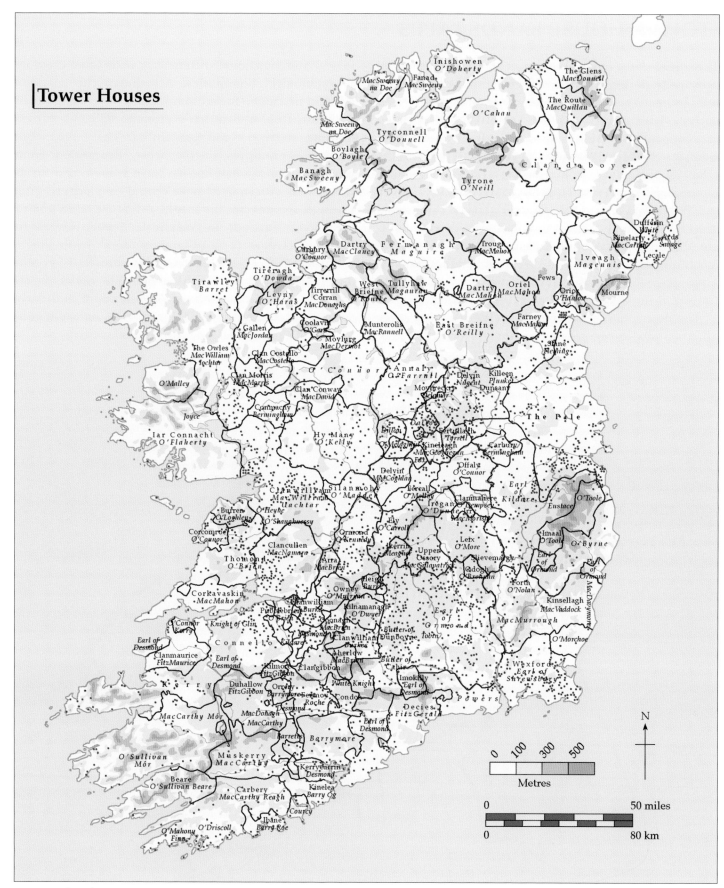

Fig. 2   Although present to some degree in all counties, tower houses are densest in areas of early Anglo-Norman settlement, including south Dublin, south Wexford, Louth, Kilkenny, Tipperary, west Limerick and Westmeath. In the west, tower houses were also constructed by Irish overlords

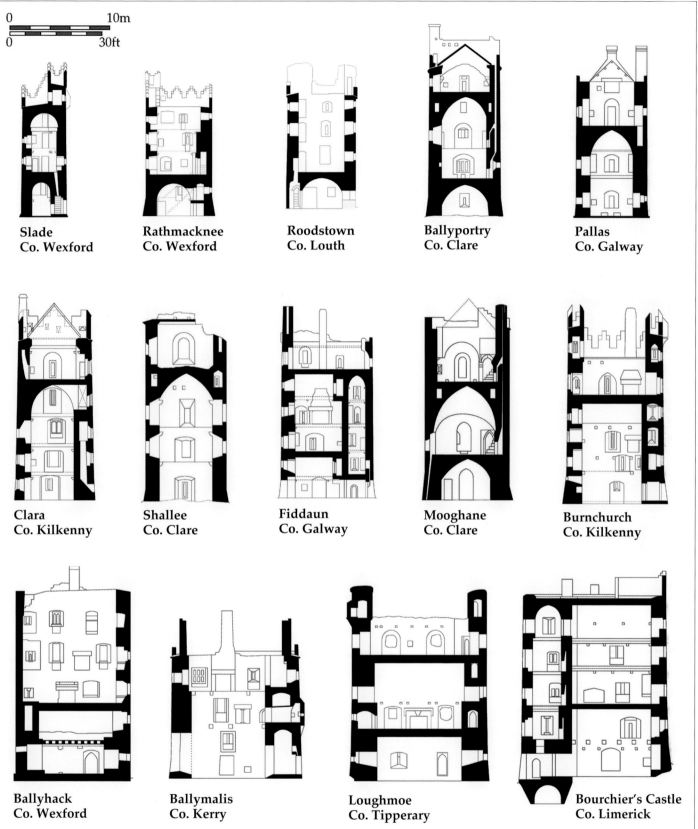

0   10m

0   30ft

Slade
Co. Wexford

Rathmacknee
Co. Wexford

Roodstown
Co. Louth

Ballyportry
Co. Clare

Pallas
Co. Galway

Clara
Co. Kilkenny

Shallee
Co. Clare

Fiddaun
Co. Galway

Mooghane
Co. Clare

Burnchurch
Co. Kilkenny

Ballyhack
Co. Wexford

Ballymalis
Co. Kerry

Loughmoe
Co. Tipperary

Bourchier's Castle
Co. Limerick

DONAL COLFER

Fig. 3 This random selection of tower-house sections from eight counties (Clare, Galway, Kerry, Kilkenny, Limerick, Louth, Tipperary, Wexford) illustrates the variations that existed within the architectural form. On average, the Wexford towers are smaller than those in other counties. The Wexford examples invariably had modest halls over a ground floor vault. Similar towers are found elsewhere in the eastern half of the country and in Munster, but they can be regarded as a Wexford type because of a universal adherence to this architectural form in the county.

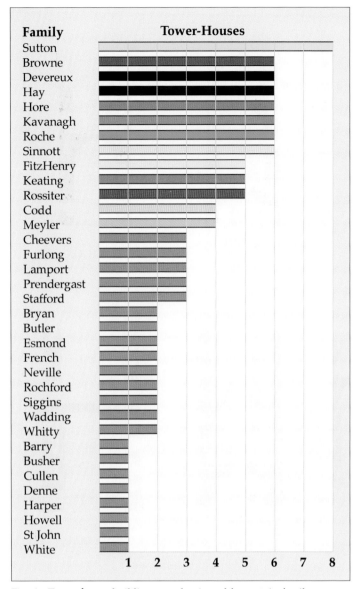

Fig. 4 Tower-house building was dominated by certain family groups. Thirty-five families built over one hundred tower houses. Sixty-seven tower houses were built by twelve of these families.

COUNTY WEXFORD TOWER HOUSES

The small Wexford towers, mostly four storeys in height but with some of three storeys, invariably had modest halls over a ground-floor vault, and, because of architectural longevity, could be of fifteenth- or sixteenth-century origin.[3] The surviving examples are almost all of a plain, rectangular or almost square plan but with design variations occurring within a common template. Exceptions occur at Ballyteige, Rathmacknee, Rosegarland and Kilcloggan, where there are slightly projecting garderobe turrets; Kilcloggan also has a minor stairway projection. Similar plain rectangular towers are found elsewhere in the eastern half of the country and in Munster but they can be regarded as a Wexford type because of a universal adherence to this architectural form

in the county. The ubiquitous preference for a single design can be attributed to the conservative ethos of the isolated Wexford Pale. This attitude was manifested in other deep-rooted characteristics of the region, including the Yola dialect, the surname profile, the use of windmills, the art of mumming and the placing of funeral crosses in sceach (whitethorn) bushes.

The high density of tower houses in south Wexford was a response to the achievement of the Irish in reclaiming the north of the county, resulting in the contraction of the English colony to the southern Wexford Pale. The siting of some tower houses was directly related to the landscape; the topographical features which defined and protected the Wexford Pale were strengthened by subsidised towers. The small number of tower houses built by the Kavanaghs in the county are mostly concentrated in the Fassagh of Bantry near the Pollmounty Gap, which gave access to Wexford from county Carlow between the Blackstairs and the Barrow. The impressive

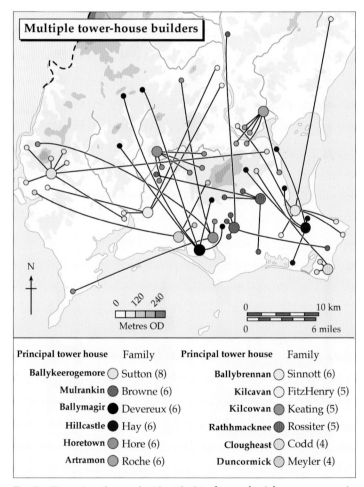

Fig. 5 'Parent' castles can be identified in the south of the county, mostly in Forth and Bargy, from which families expanded to build tower houses elsewhere in the county. The Suttons (eight) were the most prolific builders, followed by the Brownes, Devereuxes, Hays, Hores, Roches and Sinnotts (six each). A similar number is attributed to the MacMurrough Kavanaghs, principally in the Fassagh of Bantry.

Fig. 6 At Tellarought, the tower house survives beside the medieval graveyard, now occupied by the modern Catholic church. In the 1830s, Tellarought was described as 'formerly a village', which had altogether vanished. The buildings consisted mostly of clay and thatch and would have disappeared quickly, following abandonment.

visual impact of 'high rise' tower house architecture on the flat landscape of south Wexford must have augmented their effectiveness as deterrents. They also expressed the status, power and cultural identity of their occupants.

Fieldwork and documentary sources have identified 137 tower houses in county Wexford (Appendix 1).[4] Some tentative sites have been excluded due to insufficient physical or documentary evidence.[5] In sixty instances, tower house fabric still exists, in various states of preservation. In twenty-three cases, this is categorised as 'extensive', in twenty as 'significant' and in seventeen as 'fragmentary'.[6] Of the identified tower houses, seventy-eight no longer survive but are referred to in historical sources; fifty-two can confidently be described as 'definite', while there is sufficient evidence to categorise the other twenty-six as 'possible'. Statistical and distribution evidence, as well as historical sources, allow the inclusion of the 'removed' and 'possible' sites in the tower house category. Sixteen fortified houses, best described as hall-houses, have also been identified, most located near the south coast. These structures epitomise a late sixteenth-century architectural advance towards a more sophisticated living space.

The distribution of surviving tower house fabric and tower house sites are similar, both concentrated in the south of the county, suggesting that their destruction was also spread evenly across the region. This attrition is a continuing process, as evidenced by the collapse of Lingstown tower house in 1985 and the partial fall of Mountgarrett castle in 2011. There is a predominance of both partial remains and sites only in the more exposed northern part of the tower house region, reflecting the

reality of social unrest and abandonment. The dense concentration of tower houses in the southern baronies, and in particular in the Wexford Pale, contributes to the landscape character of the region, denoting the architectural response to the discord between native Irish and English colonist in the late medieval period.

The tower house builders were relatively few in number, forming a cohesive social group bound together by marriage alliances. Although not known in all instances, thirty-five settler families can be associated with the construction of 115 tower houses (out of a total of 137) over a span of two centuries, dominated by the Suttons who built eight, and the Browne, Devereux, Hay, Hore, Roche and Sinnott families, who built six each. At the other end of the scale, eight families built one each. The Kavanaghs were responsible for a possible six tower houses in the county, four of them located in the Fassagh of Bantry, close to the gap of Pollmounty between the Barrow and the Blackstairs.

Over time, members of principal colonial families built tower houses in other parts of the region. As many as thirteen of these were in the northern part of the Pale on the demesne manor of Taghmon (barony of Shelmalier) and in the parish of Kilmannan, situated on marginal land on the southern slopes of Forth Mountain. This area had not been divided initially into sub-manors but was later acquired by descendants of original Anglo-Norman settlers, principally the Rossiters and Hores. These isolated tower houses were not associated with manorial villages and some at least may have been built to strengthen security along the Pale boundary because of the subsidy available in the fifteenth century.

Where dimensions are known, these castles are small; Newcastle and Slevoy, for example, at 35m², are only slightly bigger than the ten pound castles of the Dublin

Adamstown 1669

At Adamstown there is an old Irish castle to which there was a large house or barn-like house adjoining, but down many years since, and of late rebuilt by William Meddowe, the present tenant. It is walled around with a stone wall at least fourteen foot high, the entrance by one gate with a small house over it. The yard or court within about a quarter of an acre; without [outside] is a ruined garden on the east side and on the south and west side is a fair green about two acres round, on which stands the tenants' cabins straggling. There is not any wood in all of the premises, except that of Oldcourt, little bogs, small springs, no river, much furze and generally barren. Not twenty acres of meadow can be made upon it all.

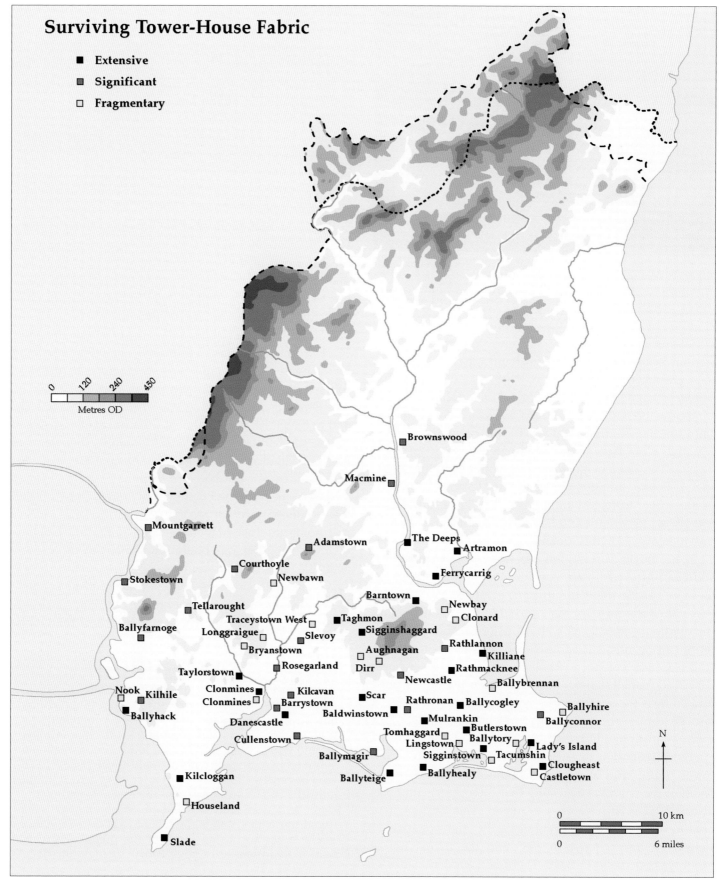

Surviving Tower-House Fabric

- ■ Extensive
- ▨ Significant
- □ Fragmentary

0 120 240 450
Metres OD

Brownswood

Macmine

Mountgarrett

Adamstown   The Deeps
                                Artramon
Courthoyle
Stokestown   Newbawn   Ferrycarrig

Tellarought   Barntown
                                        Newbay
Traceystown West   Taghmon   Clonard
Ballyfarnoge   Longgraigue   Slevoy Sigginshaggard
              Bryanstown   Aughnagan   Rathlannon
                                          Killiane
              Rosegarland   Dirr   Rathmacknee
Taylorstown   Newcastle
Nook Kilhile Clonmines Kilcavan   Ballybrennan
              Clonmines Barrystown Scar Rathronan Ballycogley Ballyhire
Ballyhack   Baldwinstown   Ballyconnor
           Danescastle   Mulrankin
           Cullenstown   Tomhaggard   Butlerstown
                                Lingstown Ballytory
                        Ballymagir   Sigginstown Tacumshin Lady's Island
Kilcloggan   Ballyhealy Ballyteige   Clougheast
                                                          Castletown
Houseland

Slade

N

0   10 km
0   6 miles

Fig. 7   The remains of sixty tower houses have been identified in the county. Of these, twenty-three are classed as 'extensive', twenty as 'significant' and seventeen as 'fragmentary'. The distribution of the different categories is spread across the tower house region.

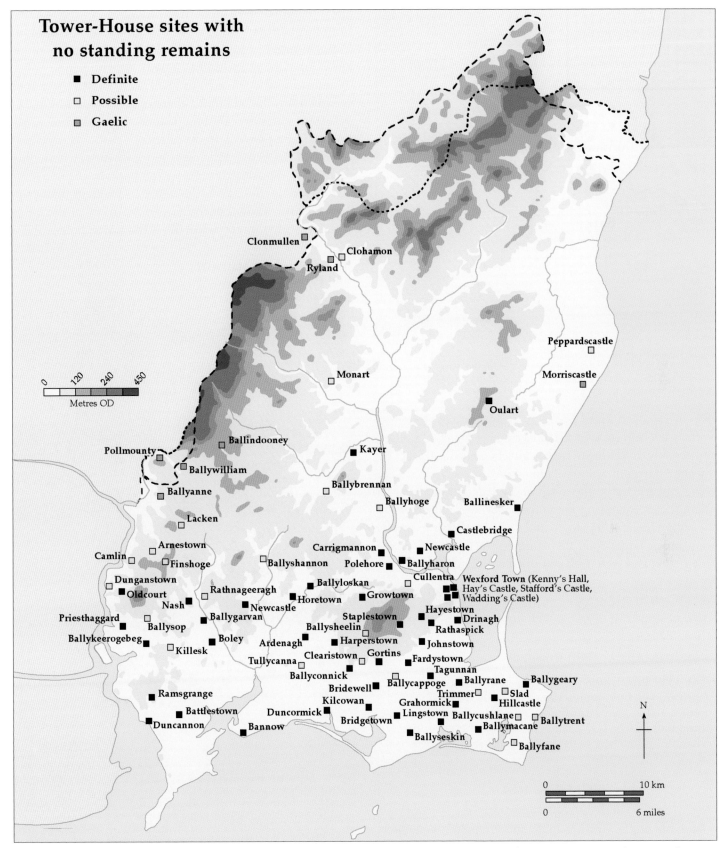

Tower-House sites with no standing remains

- ■ Definite
- □ Possible
- ▨ Gaelic

Clonmullen
Clohamon
Ryland
Peppardscastle
Morriscastle
Monart
Oulart
Ballindooney
Kayer
Pollmounty
Ballywilliam
Ballybrennan
Ballyanne
Ballyhoge
Ballinesker
Lacken
Castlebridge
Arnestown
Carrigmannon
Newcastle
Camlin
Finshoge
Ballyshannon
Polehore
Ballyharon
Dunganstown
Ballyloskan
Cullentra
Wexford Town (Kenny's Hall, Hay's Castle, Stafford's Castle, Wadding's Castle)
Oldcourt
Rathnageeragh
Horetown
Growtown
Hayestown
Nash
Newcastle
Staplestown
Drinagh
Priesthaggard
Ballygarvan
Ballysheelin
Rathaspick
Ballysop
Harperstown
Johnstown
Ballykeerogebeg
Boley
Ardenagh
Clearistown
Gortins
Fardystown
Killesk
Tullycanna
Tagunnan
Ballyconnick
Ballycappoge
Ballyrane
Ballygeary
Bridewell
Trimmer
Slad
Ramsgrange
Kilcowan
Grahormick
Hillcastle
Battlestown
Duncormick
Lingstown
Ballycushlane
Ballytrent
Duncannon
Bannow
Bridgetown
Ballymacane
Ballyseskin
Ballyfane

Metres OD
0 120 240 450

N

0 10 km
0 6 miles

Fig. 8 Of the identified tower houses, seventy-seven no longer remain standing but are referred to in historical sources. Of these, fifty-three can confidently be described as 'definite' while there is sufficient evidence to include the other twenty-four as 'possible'. Location and probability, as well as historical sources, allow the inclusion of the 'removed' and 'possible' sites in the tower house category. This is supported by the map of tower house sites. Apart from a few scattered northern examples, this is almost identical to that of existing tower house remains. Gaelic tower houses are focused on the Pollmounty Gap, with lone examples at Ryland and Morriscastle (Murrough's Castle).

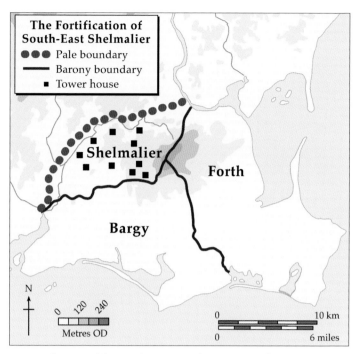

Fig. 9 The part of the Wexford Pale in the barony of Shelmalier was not initially divided into manors, as it formed part of the demesne manor of Taghmon. This vulnerable area was later occupied by existing manor-holders in Forth and Bargy, who fortified it with tower houses.

Pale. A removed tower house at Ardenagh was described in the *Civil Survey* as 'a small castle and thatched house', presumably referring to a hall attached to the tower. By the later sixteenth century, 'aggressive' tower houses were being constructed to the north of the Pale boundary in an attempt at recolonising lands that had been reclaimed by the native Irish. Adamstown and Courthoyle, for example, were much larger than the examples in the north of the Pale region and were well equipped with gun-loops.

NUCLEATED SETTLEMENT
Existing tower houses, sometimes standing alone but

Old Ross 1306

[At Old Ross there is] an old hall without a roof surrounded by stone walls, a stone house without a roof outside the gate almost razed to the ground, a little hall in which is a chapel and a kitchen in ruins, a sheepfold thatched with straw, all of no value because no one will rent them.

Old Ross 1684

About three miles eastward [from New Ross] stands a large old castle, which is quite out of repair, called Old Ross, where there is also an old ruined church, and about fifty cabins or thatched houses and has belonging to it about 1200 acres of land.

often included in a modern farm complex, are isolated from their former context. They originally formed part of a much larger complex of ancillary buildings of stone, wood and clay, including a hall, bawn, barns, mills, dovecotes and a church, as well as a cluster of cabins occupied by the manorial tenants. The morphology of deserted villages can be gleaned from documentary sources. The Down Survey refers to 'castle, church and cabins' at Ballyfane, Hillcastle and Ballyrane, where only the tower house sites are now known. A house is mentioned in five instances, either slated or thatched, presumably attached to the tower. A survey of the lands of Adamstown in 1669 described the tower house and a

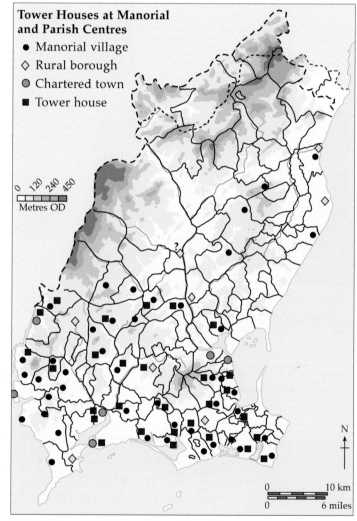

Fig. 10 Manorial villages and rural boroughs were established around a nucleus of church, castle and mill. The village settlements were mostly situated on the small manors in the south of the county where tenants could return to their dwellings at the manorial centre after a day's work. On large manors, moated sites on the periphery were the norm. Most modern villages that originated as manorial centres or granges are close to the south coast and on the Cistercian estates. Two inland examples exist at Adamstown and Newbawn, with Kilmuckridge a solitary east-coast survival. There was a close relationship between manorial villages, parish churches and tower houses, with townland, village, parish and tower house frequently sharing the same name.

Fig. 11   Of six surviving manorial villages on the south coast, Duncormick retains the best evidence of medieval origin. Diagnostic features include **A** The medieval church site. **B** The mound of the early motte castle. **C** The mill site **D**. The tower house site.

large hall attached, with a bawn surrounded by a stone wall. The fair green outside the wall was surrounded by the 'tenants cabins straggling'.[7]

The early eighteenth-century Edwards of Ballyhire estate map depicts what is essentially a late medieval barony of Forth landscape. Three tower houses are shown at Ballyhire, Ballygeary (both since removed) and Ballyconnor, with attached halls and surrounding cabins.[8] In the 1830s, Tellarought, where the tower house still stands, was described as 'formerly a considerable village, which, with the church, has altogether disappeared, and the site has been turned up by the plough, which is frequently obstructed by the foundations of old buildings'.[9] The descriptions of Adamstown and Tellarought depict a nucleated settlement associated with the church and tower house. In each case, rather exceptionally, the modern Catholic church occupies the site of the medieval parish church.

The repeated description of a 'straggle' of tenants' cabins around a tower house and church suggest that a medieval system of manorial agriculture was still being practised, with tenants travelling out from a nucleated centre to cultivate fragmented holdings. Living close to the tower house and bawn ensured security in times of danger. In the 1570s, Richard Stanihurst observed that the villagers retreated to the castle at night, after spending their days in adjacent thatched cabins.[10] The ephemeral

Fig. 12   A stylised reconstruction of the manorial village of Duncormick in south Wexford, as it might have looked in the sixteenth century.

CON BROGAN, NMSPU

Fig. 13   The tower house and bawn at Rathmacknee, with the adjacent sites of a medieval church (now occupied by a later church) and a mill, provide an excellent example of a deserted manorial village. As with many other parish centres, Rathmacknee retained its pre-colonial Irish name.

Fig. 14   Most placenames recorded on sixteenth-century maps of County Wexford refer to townlands in which tower houses were situated. This reflects the high visibility of tower houses in the landscape and their vital role as components of nucleated settlement. The tower house related placenames on this re-drawn version of Boazio's map are taken from Lythe (1569), Mercator (1595) and Boazio (1599), converted to Ordnance Survey spelling.

nature of these villages was noted in 1620: 'In every village, is a castle and a church, but both in ruin. The baser cottages are built of underwood, called wattle, and covered some with thatch and some with green sedge, of a round form and without chimneys, and resembling so many hives of bees about a country farm'.[11]

Tower houses were inserted into a well-defined settlement infrastructure established over several centuries of colonial activity. In south Wexford, they typically replaced earlier dwellings at existing villages, which were the social, economic and administrative hubs

of the manors. Although most of these villages did not endure as settlements in the landscape, it is possible to identify their locations by the presence of typical diagnostic features.[12] Documentary sources, augmented by fieldwork, suggest the locations of forty medieval village sites in county Wexford where a church and either an earthwork or stone castle, and at times a mill, are found in close proximity, identifying them as manorial/parish centres. These nucleated settlements contained the parish church and gave the parish its name. In twenty-nine instances, tower houses were situated at these centres, sharing the name of the settlement and the parish. Twenty-two retained the pre-colonial Irish name, indicating continuity of settlement, particularly true in the case of early medieval church foundations which were adopted as parochial centres.

All forty of these settlements contained a castle of some kind, consisting of seven earthwork castles, twenty-nine tower houses (thirteen sites only) and four fortified hall-houses. Not all settlements fit into the manor/parish pattern. The villages of Ballyhack, Ramsgrange,

Battlestown, Rathumney and Nash originated as monastic granges; strictly speaking, they were not manorial centres. Villages at Ballymore, Ballyorley, Bridgetown, Courthoyle and Oldcourt were not situated at parochial centres. The manorial village of Ballykeerogemore, situated in the parish of Ballybrazil, was unusual as its name was not given to the manor or the parish.

In cases where the tower house was built at a distance from the church, the original earthwork defences may have been abandoned in favour of a 'modern' residence. Examples of this include Templetown (1km), Adamstown (.8km), Ballyhealy (.5km) and Ballybrennan (.5km). The association of both a motte and a moated site with some church sites shows a progression of settlement from the initial motte to the later, perhaps more accessible, moated site. This is evident at Ballymore, Ballymoty More and Killegney, all in the frontier area of the county. A progression from moated site to tower house may have occurred at Ballyanne, Ballyconnick (both Boscher [Busher] manors), Newbawn, Kilcowan and Slevoy. The

Fig. 15 An aerial view from Carnsore, looking west across Forth and Bargy, with Lady's Island lake in the middle distance and Tacumshin Lake in the far distance. Wexford Harbour is at top right, with Forth Mountain on the horizon. This lowland region constituted the Wexford Pale. By the end of the sixteenth century, it could be described as a tower-house landscape, with the low-lying nature of the topography emphasising the verticality of the towers. The barony of Forth, in the foreground, had the greatest density of tower houses. Traditional windmills have been replaced by the wind turbines at Carnsore, now the most prominent vertical element in the landscape. Tower houses were located at: (*site only*) **A** *Ballybrennan* **B** Ballycogley **C** Ballyconnor **D** *Ballyfane* **E** *Ballygeary* **F** *Ballymacane* **H** Ballytory **I** Butlerstown **J** Castletown **K** Clougheast **L** *Hillcastle* **M** Lady's Island **N** *Lingstown* **O** Sigginstown **P** Tacumshin **Q** *Tagunnan*.

deserted site of Kilcowan in Bargy, on the Keating manor of the same name, where the parish church (of Early Medieval origin), a motte, moated site and tower house, all in close proximity, suggests a succession of manor houses spanning several centuries.

The distribution of manorial village sites shows a definite bias toward the southern cantreds of Forth and Bargy and on the manor of the Island in the cantred of Shelburne. They are noticeably absent from the seignorial manors of Old Ross and Taghmon, presumably because the population on these manors was focused on the rural boroughs of Old Ross and Taghmon, accompanied by dispersed settlement in moated sites. In fact, apart from the north of the county where both settlement forms are scarce, the locational patterns of manorial villages and moated sites are complementary. Dispersed settlement in moated sites was the norm in the centrally placed manors, particularly Duffry, Schyrmal, Fernegenel and Kayer, with nucleated manorial villages dominating in the south. The tendency towards larger manors in the centre and

north of the county required dispersed settlement, as a central nucleus would have been too far from the periphery of the manor.

Conversely, in the south, small manors encouraged the proliferation of villages and subsequently tower houses. Of the twelve manorial settlements functioning as villages in the present-day landscape, nine are in the south, on or near the coast, indicating continuity of settlement in this more secure part of the county. Adamstown and Newbawn are in an inland location, with Kilmuckridge a lone example on the east coast. The network of manorial villages in Wexford supported the continued existence of the colony. Tenants living in a village, with access to the tower house, were more secure than those isolated in moated sites. A late sixteenth-century description of Ireland records that the villagers lived in thatched, mud-walled houses, except in times of alarm, when they drove their cattle into the bawn and spent the night in the castle.[13]

Another fourteen nucleated settlements were granted borough privileges but eight of these never grew beyond

the status of village.[14] These rural boroughs served as centres for manorial markets and administration. Only one of them, Taghmon, still a thriving village, is the site of a tower house, while Old Ross had a thirteenth-century stone castle. Remnants of settlement endured for centuries at now deserted rural borough sites. At Old Ross, for example, late thirteenth-century accounts refer to the castle with a wooden palisade, a hall and moat, a dairy, sheepfold, falconry and three mills.[15] The castle continued in use until the sixteenth century but it was described as 'a large old castle quite out of repair' by 1684. The same account mentions 'an old ruined church and about fifty cabins or thatched houses'.[16] At the present time, a motte, a thirteenth-century castle site, a medieval church site, a water-mill (in working order until recently) and a scattering of houses signal Old Ross's former borough status.

SETTLEMENT ON THE MONASTIC ESTATES

The granting of large estates to the Cistercians at Dunbrody and Tintern, and to the Knights Templars (and subsequently the Knights Hospitallers) at Kilcloggan, exerted a dramatic influence on south-west Wexford.[17] Episcopal manors at Fethard and Kinnagh meant that almost all of the region was held by the church. Detailed surveys of the Templars' lands (after their fall in 1307)[18] and of all monastic possessions in 1541, following the dissolution of the monasteries,[19] provide extensive information on settlement on these church estates.

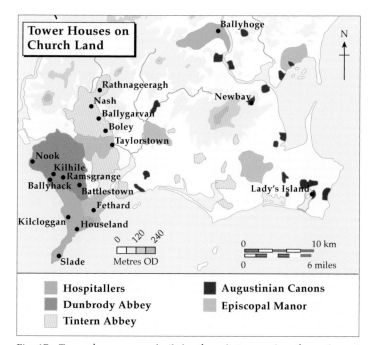

Fig. 17 Tower houses were built by the religious orders themselves at Ballyhoge, Kilcloggan and Ballyhack, or elsewhere by their tenants. There is a predominance of church land and tower houses in the south-west.

The two orders implemented different landholding regimes. The Cistercian rule did not permit lay tenants on monastic lands. Instead the outfarms, known as granges, were worked by numerous lay brothers, in line with the Cistercian philosophy of *laborare est orare* (to work is to pray). However, because of the difficulties experienced in recruitment, this rule was relaxed and by the thirteenth century the practice of renting the monastic granges to lay

Fig. 16 The thirteenth-century hall (**A**) and a church site (**B**) indicate the origin of the village of Rathumney as a grange on the Tintern Abbey estate.

R.S.A.I.

Fig. 18   Buttermilk Castle, built by the Cistercian monks of Dunbrody, was part of the grange of Nook. The tower house, with what appears to be an annex, functioned as a headquarters for the fishing industry on the estuary, particularly for salmon. A weir positioned at the headland during the monastic period is still in existence. The point was formerly known as Skeroirke (presumably from the Norse 'sker/skar' meaning 'rock').

tenants was permitted, effectively converting the granges to manorial villages.[20] This prompted the introduction of numerous lay tenants on Cistercian lands during the fourteenth century, after which there was little to distinguish the abbot from a secular landlord. The granting of lands to lay tenants was accompanied by the imposition of feudal rights and privileges, although these were officially banned by the statutes of the order.[21]

The sites of some monastic granges at Dunbrody and Tintern can be identified. On the lands of Dunbrody, out-farms were situated in the townlands of Grange, Ramsgrange, Kilhile, Battlestown and Haggard. Settlements at Ballyhack and Nook were commercial granges, sited on Waterford Harbour to take advantage of the economic opportunities offered by the estuary. The Tintern estate was divided by the episcopal manor of Kinnagh. Rathumney, which contains the remains of an early thirteenth-century hall-house and a church site, presumably functioned as the headquarters of the detached portion of the estate.[22] The principal granges on the Tintern Abbey estate were Rathumney, Dunmain, Nash, Rathnageeragh, Ballygarvan, Boley and Yoletown, all on the detached northern portion of the lands.

The Templars, true to their feudal origins, organised their estate according to conventional manorial practice.

R.S.A.I.

Fig. 19   Boley tower house, with an entrance to the bawn, was drawn by Du Noyer *c.* 1850. Built on the lands of Tintern Abbey, it was part of a defensive line along the Owenduff river. In apparently good condition in the mid-nineteenth century, not a trace remains at the present time.

Fig. 20 Ballyhack Castle, built by the monks of Dunbrody to exploit the economic potential of the estuary, was well placed to control fishing activities and the ferry crossing to Passage. The original, higher approach road can be seen at the top centre of the picture.

The core of the manor (the townland of Templetown) was retained as demesne land, some of it held by tenants-at-will, with the rest of the estate granted to free tenants holding in perpetuity. An inventory of the Templars' possessions in 1307 provides an insight into the demesne lands of the manor of Kilcloggan early in the fourteenth century.[23] It paints a picture of a highly organised, self-sufficient community, involved principally in agricultural production rather than military activities.

The 1541 post-dissolution surveys contain considerable detail on the three monastic estates, notably on the land held by various tenants, where it was located, and the rents and services.[24] The manor of Kilcloggan, where the surname evidence reveals that a mere 12% of the tenants were native Irish, was the only church estate where land was held by free tenants. The grange of Kilcloggan may have been in the adjacent townland of Haggard (hay garth; a hay yard) where a moated site (since removed) was recorded on the first edition of the Ordnance Survey. Old field patterns and possible house plots revealed by aerial photography adjacent to Templetown church, together with stray finds of medieval pottery shards, identify the presence of an associated village. A farmhouse cluster at Broomhill, the townland beside Kilcloggan, where the land was held in dispersed fragmented plots until recent times, could denote the Irish quarter on the manor, as many of these clusters are considered to be medieval in origin.[25]

TOWER HOUSES ON MONASTIC ESTATES

The rich agricultural granges on the Cistercian estates were vulnerable to raiding from the Fassagh of Bantry by the Kavanaghs and the Butlers. Some protection was afforded by up to nine tower houses on the small lay manors to the immediate north. This may explain why the three tower houses at Kilhile, Battlestown and Ramsgrange were located on the southern part of the Dunbrody estate. These were presumably built by lay tenants; John Battaile was a tenant on the Dunbrody estate in 1390.[26] The castles at Nook, Ballyhack and Duncannon related to economic activities on the estuary.[27]

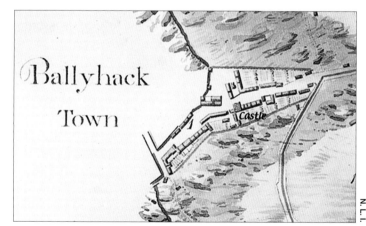

Fig. 21 The 1803 Dunbrody estate map shows the village of Ballyhack with a row of houses, which no longer exist, along the water's edge. The modern approach road along the cliff-edge had not yet been made.

Fig. 22   Templetown is a good example of a deserted medieval village based on the medieval church (**A**) and the possible site of the early Templar castle, known locally as 'the hill o' the moat' (**B**). The fields around the church contain cultivation ridges and possible house plots. The field above the church was recently cultivated and yielded numerous medieval pottery shards. A tower house is situated at Kilcloggan, two kilometres to the north.

All of the tower houses on the Tintern estate were on the detached northern portion. These lands were bordered on the east by the Owenduff river, flowing from Old Ross to Bannow Bay. In a strategy similar to that adopted along 'the water of Taghmon', which defined the Wexford Pale, four tower houses were located on Tintern granges following the line of the Owenduff river. These were located at Rathnageeragh, Nash, Ballygarvan and Boley, presumably occupied by lay tenants who were farming the granges.[28]

None of these remain, but masonry rubble in a large circular earthwork at Rathnageeragh (possibly a re-used ringfort), with a wide stream-fed fosse, could represent the remains of the later tower house. A mid-ninteenth-century drawing was made of Boley Castle before its subsequent removal. A tower house, with attached house and bawn, was built at Taylorstown in the late sixteenth century on land held by a lay tenant in the episcopal manor and parish of Kinnagh. This tower was well equipped with gun-loops, and it was strategically placed near the head of Bannow Bay, overlooking a crossing point on the Owenduff. Following an incident at the crossing during the Rebellion of 1798, the river was bridged as part of the military New Line road, connecting Wexford town to Duncannon Fort.

Ballyhack Castle is the only extant tower house on the Cistercian estates, possibly because it was occupied until the middle of the seventeenth century. Apart from one wall at Kilhile, none of the towers erected by lay tenants are still standing, perhaps suggesting a fifteenth-century

R.S.A.I.

Fig. 23   The small tower house at the manorial centre of Kilcloggan, presumably built in the fifteenth century, a short distance north of Templetown, was drawn by Du Noyer *c.* 1850. The early house, originally in the castle bawn, has been renovated as a modern dwelling.

Fig. 24 Several farmhouse clusters survive near manorial centres in south-west Wexford, particulary on the Hospitaller manor of Kilcloggan. The holdings associated with these farm villages consisted of dispersed parcels of land. In south-east Ireland, this form of archaic landholding evolved from the open-field agriculture practiced on medieval manors. The farm village of Broomhill, adjacent to the tower house at Kilcloggan, is a good example, suggesting that, in some instances, this form of communal farming existed in the locality of tower houses, perhaps confined to a particular class of tenant.

construction date. This timescale is hinted at by John Battaile's late fourteenth-century presence at Battlestown.

Three tower houses were located on the Hospitaller manor of Kilcloggan. The small tower at Kilcloggan, complete with battlements and two lookout platforms, was constructed by the Hospitallers themselves. Elements of a contemporary bawn wall and gateway are evident at the north angle. A first-floor doorway opened to the bawn wall-walk. The small size and absence of a loft under the vault could imply an early date. The tower at Kilcloggan is the only one in the county with two projecting turrets, one containing the garderobes, the other the stairway. This atypical design might hint at Hospitaller expertise imported from outside the county. At dissolution, Kilcloggan was valued at £19 7s 11d, with a 'castle or fortilage in good repair, very necessary for the defence of the country in time of war of the Kavanaghs and other Irish, near whose countries the castle lies'.[29] The *Civil Survey* also records a castle (presumably a tower house) on the Hospitaller manor of Ballyhoge (formerly confused with Ballyhack).

The castle attributed to the Keatings at Houseland no longer exists but it was recorded in a mid-nineteenth-century drawing. The complex of tower and fortified house at Slade, associated with the Laffans, was presumably built with support from the Hospitallers. The Redmond family, the principal tenants on the Templar manor, occupied a thirteenth-century hall on the Hook peninsula and by 1281 the family was referred to as *de Aula* (of the Hall).[30] The structure may have resembled Rathumney Hall on the lands of Tintern Abbey. Redmond

Hall has been replaced by Loftus Hall, built by the Loftus family who acquired the estate after the Cromwellian confiscations.[31] The episcopal manor of Fethard was also fortified, in the late fourteenth/early fifteenth century, by the construction of a high-status, L-shaped, fortified house with a round tower at the angle serving as a belfry and gaol. The structure incorporated the gatehouse and other elements of an earlier castle. The bishop erected a castle on his lands at Mountgarrett during the same period.

Two tower houses in the county are connected with the Augustinian Canons. A castle on the lands of SelskarAbbey, at Newbay, south-west of Wexford town, was referred to as a 'fortaligium' in 1540. The Down Survey described it as a

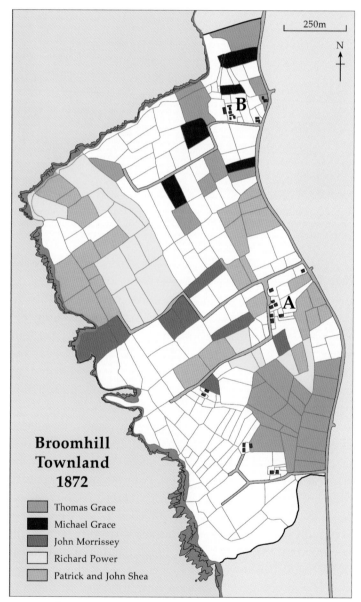

Broomhill Townland 1872

- Thomas Grace
- Michael Grace
- John Morrissey
- Richard Power
- Patrick and John Shea

Fig. 25 The farming pattern in the townland of Broomhill was recorded on the Loftus estate maps of 1872. This map illustrates the dispersed nature of the landholding, based on a sample of five tenants. In 1841, the townland had 143 occupants, living mostly in the farmhouse clusters of Broomhill (**A**) and the Spring (**B**).

Fig. 26 The tower house on Lady's Island has an attached gatehouse, a unique feature in county Wexford. A doorway from the tower gave access to the top of the gatehouse and to the bawn wall-walk. Remnants of the bawn wall can be seen attached to the tower and the gatehouse.

R.I.A.

Fig. 27 This mid-nineteenth-century evening perspective by Du Noyer, across the Bannow estuary, captured the dramatic 'high-rise' aspect of tower architecture at Clonmines as it must have appeared centuries earlier, when it was a thriving town.

castle and large stone house. Nothing remains except a possible fragment incorporated in a stable wall. The tower house at Lady's Island is associated with the Augustinian canons, who established a foundation at the well-known pilgrimage site in the mid-fifteenth century.[32] The pilgrimage was thriving in the late seventeenth century when it was derided by the governor of Wexford.[33] The Lambert family, who may have occupied the castle for a time, was long identified with the island. The castle was strategically situated at the end of a long causeway connecting the island to the mainland. A small tower (now leaning) protected the island end of the causeway, with a battlemented wall extending from the tower to the water's edge, forming a bawn in front of the castle.[34] The four-storey tower house has a gatehouse attached to its western side, giving access to the monastic site, with another wall running down to the water on either side. A first-floor doorway led to the top of the gatehouse and bawn wall-walk.

Owners and tenants of church lands were equally as concerned about security as their lay counterparts. This

---

Lady's Island Pilgrimage: Solomon Richards 1680

In this Barony of Forth is a Lough called Lough Togher, about two miles in length, and a mile in breadth, replenished with divers sorts of fish. In this Lough is an Island called Lady's Island, containing about twelve acres of land, in former times of ignorance highly esteemed, and accounted holy, and to this day the natives, persons of honour as well as others, in abundance from remote parts of the kingdom, do with great devotion, go on pilgrimage thither, and there do penance, going bare-leg and bare-foot, dabbling in the water up to mid leg, round the Island. Some others go one foot in the water, the other on dry land, taking care not to wet the one nor to tread dry with the other. But some great sinners go on their knees in the water round the Island, and some others that are greater sinners yet, go three times round on their knees in the water. This I have seen, as also I have seen persons of no mean degree leave their hose and shoes in Wexford, and go bare-footed in dirty weather from Wexford to this Island, which is eight miles, and, having done their penance, make their offering in the chapel, and return to Wexford in the same posture. This, abundance of people (not the wisest) do every year, towards the end of summer, but the chiefest or most meritorious time is betwixt their two Lady days of August 15, and September 8. If any lady, through indisposition, be loath to wet her feet, there are women allowed to do it for them, they being present and paying half-a-crown for a fee. And this penance is effectual enough.

R.S.A.I.

Fig. 28 Lady's Island was associated with the Augustinian canons, who established a foundation at the well-known pilgrimage site in the mid-fifteenth century. The tower house, possibly attributable to the Lambert family, was approached by a causeway, connecting the island to the mainland. A flanking tower (now leaning) protected the island end of the causeway, with a battlemented wall extending from the tower to the water's edge. This 1840 drawing by Wakeman shows the bawn wall with flanking tower at the end of the original causeway leading to the island.

anxiety is highlighted by the predominance of fortified churches in the south-west of the county, as well as the presence of tower houses. Church lands, frequently better documented than lay holdings, have the capacity to be more revealing about settlement. Similarly, physical evidence such as relic field systems and infrastructure on former church estates, created by seven centuries of pre- and post-dissolution continuity, is better preserved in the landscape.

WEXFORD TOWER HOUSES: ARCHITECTURE AND TYPOLOGY

At a national level, 1,100 (out of a possible 3,100) tower houses are extant in various stages of conservation, constituting the biggest group of castles in Ireland.[1] Tower-house design was dictated by the often conflicting requirements of domesticity and defence. The vertical arrangement of living spaces was a basic security element but this resulted in awkward access to stacked domestic quarters via narrow mural and spiral stairways. Household facilities included fireplaces, garderobes (latrines), window seats to maximise light in dimly lit rooms, mural chambers and storage space in vaulted ground floors.

Without documentary or archaeological evidence, tower houses are impossible to date accurately. The longevity of standard design features makes it surprisingly difficult to distinguish work of 1350–1450 from that of 1450–1550.[2] This inevitably generates conflicting theories as to their origins and development. Some argue that the earliest, simple tower houses, found in the eastern part of the country, are of fifteenth-century origin, becoming larger and more sophisticated as their construction spread to the west.[3] Conversely, a recent survey postulates that the larger, more sophisticated western towers are predominantly fifteenth-century, while the majority of eastern towers are later. This conclusion is based on early fifteenth-century radiocarbon dates and the location of the hall, or public space, between a high-level vault and the roof. In these towers, the hall was heated by a central hearth, with the smoke escaping through a roof vent.

The seven Wexford towers surveyed are included in an eastern group, mostly found in Leinster and east Ulster but with some examples in Munster. These can be both early and late and are smaller and less impressive than other towers, with the hall usually situated over a ground-floor vault. Unlike the western examples, towers in this group had fireplaces and chimney flues in the external walls.[4]

Fig. 1 Ballyteige tower house with bawn, now partially occupied by a succession of later houses. The presence of gun-loops in the bawn wall indicates that it was built after the tower, which has none. The bawn has two circular towers (one with a well) on the west end, now somewhat obscured by trees.

Fig. 2   The Deeps Castle, on the banks of the Slaney, is by far the largest structure in the county to be classified as a tower house. However, it does not fit comfortably within the group, as it is atypical in several ways. Sited on a demesne manor of the palatine lords, it was initially built as a single storey double-vaulted structure with pronounced base-batter. In the late sixteenth century, several storeys were added on, with distinctive Tudor features.

WEXFORD TOWER HOUSES

Apart from a few late sixteenth-century examples, Wexford tower houses have a hall over a ground-floor vault with fireplaces and chimneys in external walls, suggesting that the more basic Wexford tower house architecture was influenced by the subsidised 'towers and castles' built following the 1441 Act of Parliament establishing the Wexford Pale. Although tower house builders in the Wexford Pale had recognised social pedigrees, the modest resources generated by their small estates influenced the scale of their dwellings. The expenditure on the construction of multiple tower houses by some higher profile families, within and without the Pale, may also have been a factor. The limited domestic amenities provided by the typical Wexford tower house encouraged the proliferation of attached halls. The evolution of this architectural assemblage culminated in the south Wexford fortified hall-house in the late sixteenth century.

The small towers of south Wexford, normally three to four storeys high, form a distinctive sub-group. The small castles associated with the Dublin Pale typically had one or more projecting turrets at the angles, housing stairway and garderobe chutes. These are almost completely absent from the Wexford examples, where the stairs and garderobe are incorporated within the main structure. Where they do feature in the county, these turrets protrude only slightly; Kilcloggan Castle has small projecting stairway and garderobe turrets at the north and west angles, while the tower houses at Ballyteige, Rathmacknee and Rosegarland have small garderobe projections. A design variation occurs at Ballycogley tower house. The garderobe is placed in the loft over the vault, less convenient to the living quarters on the first and second floors but certainly more hygienic.

Although simple rectangular towers, without projections, can be found elsewhere, their predominance in south Wexford implies adherence to a specific design, dictated by the preference of local craftsmen. The geographical seclusion of the Wexford Pale encouraged a conservative adherence to the basic layout of early towers.

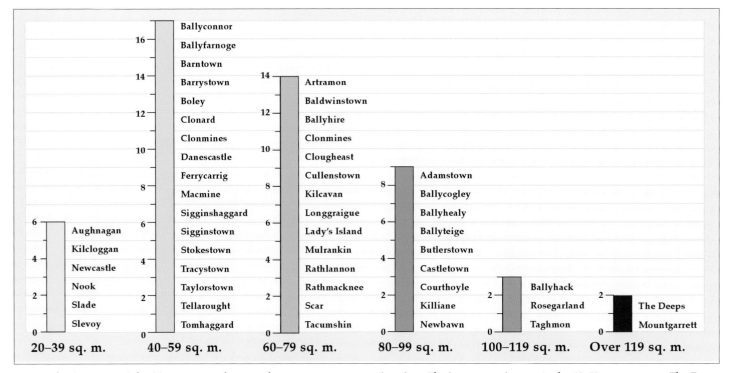

20–39 sq. m.	40–59 sq. m.	60–79 sq. m.	80–99 sq. m.	100–119 sq. m.	Over 119 sq. m.
	Ballyconnor				
	Ballyfarnoge				
	Barntown				
	Barrystown	Artramon			
	Boley	Baldwinstown			
	Clonard	Ballyhire			
	Clonmines	Clonmines			
	Danescastle	Clougheast			
	Ferrycarrig	Cullenstown	Adamstown		
	Macmine	Kilcavan	Ballycogley		
	Sigginshaggard	Longgraigue	Ballyhealy		
Aughnagan	Sigginstown	Lady's Island	Ballyteige		
Kilcloggan	Stokestown	Mulrankin	Butlerstown		
Newcastle	Tracystown	Rathlannon	Castletown		
Nook	Taylorstown	Rathmacknee	Courthoyle	Ballyhack	
Slade	Tellarought	Scar	Killiane	Rosegarland	The Deeps
Slevoy	Tomhaggard	Tacumshin	Newbawn	Taghmon	Mountgarrett

Fig. 3   The footprints of the fifty-one tower houses where measurements can be taken. The largest number are in the 40–59 sq. m. group. The Deeps Castle is the anomalous example at over 200m², with Mountgarrett, at 149m², in second place.

The footprint measurement of fifty-one tower houses in the county can be established. The almost square or rectangular towers had a ground-floor area of between 20 and 210m² square metres, with the majority between 50 and 70m². Six towers in the 20–39m² group are at the lower end, with the atypical multi-period tower house at the Deeps (200m²) the extreme example in the county. The most extensive group of seventeen tower houses occurs in the 40–59m² group. Ten tower houses can be identified as being three storeys in height, concentrated in the 40–59m² group; nineteen were four-storey, in the range 50–80m², with a larger average footprint.

The builders of five of the largest tower houses had substantial resources at their disposal. The Deeps, on a demesne manor of the Lords of the Liberty, and strategically placed on a bend of the Slaney, was held by various tenants, principally the Devereuxes. It does not fit naturally into the tower house category, as it consists of a late sixteenth-century fortified house, built over the double-vaulted ground floor of an earlier building.[5] The tower house at Mountgarrett was associated with the Butlers of Ormond, and the tower house at Taghmon, held as a demesne manor by descendants of the Marshals and defensively situated on the frontier of the Wexford Pale, was presumably built by the Lords of the Liberty. Also in the largest group, the tower house at Ballyhack, similar in size to Taghmon, was erected by the Cistercians of Dunbrody, while the Neville tower house at Rosegarland

was sited on an extensive manor of the same name. A stone head glared balefully from the external walls at Taghmon and Ballyhack, a symbolic signal of watchful vigilance.

The forty-three substantially existing tower houses in the county show that, while construction followed a standard design, variations in architectural elements gave

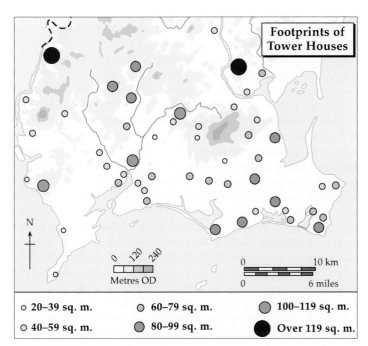

Fig. 4   Available tower house footprints reveal a tendency towards more substantial structures in the south-eastern part of the county and along the border of the Wexford Pale. Size was dictated by a combination of social, economic and strategic factors.

Fig. 5   The four-storey tower house at Ballyteige, near Kilmore Quay, one of the finest in the county, is complete with three lookout turrets. Unusually for county Wexford, the garderobe is housed in a projecting annex and the tower has two murder holes, one protecting the main entrance. Unlike the tower, the later bawn has gun-loops, suggesting a date post 1550. The tower itself may be late fifteenth/early sixteenth-century.

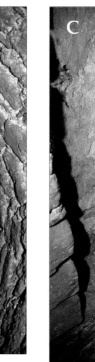

Fig. 6   Aspects of tower house architecture.   **A** Angle-loop, Ferrycarrig. **B** Spiral stairs, Kilcloggan. **C** Garderobe, Ballyteige. **D** Lookout platform, Rathmacknee. **E** Fireplace, Baldwinstown. **F** Angle-loop, Sigginstown. **G** Internal doorway, Taylorstown. **H** Cross-loop, Lady's Island. **I** Gun-loops, Sigginshaggard. **J** Battlements, Slade. **K** Machicolation, Rathmacknee. **L** Double murder-hole, Tellarought. **M** Corner machicolation, Taghmon. **N** Mural stairs, Slade. **O** Ground-floor vault with impression of wicker-work, Slade. **P** Hanging-eye for door, Baldwinstown.

BERNARD BROWNE

Fig. 7 The tower house at Lingstown survived in very good condition until its sudden collapse in 1985, possibly due to the removal of a heavy growth of ivy. The doorway was protected by a machicolation, portcullis and murder-hole. Four storeys in height, with a vaulted ground floor, the upper floors were reached by a combination of mural and spiral stairs, leading to stepped battlements and lookout platform. Wexford artist, Mai McElroy, sketched the tower while it was still standing.

each structure an individual character. Typically, Wexford tower houses were three or four storeys in height, rising from a battered base to a parapet with stepped battlements and one or more lookout platforms. Many of them, built with hammer-dressed rubble with chiselled stone at corners, doors and windows, conform to standard fifteenth-century towers.[6] Entrance doorways, usually pointed, were defended externally by a feature known as a machicolation, an open-bottomed projection over the doorway at wall-walk level, from which projectiles could be launched. Corner machicolations are features at parapet level angles of the tower houses at Ballyhack and Taghmon. Entrance doorways were usually protected internally by a square overhead chute in the entrance lobby, known as a murder-hole, through which projectiles were dropped from upper floors. However, there were exceptions. At the late sixteenth-century tower houses at Ballyconnor, Ballyfarnoge and Taylorstown, as well as the probably fifteenth-century example at Kilcloggan, there is no evidence of murder-holes; Tellarought had three while Ballyteige, Danescastle and

Killiane had two. The absence of a murder-hole is a feature of later towers but the presence of multiple examples was apparently indiscriminate.

A door from the entrance lobby gave access to the vaulted ground floor, a feature considered to be of fifteenth-century origin.[7] However, vaulting was used in county Wexford well into the following century, as it is present in all surviving Wexford tower houses, apart from the late sixteenth-century example at Stokestown and possibly at Kilcavan. Vaulting was constructed over a timber framework covered with mats of wickerwork, woven from pliable sally or hazel rods, which could be shaped to the curve of the vaulting. The mats were covered with a thick layer of mortar into which the stones were bedded. When the mortar had set, the timber was removed but the mats remained embedded in the mortar. The impressions of the wickerwork in the vaulting, and occasionally the rods themselves, are regarded as a diagnostic feature of tower house architecture.[8] Although no longer present, other timber features can still be identified from features in the masonry. These include beam sockets, stone corbels and rebates for doors.[9]

Almost invariably, a sleeping loft under the vault was entered through a door on the stairs. Kilcloggan and Rosegarland were exceptions, as the vaults were not lofted. At Kilhile, a separate stairs rose as far as the loft, also accessing a garderobe. Loft floors were supported on heavy beams resting on stone corbels. In some instances, as at Danescastle and Slevoy, the ends of the beams were also inserted into wall-sockets. At Clonard and Traceystown,

Fig. 8 The tower house at Barrystown, overlooking Bannow Bay, survives to the vault over the ground floor. Twelve gun-loops on the ground floor imply a date in the mid-sixteenth century.

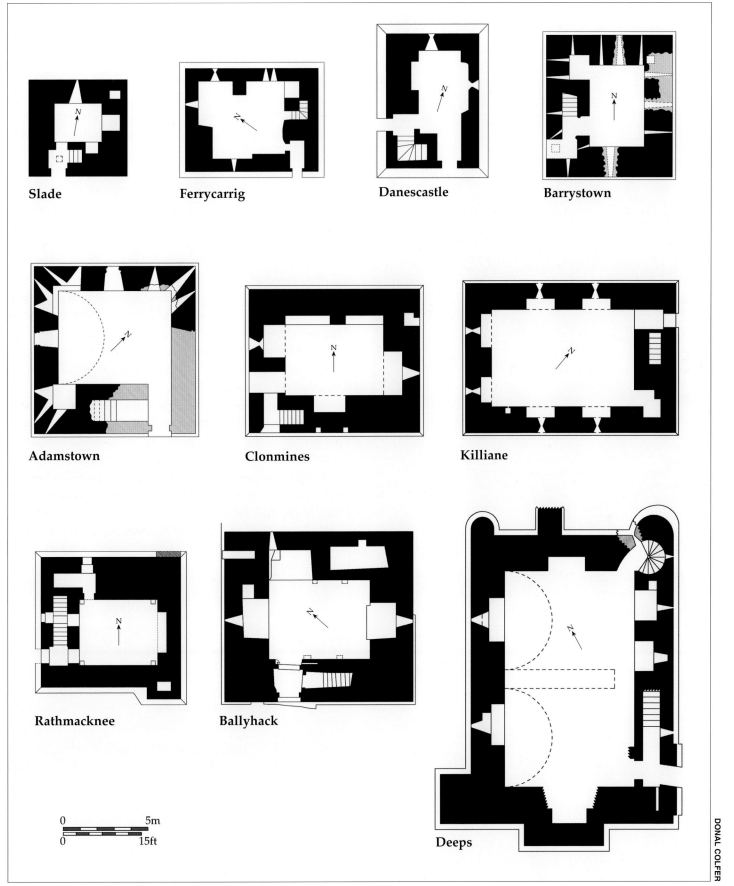

Slade

Ferrycarrig

Danescastle

Barrystown

Adamstown

Clonmines

Killiane

Rathmacknee

Ballyhack

Deeps

0   5m

0   15ft

DONAL COLFER

Fig. 9   Comparative ground-floor plans of a selection of county Wexford tower houses, ranging from the smallest (Slade) to the biggest (the Deeps).

Fig. 10 The three-storey tower house at Taylorstown, overlooking the Owenduff, was built with an attached hall, as the tower was entered from the hall and the first floor of the hall was accessed from the stairway of the tower (**A**). The ground floor had unusual horizontal gun-loops, indicating a mid-sixteenth-century date, or perhaps slightly later.

the joists for the loft were set directly into the walls, possibly a late technique, as Clonard had no base batter, a feature usually associated with late examples. Vaulting on upper floors is almost absent in the county, the exception being the tower at Slade, which has a second vault over the fourth floor, forming the roof of the tower. This technique is rare in Ireland[10] and it may have been used at Slade due to the easy availability of suitable limestone slabs on the cliffs around the Hook. The durability and efficiency of the stone roof at Slade has aided the preservation of the tower.

Stone vaulting over the ground floor possessed obvious advantages as a fire-proofing feature, as well as creating a fortress-like chamber, normally used for storage. The space was lit by slit windows, set in alcoves known as embrasures. The sides of the windows were splayed internally to command a wider field of vision. Double-splay loops are also common in Wexford, splayed on the outside and inside, with the narrow opening in the centre of the wall. Narrow loops were also utilised elsewhere, particularly on stairways, in garderobes and in mural chambers. The absence of larger windows should not be

taken as evidence of a fifteenth-century date; the tower houses at Sigginshaggard, Ferrycarrig and Sigginstown, all equipped with original gun-loops, were lit throughout by narrow slit windows for security purposes.

The upper storeys in Wexford tower houses were generally reached by a combination of mural and spiral stairways, typically rising from the entrance lobby. Ferrycarrig tower, where the stairs was accessed from the vaulted ground floor chamber, is an exception. The most common combination, present in ten of the surviving towers, was a mural stairs to first-floor level, with a spiral continuing to the parapets. However, some surviving towers, including Artramon, Ballyhealy, Ballyteige, Clonmines, Clougheast, Mulrankin and Rathmacknee, have steep mural stairways ascending through the walls to parapet level with no spiral element.

The principal living quarters, immediately over the vault, on the first and second floors, usually had some bigger single- and double-light windows, sometimes of ogee-headed design. These rooms were normally equipped with fireplaces and garderobes as well as window-seats. The fourth floor was presumably used as a bedroom by the owner's family. As well as housing the stairway and garderobe chute, the thick walls also contained mural chambers, some big enough to be used as sleeping quarters. Secret chambers, known as oubliettes, which could function as strong-rooms or prisons, are found in Wexford towers, including Ballycogley, Ballyhack, Clougheast, Rathmacknee, Taghmon and Taylorstown.

In some county Wexford tower houses, yetts and portcullises were installed as defensive features at the entrance doorways. The yett was an iron grid which was pulled into a rebate (recess) on the outside of the doorway by chains passing through holes in the doorjamb.

Fig. 11 One of the horizontal gun-loops on the ground floor of Taylorstown tower house, situated on a slope near the head of Bannow Bay, overlooking a crossing point on the Owenduff river.

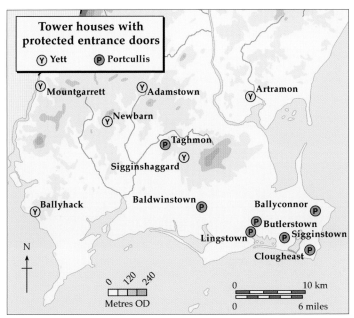

Fig. 12 The portcullis and yett both consisted of a metal grid that was used to guard the entrance. The yett was pulled into place by chains that were passed through holes in the doorframe; the portcullis was dropped into place from above through grooves in the stonework. Towers with portcullises were grouped in the southern part of the barony of Forth, suggesting a local preference or custom and possibly affluence. The castles of Ballyconnor and Sigginstown, both fitted with portcullises, belonged to the late group, implying that the use of a portcullis was a local rather than a chronological preference. Yetts were generally in tower houses with gun-loops as well as late sixteenth-century fortified hall-houses.

Doorways fitted with yetts had granite surrounds, mostly pointed, presumably because the activity associated with the yett required substantial support and the durable granite also made the removal of the protective grid more difficult. Yetts were fitted to tower houses at Adamstown, Artramon, Ballyhack, Mountgarrett, Newbawn and Sigginshaggard, all in the northern sector of the tower house zone. Ballyhack, presumably of fifteenth-century date as it was claimed in 1515 that 'the king's commissioners always used to sit there',[11] may have been the earliest of these and it is also the only example with a rectangular doorway. Adamstown and Sigginshaggard, equipped with numerous gun-loops, date to c. 1550.

The portcullis, a rare defensive feature in tower houses, was found in small numbers in Cork as well as the examples in Wexford.[12] This device, also consisting of a metal grid, was lowered from above into a channel in the doorframe. These channels survive in seven Wexford tower houses: Ballyconnor, Butlerstown, Baldwinstown, Clough-east, Lingstown (recorded before its collapse), Sigginstown and Taghmon. Apart from Taghmon, the use of the portcullis was confined to the south-east of the county, suggesting that it was a localised feature, perhaps dictated by the preference of owners or craftsmen. The idea may have originated at Taghmon, attributed to the Lords of the

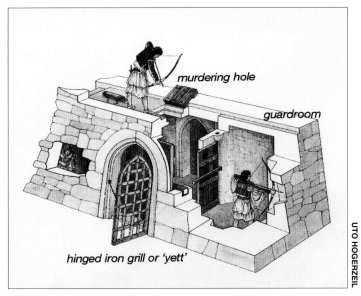

Fig. 13   This illustration shows the use of a metal grill, or 'yett' to protect the entrance doorway of a tower house. The yett is being pulled into position by a metal chain passing through a hole in the wall. Overhead, a defender is preparing to shoot arrows through the murder-hole.

Liberty; like Ballyhack it was an 'institutional' rather than a privately owned tower house, both similar in size and of probable fifteenth-century origin. Taghmon and Ballyhack, unusually for towers in Wexford, had corner machicolations, a feature of early tower houses elsewhere.[13] The portcullis, as well as angle gun-loops in Sigginstown tower house, implies that this feature could have remained part of tower house design in county Wexford for a century.

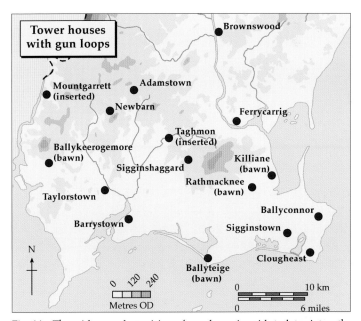

Fig. 14   The widespread provision of gun-loops in mid- to late sixteenth-century tower houses and bawns reflected the high level of social unrest in the county and the escalating use of firearms. These included towers at Barrystown, Taylorstown and Sigginstown on the south coast, as well as frontier towers, with multiple gun-loops at Adamstown, Courthoyle, Ferrycarrig and Brownswood.

Fig. 15 The substantial tower house at Adamstown guarded the Devereux manor, isolated outside the Wexford Pale. Its defensive capabilities included seventeen gun-loops and a fortified bawn.

Fig. 17 Triple gun-loops in a corner embrasure on the ground floor of Adamstown tower house. The other angles enjoyed similar protection.

By the second half of the fifteenth century, the spread of artillery impacted on the design of fortifications, with the first recorded use of cannon in Ireland occurring in 1488. Although handguns were deployed on the battle-fields of Europe in the fifteenth century, the longbow remained the preferred weapon of the English, until it was finally abandoned in favour of handguns following the advent of the musket in the 1550s.[14] Artillery and firearms were used in an attack on Ferns Castle in 1536, the first known example in the county.[15] Tower houses, mostly isolated in a rural environment, were subjected to sporadic raiding rather than sustained attack, and they were not normally menaced by heavy siege guns or artillery.[16]

Fig. 16 A plaque, containing the Devereux coat-of-arms, commemorated the building of Adamstown Castle in 1556, by Sir Nicholas Devereux of Ballymagir and his wife Catherine Power. Formerly on the wall of the castle or bawn, it is now preserved in a private dwelling near the village. The words are inscribed on part of a recycled medieval graveslab, presumably from the early medieval church site and graveyard at Adamstown. The modern painted surface, which makes the inscription more legible, may reflect the stone's original appearance.

Fig. 18   The semicollapsed nature of the tower house at Kilhile presents a convenient vertical section through the interior of the building. Details include the vaulted ground floor with entrance and doorway to the loft; corbels for supporting floors; windows on the first and second floors and access to the machicolation on the third floor. The tower was ruggedly constructed of old red sandstone, sourced on the cliff at nearby Ballyhack.

Fig. 19   Slade Castle is a multi-period structure built on the cliff-edge above a sheltered beach. The well-preserved tower, the smallest in the county, with slit windows throughout, appears to be early but lacks a significant base-batter. Its preservation has been aided by the vaulted roof which still keeps the structure dry. The fortified house, with vaulted ground floor, was added later, with a projection brought in halfway on the north wall of the tower, presumably to provide access between the two, which was never implemented. The hall was on the first floor of the house with what may have been a free-standing fireplace and chimney. In the eighteenth century, the complex became an 'apartment block' accommodating four or five local families. A massive chimney breast and an annex was added to the west of the house and an annex and external stairway to the east.

The escalating use of firearms, however, posed a direct threat and stimulated new design elements, both defensive and offensive. From the second quarter of the sixteenth century, loops for firearms were included in new Irish tower houses and inserted in some of those already constructed. In county Wexford, fifteen tower houses have gun-loops. In two instances, at Taghmon and Mountgarrett, loops were fitted into existing structures. The bawns (but not the towers) at Ballyteige, Killiane and Rathmacknee contain gun-loops, signalling that the bawns are later than the towers. Even in the secure south-east of the county, security concerns were expressed by the inclusion of gun-loops in the tower houses of Clougheast, Ballyconnor and Sigginstown. In the 1550s, 'offensive' tower houses were constructed by denizens of the Wexford

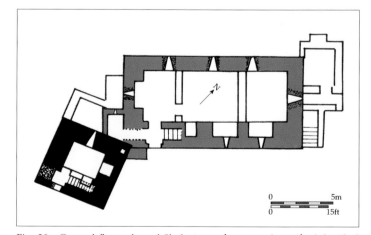

Fig. 20   Ground-floor plan of Slade tower house and attached fortified house. The original tower house is shown in black, the later fortified house in grey and eighteenth-century additions in white.

Fig. 21 Remains of original wickerwork (used in the construction process) survive over a window opening in the fortified house at Slade.

Pale to infiltrate lands to the north controlled by the Irish. In 1556, the Devereuxes of Ballymagir erected a tower house at Adamstown, the Brownes of Mulrankin built at Brownswood, and the Siggins of Sigginstown at Sigginshaggard near Taghmon. These three towers were plentifully supplied with gun-loops, particularly

Fig. 22 Ferrycarrig tower house, built in the mid-sixteenth-century, is tactically sited on a rock overlooking the Slaney gorge. Fitted with narrow slit windows and gun-loops, its primary function was the protection of the ferry crossing and river traffic from the port of Wexford, which was essential for the security of the upriver town of Enniscorthy.

Sigginshaggard which had twenty-nine and Adamstown with seventeen.

The small tower overlooking the Slaney on a rock at Ferrycarrig was also built (probably by the Roches) for offensive as well as defensive reasons. Raised in the second half of the sixteenth century, when the river link with Wexford was essential to Enniscorthy, the castle was well placed to guard the narrow Slaney gorge, where river traffic was vulnerable to attack from the cliffs at either side. The tower has slit windows throughout, with gun-loops on the ground floor and angle-loops on the first floor, covering the land approaches on the left bank of the river. Like the tower house at Taghmon, it was probably designed specifically as a fortress rather than as a residence. Three other castles had obvious military capabilities. A flanking tower of the Suttons' courtyard castle at Ballykeerogemore contained sixteen gun-loops and the surviving ground floor of Barrystown tower house in Bargy had an elaborate system of twelve gun-loops. The small tower house at Taylorstown, commanding a ford on the Owenduff river just before it enters Bannow Bay, has four gun-loops on the ground floor, two of an unusual horizontal shape, permitting a wider field of fire.

ANCILLARY FEATURES

The iconic image of a crumbling tower house standing isolated in the landscape is evocative but misleading. When tower houses were built, they were normally integrated into an extensive complex of domestic and agricultural structures. With a single entrance doorway defended by an overhead machicolation, the architecture intimates that they were intended to be self-contained structures with no direct communication with other domestic buildings, such as a hall and kitchen, which initially may have been detached or added as a lean-to against the tower. Some early halls adjoining tower houses were of mud and timber, reflecting the pre-tower type of residence. A 1617 account described Irish castles as being 'built strong for defence in time of rebellion and

---

Stanihurst (1584) on Irish Castles

The Irish held castles 'strongly constructed and fortified with masses of stone'. Adjoining the castles were 'reasonably big and spacious palaces made from white clay and mud. They are not roofed with quarried slabs or slates but with thatch. [There] they hold their banquets but they prefer to sleep in the castle rather than the palace because their enemies can easily apply torches to the roofs which catch fire rapidly if there is but the slightest breeze'.

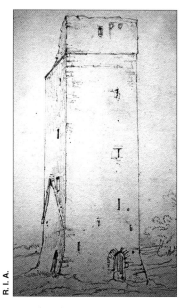

R. I. A.

Fig. 23 The existence of a second doorway at Danescastle was so unusual that it elicited two drawings by Wakeman in 1840, depicting the two entrance doors and the stone flashing of the attached house.

commonly with a spacious hall joining to the castle and built of timber and clay, wherein the family eats'.[17] Some halls were thatched. In 1584, Stanihurst, writing about Ireland in general, observed that the Irish held stone castles with adjoining thatched houses made of clay and mud.[18] The use of thatch in county Wexford is confirmed in the *Civil Survey* which recorded 'a castle and thatched house' at both Tacumshin and Ardenagh.

Twenty-seven tower houses exhibit evidence for attached halls, either documentary or in surviving fabric. Six of the towers were three-storey, eleven four-storey. The early houses or halls may have consisted of timber and clay, later replaced by more durable buildings of stone. The architecture of the surviving tower house at Danescastle, near Carrig-on-Bannow, provides evidence for a contemporary clay house. Unusually for county Wexford,

the tower has two original ground-floor entrances, the main one protected by a machicolation, the other giving entry to a one-storey house formerly against the east wall, as indicated by the stone flashing for the roof.

Wickerwork centering in the roof of the passage to this doorway indicates that it was part of the original construction. Unusually, the stairway rises from the wall passage to this doorway. A mid-nineteenth-century plan of the tower features the walls of a 'house attached to tower'.[19] No sign of these walls remain and no scar is evident on the side of the tower, as would be the case if stone walls had been keyed in or built against it. Presumably the house was actually of clay, with all traces subsequently weathered away from the tower wall. This is also intimated by the house's single-storey plan. In 1840, the unusual architecture prompted Wakeman to make two drawings illustrating the doorways on the east and north walls of the tower.[20] At nearby Scar, the three-storey tower house has a second original doorway at ground level, leading to an adjoining fortified house with a large chimney on the gable.[21] The house was not bonded with the tower, implying that the two were not contemporary. As at Danescastle, a 'soft' house of timber and clay presumably preceded the partially extant stone structure.

Fig. 24 The passage leading to the second door on the ground floor of Danescastle tower house has wicker centering, showing that it was an original feature, intended to connect with a contempory attached house.

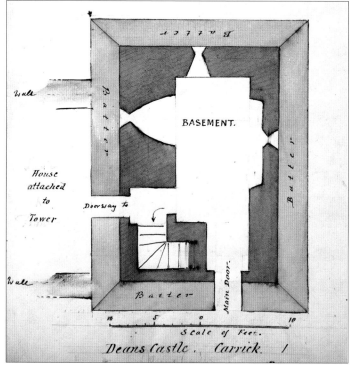

R. I. A.

Fig. 25 Du Noyer produced a ground-floor plan of the tower at Danescastle, illustrating the pronounced base-batter. It depicts the arrangement of the doors and the location of the attached hall. The stairway of the tower rose from the passageway to the hall, making it accessible to both tower and hall. The rectangular tower accommodated the house on the long wall. The window and embrasure on the left should be on the right wall, a rare mistake by the usually meticulous artist.

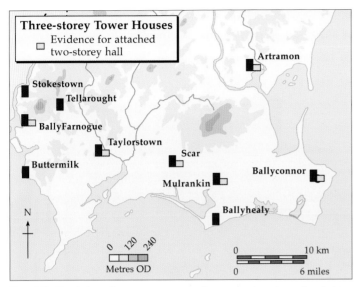

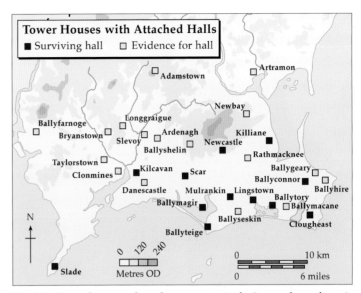

Fig. 26 Surviving three-storey tower houses are not confined to a particular period. Tellarought appears to be fifteenth-century, while Taylorstown, well equipped with gun-loops, is mid-sixteenth-century.

Fig. 27 Tower-houses where houses are attached, or where there is evidence for the previous existence of adjoining halls/houses. Extant examples, some still occupied, are concentrated in the south-east.

In a survey of the Albemarle estate in 1669, houses attached to the tower houses at Adamstown and Ballybrennan were of the timber and clay type.[22] At Adamstown, there was 'an old range house or barn-like house adjoining the castle, down many years since but recently re-built'. At Ballybrennan the castle had 'a long barn-like house joining it, but in a ruinous condition, little standing but the walls and barn timber'. At least some halls were fortified. A drawing of Ballygeary castle in 1727 shows a battlemented house, while blocked-up doorways at first-floor level in the tower houses at Ballyfarnoge and Mulrankin must have opened to the wall-walk of fortified houses.

A late seventeenth-century account of the barony of Forth observed that 'The mansion houses of most of the gentry were fortified with castles'. The house was the principal living space, with the towers used in times of danger and for sleeping. At that stage, houses were 'stone-walled with slated roofs', while some halls originally had fire-hearths in the centre of the floor. These were replaced by 'spacious chimneys', which may be represented by the massive chimneys projecting from the gables of halls at Scar, Ballyconnor and Mulrankin.[23] The stone flashing of a single-storey hall projects on the remnants of the tower house at Kilcavan. Part of the hall is incorporated in the modern long, low dwelling connected to the tower, including the Tudor hood-moulding of the original entrance doorway. At Mulrankin, Clonmines and Kilcavan, projecting stone flashing marking the roof line of the hall on the side of the tower was part of the original ensemble, signifying that a hall was at least planned, if not erected, at the same time as the tower.

In eleven instances, there are cartographic and documentary references to 'castle and house/hall'.[24] The tower houses of Ballyhire and Ballygeary in Forth have both been removed but they are depicted on a 1727 estate map with attached halls.[25] Significant remains of halls are present at twelve towers, Ballymagir, Clougheast (both recently restored), Mulrankin, Newcastle, Killiane, Kilcavan, Ballyconnor, Scar, Ballyteige, Sigginstown, Slade and Lingstown (which fell in 1985).[26] The modernised halls at Ballymagir, Clougheast, Kilcavan, Killiane, Mulrankin and Newcastle are currently occupied. The tower house at Ballyconnor survives to first-floor level. The hall has a four-light, ogee-headed window.[27] A date stone, now lost,

Fig. 28 On the Edwards estate map of 1727, the four-storey tower house of Ballyhire is depicted with a two-storey hall attached and surrounding cabins. The hall is shown with chimneys and battlements.

N.A.I.

Fig. 29   An early hall adjoining the tower house at Kilcavan, near Wellington Bridge, is still used as a family home. Stone flashing on the tower suggests that the hall was originally a two-storeyed building. Hood moulding over a window, formerly a doorway, indicates a late sixteenth-century date.

commemorated the building of the hall in 1570 by Dionysius (Denis) Stafford and his wife Katherina Sinnott.[28] The tower, with multiple gun-loops, pre-dated the hall by a short period only.

A progression in the architecture of the domestic and defensive integration of the hall and tower is evident in the changing significance of the machicolation over the tower's entrance doorway. A two-storey fortified house was joined to the fifteenth-century tower house at Slade, probably in the early sixteenth century.[29] This is possibly the earliest existing example in the county. The house, with a first-floor hall and battlements, matching those on the tower, has a

The barony of Forth c. 1680 (H. F. Hore, 1862)

The mansion houses of most of the gentry in said barony were fortified with castles, some near sixty feet high, having walls of at least five feet thick, of quadrangle form, erected – as is supposed – by the Danes, to the number of thirty, of which few are as yet become ruinous. Their houses built with stone walls, slated; having spacious halls, in the centre of which are fire-hearths, according to the ancient English mode, for more commodious extension of heat to the whole family surrounding it (but that form is antiquated) all houses at the present day having spacious chimneys. Plebians have their habitations completely builded with mudwalls, so firm and high, as there are frequently lofts thereon, after that form they find most convenient for husbandry's business, neat, well accommodated with all necessary implements, more civil and English-like contrived than vulgarly elsewhere in many parts of Ireland.

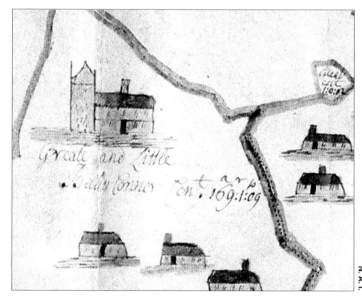

Fig. 30   The 1727 Edwards estate map contains a sketch of the tower house at Ballyconnor with a two-storey house attached. An inscribed stone, possibly from the house, gives 1570 as the construction date.

Fig. 31   The house adjoining the three-storey tower house at Mulrankin, still occupied as a modern residence, is based on an early hall mentioned in the *Civil Survey*. A blocked-up doorway (**A**) on the first floor of the tower led to the wall-walk of the earlier hall.

stone vault turned on wickerwork centering. The first-floor hall had a free-standing fireplace and chimney, which also supported the roof. A projecting chimney was added to the west wall of the house, probably in the eighteenth century, to cater for a fireplace inserted on the ground floor. The off-set nature of the design at Slade, with the tower and house connected only at one corner, facilitated protection for the doorway of the house. Both structures functioned as independent entities with no direct access between them. The ability of the machicolation to defend the entrance to the tower was not compromised. The L-shaped design is replicated at Athlumney Castle in county Meath.[30]

During the following centuries, a reluctance to abandon early tower house sites persisted, resulting in the positioning of halls against existing towers in an effort to create a more comfortable living environment. In the early seventeenth century, a very different method to that used

Fig. 32   The Edwards estate map of 1727 shows the tower house of Ballygeary with a battlemented hall attached, similar to Mulrankin.

BERNARD BROWNE

Fig. 33   The ivy-covered Rathronan tower house near Bridgetown with substantial thatched house adjoining. The tower, standing to three storeys with vaulted ground floor, has been converted as a dwelling. The thatched house may be the successor of an early thatched hall, as there are records of some halls being roofed in this way.

at Slade was employed when adding a house to the tower at Lingstown near the south coast of the barony of Forth.[31] In this instance, the house was an extension to the side-wall of the tower, which was breached to make a connecting doorway. The entrance to the tower and its machicolation remained in use as before.

A more logical architectural approach was adopted when houses were appended to towers by attaching the new structure on to the side with the entrance doorway. This was a deliberate strategy. Although rendering the machicolation obsolete, it compensated by avoiding the need for a second entrance which weakened the tower's defences. In effect, the house became the first line of defence, which could be abandoned *in extremis* for the greater security of the tower, replicating the concept of the motte-and-bailey castle of earlier centuries.

Fig. 34   The three-storey tower house at Scar, near Duncormick, has an offset, two-storey hall attached, with remains of a gable chimney, both consisting of old red sandstone (the local bedrock). Original doorways on the ground floor and first floor of the tower connect with the hall. As the hall is not bonded with the tower, it may have replaced an earlier 'soft' building, similar to one at nearby Danescastle.

Unusually, this innovation was carried a step further at Killiane tower house by omitting the machicolation over the entrance and compensating by the inclusion of a second internal murder-hole. At Rathmacknee, a more ambivalent approach left an opening in the battlements of the tower which accommodated a wooden machicolation.[32] The defence system was refined even further in the tower with attached fortified house (now removed) at Taylorstown, dating to the second half of the sixteenth century.[33] The walls of the house were bonded into the angles of the small three-storey tower, signifying that the two were contemporary. The complex was entered through the house, with a further defensive element created by placing the entrance to the first floor of the house on the stairway of the tower. This solution would be elaborated further in late sixteenth-century fortified hall-houses with service towers at Coolhull, Bargy and elsewhere.

BAWNS

In most cases, tower houses had associated courtyards known as bawns (derived from the Irish badhún, a cattle enclosure), with defences of clay, wood, or stone.[34] A 1570s account described the bawn as 'surrounded by a hedge and ditch into which the cattle were driven in time of alarm'.[35] There is evidence for twenty-nine bawns in county Wexford. Ten survive, varying from almost complete structures to fragments. The enclosed area of existing Wexford bawns are at the lower end of the national scale.[36] Of twelve removed Wexford bawns recorded in documentary sources, seven of their tower houses no longer stand. Archaeological evidence has identified seven more bawns, possibly of the 'soft' variety.[37] In some cases, partial traces of fabric allows for speculation on the nature of the bawn. Fragmentary remains of the wall and doorway of the bawn at

---

Fynes Moryson 1617

Neither can the cattle possibly be great since they eat only by day, and then are brought at evening within the bawns of castles, where they stand or lie all night in a dirty yard without so much as a lock [handful] of hay, whereof they make little for sluggishness, and their little they altogether keep for their horses; and they are brought in by nights for fear of thieves, the Irish using almost no other kind of theft, or else for fear of wolves, the destruction whereof being neglected by the inhabitants, oppressed with greater mischiefs, they are so much grown in number as sometimes in winter nights they will come to prey in villages and the suburbs of the cities.

Fig. 35 The Hospitaller tower house at Kilcloggan has a doorway in the stairway turret on the first floor, giving access to the bawn wall-walk. Broken masonry below the doorway shows where the the bawn wall was bonded with the tower, indicating that both were contemporary. Remains of the bawn gateway survive, including the square boltholes into which the timber draw-bars for securing the gate were slotted.

Fig. 36 This mid-nineteenth-century drawing of Baldwinstown tower house by Du Noyer depicts part of the bawn wall with a circular flanking tower (now covered with ivy) with intact crenellations.

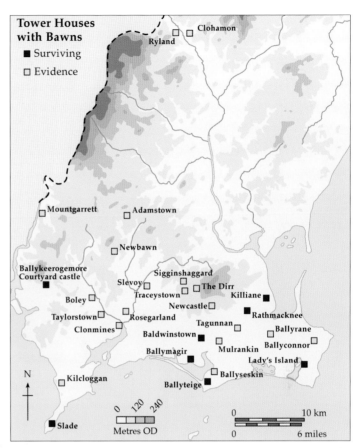

Tower Houses with Bawns
■ Surviving
□ Evidence

Fig. 37 Tower houses where a bawn exists or where evidence records the former presence of a bawn of clay, timber or stone.

Kilcloggan Castle indicate that it connected with the north-east angle of the tower. An original door from the first floor of the tower, opening to the bawn wall-walk, indicates that the two structures were contemporary.

The tower house on Lady's Island exploited the insular location by having one battlemented bawn wall, with a mural tower, across the end of the approach causeway and another running from the tower house to the water's edge.[38] A doorway from the first floor of the tower to the top of the attached gatetower gave entry to the wall-walk of the bawn. Fragments of a large bawn (28m x 22m) exist at the unique Sutton courtyard castle of Ballykeerogemore near Campile, where only part of the wall remains standing. An exceptionally high circular lookout turret, originally with two stone vaults, which partially collapsed in the 1970s, is situated at the south-east angle. A three-storey rectangular flanking tower, with multiple gun-loops, projects at the north-west corner. This tower was entered at first-floor level from the wall-walk of the bawn. The west of the bawn consisted of a later two-storey house, probably of seventeenth-century date; only the west and south walls, with projecting chimney stacks, are still standing. There is no evidence for the existence of an earlier tower house within the bawn.[39]

Fig. 38 Ballykeerogemore Castle consisted of a bawn (28m x 22m), possibly sixteenth-century, with a four-storey circular tower at one corner and a three-storey rectangular flanking tower, with multiple gun-loops, on the opposite corner, reached from the bawn wall-walk. Part of the east wall of the bawn survives. A later two-storey house formed the west wall, of which only the west and south walls are standing, both with projecting chimney stacks.

At Adamstown, the tower house was 'walled around with a stone wall at least fourteen foot high', with the entrance defended by a gate tower.[40] This arrangement was unusual for county Wexford. In the case of the three extant bawns, the tower houses, situated at an angle on the perimeter of the bawn, form part of the defences. These bawns, at Ballyteige, Killiane and Rathmacknee, are all

ROLF LOEBER

Fig. 39 The circular lookout tower at Ballykeerogemore Castle with part of the house to the right. The tower partially collapsed in the 1970s.

well-preserved and possibly date to the 1550s.[41] Gun-loops in the bawn walls indicates that they are later than the tower houses. The bawn entrances, each protected by a machicolation, are all adjacent to the tower wall, allowing flanking fire to be directed at the gateway. At Ballyteige, where the bawn meets the centre of the tower wall, a late sixteenth-century window with hood moulding was inserted in the tower, overlooking the outside of the gate.

Although broadly similar in design, the three bawns differed significantly in detail. At Killiane, only the west wall of the bawn (34m x 25m) remains standing, with stairs leading to the wall-walk and three gun-loops in the parapet. A remnant of a rectangular tower marks the south-west corner, as well as an almost complete circular tower at the south-east corner. Unusually, the upper part of the circular tower holds a fine dovecote, with access through an aperture in the corbelled roof. A large house (still occupied as a residence) was inserted along the north wall of the bawn, covering the original entrance to the tower, possibly incorporating an earlier house on the same site.

The south wall of the bawn (30m x 22m) at Ballyteige contains the entrance, machicolation, wall-walk and gun-loops. The lower parts of the walls stand to the west and

Fig. 40   The tower house at Rathmacknee, complete with battlements and two lookout turrets, is one of the best preserved in the county. The later bawn is the finest example in the county. The bawn wall-walk, accessed by a stairway, survives, including a corner machicolation with gun-loops at the north-east angle (below). A house once stood where the wall is missing. A modern dwelling stands against the west wall.

north, with circular flanking towers at the north-west and north-east angles. The east of the bawn is occupied by a series of houses, representing continuity of occupation, with facades to the outside. The houses mask the tower house entrance, rendering the machicolation obsolete.

The impressive bawn at Rathmacknee, where the tower house occupies the south-east angle, is almost intact, except at the south where a house was formerly attached to the tower wall. The bawn entrance, with machicolation, was covered by a (possibly inserted) double-splay loop in the ground floor of the tower. A stairs beside the entrance of the bawn rises to the wall-walk, with destroyed battle-ments and a semicircular machicolation fitted with gun-

Fig. 41 The tower house at Killiane is substantially complete, although modified. The early hall has been transformed into a modern dwelling. Two walls of the bawn survive, including the entrance with machicolation. The bawn, which contains gun-loops, is later than the tower, covering one of the windows. As at Ballyhack and Taghmon, a head (below) glares from the wall of a lookout turret, presumably as a symbol of constant vigilance.

loops at the north-east corner; the remains of a second machicolation can be seen on the north-east angle. A modern dwelling house stands against the west wall. The tower house and bawn are preserved as a National Monument and are accessible to the public.

CONCLUSION

In county Wexford, the basic tower house design, which emerged in the fifteenth century endured, with minor modifications, until late in the sixteenth century. A denizen of a fifteenth-century tower would have felt at home in one built a century later. Architectural innovations related mostly to the increased use of handguns in the sixteenth century, which prompted the insertion of gun-loops in some existing tower house, and their inclusion in new ones. Other innovations improved the security of the entrance doorway by the installation of a yett or portcullis. The greatest change occurred in the provision of enhanced luxury in domestic arrangements by the creation of extra living accommodation. Following a period of experiment-ation, a consensus emerged that the most suitable place for a hall was against the entrance side of the tower. This rendered the machicolation redundant but compensated by making the tower even more secure. This arrangement was perfected at Taylorstown, where the tower and hall were integrated, with access to the first

Fig. 42 The bawn gateway at Rathmacknee, with overhead machicolation. The bawn wall, constructed later than the tower, with wall-walk and corner machicolation, is largely intact.

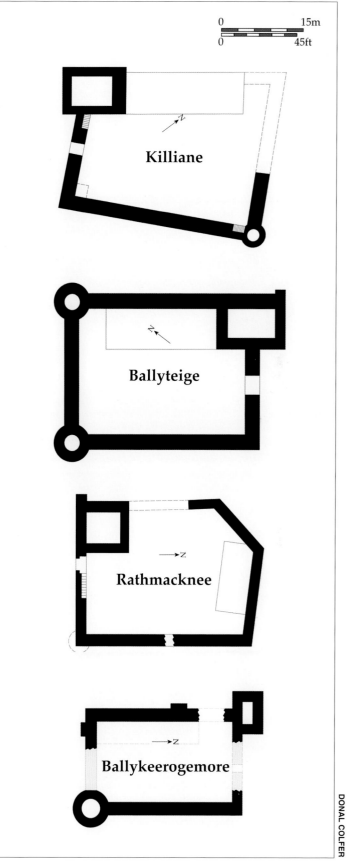

Fig. 43 Surviving bawns in County Wexford, three of which have associated tower houses. There is no evidence for a tower house at Ballykeerogemore, which is described as a courtyard castle.

floor of the hall from the tower. This design may also have been present in other non-surviving complexes.

Even when this approach became well-established, machicolations over entrance doors were installed in late towers such as Sigginstown and Clougheast. Perhaps this reflected a lingering regard for the effectiveness of the machicolation in deterring unwanted visitors if the tower remained freestanding. As well as architectural innovations, there was also a modification of emphasis in the political rationale for building tower houses. As the sixteenth century progressed, the colonists of south Wexford began to build 'offensive' towers to the north of the Pale to prevent incursions by the Irish but also to re-occupy land that had been reclaimed by them. Examples exist at Adamstown, Brownswood, Courthoyle, Sigginshaggard and Ferrycarrig. Initially at least, they were intended to be stand-alone fortresses, as all sides were well equipped with gun-loops.

In the later part of the sixteenth century, social demands, combined with a desire for more comfortable domestic arrangements, prompted an evolution in the

DONAL COLFER

Fig. 44   This remarkable circular dovecote (with resident pigeon) is located in the bawn tower at Killiane Castle. The holes for the birds are built-in around the inner wall on the top floor; an opening in the vaulted roof allowed the birds access. Pigeons played a significant part in the medieval diet.

concept of the tower house with attached hall. A more cohesive design merged the functions of both elements, reducing the status of the tower but retaining many characteristics of the tower and hall. This evolution culminated in the emergence of the late sixteenth-century fortified hall-house. This innovative building type is exclusive to south Wexford and adds a distinctive element to its landscape.

R. I. A.

Fig. 45   The insular location of the tower house on Lady's Island was strengthened to create further security. A flanking tower (now leaning) at the end of the causeway approaching the island was linked to the shore by a battlemented wall. The tower house and the attached gatetower (unique in the county), giving access to the monastic site and the rest of the Island, were also connected to the shoreline by walls.

Lady's Island 1680

In the south of the barony [of Forth] there is a lake called Lough Togher into which is extended an isthmus or tongue of land named Our Lady's Island. At the entrance [to the island] is a long causey or bridge, from which the lake gets its name [the Irish word 'tóchar' means a causeway]. At its end a small turret is erected before the castle gate in the midst of a strong stone wall with battlements extending from the east side into the water. Within the isthmus is a church dedicated to Our Lady, daily frequented by infirm pilgrims from all parts of Ireland who, by praying and making offerings, have been cured of various maladies and infirmities.

THE WEXFORD FORTIFIED HALL-HOUSE:
LATE SIXTEENTH-CENTURY TRANSITIONAL RESIDENCES

In a logical sequence from the attachment of houses to towers, an original building type emerged in county Wexford in the late sixteenth century. These new structures, best described as fortified hall-houses, signalled a transition from the iconic tower house form that had dominated the landscape for two centuries. This development was stimulated by an escalating evolution in social and household requirements, as well as dramatic changes in military technology due to the rapidly improving design of firearms and artillery. The latest formal architectural elements were adapted to meet local requirements, representing a pronounced move towards a more sophisticated domestic arrangement. Combined with co-ordinated defensive features, this progression resulted in the emergence of a sub-typology, unique, not only to Ireland, but to county Wexford.[1] The buildings consisted of an elongated rectangular three-storey block, lacking a stone vault, with the hall occupying the first floor, accessed from a small four-storey entrance tower, offset at one end.[2] In silhouette, the new hall-houses echoed the fortified churches of the fourteenth and fifteenth centuries.

Fig. 1 Coolhull Castle consists of a hall-house of two storeys and an attic, with an offset service tower at one end. The tower contains the entrance, a spiral stairway leading to the rooms in the house, a garderobe and a lookout turret. The round-topped, granite doorway, is protected by a gun-loop in the house, a yett and a machicolation. The ground floor of the house has no vault and is lit by slit windows. The hall, on the first floor, is lit by single-light, round-headed windows, with the exception of two which have two lights. The wall-walk, accessible from the tower, has a square corner machicolation, with gun-loops, on the north-east angle. The hall has a fine fireplace with the chimney corbelled out on the inside of the wall-walk.

R. I. A.

Fig. 2 Wakeman's 1840 drawing shows Coolhull with a hipped roof, possibly of thatch and in poor condition. The battlements on the left of the tower, since fallen, were still in place.

HALL-HOUSE ARCHITECTURE

The design of the hall-houses differed significantly from the traditional tower house. The absence of a stone vault over the ground floor marked a fundamental change from the defensive arrangements of tower-house design. The use of a service tower to access upper floors, as well as providing covering fire, was an innovative element in defensive building.[3] As well as providing some accommodation, the tower also acted as a lookout platform. The principal examples of these distinctive residences are Coolhull, Bargy, Hilltown and Dungulph.[4] These hall-houses were all erected by families with an established tradition as tower-house builders (Devereux, Rossiter, FitzHenry, Whitty). None were sited at established manorial centres. All were on 'green field' sites, presumably because they were constructed on newly acquired lands.

This opportunity facilitated modern buildings with an enhanced emphasis on comfortable domestic arrangements, inevitably compromising the defensive capabilities. This was obviously a concern, as security elements were carefully integrated into the architecture of the new layout, resulting in a more cohesive arrangement than the one utilised in tower houses. Typical tower-house features were retained, including battlements, machicolations, yetts, ground floor loops and lookout platforms. The ever-increasing prevalence of firearms necessitated a coordinated system of tactically located gun-loops. The offset nature of the tower allowed for flanking fire along one wall of the house. The re-introduction of the corner machicolation on the opposite angle, a feature rarely seen in Wexford tower houses, provided cover for the other two walls.

The Devereuxes of Ballymagir built the fortified hall-house at Coolhull, probably the prototype of the group, in the later part of the sixteenth century. It presents an intriguing comparison with the traditional tower house on their frontier manor of Adamstown. The few remaining round-headed windows at Adamstown provide an architectural link between the two buildings. Exposed to raids from the Fassagh of Bantry, the Adamstown tower house had at least seventeen gun-loops. A datestone, now preserved in a nearby private residence, records that it was built in 1556.[5] In marked contrast, a few decades later the same family had the confidence to erect a very different, but still fortified, residence, at Coolhull near the south coast, incorporating the latest fashion in domestic and social arrangements. The layout may have been influenced by the principal Devereux residence at Ballymagir, which comprised a tower house with a later hall offset at one end. A similar arrangement was used at the nearby castle of Scar.

The Coolhull building consists of a rectangular three-storey house, with a small entrance tower offset to the west. The masonry of both elements is relatively intact, including stepped crenellations on house and tower. The arched entrance doorway of dressed granite was fortified by a machicolation and yett, and it was also covered by a gun-loop in the ground floor of the house. All levels were reached through doorways from a spiral stairway ascending through the tower. The first floor of the tower has a garderobe with a large oubliette underneath, reminiscent of the tower at Fethard. The first and second

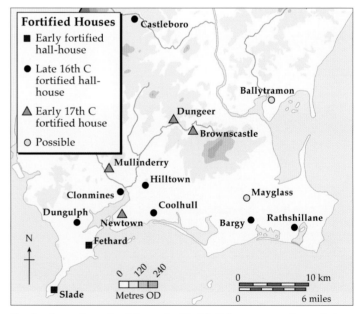

Fig. 3 Apart from Castleboro, fortified hall-houses were located close to the safety of the south coast. Several early seventeenth-century fortified houses were adjacent to the fringe of the Pale.

NEVILLE DUKES

Fig. 4   An interior view of Coolhull, showing two roof lines from different phases on the side of the tower; doorways from the tower to the house; corbels for supporting the first and attic floors, and the fireplace and chimney on the right. A gun-loop to the right of the ground-floor doorway covers the main entrance. The lookout turret can be seen at top left.

Fig. 5   Coolhull fortified hall-house from the rear. Gun-loops in offset of the tower, in the angle of the battlements, and in the corner machicolation on the right, provide cover for the house wall.

Fig. 6   Coolhull details: **A** Granite doorway with holes for yett and gun-loop on the left. **B** Corner machicolation with gun-loops. **C** Spiral stairway with generous steps in the tower.

N. L. I.

Fig. 7   As this late eighteenth-century image shows, Bargy Castle was very similar to Coolhull. Although now restored and modified as part of a dwelling, with several extensions, the fabric of the late sixteenth-century fortified house, retaining many original features, can still be identified.

floors have small chambers, with a larger one on the third floor. A doorway from this level leads to the wall-walk and battlements of the house. A narrower spiral stairs continues to the top of the tower and lookout platform. All windows, including a gun-loop on the first floor, are narrow slits.

The ground floor of the house has eight slit windows, as in tower houses, but lacked vaulting. The hall was positioned on the first floor, with five single- and two double-light windows, all round-headed. The north wall contains an impressive fireplace but a second one in the east wall has been removed. The second fireplace implies that part of the hall was partitioned off as a private space for the immediate family. The attic on the second floor has four slit windows. The battlements have a gun-loop at the south-east angle and a square corner machicolation with gun-loops at the north-east.[6]

The Rossiters of Rathmacknee Castle were responsible for erecting the fortified hall-house at Bargy, three miles to the south of their main residence. Now incorporated in a

Fig. 8   The lookout platform at Bargy Castle, manned by three trustworthy and ever-vigilant retainers. The turret affords extensive views over the south of the county.

Fig. 9 This plaque over the doorway of Bargy Castle formerly bore the Rossiter coat-of-arms surrounded by heads with Elizabethan ruffs, possibly representing members of the Rossiter family, the builders of the castle. This was replaced by the de Burgh coat-of-arms, presumably in the 1960s, when the property was acquired by a member of that family.

Fig. 10 The tower of Bargy Castle from the wall-walk, showing the original roofline on the Elizabethan chimney stack. The door from the tower to the wall-walk is at bottom, right of centre.

modern residence and extensively altered and extended, many features of the original edifice can still be recognised. In general, the design and size resembles Coolhull but some variations are apparent. Unlike Coolhull, one of the fireplaces in the hall was placed against the tower wall. It is set in a massive chimney breast which also supported the roof. Most windows have been enlarged except for those in the tower, some of which were mere gun-loops. As at Coolhull, the first floor of the tower has a garderobe and oubliette. A doorway from the second floor of the tower leads to the wall-walk, which has a corner machicolation on the north-east angle. The entrance doorway, protected by a yett and machicolation, has a curved top and hood moulding, signifying a later date than Coolhull. The doorway and moulding at Enniscorthy Castle, re-built in the mid-1580s, are almost identical, placing Bargy Castle in the same timeframe. A date of 1591, preserved on wooden panelling in the castle, must therefore record the construction date.[7]

The fortified hall-house at Dungulph, near Fethard in the barony of Shelburne, was erected by a branch of the

Whittys of Ballyteige.[8] This structure, although smaller, is similar to Coolhull and Bargy, with one significant variation. At Dungulph, the offset service tower is replaced by a circular tower at the north-east angle, housing a spiral stairs leading to the upper floors and presumably to the wall-walk and corner machicolation. It also gave entry to a garderobe from which gun-loops covered the north wall. Renovation as a dwelling in 1917 modified and obscured many original features.

Some are illustrated in mid-nineteenth-century drawings. These show that the entrance doorway, with hood moulding, resembled both Bargy and Enniscorthy, indicating a date in the last decades of the sixteenth century. The doorway, guarded by a machicolation and

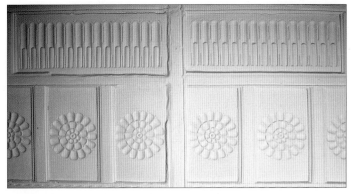

Fig. 11 A date of 1591 (not shown) is preserved on panelling at Bargy Castle, indicating its construction in the late sixteenth century.

R.S.A.I.

Fig. 12 This drawing by Du Noyer from the mid-nineteenth-century shows that the fortified hall-house at Dungulph differed significantly from Coolhull and Bargy. The circular stairway tower is at the north-east angle and does not contain the entrance. Note the hood moulding over the windows and doorway, dating the structure to the late sixteenth century.

yett, is not positioned in the tower but gives direct entry to the house. Historic drawings show that the larger windows of the first-floor hall originally had hood mouldings also. The slit windows lighting the stairway in the tower are intact, as well as gun-loops covering the doorway and east wall. The west and south walls were guarded by the corner machicolation on the south-west corner. The unusual circular tower may have been influenced by the similar, but earlier, tower at nearby Fethard Castle.

The fortified hall-house at Hilltown, a short distance south of the river Corock, which formed the boundary of the Wexford Pale, is attributed to the FitzHenrys of Kilcavan. Like Coolhull and Bargy, it is a three-storey house with a four-storey tower offset at one end. Hilltown

Fig. 13 A modified corner machicolation at Dungulph, positioned to provide cover for the doorway and the front and side walls.

R.I.A.

Fig. 14 Wakeman's 1840 drawing depicts a roofed Hilltown Castle with architectural features, including an entrance doorway in the tower but no machicolation. The offset tower has two chimneys, one serving a fireplace on the first-floor hall of the house. The house has slit windows on the ground floor and windows with hood moulding in the hall. The crenellations are lacking but a corner machicolation is positioned on the angle of the house, which has a pronounced base-batter.

is the smallest of the group, with plain battlements and a gentle wall batter. Part of a farmyard complex, it has been considerably altered, particularly by the insertion of an nineteenth-century corn mill in the tower. The internal arrangements are not clear as the tower was completely gutted to facilitate the mill, and walls have been breached in several places. However, sufficient original features survive to allow for a tentative description of the building, facilitated by two historic drawings from the mid-nineteenth century.[9]

The original doorway has been removed but its position is marked by a breach in the tower wall, corresponding to the doorways at Coolhull and Bargy. This opening is protected by a loop in the first-floor wall of the house. The tower has two original double-light and several slit windows, mostly blocked up. Unusually, a chimney stack in the tower wall serviced a first-floor fireplace in the hall. The windows in the house reveal that the hall was on the first floor, as in the other three hall-houses. Three slit windows are shown on one wall of the ground floor in historic drawings, with presumably a similar number on the opposite wall. The first floor has four rectangular matching windows, two with double lights and all with square hood moulding. One on the east wall has been extended downwards to create a doorway reached by external stone steps, probably when the building operated as a mill.

The fireplace is on the first floor of the house on the north wall, with the chimney flue in the tower wall. The fenestration on the second floor is more generous than in

R.S.A.I.

Fig. 15   This *c.* 1850 watercolour of Hilltown Castle by Du Noyer shows some changes since Wakeman's drawing of 1840. A building with a bellcote has been added on to the tower. The hall is still roofed but much of the tower, including the entrance, is obscured by the attached building.

R.I.A.

Fig. 16   Similar doorways with hood mouldings in the castles of (from left) Dungulph, Bargy and Enniscorthy, intimating that they were contemporary. Enniscorthy Castle has an established date, as it was built by Henry Wallop in the 1580s, which places the fortified hall-houses in a similar timeframe, corresponding with a 1591 date preserved on wooden panelling in Bargy Castle.

Fig. 17 Hilltown Castle at the present time. The structure was much altered by the insertion of a corn mill in the nineteenth century, which resulted in the blocking up of windows and the removal of all internal features from the tower. A window at first-floor level was enlarged to make a door, reached by stone steps. A blocked-up doorway (**A**) in the tower opened to the wall-walk.

the rest of the group. Three double-light and two single-light windows hint at a greater domestic use for this floor and perhaps a slightly later date. A fireplace, with projecting flue on the west wall, is another indication that this space was used extensively as a family area. No evidence of vaulting, garderobes, stairway or comm-unication between tower and house can be detected, apart from a blocked-up doorway at second-storey level in the wall of the tower. This led to the wall-walk of the house and the corner machicolation on the south-west corner. The destroyed battlements of the house were presumably similar to the extant plain ones on the tower.[10]

All four buildings in this group were constructed by leading settler families in the south of the county. The new design was inspired by a desire for enhanced household comfort but also with the purpose of proclaiming social standing. In an environment of sporadic raiding, the opportunity to implement an integrated defence system based on the wholesale

Fig. 18 Rectangular mullioned windows with hood moulding in Hilltown Castle indicate a late sixteenth-century construction date.

Fig. 19 A gable of a two-storey Jacobean house at Clonmines. The remains of a corner machicolation can be seen on the left side of the wall.

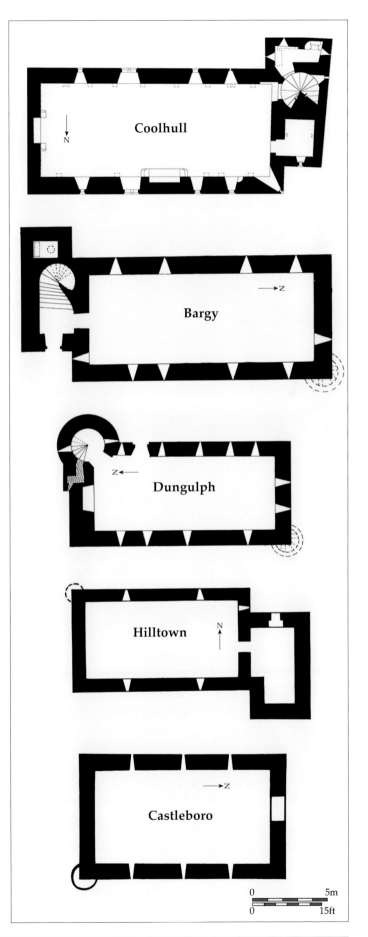

adoption of handguns was also a factor. The design of the windows and traditional tower-house doorway at Coolhull, erected by the Devereuxes of Ballymagir, point to it being the prototype for the group. As the Devereuxes were among the elite in the county, this set an architectural standard to be emulated by their peers, motivated by both practical and social considerations.

Compared to the longevity of the tower house, the life-span of the fortified hall-house was short. The evolution in design implies that the Coolhull-type castles represented an architectural transition from tower houses with attached halls to the residences of the seventeenth century. After a sustained period of enforced spartan living conditions in cramped tower houses, this rapid change can be attributed to the defensive potential of firearms, as well as an awareness of how improving standards in design enhanced domestic comfort and social status. The new architectural model did not remain static but was subject to experimentation, particularly in relation to the service tower. A further phase in that progression consisted of the tower being abandoned altogether. This is evident in two late sixteenth-, early seventeenth-century buildings in contrasting landscapes.

Fig. 20 The relative footprints of fortified hall-houses. The structures at Coolhull and Bargy are similar in size and design. Windows and internal door at Hilltown, and windows at Dungulph and Castleboro Demesne, are speculative. An architectural progression can be seen from the complex structure at Coolhull to the simplified layout at Castleboro.

CON BOGAN, NMSPU

Fig. 21   The fortified house at Rathshillane, on the western shore of Lady's Island lake, represents another step in the progression from late medieval tower house to eighteenth-century 'big house'. The tower element is discarded altogether in favour of a rectangular, but heavily fortified, house. This view from the west shows the house with slight batter, one- and two-light rectangular windows and corbelled chimneys at west and east, projecting high above the battlements. The presence of two fireplaces on the first floor indicates that this was the principal domestic space.

Fig. 22   This view of Rathshillane reveals the doorway with remains of a machicolation. A niche over the door presumably contained the coat-of-arms of the French family. The building was equipped with fifteen gun-loops on the ground floor, with corner machicolations on the angles. The damage to the south wall was caused by the collapse of the garderobe chute. The fabric of this unique transitional house has been seriously compromised by recent intrusive development.

Fig. 23   **A** Corner machicolation. **B** First-floor fireplace with granite lintel at Rathshillane.

Fig. 24   The modified, three-storey house at Castleboro, lacking a vault, was probably built by the Butlers in the late sixteenth/early seventeenth century. Defensive features included a yett protecting the entrance, a bartizan (below right) supported on corbels, and a lookout platform.

At Rathshillane, on the western shore of Lady's Island lake, a dwelling attributed to the Frenchs of Ballytory consisted of a fortified house without the service tower of the earlier examples. The three-storey house, similar in size to Dungulph, is entered by a doorway with a curved lintel, guarded by the ubiquitous machicolation. The entrance leads directly to the ground floor, lacking a vault, with up to six single-light rectangular windows. There is no evidence for the stairway, which was presumably made of timber.

Although situated in the secure south-east of the county, concern for protection is shown by the presence of fifteen gun-loops in the external walls of the ground floor. The first floor was supported on joists inserted directly into the wall. The hall, situated on this floor, had one single-light and five two-light rectangular windows. Fireplaces on the east and north walls indicate that the room was divided into two living areas. The second floor, with two double-light and three single-light windows, had a fireplace and garderobe, showing that it was also used as a living space. The stepped battlements are substantially intact, with corner machicolations at the north-east and south-west angles. The fabric of this small elegant structure has been compromised by regrettably intrusive development.

The only other building comparable to Rathshillane is found in the west of the county, at Castleboro in the

Fig. 25   The first edition of the Ordnance Survey records a 'castle in ruins' at Newtown, Bannow. The ruins have been removed but a mid-nineteenth-century drawing by Du Noyer depicts a two-storey fortified house. This is suggested by the string-course marking the roofline and by the corbelled-out feature on the side of the wall, which may have been a machicolation. The structure may have been similar in design to Rathshillane.

foothills of the Blackstairs. Probably built by the Butlers in the early seventeenth century, it has a somewhat bigger footprint than Rathshillane, with three floors and an attic but no vault. Windows and other original features have been altered. A fireplace at second-floor level indicates that this was the principal living space. The use of a yett to defend the entrance doorway hints at the threat posed by the proximity of the forests of the Duffry and the Fassagh of Bantry. This is also shown in the bartizan rising on corbels from second-floor level and a small lookout platform on the parapet at the south-west angle.

The possibility that other similar buildings have been removed from the landscape is intimated by an illustration of a now vanished edifice, at Newtown, Bannow.[11] The two-storey structure, described as 'the ancient house of the Siggins', had a rectangular two-light window at second-floor level, with a machicolation-like feature on one wall. The fragmentary remains of a structure at Brownscastle, overlooking the 'pill' which formed the boundary of the Wexford Pale, may have been in the same category.[12]

The concept of the fortified hall-house evolved from a series of strategies used to integrate a house with an existing tower house. This process went through several iterations, perhaps culminating in the late sixteenth-

century example at Taylorstown. This architectural model was refined in the fortified hall-houses at Coolhull, Bargy and Hilltown, where a door in the tower controlled admission to the whole complex. This approach was short-lived. At Dungulph, the tower was reduced to a stairway turret with the doorway in the wall of the house, while the tower was dispensed with completely at Rathshillane. In spite of other design changes, the corner machicolation was retained into the early seventeenth century as an indispensable defensive (and perhaps decorative) element.

The survival of only four examples of this building type suggests that there was no widespread inclination to abandon traditional tower houses with their attached halls. The fact that these were typically situated at manorial and parish centres with an established infrastructure while the new hall-houses were all on 'green-field' sites supports this view. The small number of fortified hall-houses suggests that most families were content to remain in their traditional dwellings, sometimes abandoning the tower house and developing the attached house, several of which are still occupied. This continuity is evident from the number of surviving tower houses that have an adjoining or adjacent house, mostly in ruins and frequently associated with a farmyard complex.

ENDGAME

At a national level, the movement away from tower house construction was stimulated by an inevitable progression in social and domestic requirements, as well as innovations in the design of firearms and artillery. In many instances, by the 1590s, earlier tower houses were old, decrepit and no longer desirable for domestic use. Everyday living was normally conducted in the adjoining house, with the tower retained as a place of refuge should the need arise. In county Wexford, the defensive use of firearms was reflected in the design of some late tower houses, mostly in strategic frontier locations. The impressive tower house at Adamstown, located north of the Wexford Pale, combined generous domestic arrangements with a complex array of gun-loops. However, in the small, fortress-like tower houses at Ferrycarrig and Sigginshaggard, both equipped with gun-loops and near the borders of the Pale, defence took precedence over domestic comfort.

The emergence of fortified hall-houses in south Wexford in the late sixteenth century signalled a move from the iconic tower house form that had dominated the landscape for two centuries. Elsewhere in Ireland, there is some evidence for the building of tower houses in the early seventeenth century.[1] Surviving examples in county Wexford suggest that tower house building was contemporaneous with fortified hall-houses, but was phased out by the end of the sixteenth century.

A late example at Stokestown, close to the Barrow just south of New Ross, with no vaulting or base- batter and mullion and transom windows, with hood moulding, still retained the traditional verticality of the tower house. This was possibly an expression of the awareness of the dangers associated with the Fassagh of Bantry, a short distance to the north. A drawing of a small tower (now removed), possibly at Tullycanna, depicts it with Tudor style diamond-shaped chimney stacks. The 'pacification' of Wexford by the plantation in 1610 may explain the apparent absence of early seventeenth-century tower houses in the county.

As well as rendering tower houses ineffective, the escalating capabilities of firearms (particularly artillery) led to a divergence of defensive and domestic requirements. These provoked the emergence of new, non-domestic military fortifications at strategic locations, designed to withstand assault by cannon.[2] In 1581, access to the county was defended by a fort, erected by Henry Wallop and Anthony Colclough at Coolyhune, near St Mullins in the present county Carlow, to control the Barrow valley and the Pollmounty Gap between the river and the Blackstairs. By the end of the sixteenth century, there were forts at the entrance to Wexford Harbour, at Duncannon on Waterford Harbour and at Passage on the opposite side.[3]

Fig. 1 In the late sixteenth century, the increasing use of firearms and artillery led to the construction of purpose-built military forts, which were better able to withstand bombardment by cannon. Duncannon Fort, shown here in a 1680s drawing by Thomas Phillips, was built in 1587 on a promontory on the eastern shore of Waterford Harbour to control the shipping lane, which was within easy range of its guns. Features depicted include a chapel, the barracks, the defences around the headland, and a dry moat and rampart on the landward side. The flag is an early version of the Union Jack. The weir in the foreground, dating to Cistercian times, supplied fish for the garrison. The fort was the focus of military activity in the county during the 1640s.

Fig. 2 The late three-storey tower house at Stokestown, overlooking the Barrow to the south of New Ross, with no batter or vault, has a two-light, mullioned window, with hood-moulding, on the second floor.

THE NINE YEARS WAR

As the sixteenth century neared its end, the New English officials became increasingly aggressive in their efforts to accumulate land and to impose English law on the 'Irish enemies' and 'English rebels'. This was opposed by both groups, united by their adherence to the old religion, resentment of the rigid imposition of English law and the denial of their civil liberties and religious freedom. In

Fig. 3 About 1620, the Etchinghams began the construction of a castle at Dunbrody. Apparently never completed, the existing remains, situated at the east end of a U-shaped court, have drum towers with gun loops, and fragments of three gables with projecting chimneys.

Gentlemen of the Barony of Forth 1608
(Hore, 'Forth', i, p. 97)

James Butler Butlerstown	**Hugh Rochford** Tagunnan
George Cheevers Killiane	**Richard Rochfort** Pettitstown
James Codd Ballyfane	**Matthew Shiggin** Sigginstown
Jasper Codd Clougheast	**Jasper Sinnott** Rathdowney
Martin Codd Castletown	**James Stafford** Grageen
Nicholas Codd Ballymacane	**John Stafford** Furziestown
John Devereux Mayglass	**Henry Synnott** Grahormack
John Esmond Rathlannon	**James Synnott** Bearlough
Robert Esmond Johnstown	**Martin Synnott** Ballybrennan
Patrick Fitznicholl Ballyconnor	**Nicholas Synnott** Ballyell
Walter French Ballytory	**Robert Synnott** Ballyrane
Matthew Hay Hayestown	**Simon Synnott** Ballygeary
Richard Hay Reedstown	**William Synnott** Grogan
William Hay The Hill	**John Turner** Ballysheen
William Hay Slad	**Philip Wadding** Assaly
John Hore Jonastown	**John Walsh** Pollrankin
Edward Keating Ballymacane	**Nicholas Walsh** The Bush
Paul Keating Ballybeg	**Nicholas White** Trimmer
Derry O'Doran Redmondstown	**Patrick Whitty** Ballycushlane

Fig. 4 A 1608 list of Gentlemen of the barony of Forth, with the townlands where they resided, shows that a number of families (Butler, Codd, Esmond, French, Hay, Siggin, Sinnott) continued to occupy lands granted to them in the early days of the colony. Tower houses were located at twenty of the locations mentioned. Derry O'Doran was the sole representative of the native Irish. The Sinnotts (7), Codds (4) and Hayes (4) were particularly prolific. Most of these were later involved in the Confederate War of the 1640s and subsequently lost their lands.

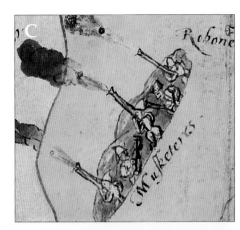

Fig. 5   During the Nine Years War, the siege of the Maguire castle at Enniskillen epitomised the impotence of a tower house against a modern army using firearms and artillery. The attacking army (**A**) is drawn up in battalions with flags flying, near their tented camps, armed with halberds and swords. A small number of musketeers, protected by trenches and a breastwork on wheels (known as a 'sow') are laying siege to the tower house (**B, C**). The defenders in the tower house are returning fire. A battery of five cannon has succeeded in breaching the bawn wall (**D, E**). Some of the attackers are in boats, one with a protective covering fitted with gun-loops. Boats on the river are moving supplies and firewood. The castle fell to the English in 1592 but it was retaken by the Irish in the following year. A gruesome detail (**F**) illustrates the barbaric English custom of impaling the heads of captured opponents on spikes. The siege emphasised the inadequacy of medieval fortifications against a modern European army equipped with the latest technology. This unequal conflict resulted in the abandonment of traditional castles and ultimately signalled the end of Gaelic Ireland.

Fig. 6 Bargy Castle, with various later extensions, continues to be occupied as a dwelling house. Although modified, the late sixteenth-century fortified hall-house at its core (similar to Coolhull Castle in design) is still identifiable. Many original architectural features survive, particularly in the tower.

1579, the growing provocation ignited a rebellion in Munster; a force of Spaniards and Italians landed at Smerwick, confirming English fears of an attack by their Catholic enemies in Europe, using Ireland as a point of entry. The rebellion was crushed with brutal severity, followed by the dispossession of participating landowners. The subsequent plantation was unsuccessful, but set a template for similar strategies in the future.[4] By the 1590s, Ulster remained the last bastion of Irish control, where the great lords were determined to maintain their sovereignty and to resist the encroachment of English law and ownership. By 1595, the Ulster lords were in rebellion, led by Hugh O'Neill, earl of Tyrone, and Red Hugh O'Donnell of Tír Chonaill, engaged in a contest that would decide the future of Gaelic Ireland and the outcome of the Tudor conquest.[5]

Confining his activities to Ulster, O'Neill enjoyed considerable success in the early years of the war. In Wexford, Dómhnall Spáineach Kavanagh rose in rebellion, supported by the O'Byrnes and O'Tooles, in an attempt to recover his former lands. In 1598, he inflicted a heavy defeat on a force led by Wallop, Masterson and Colclough and re-occupied his lost lands, until ousted by Wallop and Masterson following the Treaty of Mellifont (1603). After the war, the lands of some Irish landowners were confiscated, particularly in the Duffry, most of which were acquired by Thomas Colclough of Tintern Abbey.[6] However, not all Irish landowners were dispossessed. In

Fig. 7 Only the ground floor, with a double barrel-vault, remains of the Devereux tower at Ballymagir. The early, offset hall has been re-modelled as a modern dwelling. Some original details are still in evidence.

Fig. 8   Conservation works carried out by successive owners, particularly the Boxwells and Skrines, have made the four-storey Butlerstown Castle, with restored roof, loft floor and portcullis, one of the best maintained tower houses in the county. The roof, in particular, contributes to the preservation of the fabric by keeping out the rain. A lowering of the external ground level resulted in the construction of the plinth and steps up to the doorway.

Fig. 9   In some instances, as at Butlerstown, an eighteenth- or nineteenth-century residence was constructed within the same farmyard complex, but not connected with the late medieval tower house.

Fig. 11   The French tower house at Ballytory, which probably had an attached hall, was integrated with a later dwelling. Original fabric can be identified in the modified tower house (at right of picture).

1635, Sir Morgan Kavanagh, living in his 'old, high, narrow castle with narrow and steep stairs', still held lands at Clonmullen in County Carlow near Bunclody.[7]

In 1601, the long awaited aid from Spain finally landed at Kinsale on the south coast, where the Spanish force was besieged by the English army. O'Neill, forced to march south to relieve the Spaniards, was defeated by the English just outside Kinsale. Tyrone continued in arms until 1603 when he submitted under the terms of the Treaty of Mellifont (1603). Four years later, unable to accept the new order, O'Neill took ship from Lough Swilly, accompanied by Rory O'Donnell, earl of Tír Chonaill and ninety of the leading men of Ulster, and sailed into voluntary exile on the continent. The Battle of Kinsale and the subsequent 'flight of the earls' gave England control over all of Ireland, signalling the end of the Gaelic lordships and the demise of the old Irish world.[8]

Fig. 10   At Longgraigue, the tower house (with pointed roof) was integrated with a later dwelling. Some original features survive.

In the turbulent political situation following the Nine Years War, defended residences continued to be built in Wexford into the early seventeenth century. At Clonmines, a fragment of a small Jacobean dwelling, probably of one storey and attic, has the remains of a corner machicolation on one angle, suggesting that it was fitted with the usual defensive features. Likewise, at Dungeer, just north of Taghmon, a surviving section of the walls of a T-shaped house has gun-loops on the ground floor. An early seventeenth-century house at Mullinderry on the east bank of the Owenduff river is still occupied. Similar in size to Coolhull and consisting of two storeys and an attic, the building has a large chimney projection on the south gable and the remains of a corner machicolation on the north-west angle.[9]

The Plantation of North Wexford
In the aftermath of the Nine Years War, the English authorities believed that the best tactic for anglicising the Irish was via 'control through acculturation'. In the early seventeenth century, a policy of plantation was revived to attract colonists and settlers from Britain. The population of Ireland, as low as 750,000 in 1600, had been reduced even further by emigration to continental Europe and America. Apart from the organised plantations, individual landlords promoted a movement of British tenants and artisans to Irish estates. In 1608, a plantation was initiated in Ulster which involved the relocation of the native Irish into specified areas and the 'planting' of the cleared lands with English and Scottish owners (known as undertakers and servitors) with their imported tenants. The scheme was widely implemented but the removal of all of the Irish proved to be impractical and many remained in place.[10]

Early Seventeenth-Century Plantation Castles

Wingfield
(Ballynabarney)
Wingfield
Newtown
Coole-
*Sexton-
Ford*
Carnew
Limerick *Esmond*
Huntington *Esmond*
Monaseed
*Marwood-
Masterson*
Prospect
*Fisher-
Chichester*
Clohamon *Calvert*
Monasootagh
*Hibbotts-
Annesely*
Middletown
*Jones-
Esmond-
Sinnott*
Mountfin *Molyneux*
Milshoge
*Pierse-
Medhop-
Annesley*
Tomduff
*Parsons-
Cooke*
Ballycarney
*Corroll-Thornetone
Wade-Beirne*
Castleannesley
Annesley
Drumgold
Blundell-Wallop
Chichester-Trevelyan-
Fortesque-Annesely
Edermine *Kenny*
Ballyvoodock
Rahale
*Loftus-
Stafford*
Ballynaclash
*Langhorne-
Loftus-Cheevers*

0 120 240 450
Metres OD

N

0   10 km
0   6 miles

Fig. 12 Grantees who acquired land in the Wexford plantation were obliged to build castles 'to make that part of the county strong and defensible against an Irish enemy'. These castles were in the north and east, an area almost completely devoid of tower houses, resulting in the effective fortification of most of the county.

In county Wexford, a small settlement of English tenants had already been introduced around Enniscorthy by Henry Wallop. After the war, presumably because of the involvement of the Kavanaghs, a large plantation was proposed to pacify the Irish region of north Wexford. The crown already claimed title to considerable lands in the county following the dissolution of monastic land in 1541 and on the back of 'surrender and re-grant' schemes which began as early as the 1540s. The crown's claim was enhanced in 1610 by the 'discovery' of a dubious legal title to all the land between the Slaney and the sea, dating back to Richard II's confiscation in 1395. This region became the focus of the plantation of north Wexford by the Jacobean administration between 1610 and 1618.[11]

The implementation of the plantation was complex. The land was parcelled out in large estates to eighteen New English, known as undertakers, and in smaller estates to New English servitors and to existing

Fig. 13 The plantation castle at Ballycarney no longer exists but it was recorded by Wakeman in 1840. The complex consisted of a three-storey tower house and a bawn, of which one flanking tower is shown.

landowners (three Old English, three New English and four Irish). New boroughs were established at Enniscorthy and Newborough (Gorey) as centres of security, commerce and administration. The plantation revolutionised land ownership in the northern part of the county, with fewer people owning larger estates and the Irish share dropping to thirty-six per cent. However, there was little change in occupancy, as the native Irish remained as workers and tenants without title, although the Kavanaghs, 'a hardy and unquiet people', succeeded in recovering some lands in the Duffry.

In the expectation of inevitable opposition from the dispossessed Irish, grantees were instructed to finance

Fig. 14 The Wexford plantation served as a model for similar initiatives in the New World. George Calvert (Lord Baltimore), who acquired the manor of Clohamon in north County Wexford, also received a grant of land in Newfoundland, where he established a settlement at Ferryland on the Avalon peninsula. Archaeological excavations have uncovered extensive remains of Baltimore's settlement, which is well documented. The stone quayfront of Ferryland is shown above.

Fig. 15   The well-preserved Huntington Castle, just across the border in county Carlow, was built in 1625 by the Esmonds, an Old English family from Johnstown in south Wexford, on lands acquired at the time of the plantation. The original structure consisted of a rectangular three-storey tower with a half-circular staircase projection, with bartizan-like features on two corners.

'faire and strong castles, houses and bawnes' on their new estates. Eighteen plantation castles were built by recipients of lands in the Wexford plantation. Described as 'making that part of the county strong and defensible against an Irish enemy', they were predominantly in the region which was previously devoid of tower houses.[12] The whole county was now effectively fortified, eventually resulting in the demise of a Gaelic society that had persisted in the north of the county for centuries.

Apart from some pictorial evidence, little remains of plantation castles in the county. The well-preserved Huntington Castle at Clonegal, just across the border with county Carlow, presents an excellent example of the period. It was built c. 1625 by the Esmonds on lands acquired at the time of the plantation, a late example of an Old English family from Johnstown in south Wexford being involved to the north of the county. The original structure consisted of a rectangular three-storey tower with a half-circular staircase projection. It has affinities with plantation castles elsewhere in Ireland.

Fig. 16   Built before 1619, by Sir Henry Harrington, seneschal of the O'Byrne country, Carnew Castle, just over the Wicklow border, is a good example of a still substantially surviving plantation castle.

Fig. 17 Following the construction of a dwelling house close by, the fortified house adjoining the tower house at Slade was converted into apartments and rented to tenants on the Loftus Estate. This involved the insertion of doors and windows, the addition of annexes at each end and an external stairway giving access to the first floor. The building, shown here in a *c.* 1870 photograph, was occupied by tenants until the early twentieth century.

PRIVATE COLLECTION

Dunbrody Castle on the Etchingham estate also belongs to this period, although not associated with the plantation. Apparently never completed, the existing house, of at least two storeys, situated at the east end of a U-shaped court, has drum towers with gun-loops at each angle, as well as fragments of three gables with projecting chimneys.[13]

The Wexford plantation served as a template for similar initiatives in Ireland and also for successful colonies in the New World.[14] This was epitomised by the foundation of a settlement at Clohamon on the east bank of the Slaney, not acquired during the plantation, but purchased by George Calvert, Lord Baltimore, in 1625, who, as a Catholic, had left England in search of religious freedom. After a short stay at Clohamon, Calvert sailed for Newfoundland, where he had been granted a large estate. He decided to settle at Ferryland on the Avalon Peninsula. He later acquired land in Maryland, where a colony which became the city of Baltimore was established by his sons. The family retained an interest in the Baltimore estate at Clohamon until the 1740s.[15]

Hopes for a relaxation of anti-Catholic legislation on the accession of James I in 1603 were not realised and political and religious tensions in Ireland intensified. Although religious oppression continued to be of paramount concern, a renewed focus on the confiscation of land held by Catholics caused widespread consternation. Spectacular change was epitomised by the

wholesale transfer of land from Catholic to Protestant ownership.[16] The Catholics were mostly of old stock, either Gaelic or Anglo-Norman, who increasingly called themselves Old English to distinguish themselves from the native Irish and the newly arrived Protestant English. They also sought to exhibit their loyalty to the crown, even though by that time they had assimilated much of

KEVIN WHELAN

Fig. 18 Derelict castles were converted to many uses, particularly as farm buildings and storage areas. In the early twentieth century, Ferns Castle became the focus of a popular sporting activity, when the castle wall was used as the front wall of a handball alley.

Clonmullen Castle: William Brereton 1635

In this wood there runs a little river [the Clody] which divides the counties of Wexford and Carlow, over which when we had passed we went to Clonmullen, the castle and seat of Sir Morgan Kavanagh, who seems to be a very honest, fair-dealing man, and his lady a good woman, but both recusants [Catholics]. Here we were entertained with good beer, sack and claret, whereof he was no niggard. This castle and seat of Sir Morgan Kavanagh is an old, high, narrow, and inconvenient building; the stairs leading up into the dining-room mid chambers being narrow and steep, like a steeple stair; this also seated in a most solitary, melancholy place, woods on two sides and plains on the other; these are moors and mountains, whereon they say there are wolves. This also is in the Dufferie, which hath always been reputed a thievish place, but Sir Morgan being demanded, said that the sixteen rebels before-named were most conversant about Ross and in the county of Kilkenny.

Fig. 19   Fethard Castle was taken and garrisoned by the Confederates and subsequently used by them as a rendezvous and recruiting centre.

Gaelic culture. Following the accession of Charles I to the throne in 1625, the political situation in England unravelled rapidly and the king offered concessions, known as 'the graces,' to Irish Catholics in return for £40,000. The inevitable resentment generated by the failure to implement the promised reforms further alienated the Catholic community.[17]

THE REBELLION OF 1641

Against a background of political, economic and religious friction in Britain and Ireland, the native Irish and Old English, forced into an uneasy alliance, contemplated rebellion. From 1620 to 1650, political upheaval was widespread across Europe, where the Thirty Years' War was raging. The situation was exacerbated by the eruption of Civil War in England between king and parliament in 1642, with the Scots entering the war on the side of parliament. In Ireland, the rising had started in Ulster in 1641, the insurgents claiming not to be rebels but supporters of the king.[18] In the early years, the response to the repression and violence of the previous century exploded in vicious retaliations against Protestant settlers, particularly in Ulster. This onslaught was flagrantly exaggerated to create a massacre myth for propaganda purposes.[19]

In 1642, a meeting of the Confederate Catholics at Kilkenny established an executive supreme council as well as a legislative general assembly. The rebellion spread quickly to county Wexford, where 2,300 men were mustered: Wexford town became one of the principal ports of the Confederation.[20] In anticipation of a siege,

extensive work was carried out on the town defences and the harbour was fortified by a timber boom stretching from Ferrybank towards Pole (now Paul) Quay. The fort at the mouth of the harbour on Rosslare Point was reinforced and armed with nine cannon guns. A fortification known as Fort Margaret was begun on the Raven Point, the northern arm of the harbour entrance.[21] However, it is not clear if it was ever completed as it apparently played no part in subsequent events. The traditional empathy with Catholic Spain was expressed in the town by displaying the Spanish colours, with the slogan 'God bless the king of Spain, for but for him we should all be slain'. [22]

The next decade brought the most dramatic period of conflict and social upheaval in the history of the county.[23] Duncannon Fort, dominating access to the ports of Waterford and New Ross, was the focus of initial military activity. The only modern military fortification in the county, the high-profile fort was besieged sporadically by

Fig. 20   When a company of government soldiers attacked the Whitty castle at Dungulph, sixteen of them were killed by Confederate troops.

Fig. 21   A fanciful impression of the attack on Redmond Hall, showing the soldiers from Duncannon Fort under attack from a Confederate force, which came to support the Redmonds, alerted by the sound of gunfire. The family continued to occupy the Hall but surrendered to Cromwellian forces in 1649. This image of the hall, with the wool-sacks that allegedly blocked the windows, was used in the design of the Redmond coat-of-arms.

Confederate forces.[24] During endemic skirmishes in the vicinity, tower houses and fortified houses were occupied and targeted by both sides, signalling the dying throes of medieval fortifications in the face of ever-improving firearms and artillery. Fethard Castle was taken by a group of rebels and held as a Confederate headquarters.

Ballyhack Castle, another Confederate strongpoint just up-river from Duncannon Fort, was pounded by cannon fire from a parliament ship in the estuary and the village was burned by a raiding party. In 1642, a detachment of soldiers from Duncannon captured twenty-three Confederate troops in Ramsgrange Castle; the castle and village were burned and eighteen of the prisoners were hanged. When a company of government soldiers laid siege to the Whitty castle at Dungulph, sixteen of them were killed by a group of Confederate troops. Tintern Abbey (referred to as Tintern Castle), garrisoned by thirty soldiers from Duncannon Fort, was attacked by a group of Confederates and, after a siege lasting a fortnight, was obliged to surrender.[25]

The bloodiest skirmish took place in July 1642, when Captain Ashton brought ninety men by sea from Duncannon Fort to attack Redmond Hall on the Hook, where the occupants put up a stiff resistance. When a heavy fog descended, a party of 200 Confederates approached the hall unseen and defeated the attackers with great loss of life. Seventeen were taken prisoner and later hanged, some at Ballyhack Castle, in retaliation for the earlier hangings at Ramsgrange. In 1645, after two months of fierce exchanges, Duncannon Fort surrendered and it was occupied by the Confederates, who held it until the arrival of the Cromwellian forces.

The revenues from the Etchingham, Colclough and Loftus lands were requisitioned for the support of the fort. By the end of the decade, the Confederacy had degenerated into acrimonious factions and the country was reduced to destitution by war. Nevertheless, the Confederate Catholic regime that controlled much of Ireland from 1642 until 1649 has been described as 'one of the most successful revolts in early modern history'.[26] The ultimate failure of the rebellion proved to be devastating, as it prompted Cromwell's brutal campaign of retribution and the annihilation of the Catholic landowning elite.

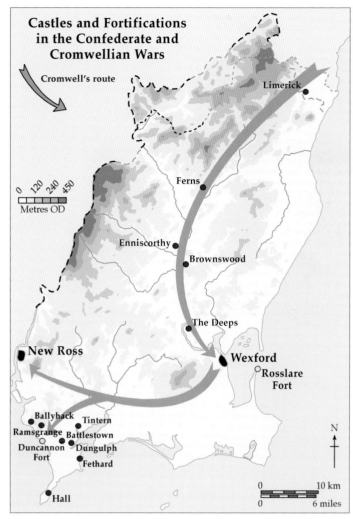

Castles and Fortifications in the Confederate and Cromwellian Wars

Cromwell's route

Metres OD
0 120 240 450

Limerick

Ferns

Enniscorthy

Brownswood

The Deeps

New Ross

Wexford

Rosslare Fort

Ballyhack
Tintern
Ramsgrange
Battlestown
Duncannon Fort
Dungulph
Fethard

Hall

N

0   10 km
0   6 miles

Fig. 22 Castles involved in the Confederate War and the Cromwellian campaign are concentrated in the vicinity of Duncannon Fort and along the route of Cromwell's march from Drogheda to Wexford town.

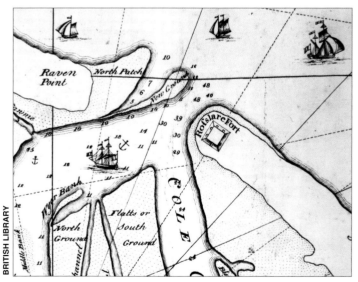

Raven Point
North Patch
New Ground
Rosslare Fort
Wyer Bank
North Ground
Flatts or South Ground
COLE

Fig. 23 A late eighteenth-century map shows the commanding position of Rosslare Fort at the entrance to Wexford Harbour. The late sixteenth-century fort was reinforced by the Confederates and armed with nine cannon. It quickly fell to Cromwell's troops, giving his ships free access to the harbour.

Fig. 24 Brownswood Castle, on the east bank of the Slaney below Enniscorthy, was taken from the Confederates by Cromwellian soldiers. During the siege, the occupants blew up two barrels of gunpowder, which may have contributed to the present dilapidated state of the structure.

CROMWELL

In 1649, Oliver Cromwell, leader of the victorious parliamentarian army, landed at Dublin with a highly trained, well-equipped army of 12,000 men, determined to avenge alleged massacres of Protestants and to impose government authority by implementing a policy of 'conquest, confiscation and colonisation'.[27] After the ruthless sacking of Drogheda, Cromwell marched south to lay siege to Wexford, the 'Dunkirk of Ireland and a place only famous for being infamous' and made camp outside the town.[28] On route, the castles of Limerick, Ferns and Enniscorthy were taken and garrisoned. Brownswood Castle, on the east bank of the Slaney below Enniscorthy, was later recovered from the Confederates.[29]

Cromwell's army camped outside Wexford and prepared for a siege. The garrison abandoned the fort on Rosslare Point, which was then occupied by the Cromwellians.[30] This allowed siege guns to be landed, which were positioned on Trespan Rock to the south of the town. As the town wall had been ramparted with clay, cannon fire was directed on the castle, which was quickly breached.[31] The Cromwellian soldiers took the castle, stormed the walls and sacked the town. In Cromwell's own words, his soldiers 'put all to the sword that came in their way … not many less than 2,000'. A selfish regret was expressed by Cromwell himself for the destruction of the town, as it would have made excellent winter accommodation for his army, but its tribulations were seen as a 'just judgement' by God on the greedy inhabitants for the way that they had mistreated 'divers poor Protestants'.[32]

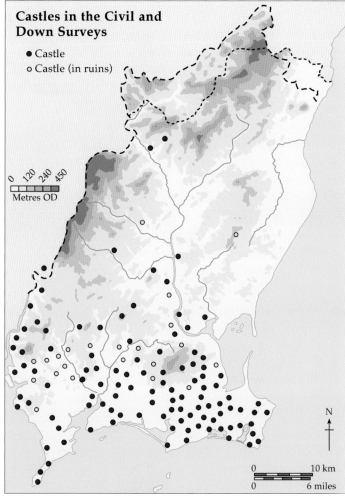

Castles in the Civil and Down Surveys

- ● Castle
- ○ Castle (in ruins)

0 120 240 450
Metres OD

N

0   10 km
0   6 miles

Fig. 25 The locations of 'castles' recorded in the mid-seventeenth-century *Civil Survey* correspond closely to the distribution of tower houses. Castles described as being in ruins are concentrated in the frontier region between the Irish north and the southern English Pale.

From Wexford, Cromwell marched on New Ross where a surrender was negotiated.[33] The garrison at Duncannon was an obvious target and, after the fall of Ross, the fort was besieged by 2,000 troops, accompanied briefly by Cromwell himself and initially under the command of General Michael Jones. The Cromwellian forces occupied Tintern Abbey and other small castles in the vicinity, and they controlled the river from Ballyhack Castle and the fort at Passage. As the situation became hopeless, Duncannon Fort was eventually surrendered in 1650.

The aftermath of the Confederate rebellion revolutionised subsequent political and social life.[34] After 'the war that finished Ireland', the Act of Settlement decreed that the lands of more than 10,000 Catholic landowners were to be confiscated and granted to the Cromwellians who had helped Parliament to defeat the Confederates, either as investors (known as 'adventurers') or soldiers who were to be paid in land. A small fraction of the dispossessed, with their families, were transplanted to

Connacht, where they received meagre lands in exchange. The demographic disaster was compounded by the shipping of up to 60,000 Irish soldiers to serve in continental armies and the transportation of 25,000 Irish men, women and children as cheap labour to the plantations of Virginia and the West Indies.

Two surveys were implemented to facilitate the confiscation of land: the *Civil Survey* (1654–56) established land ownership and value in 1640, while the *Down Survey* of 1654 mapped the lands that were to be forfeited.[35] The confiscations terminated four centuries of ownership by the descendants of the original Anglo-Norman colonists on the small manors in the southern part of the county, most of whom had assumed their hereditary leading role in the Confederate army.

THE TOWER-HOUSE GENTRY

The dispossessed families had an intimate association with tower houses over two centuries and their departure changed how tower houses were perceived and used by new owners. The *Civil* and *Down Surveys* recorded 130 'castles', most of them tower houses, with only twenty-one described as being 'in ruins'. The ruins were mostly

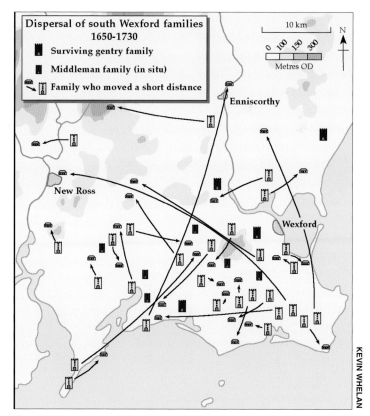

Dispersal of south Wexford families 1650-1730

- 🏰 Surviving gentry family
- 🏰 Middleman family (in situ)
- 🏰 Family who moved a short distance

0 100 150 300
Metres OD

10 km   N

Enniscorthy

New Ross

Wexford

Fig. 26 The impact of the Cromwellian confiscations disrupted a deep-rooted landowning class. However, many remained in the county and succeeded in renting alternative property. Some travelled considerable distances to acquire leaseholds but others became tenants close to their former holdings. This propinquity allowed the dispossessed to continue as a cohesive group and to maintain their sense of community.

KEVIN WHELAN

KITTY KEATING

Fig. 27   Many of the dispossessed remained as tenants on the lands which they formerly owned, and continued to be regarded as the legitimate leaders of their communities. Their residences in the baronies of Forth and Bargy are typified by this substantial thatched house at Yoletown with its courtyard enclosure, which echoes the medieval moated sites and tower-house bawns of earlier centuries.

sited along the border of the Wexford Pale and in the northern part of Shelburne, exposed to raids from the Fassagh of Bantry. Their dilapidated condition might indicate a combination of an early building date and abandonment. More than 100 tower houses, with attached dwellings, mostly in the southern baronies, were available as residences to the recipients of the confiscated lands and it would have been practical to occupy them for a considerable time.

The vivid memories of the 1640s and an awareness of the inevitable resentment of the dispossessed encouraged the retention of the tower houses as places of refuge. An account of the barony of Forth written in the 1680s shows that this was the case. It stated that the mansion houses of the gentry were fortified with quadrangular castles, nearly sixty feet high. The houses, built with stone and slated, formerly had fire-hearths in the middle of the halls but these had been replaced by spacious chimneys, possibly by the new owners.[36] These 'spacious chimneys' survive at several sites, including Mulrankin, Skar and Slade.

The dispossessed Catholic elite in county Wexford and elsewhere continued to be regarded as an 'underground' gentry, either as tenants on the lands which they had formerly owned or in exile. They were viewed with suspicion by the authorities because of their perceived connections with England's Catholic enemies on the continent. However, not all of the dispossessed left Wexford. Many remained as tenants on their former lands or in the near vicinity, and they continued to provide priests for the church and political leadership for their communities.[37] They retained their identity as a cohesive grouping, preserving their distinctiveness as descendants of the first Anglo-Norman colonists.

For example, in the late seventeenth century, Nicholas French, bishop of Ferns, left a bursary to the Irish College in Louvain for the education of young Wexford men, with preference given to the families of French, Rossiter, Browne and Devereux.[38] In his account of the 1798 Rebellion, Edward Hay established his pedigree by stating that his ancestors came over with Strongbow and held land in south Wexford by knight's fee until dispossessed by Cromwell.[39] This enduring sense of loss has been aptly expressed by the phrase 'only the dispossessed people know their lands in the dark'.[40] As late as 1900, this feeling of entitlement was demonstrated by a rebuke written on the margin of the 1771 estate maps of Loftus Hall by a descendant of the original Redmond owners, stating that 'Redmond Hall it was and Redmond Hall it will remain. The Loftus family obtained it by plunder and disloyalty'.[41]

Fig. 28   This late eighteenth-century illustration of Killiane Castle provides an excellent example of progressive development. The tower house was secured by the addition of a later bawn. An eighteenth-century house, with external doorway and connected to the tower by a passageway, was inserted along one side of the bawn wall. The exterior of the tower is maintained in good condition and the house has been refurbished to a high standard.

TOWER HOUSES ABANDONED

By the late seventeenth century, tower houses were old, dilapidated, uncomfortable and no longer suited to continuous occupation. An observation that 'the reason for the abandonment of castles was not Cromwell but neglect, damp and the inconvenience of climbing spiral staircases' offers an accurate assessment of the situation. The fate of the tower house depended on how they were regarded by the new owners. The creative use of the late medieval castles meant that tower houses were 'quarried, abused, adapted and reshaped', reflecting the architectural preferences of succeeding generations.[42]

The end result varied, depending on the preferred approach. The practicality of using the tower-house site with associated infrastructure was generally recognised but implemented with different strategies. In some instances, the attached house was upgraded, leaving the tower to deteriorate but retained as a symbol of inherited status. This approach was frequently adopted, with some houses occupied down to the present time, notably at Newcastle, Mulrankin, Ballyteige and Killiane (the best

Fig. 29   The vulnerability of surviving late medieval structures was demonstrated by the partial collapse of Mountgarrett tower house in 2011, following damage inflicted by sustained heavy frost.

example). At Ballybrennan, Ballytory, Bryanstown and Longgraigue, the tower and house were eventually integrated as one building, with many original features modified or removed. At some sites, notably Butlerstown, Ballycogley and Baldwinstown, the tower house was eventually abandoned in favour of a new dwelling within the same precinct. During the late seventeenth and early eighteenth centuries, dwellings were being constructed on sites not associated with tower houses. These houses, which retained some defensive features, for example at Clohamon and Dunmain, were the forerunners of the Georgian 'Big Houses' that would dominate the landscape of the county during the 1700s.[43]

Reflecting the suitability of their late sixteenth-century design, the fortified houses at Ballymagir, Bargy and Dungulph retain many original features but have been modified as modern residences. The most unusual adaptation occurred at Slade. Following the construction of a new dwelling in the early eighteenth century, the tower house and associated fortified house were converted into a 'tenement' by the Loftus estate. This involved the insertion of internal dividing walls and the addition of an external chimney and outside stairway, giving access to the first floor of the house. The 1872 estate papers recorded three families paying five shillings each per annum for accommodation in the 'old castle'.[44]

The enduring attraction of the tower house as an iconic landscape feature has led to their conservation at Ballyhealy, Butlerstown, Clougheast and Killiane. Conversely, the collapse at Lingstown in 1985 and Mountgarrett in 2011 highlights their vulnerability. Of sixty surviving towers, with fabric ranging from fragmentary to substantially complete, only three (Ballyhack, Rathmacknee, Slade) are in State care, plus the hall-house at Coolhull.

LEGACY

The imposition of Anglo-Norman feudalism on Ireland was a pivotal event that fundamentally influenced the subsequent evolution of political, social and cultural affairs, as well as the development of landscape character. In county Wexford, the pattern of settlement was dictated by geographical location and topographical variation. Proximity to Britain facilitated contact and made the county an attractive destination for prospective colonists, providing a sense of security, real or imagined. Landscape was an influential factor, with the heavily wooded, mountainous north and west contrasting strongly with the low-lying east and south.

However, the incomplete nature of the conquest generated inevitable confrontation with the Irish. The eventual control of the woods and mountains by the Irish and the occupation of the south by the colonists resulted in antagonism between upland and lowland, a widespread phenomenon not confined to county Wexford. Political control is easier to impose on lowland people, rather than on the dispersed populations of uplands, who can frustrate the expansionist ambitions of their lowland adversaries for centuries.[1] In county Wexford, the situation was exacerbated by the fact that the lowlanders were interlopers who had driven the mountain dwellers from their former territories. The colonists' use of English

Law, which differed greatly from the Brehon Law of the Irish, created a two-tier structure, which effectively underpinned a system of apartheid. The inexorable clash between the two cultures determined the political and social future of the county and of Ireland.

The legacy of the Anglo-Normans is manifested in the surviving landscape infrastructure and in cultural traits. The feudal landholding and administrative system created by their arrival established the matrix for castle building, which consolidated control over their conquered territory. In county Wexford, the conflict between colonist and native Irish was initially charted by the construction of a diagonal network of earthwork fortifications and thirteenth-century stone castles across the centre of the county, dividing the wooded and mountainous north and west from the settled regions to the south and east. However, these defences proved to be porous. By 1389, when Taghmon was described as being 'in the marches', the frontier between Irish and colonist had shifted even further south. From the late fourteenth century onwards, the settlers were confined to this southern region, consisting principally of the baronies of Forth, Bargy and the southern part of Shelmalier West, with an outlying group in the northern part of Shelburne, formerly the manor of the Island.

Fig. 1   The remaining stone elements in the deserted medieval town of Clonmines provide a sequence of fortified structures built over two centuries, collectively reflecting the former status of the town. These include the tower added to the medieval parish church (**A**), which is dated to *c.* 1400 by the presence of Dundry stone; a unique, fifteenth-century, fortified chapel/meeting house (**B**); two possibly fourteenth-century towers added to the Augustinian Priory (**C**); two fifteenth-century tower houses (**D**), and an early seventeenth-century fortified house (**E**).

Fig. 2 The use of Dundry stone in the tower added to Selskar Abbey in Wexford town suggests a construction date *c.* 1400. This is a clear indication that the expertise required to build tower houses was available in the county at that time. The battlements on the tower were restored in the early nineteenth century.

ARCHITECTURAL LEGACY

Unlike the Dublin Pale, which was fortified by a man-made bank and ditch, the English enclave in county Wexford was defined by topographical features. Bounded by the sea to the east, south and west, the survival of the colony owed much to the protection of river, gorge and high ground to the north. As in the Dublin Pale, a decision was made in 1441 to augment the natural defences of the 'English baronies' in county Wexford through a subsidy for building 'towers or castles' along the river known as the 'water of Taghmon', which formed the boundary of the Pale. The river was also dammed to create a more formidable obstruction. In 1552, the first recorded description of the region as the 'English Pale' acknow-ledged its exclusiveness.

The stimulus of a subsidy suggests that landholders had been slow to fortify their manors. There is no direct evidence that the incentive was crucial but it must have contributed to the profusion of towers, which gave the low-lying landscape of the Wexford Pale such a distinctive character. A combination of factors influenced the building and distribution of Wexford tower houses. These included the final division of the county between native

Irish and English colonist and the modest nature of medieval land grants in the south. The holders of these small manors remained in possession of their lands for four centuries and became the dominant force in the maintenance of the colony. They were the principal builders of tower houses, which became the favoured defended residences and status symbols in the turbulent late medieval period.

The descendants of early settlers in county Wexford preserved the tradition of their European origins, out of which the tower house evolved, both as emblems of prestige and as defences against incursions by Irish and English warlords. Similar to earlier keeps but smaller and more intimate, the tower house achieved a balance between domestic and defensive requirements. The origin of these small castles remains contentious, although there is some consensus that they first appeared in the late fourteenth century.[2] Around 1400, the south of the county was under constant threat and it is clear that some defended residences were constructed. Churches were fortified by the addition of towers and the bishop of Ferns was raising castles at Mountgarrett and Fethard, an indication that tower-building expertise was available. The surviving stone buildings in the deserted medieval town of Clonmines illustrate a tradition of tower building

Why civilisations can't climb hills by James Scott (2010)

State-making has always been the business of plains and lowland people. Inevitably, the process of expansion comes up against physical limits: elevated territories are intrinsically less accessible to their technologies and also less interesting economically in terms of their tax yield. For long centuries upland regions defined the limits of civilizations – political control sweeps readily across a flat terrain. Once it confronts the friction of distance, abrupt changes in altitude, ruggedness of terrain, and the political obstacle of population dispersion and mixed culti-vation, it runs out of political breath. In sum, lowland-based polities and their associated civilisations suffer from altitude sickness. What is involved are deliberate strategies of state evasion or state prevention, not chance movements of population. Hill societies operate in the shadow of lowland states. Hill peoples are best understood as runaway, fugitive, maroon communities who have, over the course of millennia, been fleeing the oppressions of state-making projects in the valleys – slavery, conscription, taxes, corvée labour, epidemics and warfare. Each represents an alternative pattern of subsistence, social organisation and power; each shadows the other in a complex relationship of mimicry and contradiction.

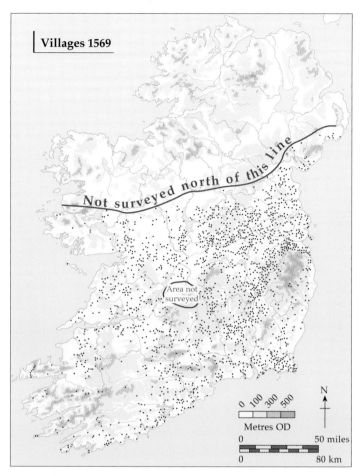

Villages 1569

Not surveyed north of this line

Area not surveyed

N

0 100 300 500
Metres OD

0   50 miles
0   80 km

Fig. 3   The sites of villages recorded on mid-sixteenth-century maps are mostly grouped around the Dublin Pale and also in the Wexford Pale, where their distribution corresponds to that of the tower houses around which the manorial villages were huddled.

Because of the late transition, many towers have survived, either as part of a later house or attached to it, frequently the habitations of lesser gentry. The proximity of new and old testifies to the long survival of an archaic lifestyle and an abrupt but uneven transition to the modern.[3]

Tower houses are the most prominent late medieval architectural features in the south Wexford landscape. Because of their ubiquity, they can be taken for granted but an appreciation of the complex reasons for their presence illuminates a crucial period in Wexford's history. Examples in the lowlands of south Wexford, especially in the context of ancillary buildings, emphasise their symbolic power and echo a former distinctive landscape character. Treatment of upstanding examples ranges from conservation to benign neglect and even destruction. An archaeological survey of existing towers and sites would facilitate a greater understanding of their origin and function. Apart from a few examples, the manorial villages associated with the tower houses, principally in Forth and Bargy, no longer exist. Their inclusion on several sixteenth-century maps proves that they were significant centres of late medieval settlement.[4]

The tower house spans the transition between medieval castles and the 'big house' of the eighteenth and nineteenth centuries. The presence of defensive features in some 'big houses', reflecting a lingering concern about security, provides an architectural link with the earlier defended residences. Clohamon House (near Bunclody)

extending over two centuries. The limited domestic arrangements in county Wexford's small tower houses prompted the construction of adjoining halls at an early date. Halls became the normal residences of the occupants, with the towers reserved for sleeping or when danger threatened. The complex was defended by an enclosure known as a bawn, initially of clay and timber but later of stone.

In other parts of Ireland, tower houses were built into the 1600s but in county Wexford they were superseded by fortified hall-houses after the late sixteenth century. Following the catastrophic 1640s, which resulted in widespread confiscation of Catholic-owned property, the prominence of ancestral tower houses in the landscape provided the dispossessed with enduring reminders of the loss of lands that had been held by their families for four centuries. During the seventeenth and early eighteenth centuries, tower houses were abandoned for more modern dwellings. This was particularly apparent in south Wexford after the transfer of ownership to new colonists subsequent to the post-Cromwellian dispossessions.

Fig. 4   The appeal of the architecture and heritage of tower houses has resulted in several restoration projects in the county. Conservation work has been carried out on the well-preserved tower house at Clougheast, near Carne, where the adjoining house has been restored as a dwelling.

Fig. 5   The existence of 137 tower houses has been identified in the Wexford landscape, with the substantial survival of forty-three providing an evocative architectural reminder of the county's turbulent past. Frequently visible in the southern lowlands, like the one shown here at Clonmines, viewed from across the Owenduff river, the distinctive towers constitute an essential component of the county's character and heritage.

Fig. 6   Two seven-sided turrets on the angles of the weather-slated, *c.* 1690 Dunmain House (near Campile) indicate an intention to provide defensive capabilities. The house provides an architectural link between fortified hall-houses and the 'big house' of the eighteenth century.

which incorporates elements of an earlier structure, has several such features, including gun-loops at the top of the stairs; Killowen House (near Campile) and Hillview (near New Ross) both have gun-loops covering the front door. Dunmain House, built *c.* 1690, with two seven-sided turrets conferring the appearance of a defended structure, provides the closest parallel to late sixteenth-century fortified hall-houses.[5]

CULTURAL LEGACY

The tower houses of south Wexford constitute an inescapable visual reminder of the colony that occupied the Wexford Pale in the late medieval period. Although not as immediately obvious, the cultural legacy of that unique community has resonated through the centuries. The seclusion of the colony within the Pale nurtured a deep-rooted society with a distinctive dialect, customs and traditions. The enclosed intensity of the Wexford Pale encouraged the emergence of a dialect, known as Yola, a fossilised form of Chaucerian English. The application of Yola soubriquets described the perceived hereditary characteristics of some families who were long established in the region.[6] In the conservative isolation of the Wexford Pale, this class remained steadfastly Catholic and contributed numerous priests and many bishops to the Church. The roll-call of Wexford-born bishops included

Barry, Browne, Codd, Devereux, French, Furlong, Keating, Lambert, Reville, Rossiter, Stafford, Sweetman and Wadding. This loyalty to the 'old religion' continued throughout the Penal Era and in the 1830s mass attendance in south Wexford was among the highest in the country.

By the end of the twelfth century, the Normans in England had ceased to call themselves 'Normans'.[7] In native Irish sources, the term 'Norman' referred to the Scandinavian 'Northmen', who initially arrived as raiders in 795 and were eventually absorbed into Irish society.[8] When the group of adventurers who intruded into Ireland from 1169 onwards was given a collective name, it was not 'Norman' but 'English', particularly after the loss of Normandy to the French in 1204. This was the term almost exclusively used by Gerald de Barry throughout his contemporary account *Expugnatio Hibernica* (*The conquest of Ireland*), in which some of his relations played a leading role, and in the French poem *The song of Dermot and the Earl*, and it continued to be the norm (with variations) until the middle of the nineteenth century. The *Expugnatio* quotes Maurice FitzGerald as saying 'Just as we are English to the Irish, so we are Irish to the English'.[9] Even at an early date, the English in Ireland already regarded themselves as a distinct group, a 'middle nation'.

Early charters acknowledged the disparate origins of this group by referring to its mixed ethnicity. For

Fig. 7 As part of the nineteenth-century revival of interest in medieval architecture, the FitzHenry tower house at Macmine, on the west bank of the Slaney, was adapted and integrated with a neo-Gothic house with decorative turrets and hood-moulding over doors and windows.

example, a Marshal charter to Dunbrody Abbey was addressed to all his men, French, English, Welsh and Irish.[10] A charter issued by Raymond le Gros referred to 'French, English, Flemish, Welsh and Irish'.[11] However, the term 'Norman' is noticeably absent from the charters issued by the new arrivals. For political and cultural reasons, the nomenclature used to describe the multi-ethnic settlers has gone through several transitions. The term 'English' rather than 'Norman' remained the conventional term, when referring to the colonists and their descendants, until the mid-nineteenth century, in conformity with predominant usage in contemporary medieval sources.[12] The colony was reinforced by subsequent waves of settlers, most of them English peasants but the focus has usually been on an aristocratic elite. Their identity was emphasised by the extension of English law to the settlers to the exclusion of the native Irish. Their separateness was reinforced by a siege mentality, a defensive response as the colonial settlement was eroded by the resurgent Irish.[13]

A document known as the Remonstrance, sent to Pope John XXII (1316–34) in 1317 from the Irish people, referred to the Irish and to the 'English of Ireland' as distinct nations. It also stated that the English inhabitants of Ireland claimed to be a middle nation, different in behaviour from the English of England and from other nations. This document proves that the English colonists

Some Yola Soubriquets

Stiff Stafford	Stiff Stafford
Dugged Lamport	Dogged Lambert
Gay Rochfort	Gay Rochfort
Proud Deweros	Proud Devereux
Lacheny Cheevers	Laughing Cheevers
Currachy Hore	Obstinate Hore
Criss Colfer	Cross Colfer
Valse Furlong	False Furlong
Shimereen Synnott	Showy Sinnott
Gentleman Browne	Gentleman Browne

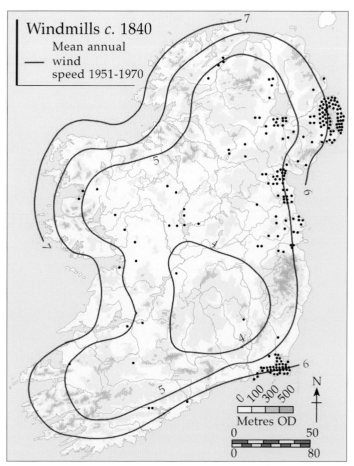

Windmills *c.* 1840

Mean annual wind speed 1951-1970

Metres OD

N

Fig. 8   The distribution of windmills in Ireland was greatest in south Wexford, in county Down and to a lesser extent in the Dublin Pale. The use of windmills, like the restored example at Tacumshin (left), was one of the distinguishing characteristics of the Wexford Pale.

Fig. 9   Mumming consists of a 'sword-dance' performed by dancers, who also recite rhymes portraying characters from Irish history. Thought to have originated in England, its survival in south Wexford is another example of inherited cultural practices and an enduring tradition.

Fig. 11   Johnstown Castle represents the most dramatic move from tower house to 'big house', the Gothic Revival style influenced by the Victorian fascination with medieval castle architecture. This was also articulated in the retention of the ivy-covered tower house, formerly the home of the Esmonds, shown at centre of picture. The removal of the tower house coincided with the presentation of the castle to the nation in 1945.

Fig. 10   Seathrún Céitinn's *Foras feasa ar Éirinn* (1634) was an enduring success and a great number of manuscript copies were made. This excerpt is from a signed copy by the famous eighteenth-century Gaelic poet, Aodhgán Ó Rathaile (c. 1670–1729) written in an Irish script. It lists some of the principal Anglo-Norman families, including the Barrys, Devereuxes, Prendergasts, Roches and Walshes, all of whom were established in County Wexford.

in Ireland regarded themselves as a distinct group with a pronounced identity. This enduring distinctiveness was subsequently highlighted by descriptions such as 'the English of Ireland', 'the English born in Ireland' and 'the English by blood' as opposed to 'the English by birth'.[14] Those who adopted the culture and customs of the native Irish were regarded as 'degenerate' by their own, fomenting divisions among the colonists. From 1297 onwards, attempts were made to stifle this acculturation by legislating against association with Irish culture, including intermarriage, language, dress, literature and music.[15] In 1366, these laws were consolidated in the Statutes of Kilkenny, in an effort at uniting all of the English in Ireland.[16]

In 1584, Stanihurst used the more collective term *Britannis* to describe the colonists and Boazio's map of 1599 records the landing of the 'Englishmen' at Bannow. Late in the sixteenth century, the region occupied by the colony in south Wexford was known as the 'English Pale' or the 'English baronies'.[17] By the seventeenth century, as the post-Reformation world brought about shifting political and religious allegiances, the descendants of the first invaders regarded themselves as 'Old English' and were identifying with early rather than contemporary

English connections. This can be seen in Seathrún Céitinn's (Geoffrey Keating) *Foras feasa ar Éirinn*, in 1634, where he mentions 'Norman' (once) but usually uses 'foreigner' when referring to the early settlers.[18] A member of an early settler family, who acquired several manors in county Wexford, Keating's attitude marked a transition from the entrenched division between Irish and English (sean Ghaill) by placing a new emphasis on a common Irishness, united by a shared Catholicism, referring to them collectively as 'Éireannaigh'.[19] His list of 'noble descendants' of the Old English included the Barrys, Devereuxes, Prendergasts and Roches, all prominent in county Wexford.

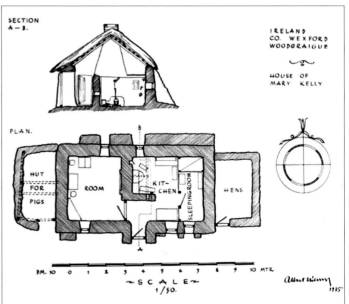

Fig. 12   The thatched, mud-walled house (shown here in plan and section) occupied by Mary Kelly, which survived in Woodgraigue (parish of Ambrosetown) in Bargy into the 1930s, resembled the cabins of the late medieval manorial villages that clustered around tower houses.

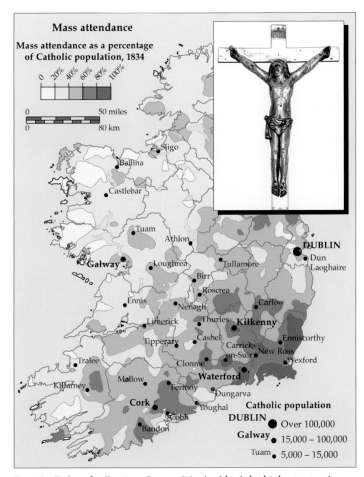

In the charged political and religious atmosphere of post-Union, nineteenth-century Ireland, there was an increasing romantic awareness of a medieval 'Norman' heritage. This emerged against the backdrop of the Gothic Revival movement, which generated a cachet for all things medieval, particularly architecture. This was typified in county Wexford by Johnstown Castle, which represented three generations of building by the Knox Grogans, beginning in 1810, and incorporating the original tower house. The architect Daniel Robertson worked there from 1835–1850 to create a fantasy landscape. The massive artificial lake was dug out in 1842, and a neo-Norman house was added, with neo-medieval fortifications, a castellated stable block, embattled gate lodges and turrets over the water, creating romantic reflections in the lake and a striking silhouette. Robertson also designed a fantasy Early English castle at Wilton in 1838, elevated on a platform with dry moats, battlements, machicolations, parapets and turrets. He also worked at Castleboro (now a

magnificent ruin) and Ballinkeele. Other Wexford castellated houses from this period include Bloomfield, Macmine and Cahore.[20]

This secular work coincided with the ecclesiastical work in county Wexford of renowned English architect, Augustus Welby Pugin (1812–1852), whose intention was to create atmospheric, dim, mysterious churches, which appealed to the senses rather than the intellect. Pugin rejected the sterility of the Enlightenment, and turned decisively away from the formal coolness, clarity and restraint of the Georgian style. He discarded the tyranny of symmetry, and sought to create emotional buildings, cloaked in a spiritual aura, and breathing a sense of age-old continuity. His Gothic style elevated the native medieval tradition over the classical antiquity which so appealed to the Enlightenment. By re-establishing the architectural link with medieval England, he also

N.G.I.

DEAN AND CHAPTER OF WESTMINSTER

Fig. 15   The Gothic Revival was promoted in county Wexford by the renowned architect Augustus Welby Pugin, who designed several Catholic churches in the diocese, including Enniscorthy Cathedral, St Peter's College and the parish churches at Gorey, Tagoat and Barntown. A comparison of the original Pugin altar in the chapel at St Peter's College with the elaborately designed early fourteenth-century tomb of Aymer de Valence (formerly Lord of Wexford) in Westminster Abbey, illustrates the influence of medieval Gothic on Pugin's nineteenth-century churches.

reasserted the continuity of the Catholic church from the pre-Reformation period.

In Wexford, where he had many commissions due to the patronage of the Talbot family, his principal models were the abbeys of Tintern and Dunbrody. His most impressive Wexford achievements were the Norman style church at Gorey and the (recently renovated) cathedral in Enniscorthy. He also designed the churches at Barntown, Tagoat and St Peter's College.[21] This movement influenced the restoration of some late medieval structures, including Butlerstown Castle, Bargy Castle, Enniscorthy Castle, Dungulph Castle and Huntington Castle in Clonegal.

The medieval theme also surfaced in art and literature. For example, in his well-known painting, 'The meeting on the turret stairs', the artist Frederick Burton (1816–1900) used a typical tower-house spiral stairway as the setting for a rendezvous between a knight and his lady, portraying a romanticised and enduring image of medieval courtly love. The Normans became a crucial part of the personal mythology of the poet William Butler Yeats (possibly influenced by the contemporary publication of Orpen's *Normans*). Keen to be regarded as Irish rather than English, Yeats chose to highlight his alleged aristocratic Norman ancestry. In 1917, he even

PRIVATE COLLECTION

Fig. 16   A drawing of Thoor Ballylee by Lady Gregory's son, Robert, following the purchase of the tower by the poet W. B. Yeats. He composed a rhyming couplet, 'to be carved on a stone', to commemorate the restoration: I, the poet William Yeats, / With old mill boards and sea-green slates / And smithy work from the Gort forge, / Restored this tower for my wife George, / And may these characters remain / When all is ruin once again.

acquired his own tower house, known as Thoor Ballylee, near Gort in county Galway. He attributed it to the Normans although it was probably built in the sixteenth century.[22] He was attracted by the philosophical aspect of the tower, particularly the spiral stairway, – 'This winding, gyring, spring treadmill of a stair is my ancestral stair' – which he regarded as a symbolic connection with his medieval origins. In 1927, he wrote 'I like to think of that building as a permanent symbol of my work, plainly visible to the passer-by'.[23] The Tower (1928), often regarded as Yeats's finest volume, and inspired by Thoor Ballylee, contained such classic poems as 'Sailing to Byzantium' and 'Among Schoolchildren'. His poem 'The Tower' features a glossary of tower-house architecture: battlements, loophole, narrow stairs, bawn.

Perhaps influenced by the Gothic Revival, the term 'English' was replaced by 'Norman' or 'Anglo-Norman', from the second half of the nineteenth century, when referring to the group that colonised Ireland in the medieval period. This variation is attributed to Goldwin Smith (1823–1910), a professor of history at Oxford. By his own admission, he used the expression to take the heat out of contemporary political debate by minimising the period of English misrule in Ireland.[24] This shift suited the mood of Irish nationalism. County Wexford historians were to the fore in the promotion of a 'Norman' myth, presumably motivated by the county's involvement in the initial stages of the invasion. After Herbert Hore had spent decades copying medieval records relating to county Wexford, mostly in London, his son, Philip Hore,

Fig. 17   A monument was erected *c.* 1870 in Wexford town to mark the reclamation of land by the Redmond family. It included a coat-of-arms acknowledging descent from the Anglo-Norman Redmonds, who acquired land on the Hook peninsula in the thirteenth century. The coat-of-arms includes a castle and a fire-beacon, representing the medieval Redmond (now Loftus) Hall and the Tower of Hook.

published them in six volumes (1900–1911). The Hores were descended from early settlers who occupied extensive estates in the barony of Shelmalier.

Goddard Orpen, who lived in Monksgrange on the slopes of the Blackstairs, published his epic four-volume *Ireland under the Normans* between 1911 and 1920. His unequivocal use of 'Norman' (although his text also used 'English') distinguished the earlier settlers from the less prestigious later planters, especially the despised Cromwellians, 'a gentry of the sword rather than of the blood'. The Normans enjoyed the cachet of being a military aristocracy, and the Victorian period was also massively invested in medievalism and a return to the Gothic. Orpen's work mostly dealt with the invasion and colonisation of Ireland and generated controversy in nationalist circles. In response, Edmond Curtis, his trenchant critic, published *A history of medieval Ireland* in 1923, which focused on all aspects of Irish history during the period, but retained the term 'Norman' to describe the invaders.[25]

Following the publication of these two great works, the inclusive term 'Anglo-Norman' (and variants) which had appeared in Ireland as early as 1869,[26] became the

Fig. 18   The multi-ethnic nature of the Anglo-Norman colonisation of Ireland resulted in the introduction of a wide range of surnames of French, English, Welsh and Flemish origin. The retraction of the colony in county Wexford established these names in the south of the county, creating a unique surname profile. Some have not survived but are found as elements in placenames. The enduring nature of the colony meant that these distinctive surnames were embedded in the region and became part of the cultural and social fabric. The family names of the tower-house builders became synonymous with the county. In the mid-seventeenth century, the vast majority lost their lands following the Cromwellian campaign in Ireland. Most remained in the county but some were transplanted west of the Shannon. This montage demonstrates the prevalence of surnames of Anglo-Norman provenance in the county at the present time. Nearly all have been recorded on business premises or on signs and vehicles. The only exception is Cheevers, formerly a prominent Wexford family. The example shown here was recorded in east Galway, possibly a descendant of the dispossessed Wexford diaspora.

ANNE BERNSTORFF

Fig. 19   The association of south Wexford with the arrival of the Anglo-Normans is typified by the Ros Tapestry, designed by Anne Bernstorff and created in recent years by dedicated teams of community 'stitchers' under the leadership of Alexis Bernstorff. The tapestries are on display on the quays of New Ross. This panel depicts the meeting of Diarmait Mac Murchada with Robert FitzStephen in 1169, following the first landing at Bannow Island.

conventional term used to describe the medieval colonists and their descendants. Subsequent historians, conscious of contemporary political problems, and with subliminal motivations similar to that of Goldwin Smith, have been unduly hesitant about using the term 'English'. This ambivalent use of terminology is, in itself, an intrinsic element of the complicated legacy of the English intrusion into Ireland in the medieval period.

In county Wexford, the impact of the Anglo-Norman colonisation has resonated down through the centuries. The names of Bannow and Baginbun, the initial landing places, are recognised throughout Ireland. The settlers and their descendants bequeathed a striking architectural legacy, including early earthwork defences, the abbeys of Dunbrody and Tintern, the unique Tower of Hook, St Mary's in New Ross, and the frontier castle at Ferns as well as many later tower houses, parish churches and

windmills. The profusion of medieval settler names in the south, some exclusive to the county, marks the extent of the former Wexford Pale. Several later families boasted of their Norman ancestry, including the Redmonds. The family coat-of-arms on the monument at Redmond Square in Wexford town includes a fire beacon, linking them with the medieval family of Redmond Hall (now Loftus Hall) on the Hook, who were known as Réamonn an Tigh Sholais (Redmonds of the Lighthouse).

County Wexford presents a concise microcosm of the ethnic and cultural duality which resulted from the colonisation by the English in the late twelfth and thirteenth centuries. The Irish recovery generated incessant raiding, warfare, acculturation, the retraction of the colony and eventual amalgamation. A close scrutiny of the landscape reveals the impact of medieval feudalism. The colony determined the distribution of villages and towns, many of them abandoned, epitomised by the deserted town of Clonmines. The ubiquitous presence of castles in the south Wexford landscape, particularly late medieval tower houses, constitute a pervasive indication of the interaction between the two nations. Contrasting distributions of Irish and English townland names and surnames of Irish and Anglo-Norman origin chronicle the synthesis of native Irish and colonist. Further influxes from England in the sixteenth and seventeenth centuries deepened the societal mix. In that sense, county Wexford has always hosted a multi-cultural society.

A sense of a 'Norman' past has inspired the creation of the Ros Tapestry, a series of embroidered panels (fifteen when completed) depicting initial Anglo-Norman activity in the south-east. This past is also reflected in the impressive number of Wexford writers, past and present, of fact and fiction, whose surnames belong to the Anglo-Norman tradition. These include recent historians Kathleen Browne, Bernard Browne, T. C. Butler, Mark Codd, Paddy Corish, Louis Cullen, Nicky Furlong, Dick Roche, Nicky Rossiter and Dan Walsh, while creative writers include John Banville, Eoin Colfer, Billy Roche and Colm Tóibín (Tobin). The connection with the medieval is epitomised by Wexford's many historic monuments, which are now the county's principal heritage attractions. However, while the medieval period was pivotal, it was only part of Wexford's odyssey. Disparate historical influences have coalesced over the millennia to form a complex palimpsest, creating the county's enduring landscape and cultural character.

ADAMSTOWN

Sites and Monuments Record: (**SMR**) WX031-019001
Irish Transverse Mercator Co-ordinates (ITM): 686885, 628506 (Easting, Northing)
Grid Reference: 286954, 128456 (Easting, Northing)
Associated families: Devereux, Downes
Footprint: 81m² (9m x 9m)

Only the south-east wall and part of the north-east and south-west walls survive. Four storeys in height, with base batter and granite quoins, the vaulted ground floor (lacking loft) had three gun-loops at each angle. The destroyed doorway was guarded by a yett. A mural stairs, protected by a murder-hole operated from the second floor, led to the first floor which has a fireplace, one surviving window and gun loops in the south-west wall. A spiral stairs (now destroyed) continued on the second floor, which has two round-headed windows, one with two lights, a fireplace and three gun loops. The third floor has single-light windows on surviving wall. The tower house was formerly centrally placed in a bawn. A date-stone records that the tower was built by Nicholas Devereux and his wife Catherine Power in 1556.

ARTRAMON

SMR: WX037-007001
ITM: 703534, 626192
Grid: 303606, 126142
Families: Roche, Masterson, Le Hunte
Footprint: 68m² (8m x 8.5m)

The three-storey tower house, surviving to wall-walk level, has base-batter and good quoins. The pointed granite doorway is protected by a yett, machicolation and murder-hole. The entrance lobby leads to the vaulted ground floor which retains no original features. A mural stairs leads to the doorway of the loft under the vault and continues to the first floor, which has four plain windows, some with seats, a fireplace and garderobe. The stairs continues to the second floor which has three plain windows and a garderobe. A later brick vault was added to the second floor.

AUGHNAGAN

SMR: WX041-025001
ITM: 693716, 616121
Grid: 293786, 116069
Families: Hore
Footprint: 36m² (6m x 6m)

Only part of the ground floor walls survive of the small tower house which is now used as a farm building. Original features consist of two embrasures and a double-splay loop.

BALDWINSTOWN

SMR: WX047-022001
ITM: 696978, 610398
Grid: 297049, 110344
Families: Keating, Stafford
Footprint: 76m² (9.5m x 8m)

The four-storey tower house, with slight batter, survives with battlements, but with serious structural cracks. All windows are rectangular and dressed stone is granite. The round-topped entrance was protected by machicolation (destroyed) and portcullis but no murder-hole. The vaulted ground floor has two surviving double-splay loops. Mural stairs to first-floor level rises from the entrance lobby, giving access to a loft under the vault which has a stirrup-loop and two windows. The first floor has a fireplace (destroyed), a garderobe, a rectangular window with seats and two destroyed windows. A mural stairs continues to the second floor which has a fireplace, a garderobe, two windows with seats and a destroyed window. A spiral stairs rises to the third floor which has three windows, one with seats and an antechamber. A spiral stairs continues to stepped battlements, two lookout platforms and a gable with doorway to wall-walk. Part of the bawn wall runs south from the tower to a circular tower entered from the bawn wall-walk

BALLYCOGLEY

SMR: WX047–019001
ITM: 703685, 611232
Grid: 303757, 111179
Families: Wadding, Ousely, Barrington
Footprint: 87m² (10.9m x 8m)

The four-storey tower house survives to parapet level, except for the south-west angle which is damaged above the first floor. All dressed stone is granite. The destroyed entrance leads, through a lobby with murder-hole, to vaulted ground floor which has five embrasures, with one surviving double-splay loop. Stairway to first floor rises from lobby, giving access to the loft under the vault which, unusually, is equipped with a garderobe. The first floor has a fireplace (destroyed), and ogee-headed window and two slit windows. Two oubliettes are located beneath the floor. The mural stairs rises to the second floor which has a fireplace, a rectangular two-light window with seats and two slit windows. The stairway continues to the third floor which has one slit window. A spiral stairs continues to the parapet which had a lookout platform at one angle and gables inside the wall-walk.

BALLYCONNOR BIG

SMR: WX048-033001
ITM: 711742, 610655
Grid: 311816, 110602
Families: Stafford
Footprint: 49m² (7m x 7m)

The tower house survives to first-floor level with base-batter and good quoins. The pointed granite entrance was protected by a portcullis but no murder-hole. The entrance lobby leads to the vaulted ground floor, which has at least nine gun-loops, many of them blocked up. The mural stairs, which has two more gun-loops, rises to the loft under the vault which has two gun-loops. A spiral stairs continues to the first floor, which has slit windows and two gun-loops. A somewhat later house (now heavily overgrown) is attached to the north of the tower, of which one wall and a gable with chimney survives, an original four-light ogee-headed window with mullions removed, a doorway and a gun-loop. A date-stone recorded the building of the house in 1570.

BALLYFARNOGE

SMR: WX039-049001
ITM: 670876, 618647
Grid: 270941, 118595
Families: Prendergast, Glascott.
Footprint: 52.5m² (7.5m x 7m)

The three-storey tower house, with granite quoins but lacking base-batter, survives to wall-walk level. The destroyed entrance, lacking evidence of murder-hole, gave access through a lobby to the vaulted ground floor which has four embrasures but no surviving windows. A mural stairway gives access to a loft under the vault and continues on to the first floor, which has a garderobe, a fireplace and three small windows. The mural stairs continues to the second floor, which is much altered by later work. Access to the wall-walk was through an opening in the roof of a mural passage. A passage on the first floor possibly led to a doorway leading to the wall-walk of an attached fortified house, indicated by the surviving ruins and the flashing for the gable on the wall of the tower.

BALLYHACK

SMR: WX044-009001
ITM: 670512, 610969
Grid: 270577, 110916
Families: Cistercians, Etchingham.
Footprint: 106m² (10.8m x 9.8m)

Constructed of old red sandstone quarried from the adjacent cliff, the four-storey Cistercian (not Hospitaller) tower house stands to wall-walk level. The rectangular doorway is protected by a machicolation, yett and murder-hole. The vaulted ground floor has three slit windows. A mural stairs rises from the entrance lobby to a passage leading to the loft under the vault, which has a garderobe and a mural chamber. The stairs rises to the first floor from which a spiral stairs continues to the wall-walk. The first floor had two windows with seats, a fireplace, garderobe and access to an oubliette. The second floor has several ogee-headed windows, a fireplace, garderobe and an altar alcove. Another mural chamber may have been used as a sacristy. The third floor has a machicolation and several ogee-headed windows. At parapet level, there is a corbelled-out chimney stack and the corbels for a corner machicolation can be seen at the southern angle.

BALLYHEALY

SMR: WX052-022002
ITM: 700332, 605715
Grid: 300403, 105660
Families: Cheevers, Whitty
Footprint: 82m² (10.4m x 7.9m)

The four-storey tower house is complete to re-built crenellations. The interior has been converted as a modern dwelling. The round-headed doorway gave access through the entrance lobby to the vaulted ground floor, which has six embrasures, two with double-splay loops. A mural stairway continues to the loft under the vault and the first-floor hall, which has a fireplace, garderobe and slopstone, with two-light, cusped, ogee-headed windows and seats in the north and east walls. The mural stairs rises to the second floor, which has a fireplace, garderobe and two ogee-headed windows. The stairs rises to the third floor which has three slit windows. Although the battlements have been re-built, much of the four lookout platforms may be original.

BALLYMAGIR (RICHFIELD TOWNLAND)

SMR: WX046-05202
ITM: 694974, 607513
Grid: 295044, 107459
Families: Devereux, Loftus.
Footprint: 81m^2 (11.5m x 7m)

The tower house had an attached, offset fortified house, now incorporated in a modern dwelling. The tower was previously converted, with only the ground floor, with base-batter, surviving in its original form. The entrance doorway led to the ground floor, which has an unusual double vault, lacking lofts. A recent survey uncovered several other original features (Ben Murtagh, pers. comm.). The complex is located in a large moated site.

BALLYTEIGE

SMR: WX052-018001
ITM: 696629, 604493
Grid: 296700, 104438
Families: Whitty, Colclough, Meadows, Grant
Footprint: 82m^2 (10.5m x 7.8m)

The four-storey tower house stands to crenellations, with base-batter and a projecting garderobe tower. The entrance doorway of dressed granite is protected by a machicolation and murder-hole. The lobby leads to the vaulted ground floor, which has five embrasures, three with narrow loops. A mural stairway, covered by a second murder-hole, leads to the loft under the vault and to a passage which has an oubliette and a garderobe, and to the first-floor hall. The hall has two destroyed windows, a blocked ogee-headed window and a blocked fireplace. A spiral stairway continues to second floor which has a possible garderobe, blocked windows and a fireplace. A mural stairs rises to the third floor which has three slit windows, a garderobe and an antechamber. A stairs leads to the wall-walk, which has stepped battlements with lookout platforms at all four corners.

BALLYTORY

SMR: WX048-042002
ITM: 709078, 607765
Grid: 309151, 107711
Families: French, Codd, Doyle
Footprint: Not available

The tower house has been roofed down and incorporated into a modern dwelling. The remaining lower part of the tower has base-batter, pointed doorway and a ground-floor vault.

BARNTOWN

SMR: WX037-034001
ITM: 699999, 621661
Grid: 300070, 121610
Families: Roche, Wadding, Le Hunte
Footprint: 52m² (8m x 6.5m)

The internally damaged, four-storey tower house survives to wall-walk level. The doorway (destroyed), protected by a machicolation and probably a murder-hole, entered a lobby and ground floor with two slit windows. Remains of a mural stairs gave access to the loft under the vault (destroyed) and first floor, which had a fireplace, garderobe and three small windows. A spiral stairs (destroyed) rose to the second floor, which had a garderobe, fireplace and three larger windows, two with seats. The spiral stairs continued to the third floor, which had four loops, and on to (destroyed) battlements.

BARRYSTOWN

SMR: WX045-020001
ITM: 685340, 611906
Grid: 285408, 111853
Families: Barry, King, Kenny
Footprint: 56m² (8m x 7m)

This tower house survives only to top of ground-floor vault, with base-batter and granite quoins. The pointed doorway of dressed granite was protected by a yett and a murder-hole in the entrance lobby. From the lobby, a pointed doorway leads to the vaulted ground floor, with a mural chamber and three blocked windows. The ground floor has thirteen gun-loops, including one covering the entrance lobby. A mural stairs gives access to the loft under the vault, which has one surviving window and an antechamber. The stairs continued to the first floor, which no longer survives.

BROWNSWOOD

SMR WX026-022003
ITM: 697806, 635608
Grid: 297877, 135560
Families: Browne, Rochford
Footprint: Not available

The remains of the three-storey tower house, built on a rock outcrop on the banks of the Slaney, consist of parts of the east and south walls. The ground floor was originally vaulted, with an oubliette in the vault entered from the second floor. Gun-loops are located in alcoves on the south-east corner and east wall of the ground floor. Some windows survive at first- and second-floor level.

BRYANSTOWN

SMR: WX040-024001
ITM: 681941, 618004
Grid: 282008, 117952
Families: Bryan, Roche, Isham
Footprint: Not available

The small tower house, now integrated with Bryanstown House, had a vaulted ground floor with at least two upper floors. A projection at one angle contained the stairway. Most original features have been blocked up or modified.

BUTLERSTOWN

SMR: WX047-054001
ITM: 704382, 608867
Grid: 304454, 108813
Families: Butler, Herron, Harvey, Boxwell, Skrine
Footprint: 83m² (9.7m x 8.6m)

This four-storey tower house with good quoins and base-batter, survives complete to stepped crenellations. All windows are small rectangular slits. The round-headed doorway, protected by machicolation and portcullis, leads to a lobby giving access to the vaulted ground floor, which has three embrasures and one surviving double-splay loop. A mural stairs, protected by a murder-hole, leads to the loft under the vault and the first floor, which has three windows with seats, a fireplace, garderobe and antechamber. The stairs continues to the second floor which is similarly equipped. A spiral stairs rises to the third floor which has four windows. The spiral continues to the wall-walk which has rebuilt gables and a restored roof. A loop and cross-loop are inserted in the battlements. The lookout platform has three ogee-headed windows. Extensive conservation work has been carried out by successive owners.

CASTLETOWN

SMR: WX053-027
ITM: 711093, 604948
Grid: 311167, 104893
Families: Codd, Palliser, Hunt, Keane
Footprint: 82m² (9.5m x 8.6m)

Only the first storey survives of this tower house. The modified doorway led through a lobby to the vaulted ground floor, which has four embrasures, three blocked-up slit windows and one double-splay window. A secondary door has been broken through opposite the original entrance. The stairs led from the entrance lobby to the doorway (now blocked) of the loft under the vault and on to the destroyed first floor.

CLONARD

SMR: WX042-005001
ITM: 702018, 619920
Grid: 302090, 119869
Families: Sutton, Hatton
Footprint: 49m² (9.5m x 8.6m)

This tower house survives to the top of the ground-floor vault but it lacks the west wall which must have contained the doorway and stairs. There is no evidence for quoins or base-batter. The loft under the vault, with one window, was supported on joists set directly into the walls.

CLONMINES

SMR: WX045-012001
ITM: 684367, 613031
Grid: 284435, 112978
Families: FitzHenry, Annesley
Footprint: 79m² (9.8m x 8.1m)

This four-storey tower house, known as the 'Black Castle', survives to wall-walk level, with good quoins and base-batter. The pointed entrance doorway, protected by machicolation and murder-hole, leads through an entrance lobby to the vaulted ground floor which has five embrasures and one surviving double-splay loop. A mural stairway, with possible secondary doorway to the exterior, or to an attached house, at its foot, leads to the loft under the vault and the first floor which has two windows, one with seats, a fireplace, garderobe and two mural chambers. The stairs continues to the second floor which has similar features. The mural stairs rises to the third floor, which has two windows, and the wall-walk with remains of battlements and lookout platform over the stairs housing.

CLOUGHEAST

SMR: WX053-032001
ITM: 711976, 605632
Grid: 312050. 105577
Families: Codd, Waddy
Footprint: 61m² (8.7m x 7m)

This four-storey tower house survives complete with stepped battlements, good quoins and base-batter. The pointed doorway, protected by machicolation, portcullis and murder-hole, leads through a lobby to the vaulted ground floor, which has a mural chamber and three double-splay loops. The mural stairway rises from the lobby, giving access to the loft under the vault, which has a chamber from which the portcullis was operated. The stairs continues to the first floor, which has three windows, a fireplace, garderobe and an oubliette accessed from a mural chamber. The stairs continues to the second floor which has a fireplace, garderobe and four windows, one with two lights. The stairs rises to the third floor, which has two slit windows and a gallery leading to the attic, wall-walk, lookout platform and battlements, which are fitted with gun-loops. The interior gables of the attic served as a dovecote.

COURTHOYLE

SMR: WX035-014001
ITM: 681931, 624991
Grid: 281998, 124941
Families: Howell, Walsh, Devereux
Footprint: 80m² (10.3m x 7.8m)

Only the ground floor, with collapsed vault, survives of this tower house, which had granite quoins and base-batter, and a loft under the vault. The doorway was probably in the section of the east wall which is now destroyed. There are remains of a spiral stairway rising at the east angle and evidence for a garderobe chute on the north wall. The ground floor has six long loops with a cross-loop on the stairway.

CULLENSTOWN

SMR: WX046-046001
ITM: 687575, 608666
Grid: 287644, 108612
Families: Cullen, Boyse, Radford, Sparrow, Hayes
Footprint: 60m² (8.5m x 7m)

This tower house, with good quoins and base-batter, has been reduced to first-floor level and integrated with a dwelling house. The entrance, protected by a murder-hole, leads through a lobby to the vaulted ground floor, which has four embrasures but no other original features. A mural stairs rises to the loft under the vault, which has two windows. A spiral stairs continued to first floor and to a passage with a possible garderobe. The first floor has a fireplace and remains of window embrasures with seats.

DANESCASTLE

SMR: WX045-021001
ITM: 686444, 611642
Grid: 286512, 111589
Families: Denne, Cheevers, Boyse
Footprint: 52m² (8.3m x 6.25m)

The four-storey tower house survives to wall-walk level with good quoins and base-batter. The pointed doorway on the north wall, protected by a machicolation, leads to the vaulted ground floor, which has three embrasures with double-splay loops. A second doorway, on the east wall and protected by a murder-hole, leads through a lobby to the ground floor. This doorway led to a house, whose stone gable flashing survives on the tower wall. The stairway rises from the lobby and, protected by a murder-hole, gives access to the loft under the vault and the first floor. This floor has three rectangular windows with seats, a garderobe, and a destroyed fireplace. A spiral stairs rises to the second floor which has similar features. The spiral continues to the third floor which has two windows. A stairs leads to destroyed battlements where there is evidence for a lookout platform.

DEEPS

SMR: WX032-026001
ITM: 698114, 627284
Grid: 298185, 127234
Families: Sinnott, Roche, Devereux
Footprint: 200m² (15.8m x 12.7m)

This castle is is atypical among the county Wexford tower houses, and has been much altered over the centuries. The rectangular structure of three storeys and an attic, with base-batter, had two barrel-vaulted chambers at ground level (now destroyed) with two entrances, one protected by a murder-hole. Each vault had two loops, with an inserted fireplace. The first floor, accessed by two stairs, one of them spiral, has two fireplaces (one destroyed), possibly two garderobes, a mullioned window (originally two) and several defensive loops. A spiral stairs leads to the second floor, which has mullioned windows with hood mouldings and possibly three garderobes.

FERRYCARRIG

SMR: WX037-027001
ITM: 701530, 623259
Grid: 301602, 123208
Families: Roche
Footprint: 44m² (7.3m x 6m)

This tower house, strategically situated on a rock overlooking the Slaney, was well placed to protect river traffic and the ferry crossing. The tower survives to three storeys, with a pronounced base-batter securing the structure to its rock base. All windows are narrow loops. The doorway (rebuilt), protected by a murder-hole, leads to the vaulted ground floor, which has two double-splay loops and three damaged gun-loops. A mural stairs rises from the first-floor chamber, leading to the loft under the vault and continuing to the first floor, which has a fireplace, garderobe, three windows and cross-loops in two of the angles. A spiral stairs continues to the second floor, which has three windows and partly surviving walls.

KILCAVAN

SMR: WX046-001001
ITM: 687870, 613260
Grid: 287939, 113207
Families: FitzHenry, Thompson, Murphy
Footprint: 63m² (9m x 7m)

Two walls of this tower house survive in a damaged state to four-storey level, with good quoins and slight base-batter. Each wall has embrasures at all levels. There is no evidence of vaulting over the ground floor but, unusually for Wexford, the tower may have been vaulted over the second floor. A gable scar indicates the former presence of a house attached to the tower. A smaller dwelling house on the same site has hood moulding over a window (originally a door), suggesting a late sixteenth-century origin.

JOHNSTOWN (RATHLANNON)

SMR: WX042-016001
ITM: 701856, 616610
Grid: 301928, 116558
Families: Esmond, Grogan
Footprint: 69m² (9m x 7.65m)

The four-storey tower house of Rathlannon (in Johnstown townland) survives to crenellations, with good quoins and slight base-batter, but the interior has been greatly altered. The pointed entrance of undressed stone is protected by a murder-hole and machicolation, unusually located at first-floor level. A lobby leads to the ground floor where no vault survives. A mural stairs led to the first floor, with a spiral stairs continuing to the battlements. Few original internal features survive due to later work.

KILCLOGGAN

SMR: WX049-004001
ITM: 675921, 604795
Grid: 275987, 104740
Families: Knights Hospitaller, Loftus, Furlong, Power
Footprint: 35m² (6.1m x 5.7m)

This small, four-storey tower house survives to stepped crenellations. Constructed of old red sandstone from the nearby cliffs along Waterford Harbour, the tower has a slight base-batter and has two vertical projections housing the stairway and garderobes. The rebuilt entrance, protected by a machicolation, leads to the vaulted ground floor which has no loft. A damaged mural stairs leads to the first floor, which has a fireplace, garderobe (destroyed) and two rectangular windows with seats. A doorway in the stairs projection led to the removed bawn wall-walk. A spiral stairs rises to the second floor which has a fireplace, garderobe and two ogee-headed windows. The spiral stairs continues to the third floor which has four windows, two of them ogee-headed. The battlements, with two lookout platforms, survive almost intact. Fragments of the contemporary bawn wall and entrance survive at one angle.

KILHILE

SMR: WX044-003001
ITM: 671282, 611835
Grid: 271347, 111782
Families: Cistercians, Etchingham
Footprint: (6.3m x ?)

Only one wall, and parts of the adjacent walls, with good quoins and base-batter, survive at this tower house, built of local old red sandstone. The pointed entrance, protected by machicolation and murder-hole, led to a lobby and vaulted ground floor. Unusually, a separate stairway led to a garderobe and the loft under the vault. A passage in the lobby led to a second stairs (destroyed) giving access to upper floors. The surviving fabric shows fireplaces at first and second floors, an oubliette at loft level and windows on the first and second floors.

KILLIANE

SMR: WX042-020001
ITM: 705832, 616717
Grid: 305905, 116665
Families: Hay, Cheevers, Bunbury, Harvey, Mernagh
Footprint: 99m² (11.7m x 8.5m)

The four-storey tower house survives to battlements with battered walls and good quoins. The entrance (now blocked), protected by a murder-hole but no machicolation, leads through a lobby to the vaulted ground floor, which has six embrasures, each with a double-splay loop, some surviving. A mural stairway (protected by a second murder-hole) leads to the loft under the vault, which has a window with seat, and to the first floor. This floor has five embrasures with secondary windows, a fireplace and garderobe. The mural stairs continues to upper floors and wall-walk. The second floor has three windows with seats, one ogee-headed with two lights, a fireplace and garderobe. The third floor has three enlarged windows. The wall-walk has crenellated battlements and a lookout platform at each angle. A stone face is inserted on the outside of one lookout platform.

LADY'S ISLAND

SMR: WX053-014001
ITM: 710595, 607547
Grid: 310669, 107493
Families: Augustinian Canons, Lamberts, Browne
Footprint: 79m² (9.2m x 8.6m)

This four-storey tower house (associated with the Augustinian Canons) survives to wall-walk level with an attached gatehouse, a unique feature in county Wexford. The pointed entrance, protected by a murder-hole, leads to a much altered, vaulted ground floor which has one double-splay loop. A mural stairs leads to the loft under the vault, which has two windows and a mural chamber, and on to the first floor, which has a damaged fireplace, a garderobe, three damaged windows (one with seats) and a mural chamber. A spiral stairs rises to second floor, which has a fireplace and garderobe, both damaged, a window with seats and several slit windows. The stairs continues to third floor, which has three slit windows, and on to the wall-walk. The first floor and parapet of the gatehouse is accessed from the tower. A flanking tower, originally part of the bawn wall, is now leaning at an angle.

LONGGRAIGUE

SMR: WX040-012001
ITM: 684065, 618385
Grid: 284133, 118333
Families: Bryan, Leigh, Sutton, Gibbon
Footprint: 68m² (8.5m x 8m)

Longgraigue House incorporates elements of an earlier tower house. Sections of the tower walls with base-batter and granite quoins can still be identified.

MACMINE

SMR: WX032-001003
ITM: 697149, 632268
Grid: 297220. 132219
Families: FitzHenry, King, Richards, Benedictine Nuns, Flood, Dunne.
Footprint: 58m² (7.7m x 7.5m)

The much altered tower house survives to the second floor, with modern brick additions. The vault over the ground floor survives but there are no other original features at this level, apart from base-batter. A mural stairs leads to the loft under the vault and the first floor, which has a granite fireplace, a garderobe and four embrasures but no original windows. A spiral stairs continues to the second floor, where a fireplace and four embrasures may be original (but not the windows).

MOUNTGARRETT

SMR: WX029-009001
ITM: 672452, 629474
Grid: 272517, 129425
Families: Bishop of Ferns, Butlers of Ormond
Footprint: 149m² (13.8 x 10.8m)

The large five-storey tower house survived partially to wall-walk level, with good quoins and base-batter, until early in 2011, when most of the southern and parts of the adjoining walls collapsed. This account is based on the pre-collapse condition of the structure. The pointed entrance, protected by a yett, probably inserted, led through a lobby, which had a guardroom, to the ground floor, which had no evidence for a vault. A spiral stairs accessed the upper rooms. Remains of garderobes could be identified at four locations in the upper floors, with fireplaces on the first and second floors. A large mullioned window and gun-loops on the second floor were late insertions.

MULRANKIN

SMR: WX047-031001
ITM: 699682, 610166
Grid: 299753, 110112
Families: Browne, Cliffe, Furlong, Cardiff
Footprint: 65m² (9m x 7.2m)

This tower house, three storeys in height with base-batter, survives almost complete. The entrance, protected by a murder-hole, led to a vaulted ground floor, which had five embrasures, two with narrow loops. A mural stairs from the entrance lobby to the first floor gives access to the loft under the vault. The first floor has a damaged fireplace, a two-light ogee-headed window, a single-light ogee-headed window, a removed window and a garderobe. A blocked-up doorway may have led to the wall-walk of an adjacent house or of the bawn. A mural stairs leads on the second floor, which has two blocked windows. Stairs continues on to wall-walk which has damaged crenellations and lookout platform. Stone flashing on the west wall indicates the existence of an attached hall, elements of which survive in the present dwelling house.

NEWBAWN

SMR: WX035-039001
ITM: 682583, 622239
Grid: 282651, 122188
Families: Devereux, de Londres, Leigh, Browne, Ryan
Footprint: 97m² (10m x 9.7m)

Only a fragment of the tower house at Newbawn survives. This consists of part of a wall, with two double-splay loops and a pointed doorway which was protected by a murder-hole and yett. Part of another wall shows evidence for a mural stairway.

NEWCASTLE (KILMANNON)

SMR: WX042-024001
ITM: 698000, 614487
Grid: 298071, 114434
Families: Rossiter, Jennings, Lett
Footprint: 33m² (6m x 5.5m)

The tower house survives to second floor, with quoins and battered walls. The entrance (blocked) is protected by a murder-hole. A lobby leads to the vaulted ground floor, which has two double-splay loops and a mural chamber. A mural stairs gives access to the loft under the vault and the first floor, which has three window embrasures, one with a seat, but no evidence of a fireplace or garderobe. A spiral stairs continues to the second floor but no features survive.

RATHMACKNEE GREAT

SMR: WX042-029001
ITM: 703019, 614138
Grid: 303091, 114085
Families: Rossiter, Knox, Grogan
Footprint: 70m² (8.9m x 7.9m)

The four-storey tower house survives to crenellations with base-batter and projecting garderobe turret. A pointed doorway, protected by a murder-hole and an opening in the battlements, probably for a wooden machicolation, leads through a lobby to the vaulted ground floor, which has a double-splay loop covering the bawn entrance. A mural stairs rises from the lobby, giving access to the loft under the vault, which has one window and a mural chamber. The stairs continues to the first floor, which has a fireplace, garderobe, a mural chamber, another mural chamber with an oubliette and two ogee-headed windows. A blocked doorway in the external wall may have led to the wall-walk of an attached house. The stairs rises to the second floor, which has similar features, and continues to the third floor which has three windows, a slit window and two mural chambers. The stairs advances to the wall-walk, which has stepped battlements and four lookout platforms. The bawn, complete except at the south wall, has a wall-walk, corner machicolation and gateway protected by a machicolation. The tower house and bawn are maintained as a National Monument.

RATHRONAN

SMR: WX047-011001
ITM: 698460, 610922
Grid: 298531, 110869
Families: Browne, Cliffe, Hassett
Footprint: Not available.

The tower house survives to three stories but it has been integrated with a later house and few original features survive, apart from a vaulted ground floor.

ROSEGARLAND

SMR: WX040-042001
ITM: 685886, 615372
Grid: 285954, 115320
Families: Neville, Sinnott, Leigh
Footprint: 108m² (12.7 x 8.5m)

The tower house survives only to first-floor level, with battered walls and projecting garderobe chute. A pointed entrance doorway leads directly to the vaulted first floor, which has embrasures on three walls with large lights (presumably inserted) and a large inserted carriage door in the fourth wall. There was no loft under the vault. A mural stairs leads to the first floor, which has three embrasures, a cupboard and a garderobe in the projecting turret. Decorative turrets have been added to all four corners.

SCAR

SMR: WX046-007001
ITM: 693753, 612418
Grid: 293823, 112365
Families: Bryan, Wilson
Footprint: 64m² (8.8m x 7.3m)

This three-storey tower house survives to wall-walk level, ruggedly built of the underlying old red sandstone. The lintelled doorway, protected by a murder-hole, leads through a lobby to the vaulted ground floor, which has five damaged embrasures and an original doorway leading to an attached house. A mural stairs leads to the loft under the vault and the first floor which has three altered windows, some with seats, a garderobe, a destroyed fireplace, a slop-stone and a secondary door to the attached house. The mural stairs rises to the second floor, which has four destroyed windows (two with seats) and continues to the wall-walk. An offset fortified house is attached to the tower but not bonded, with one side wall, and part of the gable with large projecting chimney, surviving.

SIGGINSHAGGARD

SMR: WX041-009001
ITM: 693875, 618934
Grid: 293945, 118882
Families: Siggins
Footprint: 40m² (6.6m x 6.1m)

The four-storey tower house survives almost to the wall-walk, with quoins and base-batter. The pointed entrance of dressed granite, protected by a machicolation, yett and possibly a murder-hole, leads through a lobby to the vaulted ground floor, which has three double-splay loops and ten gun-loops. A mural stairway leads to the loft under the vault, which has two small windows, a mural chamber and six gun-loops. A spiral stairs, with two slit windows and two gun-loops, rises to the first floor, which has a fireplace, garderobe, four damaged windows and seven gun-loops. The spiral stairs (destroyed) continued to the second floor, which has three slit windows and two gun-loops, and to the third floor, which has three slits and two gun-loops, and on to the wall-walk.

SIGGINSTOWN

SMR: WX053–001001
ITM: 706246, 607072
Grid: 306319, 107018
Families: Siggins, Jacob
Footprint: 55m² (7.5m x 7.3m)

The four-storey tower house, with good quoins and base-batter, survives to wall-walk level. The pointed entrance (blocked) was protected by a machicolation, portcullis and a cross-loop from the vaulted ground floor, which has three embrasures with double-splay loops, as well as two long loops covering the angles. A mural stairs rising to first floor gives access to the loft which has a chamber controlling the portcullis. A spiral stairs gives access to the second floor, with loop windows in each wall, a fireplace, and a garderobe with a cross-loop. The spiral stairs with cross-loop rises to the third floor which has similar features and continues to the destroyed parapet, which had a lookout platform at one angle.

SLADE

SMR: WX054-008001
ITM: 674573, 598550
Grid: 274639, 98494
Families: Knights Hospitaller, Laffan, Redmond, Loftus, Mansell. Robinson, Breen, Rice
Footprint: 29m² (5.5m x 5.3m)

The small, four-storey tower house survives to battlements with good quoins and slightly battered walls. A pointed doorway, protected by a machicolation and murder-hole, leads though a lobby to the vaulted ground floor, which has one blocked window. A mural stairs leads to the loft under the vault which has one slit window. A spiral stairs rises to the first floor, which has two rectangular windows with seats, a fireplace and a garderobe with a spy hole to the stairs. The spiral stairs rises to the second floor which has two small windows with seats. The spiral continues to third floor, which is covered by a second vault, and on to the parapet, which has stepped crennellations. A further half-storey, with a lookout platform on top, contains the machicolation. A later fortified house is attached to a corner of the tower house. The complex is maintained as a National Monument.

SLEVOY

SMR: WX041-015001
ITM: 687667, 617565
Grid: 287736, 117513
Families: Rossiter, Tottenham, Pigott
Footprint: 37m² (6.5m x 5.6m)

This much altered tower house survives to first-floor level, with granite quoins but with no batter. A lintelled doorway, protected by a murder-hole, leads through a lobby to the vaulted ground floor, which has four embrasures with one double-splay loop. A damaged mural stairway gives access to the loft, with one window, under the vault and the first floor which has a gardrobe, a damaged fireplace and one large window with granite frame.

STOKESTOWN

SMR: WX034-015003
ITM: 669329, 623723
Grid: 269394, 123672
Families: Prendergast, Dormer
Footprint: 46m² (7m x 6.6m)

The three-storey tower house survives to crenellations but in a much modified condition. Lacking a vault, wall-batter and quoins, the tower has few original features, apart from some blocked lights and a large mullioned and transomed window (blocked) with square hood-mouldings on the second floor.

TAGHMON (POLEMARL)

SMR: WX041-008001
ITM: 691784, 619823
Grid: 291854, 119772
Families: Lords of the Liberty, Meyler, Hore, Holmes
Footprint: 112m² (10.8m x 10.3m)

The large, four-storey tower house survives to wall-walk level with good quoins and base-batter. The round-headed doorway, protected by a machicolation, murder-hole and portcullis, opens through a lobby to the vaulted ground floor, which has two double-splay loops and one inserted gun-loop. A mural stairway leads to the loft under the vault, from which the portcullis was operated, and continues to the first floor, which has three small windows with seats, a slit window, a damaged fireplace, a garderobe and a possible gun-loop. The mural stairs continues to second floor which has similar features to the first (apart from the possible gun-loop). A spiral stairs continues to the third floor, which has three windows with seats, a fireplace, a garderobe and an entrance to an oubliette. The spiral stairs rises to the wall-walk which has remains of corner machicolations at two angles.

TAYLORSTOWN

SMR: WX040-001
ITM: 681736, 614429
Grid: 281803, 114376
Families: Rochford, Chambers, Rossiter, Cullen, Codd
Footprint: 57m² (7.6m x 7.5m)

This tower house survives to second storey, with good quoins and base-batter. The lintelled doorway, unprotected by a murder-hole, leads through a lobby to the vaulted ground floor, which has recesses containing horizontal gun-loops and a secondary entrance through another embrasure. A mural stairway from the lobby leads to the loft under the vault, which has one window. An oubliette is accessed from the stairway outside the loft doorway. Opposite the loft entrance, a door in the external wall of the tower provided access to an attached fortified house (now removed, apart from fragments of wall attached to the tower). The mural stairs continues to the first floor, also providing access to another horizontal gun-loop and a garderobe. The first floor has two double-light rectangular windows, one single-light, a fireplace and two gun-loops. A spiral stairs rises to the second floor which has three blocked embrasures. Part of the bawn survived until recently.

TELLAROUGHT

SMR: WX034-040001
ITM: 675546, 621546
Grid: 275612, 121495
Families: Sutton, Forde, Dormer
Footprint: 54m² (7.4m x 7.3m)

This tower house, with good quoins and base-batter, survives to the damaged second floor. The destroyed entrance, protected by an unusual arrangement of three murder-holes, leads through the lobby to a vaulted ground floor, which has three embrasures but no evidence for opes. A mural stairs leads to the loft under the vault and the first floor, which has a damaged fireplace, four destroyed windows but no evidence of a garderobe. A spiral stairs continues to the partially-surviving second floor, which had two windows, one with a seat.

TRACEYSTOWN WEST

SMR: WX041-002001
ITM: 688734, 619533
Grid: 288803, 119482
Families: Hore
Footprint: 54m² (7.8m x 6.9m)

The tower house is one of a number of castles located along the valley of the river Corock which formed the boundary of the Wexford Pale. The tower survives, with quoins and battered walls, to the top of the vault, with one destroyed corner. The round-headed doorway, protected by a murder-hole, leads through a lobby to the vaulted ground floor, which has four embrasures and two surviving slit windows. A mural stairs gave access to the loft under the vault, which was supported on joists set directly into the walls.

APPENDIX 1 – TOWER HOUSES: CONDITION AND DOCUMENTATION

The following documentary sources have been used to complement fieldwork in the identification of tower houses and fortified houses.

Down Survey (DS) maps.
Du Noyer collection of drawings, R. I. A.
Du Noyer collection of drawings, R. S. A. I.
Edwards Estate map 1727 (N. A. I) 1082/3, 1/22
Hore, H. F. (ed.), 'A chorographic account of the southern part of the county of Wexford, written anno 1684: by Robert Leigh, esq., of Rosegarland, in that county' in *R. S. A. I. Jn.*, v (1858-9), pp 451–67.
Hore, H. F. and James Graves (eds.), *The social state of the southern and eastern counties of Ireland in the sixteenth century. Printed from the originals in the Public Record Office, London* (Dublin, 1870).
Hore, P. H., *History of the town and county of Wexford*, 6 vols. (London, 1900–11).
Hore, P. H., 'The barony of Forth' in *The Past*, i (1920), pp 62–106; ii (1921), pp 38–99; iii (1925), pp 9–40; iv (1949), pp 13–59.
Jeffrey, W., *The castles of county Wexford*, E. Culleton (ed.); typescript produced by Wexford Hist. Soc. (1979).
Jordan, A., 'Date, chronology and evolution of the county Wexford tower house' in *Wex. Hist. Soc. Jn.,* xiii (1990–91), pp 30–82.
Lawrence collection of photographs, N. L. I.

Leask, H., 'Slade Castle, Co. Wexford' in *R. S. A. I. Jn.*, lxxxi (1951), pp 198–202.
Leask, H., 'Rathmacknee Castle, Co. Wexford' in *R. S. A. I. Jn.*, lxxxiii (1953), pp 37–45.
Lewis, S., *A topographical dictionary of Ireland*, 2 v. (London, 1837).
Moore, M., *Archaeological inventory of county Wexford* (Dublin, 1996).
O'Callaghan, J., 'The castle of the Deeps' in *Old. Wex. Soc. Jn.*, ii (1969), pp 26–38.
O'Callaghan, J., 'Fortified houses of the sixteenth century in south Wexford' in *Wex. Hist. Soc. Jn.*, viii (1980–1), pp 1–51.
Ordnance Survey (OS) maps (1841).
O'Flanagan, M. (compiler), *Letters containing information relative to the antiquities of the county of Wexford collected during the progress of the Ordnance Survey in 1840*, 2 v. (Bray, 1933).
Scalé and Richards, Chart of Wexford Harbour, 1764, B. L.
Simington, R. C. (ed.), *The Civil Survey of the county of Wexford* (CS) (Dublin, 1953).
Wakeman collection of drawings, R. I. A.

TOWER HOUSE	FABRIC	DOCUMENTATION	STATUS	ASSOCIATED FEATURES	VISUALS	ASSOCIATED FAMILY
1. **Adamstown**	significant	CS 'a fine castle', OS 'castle in ruins'; Jeffrey 194; *Arch. invent.* 1496; *W. H. S. Jn.* (1980) 31	definite	bawn (removed) hall (removed)	Wakeman Devereux stone 1556	Devereux
2. **Ardenagh Great**	removed	CS 'small castle and thatched house'; OS 'castle site'; Jeffrey 93; *Arch. invent.* 1565	definite	hall		Hore
3. **Arnestown**	removed	CS 'castle of Arnestown'; OS 'site of Arnestown castle'; Jeffrey 196; *Arch. invent.* 1566	possible			
4. **Artramon**	extensive	CS 'castle'; OS 'Artramon castle'; Jeffrey 91, *Arch. invent.* 1497	definite	hall, church		Roche, Le Hunte
5. **Aughnagan**	fragment	CS 'castle'; OS 'castle in ruins'; Jeffrey 93 '1559, fortalice'; *Arch. invent.* 1498	definite			Hore
6. **Baldwinstown**	extensive	OS 'castle in ruins'; Jeffrey 51; *Arch. invent.* 1499	definite	bawn	Wakeman	Keating, Stafford
7. **Ballindooney**	removed	OS 'site of castle'; Jeffrey 196; *Arch. invent.* 1567	possible			Kavanagh
8. **Ballinesker**	removed	OS, 'site of Ballinesker castle'; Jeffrey 176 'castle well'; *Arch. invent.* 1568	possible	earthworks		? Sinnott, ? Cheevers
9. **Ballyanne**	removed	Jeffrey 197 late 17C refs. to 'castle of Ballyanne'	possible			Kavanagh
10. **Ballybrennan**	removed	OS 'site of castle'; Jeffrey 206 'site known'	possible			Keating, FitzHenry
11. **Ballybrennan Big**	fragment (incorporated in dwelling)	DS sketch 'castle, house, church, cabins'; OS 'site of castle'; Jeffrey 1; *Arch. invent.* 1570	definite	hall, church		Sinnott
12. **Ballycappoge**	removed	CS 'castle'; Jeffrey 54, 1634 'castle of Ballycappoge'; *Arch. invent.* 970	possible	in moated site		St John, Browne
13. **Ballycogley**	extensive	OS 'castle'; Hore, 'Forth', iii, 32; Jeffrey 2; *Arch. invent.* 1500	definite	house attached (removed)		Wadding, Barrington
14. **Ballyconnick**	removed	CS 'castle'; OS 'castle in ruins'; Jeffrey 53; *Arch. invent.* 1571	definite	moated site		Connick, Busher, Devereux, Cliffe
15. **Ballyconnor Big**	significant	DS 'castle and slate house'; Edwards Estate map 1727; *R. S. A. I. Jn.,* (1937) 298–9; Jeffrey 4; *Arch. invent.* 1501	definite	hall	Date stone 1570 Estate map 1727	Stafford
16. **Ballycushlane**	removed	Jeffrey: 1617 'manor and castle or fortalice of Ballycushlane'	possible			Browne
17. **Ballyfane** (Castlepalliser)	removed	DS sketch; DS notes 'Ballyfane castle and several cabins'; Jeffrey 10	definite			Codd, Palliser
18. **Ballyfarnoge** (Alderton)	significant	CS; Jeffrey 132	definite	hall		Prendergast, Glascott

TOWER HOUSE	FABRIC	DOCUMENTATION	STATUS	ASSOCIATED FEATURES	VISUALS	ASSOCIATED FAMILY
19. **Ballygarvan**	removed	CS 'a decayed castle'; Jeffrey 135 'castle field'; *Arch. invent.* 1572	definite	grange		Cistercians, Rossiter, Colclough
20. **Ballygeary**	removed	DS notes; OS 'site of castle'; *Arch. invent.* 1573	definite	hall	Edwards Estate	Sinnott, Edwards
21. **Ballyhack**	extensive	CS 'castle, weir, church'; OS 'Ballyhack castle in ruins'; Jeffrey 136; *Arch. invent.* 1503; *P. R. I. A.* (1975) C, 103–18	definite	grange	Du Noyer x 2	Cistercians, Etchingham
22 **Ballyharron**	removed	OS 'castle'; Jeffrey '1583 castle of Ballyharron'	definite			Sinnott, Roche
23. **Ballyhealy**	extensive (restored)	CS 'castle'; OS 'castle in ruins'; Jeffrey 56; *Arch. invent.* 1504	definite			Cheevers, Saunders Bunbury
24. **Ballyhire**	fragment	DS notes; Hore, 'Forth', iii, 46, 'castle and stone hall'; Jeffrey 7	definite	hall	Edwards Estate map 1727	Lambert, Edwards
25. **Ballyhoge**	removed	CS 'a ruined castle' Jeffrey 101; *Arch. invent.* 1574	possible			FitzHenry, Colclough Hore, Ogle
26. **Ballykeerogebeg**	removed	CS 'a ruined castle'; Jeffrey 133	definite			FitzHenry
27. **Ballyloskan**	removed	CS 'an old ruined castle'	definite			Furlong, Tottenham
28. **Ballymacane**	removed	DS notes 'castle and slate house'; OS 'castle, site of'; Hore, 'Forth', iii, 28, 40, 'castle-house with a ruined tower'; *Arch. invent.* 1577	definite	in moated site	photograph	Stafford
29. **Ballyrane**	removed	DS notes, 'castle, church, cabins'; OS 'site of Ballyrane castle'; Hore, 'Forth', iii, 10; O'Flanagan, 'tower in excellent preservation'; *Arch. invent.* 1507	definite			
30. **Ballyseskin**	removed	CS 'castle'; Jeffrey 60 'fine tower, bawn and great hall'; *Arch. invent.* 1579	definite	bawn, hall		Cheevers, Bunbury
31. **Ballyshannon**	removed	CS 'a castle in good repair'; Jeffrey 95	definite			Devereux
32. **Ballyshelin**	removed	CS 'slate house'; OS 'site of castle'; Jeffrey 1630s, 'castle and hall'	possible			Hore
33. **Ballysop**	removed	CS 'a ruined castle'; Jeffrey 137;	possible			Sutton
34. **Ballyteige**	extensive	CS 'castle'; OS 'castle'; Jeffrey 61; *Arch. invent.* 1508	definite	bawn, hall	Wakeman	Whitty, Colclough Meadows
35. **Ballytrent**	removed	Hore, 'Forth', i, 'King's castle of Ballytrent'	possible			
36. **Ballytory**	fragment (incorporated in dwelling)	Hore, 'Forth', iii, 40; Jeffrey 8; *Arch. invent.* 1509	definite	hall		French
37. **Ballywilliam** (Warren's castle)	removed	OS 'site of Warren's castle'; Jeffrey 197	possible			Kavanagh, Warren
38. **Bannow**	removed	CS; OS; Hore, *Wexford*, iv, 1616 'one ruinous castle'; Jeffrey 64; *Arch. invent.* 1425	definite	borough		Loftus
39. **Barntown**	extensive	CS 'a ruined castle'; OS 'castle in ruins; Jeffrey 98; *Arch. invent.* 1510	definite			Roche, Wadding, Le Hunte
40. **Barrystown**	significant	CS 'castle'; OS 'castle in ruins'; Jeffrey 67; *Arch. invent.* 1511	definite			Barry, King
41. **Boley**	removed	CS 'a ruined castle'; OS 'Boley castle in ruins'; Jeffrey 138; *Arch. invent.* 1512	definite	moated site, grange	Du Noyer x 2	Cistercians
42. **Battlestown**	removed	CS 'castle of Battlestown'; Leigh 'an old tower'; Hore, *Wexford*, iv, 82–3; Jeffrey 137	definite			Cistercians, Battaile, Etchingham
43. **Bridgetown**	removed	CS 'castle'; Jeffrey 68	definite			Browne, Rowe
44. **Brideswell**	removed	CS; Jeffrey 69; *Arch. invent.* 1585	definite			Devereux
45. **Brownswood**	significant	CS 'a ruined castle'; OS 'Brownswood castle in ruins'; Jeffrey 179; *Arch. invent.* 1513	definite		Wakeman	Browne, Rochford
46. **Bryanstown**	fragment (incorporated in house)	CS 'castle in indifferent repair'; OS 'Bryanstown House'; Jeffrey 100; *Arch. invent.* 1514	definite			Bryan, Roche, Isham
47. **Butlerstown**	extensive (restored)	DS castle shown; notes 'castle'; Jeffrey 11; *Arch. invent.* 1515	definite		Wakeman, Lawrence	Butler, Harvey, Boxwell, Skrine
48. **Camlin**	removed	CS 'a good castle', 'the castle of Camlin'; Jeffrey 199	possible			Dormer

Tower house	Fabric	Documentation	Status	Associated Features	Visuals	Associated Family
49. **Carrigmannon**	removed	CS 'a large ruined stone building'; Jeffrey 105 'c. 1630 castle of Carrigmannon'; 1680 'fortalice'; *Arch. invent.* 1587	definite			Devereux, Furlong
50. **Castlebridge**	removed	Lewis, i, 280	definite		Richards & Scalé map 1764	
51. **Castletown** (Carne)	fragment	DS notes 'castle of Castletown'; OS 'castle, site of'; Jeffrey 13; *Arch. invent.* 1516	definite			Codd
52. **Cleristown**	removed	OS, 'site of castle'; Jeffrey 1631, 'fortalice at Clearistown'; Hore Mss 'castle standing'	possible			Devereux
53. **Clohamon** (Castlequarter)	removed	CS; OS 'Clohamon castle in ruins'; Lyttleton 'remains of tower and bawn excavated'	definite	bawn		Grace, Masterson, Calvert
54. **Clonard**	fragment	DS castles shown; OS 'castle in ruins'; Jeffrey 17; *Arch. invent.* 1517	definite			Sutton, Hatton
55. **Clonmines**	extensive	CS 'castle in ruins'; OS 'Black castle in ruins'; Jeffrey 139; *Arch. invent.* 1433	definite	borough		FitzHenry
56. **Clonmines**	fragment (incorporated in house)	CS 'castle in ruins, OS 'castle'; Jeffrey 139; *Arch. invent.* 1434	definite	borough		Sutton
57. **Clougheast**	extensive (restored)	DS notes; OS 'castle in ruins'; Jeffrey 15; *Arch. invent.* 1518	definite	hall (restored)	Wakeman	Codd, Waddy
58. **Cullentra**	removed	OS 'site of castle'; Jeffrey 107; *Arch. invent.* 1591	possible			Roche, Hore
59. **Courthoyle**	significant	CS 'a small castle'; OS 'castle in ruins'; Jeffrey 199; *Arch. invent.* 1519	definite	church		Howell (Walsh), Devereux
60. **Cullenstown**	significant	CS 'castle'; OS 'Cullenstown castle'; Jeffrey 71; *Arch. invent.* 1520	definite			Cullen, Boyse
61. **Danescastle**	extensive	CS castle'; OS 'Danescastle'; Jeffrey 72; *Arch. invent.* 1521	definite	hall	Wakeman x 2 Du Noyer	Denn, Cheevers
62. **Deeps**	extensive	CS 'a large castle'; OS 'a large castle'; Jeffrey 108; *Arch. invent.* 1522; *W. H.S. Jn.*, (1969) 26–38	definite		Wakeman	? Lords of Liberty, Sinnott, Roche, Devereux
63. **Dirr**	fragment of bawn	CS 'the castle of Dirr'; OS 'castle in ruins'; Jeffrey 109; *Arch. invent.* 1594	definite	bawn		Meyler
64. **Drinagh**	removed	DS notes 'decayed castle and church'; Hore, 'Forth', ii, 88; Jeffrey 17; *Arch. invent.* 1592	definite	church		Roche, Hore
65. **Duncannon**	removed	Cartographic record; Hore, *Wexford*, iv, 22–3; Jeffrey 142	definite			Etchingham
66. **Duncormick**	removed	CS 'castle'; OS 'castle site'; Jeffrey 72; *Arch. invent.* 1593	definite	manorial village, motte, church, earthworks		Meyler
67. **Dunganstown**	removed	CS 'castle'	possible			? Keating
68. **Fardystown**	removed	CS 'castle of Fardystown'; DS notes 'at Fardystown a waste ruined castle'; Jeffrey 18	definite			Rossiter,
69. **Ferrycarrig**	extensive	OS 'Passage tower'; Jeffrey 111; *Arch. invent.* 1523	definite		18c etching Wakeman, Du Noyer	Roche
70. **Finshoge**	removed	CS 'butt of a castle'; Jeffrey 203	possible	earthworks		
71. **Gortins**	removed	CS 'castle'; OS 'castle, site of'; Jeffrey 76; *Arch. invent.* 1595	definite			Prendergast
72. **Grahormick**	removed	DS notes 'an old castle'; Jeffrey 19 '1840, castle in good preservation'	definite			Sinnott, Scurlock
73. **Growtown**	removed	CS 'a fair castle in good repair'; DS 'castle of Growtown'; Jeffrey 112	definite	earthworks		Cheevers, Hore
74. **Harperstown**	removed	CS 'castle'; OS 'castle in ruins'; Hore and Graves, 58; Hore 'Chor. acc.','large castle of Harperstown'; Jeffrey 76	definite			Hore
75. **Hayes' Castle** (Wexford town)	removed	Hore, *Wexford*, v, 343, 356; Jeffrey 43	definite			Hay
76. **Hayestown**	removed	DS 'castle, slate house, cabins'; Hore, 'Forth', i, 19	definite			Hay
77. **Hillcastle**	removed	DS sketch of castle; DS notes 'castle, cabins'; Jeffrey 20; *Arch. invent.* 1599	definite	hall, moated site		Hay,Nunn

TOWER HOUSE	FABRIC	DOCUMENTATION	STATUS	ASSOCIATED FEATURES	VISUALS	ASSOCIATED FAMILY
78. Horetown	removed	CS, 'a fine castle but something out of repair'; Jeffrey 113 'castle field'	definite			Furlong, Davis, Goff
79. Houseland	fragment	CS 'an old castle'; OS 'Houseland castle in ruins'; Jeffrey 151; *Arch. invent.* 1524	definite		Du Noyer photograph	Keating, Loftus
80. Johnstown	removed 1940s	OS 'castle'; Jeffrey 20; *Arch. invent.* 1526	definite		drawing, Lawrence	Esmond, Grogan
81. Kayer (Wilton)	removed	CS 'castle'; OS 'Wilton castle'; Jeffrey 205 '1618: castle of Kayer'; *Arch. invent.* 1615	definite			Furlong, Butler, Alcock, Denne
82. Kilcavan	significant	CS 'castle'; OS 'castle in ruins'; Jeffrey 79; *Arch. invent.* 1527	definite	hall (hood moulding), church		FitzHenry, Thompson
83. Kilcloggan	extensive	CS 'castle'; OS 'Kilcloggan castle in ruins'; Jeffrey 152 '1541, castle or fortalice'; *Arch. invent.* 1528	definite	bawn	Du Noyer	Hospitallers, Loftus
84. Kilcowan	removed	OS 'site of castle'; Jeffrey 78 '1548, castle and hall'; *Arch. invent.* 1600	definite	early medieval site, motte moated site		Keating, Isham
85. Kilhile	significant	CS 'castle'; OS 'Kilhile castle in ruins'; Jeffrey 156; *Arch. invent.* 1529	definite			Cistercians, Etchingham
86. Killesk	removed	CS 'a small castle' [may be confused with fortified church]; Jeffrey 154 '1562, castle of Killesk'; *Arch. invent.* 1601	possible			FitzGerald (Barron)
87. Killiane	extensive	DS 'castle and church'; *Arch. invent.* 1530; Jeffrey 23	definite	hall, bawn	Wakeman late 18c painting	Hay, Cheevers, Harvey
88. Lacken	removed	OS 'site of castle'; Jeffrey 'castle field'; *Arch. invent.* 1054	possible	moated site		
89. Lady's Island	extensive	Hore 'Forth' 1680s; Jeffrey 24; *Arch. invent.* 1531	definite	gatehouse, bawn, flanking tower	Wakeman Lawrence	Augustinians, Lambert
90. Lingstown	removed fell 1985	DS notes 'castle and watermill'; Jeffery 26 *Arch. invent.* 1532	definite	hall	photograph drawing	Lambert, Boxwell
91. Longgraigue	fragment (incorporated in house)	CS 'castle in repair'; Jeffrey 115; *Arch. invent.* 1533	definite	hall		Bryan, Leigh, Gibbon
92. Macmine	significant	CS 'a fair castle'; OS 'Macmine castle'; Jeffrey 115; *Arch. invent.* 1534	definite	hall		FitzHenry, King, Dunne
93. Morriscastle (Tinnacree)	removed 1936	OS 'site of Morris castle'; Jeffrey 'fragment removed 1936'; *Arch. invent.* 1614	definite			Ó Morchoe, Mountnorris
94. Monart	removed	CS 'castle of Monart'; Jeffrey 232; DS, sketch of castle; *Arch. invent.* 1058	possible	moated site		Colclough
95. Mountgarrett	significant (partial collapse 2010)	OS 'Mountgarrett castle in ruins'; Jeffrey 208	definite		Wakeman	Episcopal, Butler
96. Mulrankin	extensive	CS 'castle, hall, bawn'; OS 'castle in ruins'; Jeffrey 80; *Arch. invent.* 1536	definite	hall, bawn	Wakeman	Browne, Cliffe
97. Nash	removed	CS 'a decayed castle'; 'castle field'; Jeffrey 166	definite	grange, earthworks		Cistercian, Colclough
98. Newbawn	fragment	CS 'a ruined castle'; OS 'castle in ruins; Jeffrey 121; *Arch. invent.* 1537	definite	moated site		Browne
99. Newbay	fragment (incorporated in outhouse)	DS shows castle; DS notes 'castle and large stone house'; Jeffrey 28 '1562, castle or fortalice'; *Arch. invent.* 1606.	definite	hall		Selskar Abbey, Roche
100. Newcastle (Clongeen)	removed	CS; OS 'site of castle'; Jeffrey 122 'castle field'	definite	motte		Neville, Leigh
101. Newcastle (Kilmannon)	significant	CS 'castle'; OS 'castle'; Jeffrey 83; *Arch. invent.* 1538	definite	bawn, hall		Rossiter, Jennings, Lett
102. Newcastle (Tikillin)	removed	CS 'a castle indifferent in repair'; OS 'castle site'; Jeffrey 122; *Arch. invent.* 1607	definite			Roche
103. Nook (Buttermilk)	fragment	CS 'small castle and weir'; Jeffrey 169; *Arch. Ire.* Autumn, 1991; *Arch. invent.* 1539	definite	grange	Du Noyer x 4	Cistercians, Etchingham
104. Oldcourt	removed	CS 'castle of Oldcourt'; OS 'castle, site of'; Jeffrey 160; *Arch. invent.* 1609	definite	manorial village		Sutton
105. Oulart	removed	CS 'a ruined castle'; OS 'castle, site of'; Hore, 'Forth', '(d. 1618) had grant of castle of Oulart'; Jeffrey 189 'castle field'	definite			Sinnott
106. Peppardscastle	? fragment	Jeffrey 192; 'castle incorporated in house'	possible			Peppard, White

TOWER HOUSE	FABRIC	DOCUMENTATION	STATUS	ASSOCIATED FEATURES	VISUALS	ASSOCIATED FAMILY
107. **Polehore**	removed	CS 'a castle and weir'; OS 'site of Polehore castle'; Jeffrey 123; *Arch. invent.* 1611	definite			Hore
108. **Pollmounty**	removed	CS 'Pollmounty castle'; OS 'castle site'; Jeffrey 211 'part of a wall'	definite			Kavanagh
109. **Priesthaggard**	removed 1970s	CS 'castle'; OS 'castle in ruins'; Jeffrey 160 'doorway and vaulted chamber survives'; *Arch. invent.* 1541	definite			Meyler
110. **Rathnageeragh**	removed	CS 'a decayed castle'; Jeffrey 167 'castle meadow'; *Arch. invent.* 371	possible	grange		Cistercians, Power, Colclough
111. **Ramsgrange**	removed	CS 'a ruined castle'; Hore, *Wexford*, iv, 72–3; Jeffrey 163	definite	grange		Cistercians, Etchingham
112. **Rathaspick**	removed	Hore, 'Forth', ii, 37; Hore and Graves 1564, 50; Jeffrey 30; *Arch. invent.* 1612	definite			Codd
113. **Rathlannon** (Johnstown)	significant	DS notes 'Rathlannon castle'; OS 'castle in ruins; Jeffrey 31; *Arch. invent.* 1525	definite			Esmond
114. **Rathmacknee**	extensive	OS 'castle' Hore, 'Forth' iii, 21; *Arch. invent.* 1542; Jeffrey 32; Leask, *JRSAI* (1953), 37–45	definite	bawn, hall, mill church	Wakeman	Rossiter, Knox, Grogan
115. **Rathronan**	significant	CS 'castle'; OS 'castle'; Jeffrey 86; *Arch. invent.* 1543	definite	hall		Browne, Cliffe
116. **Ballymagir** (Richfield)	significant (hall incorporated in dwelling)	CS 'a fair castle and a large bawn'; Jeffrey 57; *Arch invent.* 1544	definite	in moated site (*Arch. invent.* 1084), bawn (modified), attached hall		Devereux, Loftus
117. **Rosegarland**	significant	CS 'castle and bawn'; OS 'castle'; Jeffrey 125; *Arch. invent.* 1545	definite			Neville, Sinnott, Leigh
118. **Ryland**	removed	OS 'Ryland castle in ruins'; Jeffrey 233 'part survive'; *Arch. invent.* 1613	possible			Kavanagh, Annesley
119. **Scar**	extensive	CS 'castle'; OS 'castle in ruins'; Jeffrey 87; *Arch. invent.* 1546	definite	hall	Wakeman	Meyler, Bryan
120. **Sigginshaggard**	extensive	CS 'a ruined castle'; OS 'castle in ruins'; Jeffrey 128; *Arch. invent.* 1548	definite	evidence of bawn		Siggins
121. **Sigginstown**	extensive	OS 'castle in ruins'; Hore, 'Forth', iii, 41; Jeffrey 35; *Arch. invent.* 1547	definite	hall		Siggins, Jacob
122. **Slad**	removed	Hore, 'Forth', iii, 19 'Hayes' castle at Slad'; Jeffrey 37	definite			Hay
123. **Slade**	extensive	CS 'an old castle'; OS 'Slade castle in ruins'; Jeffrey 163; *Arch. invent.* 1549; Leask, *J. R. S. A. I.* (1951) 198–201	definite	hall	Grose, Wakeman x 2, Du Noyer x 2	Hospitallers, Laffan, Redmond, Loftus, Mansell
124. **Slevoy**	significant	CS 'castle and bawn'; OS 'castle'; Jeffrey 128; *Arch. invent.* 1550	definite	hall, moated site (*Arch. invent.* 1088), bawn		Rossiter, Tottenham, Pigott
125. **Staffords' Castle** (Wexford town)	removed	Hore, *Wexford*, v, 209, 341; Jeffrey 45	definite		painting 1820	Stafford
126. **Staplestown**	removed	DS notes 'castle at Staplestown'; DS sketch of castle; Jeffrey 38 'castle field'	definite			FitzHenry
127. **Stokestown**	significant	CS 'a fair castle'; OS 'castle'; Jeffrey 212; *Arch. invent.* 1551	definite			Prendergast, Dormer
128. **Tacumshin**	fragment	DS notes 'castle and thatched house'; Hore, 'Forth' i, 18; Jeffrey 41; *Arch. invent.* 1552	definite			Hay, Parle
129. **Taghmon** (Poulmarl)	extensive	CS 'a fair castle'; OS 'castle'; Jeffrey 129; *Arch. invent.* 1466	definite	borough	Wakeman	Lords of Liberty, Meyler Hore, Holmes
130. **Tagunnan**	removed	DS castle and bawn; DS notes 'castle with slate house and cabins'; Jeffrey 39	definite	bawn, hall		Rochford, Knox, Harvey
131. **Taylorstown**	extensive	CS 'a small castle out of repair'; OS 'Taylorstown castle in ruins'; Jeffrey 171; *Arch invent.* 1553	definite	evidence of bawn, hall		Rochford, Chambers
132. **Tellarought**	significant	CS 'castle'; OS 'castle in ruins'; Jeffrey 170; *Arch. invent.* 1554	definite	manorial village		Sutton, Forde
133. **Tomhaggard**	fragment	CS 'castle'; Jeffrey 89; *Arch. invent.* 1555	definite	manorial village		Rossiter
134. **Traceystown West**	fragment	CS 'a ruined castle'; OS 'castle in ruins'; Jeffrey 131; *Arch. invent.* 1556	definite			Hore, Goff
135. **Trimmer**	removed	DS notes 'large house or tower at Trimmer'; DS tower shown; Jeffrey 41	possible			White
136. **Tullycanna**	removed	CS 'castle'; Jeffrey 89	possible			Neville

TOWER HOUSE	FABRIC	DOCUMENTATION	STATUS	ASSOCIATED FEATURES	VISUALS	ASSOCIATED FAMILY
137. **Waddings' Castle** (Wexford town)	removed	Hore, *Wexford*, v, 86, 350; Jeffrey 45	definite			Wadding

Classifications: 'Extensive': most of four walls and internal features surviving.
'Substantial': walls and internal features partially surviving (sometimes incorporated in a later building).
'Fragmentary': any identifiable surviving fabric (sometimes incorporated in a later building).

APPENDIX 2 – FORTIFIED HOUSES: CONDITION AND DOCUMENTATION

HALL-HOUSE	FABRIC	DOCUMENTATION	STATUS	ASSOCIATED FEATURES	VISUALS	ASSOCIATED FAMILY
1. **Ballytramon**	removed (fell 1940s)	CS 'a fine house'; OS 'castle in ruins'; Jeffrey 97; *Arch. invent.* 1581	definite		image Hore Mss	Sinnott
2. **Bargy**	extensive (incorporated in dwelling)	CS 'a fair castle'; OS 'castle'; Jeffrey 64; *Arch invent.* 1558; O'Callaghan 35–39	definite		Grose NLI drawings	Rossiter, Harvey
3. **Ballykeerogemore**	fragment	CS 'a large castle'; OS 'castle in ruins'; Jeffrey 134; *Arch. invent.* 1506	definite	hall in bawn, church	Wakeman	Sutton
4. **Brownscastle**	fragment	CS 'a small pile of stones'; OS 'castle in ruins'; Jeffrey 99 '1618, Browne's castle near the pill'; *Arch. invent.* 1619	definite			Browne, Sinnott, Howlett
5. **Castleboro**	significant	CS 'castle'; OS 'an old castle'; Jeffrey 201; *Arch. invent.* 1559	definite			Butler, Carew
6. **Clonmines**	fragment	CS 'castle in ruins'; OS 'castle in ruins'	definite	borough		
7. **Coolhull**	extensive	OS 'Coolhull castle in ruins'; Jeffrey 69; *Arch. invent.* 1560; O'Callaghan 26–31	definite		Wakeman Du Noyer	Devereux
8. **Dungeer**	fragment	CS 'castle of Dungeer'; OS 'castle in ruins'; Jeffrey 110; *Arch. invent.* 1623	definite			Roche, Sutton
9. **Dungulph**	extensive (incorporated in dwelling)	CS 'castle'; OS 'Dungulph castle'; Jeffrey 147; *Arch. invent.* 1561; O'Callaghan 22–6	definite		Wakeman Du Noyer	Whitty, Loftus, Cloney
10. **Fethard**	extensive	OS 'Fethard castle in ruins'; Jeffrey 148; *Arch. invent.* 1448; O'Callaghan, 16–22; Murtagh, Fethard castle (1993).	definite		Du Noyer	episcopal, Loftus
11. **Hilltown**	extensive	CS 'a fair castle'; OS 'castle'; Jeffrey 113; *Arch. invent.* 1562; O'Callaghan, 33–4	definite	evidence of bawn	Wakeman Du Noyer	FitzHenry, Esmond
12. **Mayglass**	removed	DS notes 'ruins of castle and cabins'; 'Forth' 1680 'a sumptuous ancient house'	possible			episcopal
13. **Mullinderry**	fragment (incorporated in dwelling)	CS 'a fair slate house'; Jeffrey 117; *Arch. invent.* 1630	definite			Hore
14. **Newtown**	removed	OS 'castle in ruins'; *Arch. invent.* 1608	definite		Du Noyer	? Siggins
15. **Rathshillane**	significant	OS 'castle in ruins'; Jeffrey 34; *Arch. invent.* 1563	definite			French
16. **Redmond Hall**	removed	CS 'an old castle called Redmonds Hall'; Jeffrey 161; *Arch. invent.* 1604	definite			Redmond, Loftus
17. **Slade**	extensive	CS 'an old castle'; OS 'Slade castle in ruins'; Jeffrey 163; *Arch. invent.* 1564; Leask, *JRSAI* (1951) 198–201; O'Callaghan 15–16	definite	attached to tower house	Wakeman Du Noyer	Laffan, Mansell

ENDNOTES, ATTRIBUTIONS AND BIBLIOGRAPHY

The abbreviations listed here are used for sources that occur frequently; other sources are given in full.

A. F. M. — *Annals of the Four Masters*
Arch. Ir. — *Archaeology Ireland*
Arch. inventory — *Archaeological inventory of County Wexford*
Cal. Doc. Ire. — *Calendar of Documents relating to Ireland*
N. A. I. — National Archives of Ireland
N. L. I. — National Library of Ireland
O. P. W. — Office of Public Works
O. S. — Ordnance Survey of Ireland

R. I. A. Proc. — *Proceedings of the Royal Irish Academy*
R. S. A. I. Jn. — *Journal of the Royal Society of Antiquaries of Ireland*
S. M. R. — Sites and Monuments Record
T. C. D. — Trinity College Dublin
Wex. Hist. Soc. Jn. — *Journal of the Wexford Historical Society*
G. S. I. H. S. — Group for the study of Irish historic settlement

LOCATION AND LANDSCAPE

1. M.-T. Flanagan, 'Strategies of lordship in pre-Norman and post-Norman Leinster' in *Anglo-Norman Studies*, xx (1998), p. 112.

2. A. Gwynn and R. N. Hadcock, *Medieval religious houses Ireland* (London, 1970), pp 78–9.

3. *Annals of the Kingdom of Ireland by the Four Masters*, J. O'Donovan (ed.), 7 v. (Dublin, 1851), (hereafter *A. F. M.*), ii, p. 1167. For a discussion on the trícha cét, see J. Hogan, 'The trícha cét and related land measures' in *R.I.A. Proc.*, xxxviii, C (1928–9), pp 148–235.

4. E. Culleton, *Celtic and Early Christian Wexford* (Dublin, 1999), pp 21–2.

5. E. Culleton, *The south Wexford landscape* (Dublin, 1980), pp 14–37.

6. M. J. Gardiner and P. Ryan, *Soils of county Wexford* (Dublin, 1964). See fig. 14, p. 36.

7. *A. F. M.*, ii, p. 1167.

8. Gwynn and Hadcock, *Medieval religious houses Ireland*, pp 78-9.

9. R. C. Simington, (ed.), *The Civil Survey of the county of Wexford* (Dublin, 1953), p. xvii.

10. For a full account, see B. Colfer, *Arrogant trespass: Anglo-Norman Wexford 1169–1400* (Enniscorthy, 2002), pp 23–45.

CONTINENTAL CONNECTIONS

1. N. McCullough and V. Mulvin, *A lost tradition: the nature of architecture in Ireland* (Dublin, 1989), p. 11.

2. G. Stout and M. Stout, *Newgrange* (Cork, 2008), pp 67–83.

3. M. Moore, *Archaeological inventory of county Wexford* (Dublin, 1996), no. 1; F. Mitchell and M. Ryan, *Reading the Irish landscape* (Dublin, 1997), pp 167–70.

4. Mitchell and Ryan, *Irish landscape*, pp 226–7.

5. B. Raftery, 'The medieval settlement at Rathgall, County Wicklow' in C. Manning (ed.), *From ringforts to fortified houses* (Bray, 2007), pp 95–106.

6. Moore, *Arch. inventory*, nos. 222, 223.

7. G. Stout and M. Stout, 'Early landscapes: from pre-history to plantation' in F. H. A. Aalen, K. Whelan and M. Stout (eds.), *Atlas of the Irish rural landscape* (Cork, 2011), pp 40–43.

8. Moore, *Arch. inventory*, nos 224–8.

9. Moore, *Arch. inventory*, nos. 224, 225, 226, 228.

10. Aalen, Whelan and Stout, *Atlas*, p. 51; Culleton, *Celtic and Early Christian Wexford*, pp 205, 210, 214.

11. T. Ó Fiaich, 'The beginnings of Christianity' in T. W. Moody and F. X. Martin (eds.), *The course of Irish history* (Cork, 1967), pp 74–5.

12. K. Hughes, 'The golden age of Early Christian Ireland' in *Course of Irish history*, pp 85–8.

13. M. Stout, *The Irish ring-fort* (Cork, 1997); Stout and Stout, 'Early landscapes', pp 43–7.

14. Mitchell and Ryan, *Irish landscape*, pp 254–5.

15. J. Le Goff, *The medieval world* (London, 1990), p. 50.

16. For a general background to the Vikings, see E. Roesdahl, *The Vikings* (London, 1991); P. H. Sawyer, *Kings and Vikings: Scandinavia and Europe AD 700–1100* (New York, 1994).

17. *A. F. M.*, i, p. 431; Viking activity in county Wexford is examined in Colfer, *Arrogant trespass*, pp 12–24.

18. M. Ní Dhonnchadha, 'Inis Teimle, between Uí Chennselaig and the Déissi' in *Peritia*, xvi (2002), pp 457–8.

19. J. Henthorn Todd (ed.), *Cogadh Gaedhel re Gallaibh* (London, 1867), pp xxxix, 824–5.

20. *Annals of Ulster*, W. M. Hennessy and B. MacCarthy (eds.), 4 v. (Dublin, 1887–1901), i, p. 325.

21. *A. U.*, i, p. 335; *A. F. M.*, i, p. 459.

22. *A .F. M.*, i, p. 543.

23. B. Colfer, *Wexford: a town and its landscape* (Cork, 2008), pp 30–37.

24. D. Ó Corráin, *Ireland before the Normans* (Dublin, 1972), p. 105. For the recent discovery of a Viking settlement near Waterford, see R. O'Brien, P. Quinney and I. Russell, 'Preliminary report on the archaeological excavation and finds retrieval strategy of the Hiberno-Scandinavian site of Woodstown 6, County Waterford' in *Decies*, lxi (2005), pp 13–122.

25. D. Ó Corráin, 'Nationality and kingship in pre-Norman Ireland' in T. W. Moody (ed.), *Nationality and the pursuit of national independence* (Belfast, 1978), p. 324.

26. A. Perron, 'The face of the 'pagan': portraits of religious deviance on the medieval periphery' in *Journal of the Historical Society*, ix, 4 (2009), pp 467–92.

27. D. Ó Cróinín, *Early medieval Ireland* (Harlow, 1995), pp 291–2.

28.. F. J. Byrne, 'The trembling sod: Ireland in 1169' in A. Cosgrove (ed.), *A new history of Ireland*, ii (Oxford, 1993), pp 10, 22.

29 F. X. Martin, 'Diarmait Mac Murchada and the coming of the Anglo-Normans' in *N. H. I.*, ii, p. 59.

30. Perron, 'The face of the 'pagan', pp 467–92; R. Bartlett, *England under the Norman and Angevin kings* (Oxford, 2000), pp 99–202.

31. Gerald of Wales, *Topographia Hibernia*, pp 147–66.

CASTLES IN EUROPE

1. M. Bloch, *Feudal society*, ii (London and New York, 1989), pp 443–6.

2. Bloch, *Feudal society*, i, pp 161–5.

3. F. Cardini, 'The warrior and the knight' in J. Le Goff (ed.), *The medieval world* (London, 1990), pp 50; 75–7; 93; 127.

4. R. Bartlett, *The making of Europe: conquest, colonisation and cultural change 950–1350* (Princeton, 1994), p. 1.

5. Le Goff, *Medieval world*, p. 75.

6. Bloch, *Feudal society*, ii, pp 400–1.

7. S. Toy, *Castles: their construction and history* (New York, 1985), pp 1–65.

8. C. Coulson, *Castles in medieval society* (Oxford, 2003), p. 2.

9. Bloch, *Feudal society*, ii, p. 400. For a general discussion on European castles, see J. Du Meulemeester and K. O'Conor, 'Fortifications' in J. Graham-Campbell and M. Valor (eds.), *The archaeology of medieval Europe: eighth to twelfth centuries* (Aarhus, 2007), pp 316–41.

10. Coulson, *Castles in medieval society*, p. 15.

11. Toy, *Castles*, p. 53.

12. Coulson, *Castles in medieval society*, p. 51.

13. Bartlett, *Making of Europe*, pp 65–70.

14. W. Anderson, *Castles of Europe* (London, 1980), pp 51–3.

15. Anderson, *Castles of Europe*, p. 45.

16. Bloch, *Feudal society*, ii, p. 301.

17. Toy, *Castles*, pp 141–3.

18. Toy, *Castles*, pp 90–2.

19. Anderson, *Castles of Europe*, p. 103.

20. Bloch, *Feudal society*, ii, p. 302.

21. Coulson, *Castles in medieval society*, pp 21–6.

22. Bloch, *Feudal society*, i, 29.

23. R. H. C. Davis, *The Normans and their myth* (London, 1997), pp 12, 23, 57.

24. Anderson, *Castles of Europe*, p. 38.

25. Davis, *Norman myth*, pp 7–8; Anderson, *Castles of Europe*, p. 47.

26. Davis, *Norman myth*, pp 49–58.

27. Davis, *Norman myth*, pp 31–2.

28. Coulson, *Castles in medieval society*, p. 20.

29. Le Goff, *Medieval world*, pp 80–93.

30. D. M. Wilson, *The Bayeux tapestry* (London, 2004).

31. Davis, *Norman myth*, pp 103–132.

32. M. Chibnell, *The Normans* (Oxford, 2000), pp 65–72.

ANGLO-NORMAN COLONISATION

1. J. Gillingham, 'The beginnings of English imperialism' in *Journal of Historical Sociology*, v (December, 1992), pp 392–409.

2. *The song of Dermot and the earl*, G. Orpen (ed.), (Oxford, 1892), l. 140.

3. For a full account, see Colfer, *Arrogant trespass*.

4. G. Orpen, *Ireland under the Normans*, 4 v. (Oxford, 1911–1920), i, pp 77–100. For general background, see Colfer, *Arrogant trespass*, pp 23–35.

5. *Expugnatio*, p. 29; *Song of Dermot and the earl*, ll. 325–55.

6. *Song*, ll. 441–60; *Expugnatio*, p. 31.

7. *Expugnatio*, p. 53; *Song*, ll. 1395–7. For a description of the site, see I. Bennett, 'Preliminary archaeological excavations at Ferrycarrig ringwork, Newtown Td., Co. Wexford' in *Wex. Hist. Soc. Jn.*, x (1984–85), pp 25–43.

8. Moore, *Arch. inventory*, nos. 226; 962.

9. *Expugnatio*, pp 57–9; *Song*, ll. 1404–8; 1446. For a discussion on the battle of Baginbun, see J. Gillingham, 'Conquering the barbarians: war and chivalry in twelfth-century Britain' in *Haskins Society Journal*, iv (1993), pp 67–84.

10. *Expugnatio*, pp 57, 59, 67; *Song*, ll. 1526–31.

11. *Expugnatio*, pp 67, 75; *Song*, ll. 1556–1731.

12. *Calendar of documents relating to Ireland*, H. S. Sweetman (ed.), 5 v. (London, 1875–1986), i, no. 10; *Expugnatio*, p. 71.

13. *Expugnatio*, p. 93.

14. During his stay in Wexford, his officials spent £40 on herrings to feed his retinue (*Cal. doc. Ire.*, i, no. 34).

15. Orpen, *Normans*, i, p. 274.

16. Colfer, *Arrogant trespass*, pp 194–200.

17. *Calendar of ancient deeds and muniments preserved in the Pembroke Estate Office, Dublin* (Dublin, 1891), pp 11–13.

18. *Register of Kilmainham*, C. McNeill (ed.), (Dublin, 1932), pp 138–41.

19. For the identification of Ballyhoge, see Colfer, *Arrogant trespass*, pp 200–3.

20. For early Anglo-Norman settlement in county Wexford, see Colfer, *Arrogant trespass*, pp 35–45.

21. Orpen, *Normans*, i, pp 387–93, for an account of the Gaelic districts of Uí Chennselaig mentioned in Strongbow's grants.

22. *A. F. M.* ii, p. 1167.

23. *Expugnatio*, p. 185.

24. K. Nicholls, 'Land of the Leinstermen' in *Peritia*, iii (1984), pp 556–8; C. A. Empey, 'The Norman period' in W. Nolan (ed.), *Tipperary: history and society* (Dublin, 1985), p. 73.

25. J. Otway-Ruthven, 'Parochial development in the rural deanery of Skreen' in *R. S. A. I. Jn.*, xciv (1964), pp 111-22.

26. *Expugnatio*, p. 99; Otway-Ruthven, 'Parochial development', pp 111–22.

27. *Song*, ll. 2902-3.

28. Orpen, *Normans*, i, p. 373.

29. *Song*, ll. 2157-9.

30. *Song*, ll. 2741 -6.

31. *Pembroke deeds*, pp 11–12.

32. Moore, *Arch. inventory*, no. 955.

33. Orpen, *Normans*, i, p. 374.

34. G. H. Orpen, 'Charters of earl Richard Marshal of the forests of Ross and Taghmon' in *R. S. A. I. Jn.*, lxiv (1934), pp 54–63.

35. Gardiner and Ryan, *Soils of Co. Wexford*, soil suitability map.

36. Otway-Ruthven, 'Norman settlement', pp 77–9.

37. Otway-Ruthven, 'Norman settlement', p. 76.

38. For a full description of Strongbow's land-grants, see Colfer, *Arrogant trespass*, pp 39–45.

39. Davies, *Domination and conquest*, p. 11; Song, ll, 2734-50.

40. C. Ó Crualaoich (pers. comm.): Duffry derives from Dufair<Dubhthair from an early compound of dubh and tír, which is attested in Irish literature. Internally, bh was lost in the early modern Irish period in most dialects including Wexford. Where it was retained, it usually rendered anglicised v and not f. The cluster bhth in Irish regularly developed to /f/ which is exactly what is found in Duffry.

41. Orpen, *Normans*, i, p. 231.

42. E. Curtis (ed.), *Calendar of Ormond deeds 1172–1350* (Dublin, 1932), p. 11.

43. M.-T. Flanagan, 'Mac Dalbaig, a Leinster chieftain' in *R. S. A. I. Jn.*, cxi (1981), p. 11.

44. *Song*, ll. 3034–5; 3060–69.

45. *Song*, ll. 3070–1.

46. J. C. Ward, 'Fashions in monastic endowment: the foundations of the Clare family' in *Jn. Eccles. Hist.*, xxxii (1981), p. 445.

47. *Chartularies of St Mary's Abbey, Dublin*, J. T. Gilbert, (ed.), 2 v. (London, 1884), ii, pp 151–4.; Hore, *Wexford*, iii, pp 33–44.

48. For a fuller account, see Colfer, *Arrogant trespass*, pp 184–94.

49. *Song*, l. 3072.

50. S. Ó Dubhagáin and G. Ó hUidrín, *Topographical poems*, J. O'Donovan (ed.), (Dublin, 1962), p. 91.

51. E. St John Brooks (ed.), 'Unpublished charters relating to Ireland 1177–82, from the archives of the city of Exeter' in *R. I. A. Proc.*, xxxxiii, C (1935–7), no. 24; *Ormond deeds*, i, no. 111.

52. *Register of the hospital of St John the Baptist Dublin*, E. St John Brooks (ed.), (Dublin, 1936), nos. 360–1.

53. *Chartul. St Mary's*, i, p. 112.

54. Brooks, E. St John (ed.), *Knights' fees in counties Wexford, Carlow and Kilkenny* (Dublin, 1950), p. 31.

55. *Song*, l. 3082; Brooks, *Knights' fees*, p. 146

56. *Calendar of patent rolls, Ireland, James 1*, p. 327.

57. *Song*, l. 3114.

58. *Topographical poems*, p. 91.

59. Brooks, *Knights' fees*, pp 96–99.

60. Brooks, *Knights' fees*, p. 103.

61. Brooks, *Knights' fees*, pp 43–6.

62. *Song*, ll. 2185–90.

63. *Song*, ll. 2189–90, 2199–200.

64. *Expugnatio*, p. 80

65. D. Crouch, *William Marshal: court, career and chivalry in the Angevin empire 1147–1219* (London, 1990), p. 79.

66. Orpen, *Normans*, ii, p. 207.

67. For a full account, see Colfer, *Arrogant trespass*, pp 185–94.

68. Otway-Ruthven, *Medieval Ireland*, p. 186.

69. Brooks, *Knights' fees*, pp 119–27.

70. Colfer, *Arrogant trespass*, pp 94–96.

71. P. H. Hore, 'The barony of Forth' in *The Past*, i, p. 20.

72. Orpen, *Normans*, i, p. 393; *Cal. i. p. m.*, iv, p. 307.

73. Colfer, *Arrogant trespass*, pp 98–102.

74. M. T. Flanagan, 'An early Anglo-Norman charter of Hervey de Montmorency' in M. Meek (ed.), *The modern traveller to our past: festschrift in honour of Ann Hamlin* (Dublin, 2006), pp 232–42.

75. Colfer, *Arrogant trespass*, pp 96–7.

76. Brooks, *Knights' fees*, p. 96.

77. Crouch, *Marshal*, pp 80, 138.

78. Brooks, *Knights' fees*, p. 96.

79. Brooks, *Knights' fees*, pp 10, 37, 115.

80. G. Dehaene, 'Medieval rural settlement beside Duncormick motte, Co. Wexford' in C. Corlett and M. Potterton (eds.), *Rural settlement in medieval Ireland* (Dublin, 2009), pp 59–65.

81. Brooks, *Knights' fees*, pp 21, 33–5, 108, 113.

82. J. H. Andrews, *Shapes of Ireland: maps and their makers 1564–1839* (Dublin, 1997), p. 60.

83. The origin of the placename Baginbun is not known. It is possibly a combination of Irish and Norse as there are other Norse placenames in the vicinity. The 'bag' element could derive from the Norse 'bec', a beak, which would describe the headland. 'Bun' could be from the Irish 'bun', bottom or mouth of a river. Alternatively, 'bun' might be a corruption of the Irish 'Bann', a river. Either one would roughly translate as 'The headland at the river mouth', an accurate description of this prominent topographical feature.

84. M. Hanmer, *The chronicle of Ireland* (Dublin, 1571), n. p. 272.

85. Davis, *The Normans and their myth*, p. 31.

THIRTEENTH-CENTURY CASTLES

1. Anderson, *Castles of Europe*, p. 47.

2. T. Barry, *The Archaeology of medieval Ireland* (London, 1987), pp 37–55; T. McNeill, *Castles in Ireland* (London, 1997), pp 56–74.

3. *Expugnatio*, p. 249.

4. *Expugnatio*, p. 55.

5. *Expugnatio*, p. 195.

6. M. Bloch, *Feudal society ii: social classes and political organisation* (London, 1962), pp 400–1.

7. Bloch, *Feudal society ii*, p. 301; Barry, *Arch. med. Ire.*, p. 37.

8. *La Tapisserie de Bayeux*, complete reproduction 1/7 (Ville de Bayeux), pp 19, 46.

9. Toy, *Castles*, pp 52–3.

10. Coulson, *Medieval castles*, pp 225–33.

11. *Cal. doc. Ire.*, i, nos. 2,4.

12. G. Orpen, 'Motes and Norman castles in Ireland' in *R. S. A. I. Jn.*, xxxvii (1907), pp 123–52; Orpen, *Normans*, ii, distribution map.

13. Barry, *Arch. med. Ire.*, pp 45–6; D. Twohig, 'Norman ringwork castles' in *Bull. G. S. I. H. S*, v (1978), pp 7–9.

14. *Song*, ll. 3222–5.

15. *Expugnatio*, p. 53.

16. *Expugnatio*, p. 81.

17. *Expugnatio*, p. 57.

18. K. O'Conor, 'A reinterpretation of the earthworks at Baginbun' in R. Kenyon and K. O'Conor (eds.), *The medieval castles of Ireland and Wales* (Dublin, 2003), pp 17–31.

19. *Cal. i. p. m.*, vi, p. 327.

20. Identification of mottes and ringwork castles is based on the following sources: Orpen, *Normans*, ii, distribution map of mottes; R. E. Glasscock and T. McNeill, 'Mottes in Ireland: a draft list' in *G. S. I. H. S. Bulletin*, iii (1972), p. 48; G. Stout et al., *Sites and monuments record county Wexford* (Dublin, 1987); Moore, *Arch. inventory*, pp 90–4; Barry, *Arch. med. Ire.*, pp 37–71; O. S. sheets county Wexford (1841) and field work. The placing of sites in a manorial context by reference to the historical record is an essential consideration, especially where identification is uncertain.

21. M. O'Flanagan (compiler), *Letters containing information relative to the antiquities of the county of Wexford collected during the progress of the Ordnance Survey in 1840*, 2 v. (Bray, 1933), i, p. 346.

22. O. S. Wexford, sheet 2 (1841).

23. T. Westropp, 'On Irish motes and early Norman castles' in *R. S. A. I. Jn.*, xxxiv (1907), p. 321; G. H. Kinahan, 'Sepulchral and other prehistoric relics, counties Wexford and Wicklow' in *R. I. A. Proc.*, xvi (1879-82), p. 154, where it is described as a moat with an adjoining triangular level space, known as 'the table of the moat', formerly surrounded by a fosse.

24. E. Culleton, *Early man in county Wexford 5000BC–300BC* (Dublin, 1984), p. 41.

25. R. Glasscock, 'Mottes in Ireland' in *Chateau-Gaillard*, vii (1975), p. 96.

26. *Ormond deeds*, i, no. 3.

27. Moore, *Arch. inventory*, no. 12, classes it as a tumulus; Stout (S. M. R., county Wexford, no. WX003–033) describes it as a motte.

28. Pers. comm. with local farmer.

29. *Expugnatio*, pp 171–3.

30. D. Sweetman, 'Archaeological excavations at Ferns castle, county Wexford' in *R. I. A. Proc.*, C, lxxix (1979), pp 217–45; *A. F. M.*, ii, p. 1161; Barry, *Arch. med. Ire.*, p. 49.

31. Moore, *Arch. inventory*, no. 1441.

32. Barry, *Arch. med. Ire.*, pp 52–3; Moore, *Arch. inventory*, no. 959.

33. Orpen, *Normans*, i, p. 129; I. Bennett, 'Ferrycarrig Ringwork' in *Wex. Hist. Soc. Jn.*, x (1985), pp 25–43.

34. Ó Duinnín, *Foclóir Gaeilge agus Béarla*, pp 170, 822.

35. O. S. map, Wexford, sheet 49 (1841).

36. Moore, *Arch. inventory*, no. 957.

37. Colfer, *Arrogant trespass*, pp 194–208.

38. Moore, *Arch. inventory*, no. 960.

39. T. Barry, *Medieval moated sites of south-east Ireland* (Oxford, 1977), p. 89; T. Westropp, 'Five large earthworks in the barony of Shelburne, county Wexford' in *R. S. A. I. Jn.*, xxxxviii (1917), pp 12–3.

40. Coulson, *Medieval castles*, p. 69.

41. Moore, *Arch. inventory*, no. 954.

42. Moore, *Arch. inventory*, nos. 951, 950.

43. Moore, *Arch. inventory*, no. 953.

44. *Song*, ll. 3038–43, 3052–3; p. xxi.

45. Moore, *Arch. inventory*, no. 948.

46. Brooks, *Knights' fees*, p. 137.

47. Hore, *Wexford*, vi, p. 593.

48. Hore, *Wexford*, vi, p. 337.

49. *Chartul. St Mary's*, ii, p. 99.

50. *Letter Book of Christ Church, Canterbury*, iii, p. 12.

51. Moore, *Arch. inventory*, no. 1450. Moore lists it as a possible motte, as the mound is only about 2m high. In a survey of Fethard Castle, it is described as the original earthwork castle (B. Murtagh, *Fethard Castle, Co. Wexford: an architectural and archaeological report* (1993), p. 2).

52. Hore, *Wexford*, iv, p. 312.

53. *Chartul. St Mary's*, ii, p. 154; Orpen, 'Forests of Ross and Taghmon', p. 55.

54. Moore, *Arch. inventory*, no. 953.

55. For its erection, see E. Culleton and W. Colfer, 'The Norman motte at Old Ross: method of construction' in *Old Wex. Soc. Jn.*, v (1975), pp 22–5.

56. Moore, *Arch. inventory*, no. 939.

57. Moore, *Arch. inventory*, no. 942.

58. K. Nicholls, 'Anglo-French Ireland and after' in *Peritia*, i (1982), p. 391.

59. The Barrys were recorded at Ardamine c. 1250 but were probably there before 1229 (*Reg. of the hosp. of St John the Baptist*, nos. 360–1). For a detailed description of Glascarrig motte, see C. Breen, 'An eroding earthwork castle in Wexford' in Manning (ed.), *From ringforts to fortified houses*, pp 65–74.

60. Moore, *Arch. inventory*, no. 946.

61. J. Lydon, 'Ireland in 1297: 'at peace after its manner' in J. Lydon (ed.), *Law and disorder in thirteenth-century Ireland: the Dublin parliament of 1297* (Dublin, 1997), pp 22–4.

62. Gardiner and Ryan, *Soils of county Wexford*, soil suitability map.

63. The fishery at Bannow, for example, was an important item in the manorial accounts (*38th Report of the deputy keeper of the public records of Ireland*, p. 41).

64. Simington (ed.), *Civil Survey*, p. 156.

65. Moore, *Arch. inventory*, nos. 970, 1084.

66. *Civil Survey*, p. 156; Moore, *Arch. inventory*, no. 1577.

67. Barry, *Arch. med. Ire.*, pp 84–93.

68. B. Colfer, *Wexford: a town and its landscape* (Cork, 2008), pp 64–79; *Arrogant trespass*, pp 173–6, 148.

69. Orpen, *Normans*, i, p. 373, citing *Gesta Henrici*, i, p. 30.

70. Pers. comm. Dr. Ned Culleton, earth scientist.

71. *Cal. doc. Ire.*, i, nos. 1030, 1269.

72. *Cal. doc. Ire.*, i, no. 1872.

73. *Cal. doc. Ire.*, ii, no. 1950.

74. Hore, *Wexford*, i, p. 2; *Chartul. St Mary's*, ii, p. 154.

75. Hore, *Wexford*, vi, p. 351.

76. Hore, *Wexford*, vi, p. 411.

77. H. Leask, *Irish castles and castellated houses* (Dundalk, 1941), p. 51.

78. McNeill, *Castles in Ireland*, p. 118.

79. B. Murtagh, 'The medieval castle of Enniscorthy' in C. Tóibín and C. Rafferty (eds.), *Enniscorthy: a history* (Wexford, 2010), p. 106.

80. Leask, *Irish castles*, p. 47.

81. K. O'Conor, 'The origins of Carlow castle' in *Arch.*

Ire., no. 41 (Autumn, 1997), pp 13–16. The castle was built on top of an earlier ringwork.

82. T. O'Keeffe and M. Coughlan, ''The chronology and formal affinities of the Ferns donjon, Co. Wexford' in J. Kenyon and K. O'Conor (eds.), *The medieval castle in Ireland and Wales* (Dublin, 2003), pp 133–48.

83. Down Survey Map (1655), N. L. I. Ms 725.

84. Hore, *Wexford*, v, p. 104.

85. *Cal. i. p. m.*, vi, p. 327.

86. Hore, *Wexford*, iii, p. 202.

87. *Calendar of the justiciary rolls, Ireland*, 3 v. (London, 1905–56), ii, p. 349.

88. *Cal. just. rolls Ire.*, ii., p. 347.

89. *Cal. doc. Ire.*, ii, no. 933.

90. Hore, *Wexford*, i, p. 16; ii, p. 206.

91. Hore, *Wexford*, v, p. 102.

92. Colfer, *Hook peninsula*, pp 84–91.

93. *Cal. doc. Ire.*, i, nos. 2811, 2872.

94. D. Hague and R. Christie, *Lighthouses: their architecture, history and archaeology* (Llandysul, 1975), p. 14.

95. Crouch, *William Marshal*, p. 51.

96. R. Avent, 'William Marshal's building works at Chepstow Castle' in Kenyon and O'Conor (eds.), *Medieval castle*, pp 50–71; T. E. McNeill, 'Squaring circles: flooring round towers in Wales and Ireland' in *ibid.*, pp 96–106.

97. Hore, *Wexford*, i, p. 219. Twelve medieval acres is equivalent to thirty statute acres (12ha); a similar acreage beside the tower is still referred to as 'the tower lands.'

98. T. C. D. Ms. 1209, no. 64; E. Hogan (ed.), *Description of Ireland in 1598* (Dublin, 1878), p. 57.

99. Colfer, *Hook peninsula*, pp 45–7.

100. D. Sweetman, 'The hall-house in Ireland' in Kenyon and O'Conor (eds.), *Medieval castle*, p. 128; Moore, *Arch. inventory*, no. 1495.

101. T. Barry, 'The defensive nature of Irish moated sites' in Kenyon and O'Conor (eds.), *Medieval castle*, pp 182–93.

102. McCullough and Mulvin, *Lost tradition*, p. 35.

103. Barry, *Medieval moated sites*, p. 103.

104. M. Tierney, 'Excavating feudalism? A medieval moated site at Carrowreagh, Co. Wexford' in C. Corlett and M. Potterton (eds.), *Rural settlement in medieval Ireland* (Dublin, 2009), pp 191–2.

105. Barry, 'Medieval moated sites', pp 88–90; Empey, 'Knocktopher', i, pp 334–5.

106. The archaeological evidence is summarised in Barry, *Arch. med. Ire.*, pp 85–95.

107. G. Fegan, 'Discovery and excavation of a medieval moated site at Coolamurry, Co. Wexford' in Corlett and Potterton (eds.), *Rural settlement*, pp 91–108.

108. *Chartul. St Mary's*, ii, p. 154.

109. Hore, *Wexford*, i, pp 26-34.

110. B. Colfer, 'In search of the barricade and ditch of Ballyconnor, county Wexford' in *Arch. Ire.*, xxxvi (1996), pp 16-19.

111. The mapping of moated sites is based on Moore, *Arch. inventory*, pp 95–114; T. Barry 'Medieval moated sites of county Wexford' in *Wex. Hist. Soc. Jn.* vi (1977), pp 5–17.

FERNS CASTLE

1. Culleton, *Celtic and early Christian Wexford*, pp 49, 159, 188.

2. *A. F. M.*, ii, p. 1161.

3. *Calendar of the ancient deeds and muniments preserved in the Pembroke Estate Office, Dublin* (Dublin, 1891), pp 11–12.

4. *Chronica Roger de Hoveden*, W. Stubbs (ed.), 4 v. (London, 1868–71), ii, p. 134.

5. *Expugnatio*, pp 171–3.

6. D. Sweetman, *The medieval castles of Ireland* (Cork, 1999), pp 39–40.

7. *Cal. doc. Ire.*, i, no. 1872.

8. *Cal. doc. Ire.*, ii, no. 1950.

9. K. O'Conor, 'The origins of Carlow castle' in *Arch. Ire.*, ii, no. 3 (1997), pp 13–16.

10. Leask, *Irish castles*, p. 27; Sweetman, *Medieval castles*, p. 77.

11. Toy, *Castles*, pp 83, 90.

12. Leask, *Irish castles*, pp 49–50; McNeill, *Castles in Ireland*, p. 118; O'Keeffe and Coughlan, 'Ferns donjon', p. 147; Sweetman, *Medieval castles*, p. 78.

13. Sweetman, *Medieval castles*, pp 77–8; 81–2.

14. Orpen, *Normans*, iii, pp 79–110.

15. Colfer, *Arrogant trespass*, pp 223–7.

16. Sweetman, *Medieval castles*, pp 78, 82.

17. Hore, *Wexford*, vi, p. 20.

18. Sweetman, 'Archaeological excavations', p. 240.

19. Leask, *Irish castles*, p. 50; Sweetman, *Medieval castles*, p. 81; O'Keeffe and Coughlan, 'Ferns donjon', pp 138–42.

20. Colfer, *Arrogant trespass*, pp 223–38.

21. *Cal. doc. Ire.*, iv, no. 306.

22. *Cal. i. p. m.*, v, p. 22.

23. *Cal. i. p. m.*, vi, p. 326.

24. Hore, *Wexford*, vi, pp 3–80.

25. Sweetman, 'Excavations', p. 241.

26. J. F. Lydon, 'Richard II's expedition to Ireland' in *R. S. A. I. Jn.*, xciii (1963), pp 135–49.

27. Hore, *Wexford*, vi, pp 24–5.

28. Hore, *Wexford*, vi, pp 18–21.

29. Hore, *Wexford*, vi, p. 28.

30. J. Lydon, *The making of Ireland* (London, 1998), pp 153–62.

31. H. Goff, 'English conquest of an Irish barony: the changing patterns of land ownership in the barony of Scarawalsh 1540–1640' in Whelan (ed.), *Wexford*, pp 122–49.

THE SHIFTING FRONTIER

1. Flanagan, *Irish society*, pp 108–11; Nicholls, *Gaelic and Gaelicised Ireland*, pp 170–1.

2. Orpen, *Normans*, iii, p. 291.

3. Colfer, *Arrogant trespass*, pp 71–82.

4. Smyth, *Celtic Leinster*, pp 107–17; Nicholls, 'Land of the Leinstermen', pp 540–2.

5. J. Lydon, 'The impact of the Bruce invasion' in *N. H. I.*, ii, pp 3–37; A Gwynn, 'The Black Death in Ireland' in *Studies*, xxiv (1935), pp 25–42.

6. W. Smyth, 'Society and settlement in seventeenth-century Ireland: the evidence of the '1659 census'' in Smyth and Whelan (eds.), *Common ground*, p. 61.

7. Nicholls, 'Anglo-French Ireland', pp 371–2; Lydon, 'A land of war', p. 268.

8. Lydon, 'Expansion and consolidation', p. 169.

9. *Ann. Loch Cé*, i, p. 449; Frame, *Ireland and Britain 1170–1450*, pp 59–69.

10. Lydon, 'The years of crisis', p. 188.

11. For a general account of this period, see Lydon, 'A land of war', pp 256–62.

12. *Annals of Ireland by Friar John Clyn and Thady Dowling*, R. Butler (ed.), (Dublin, 1849), p. 9; *Chartularies of St Mary's Abbey, Dublin*, J. T. Gilbert (ed.), 2 v. (London, 1884), ii, p. 290.

13. *Cal doc. Ire.*, ii, nos. 1400, 1476. See Orpen, *Normans*, iv, pp 15–8; Otway-Ruthven, *History of medieval Ireland*, pp 201–2.

14. J. Lydon, 'An Irish army in Scotland, 1296' in *Irish Sword*, v (1961–2), pp 184–90.

15. *Cal. doc. Ire.*, iv, no. 306; *38th Rep. D. K. I.*, p. 42.

16. *Cal. doc. Ire.*, v, no. 3; *Chartul. St Mary's*, ii, p. 332.

17. Kenneth Nicholls, pers. comm.

18. For an account of rebel English in Ireland, see Lydon, 'The impact of the Bruce invasion' in *N. H. I.*, ii, pp 279–80.

19. *39th Rep. D. K. I.*, pp 31, 49; *Cal. pat. and cl. rolls*, p. 12, no. 9, p. 14, no 222.

20. *Cal. just. rolls*, iii, p. 237.

21. H. Schweitzer and C. McCutcheon, 'A medieval farmstead at Moneycross Upper, Co. Wexford' in Corlett and Potterton (eds.), *Rural settlement*, pp 175–88.

22. Hore, *Wexford*, i, p. 177.

23. J. Lydon, 'The hobelar: an Irish contribution to medieval warfare' in *Irish Sword*, v (1954), pp 12–16.

24. Hore, *Wexford*, i, pp 177–8.

25. *39th Rep. D. K. I.*, p. 49; Frame, *Ireland and Britain*, p. 268.

26. *Chartul. St Mary's*, ii, pp 291, 344, 358; Lydon, 'Bruce invasion', pp 275–302; R. Frame, 'The Bruces in Ireland 1315–18' in *I. H. S.*, xix (1974), pp 3–37.

27. *Chartul. St Mary's*, ii, p. 360; *Ann. Conn.*, p. 253.

28. *Chartul. St Mary's*, p. 345; *Ann. Conn.*, p. 241.

29. See map of Bruce's campaign in Lydon, 'Bruce invasion', p. 281.

30. Lydon, 'Bruce invasion', p. 294.

31. Lydon, 'Bruce invasion', pp 297–302.

32. Hore, *Wexford*, vi, p. 10.

33. *Calendar of inquisitions post mortem* (London, 1904–74), vi, pp 324–7.

34. *Chartul. St Mary's*, ii, pp 365–6.

35. *Chartul. St Mary's*, pp 372, 376.

36. *Clyn's ann.*, p. 35. For a general account of the Black Death, see Otway-Ruthven, *Med. Ire.*, pp 267–70; Gwynn, 'Black Death in Ireland', pp 25–42.

37. For example, in 1361 and 1370 (*Chartul. St Mary's*, ii, pp 395, 397).

38. Down, 'Colonial society and economy', pp 449–50.

39. T. Barry, ''The people of the country…dwell scattered': the pattern of rural settlement in Ireland in the later middle ages' in Bradley (ed.), *Settlement and society*, pp 345–60.

40. Hore, *Wexford*, i, p. 190.

41. Hore, *Wexford*, vi, p. 197.

42. K. Nicholls, The O'Dorans and the Kavanaghs (unpublished lecture); A. Kavanagh, *The Kavanagh kings of Leinster* (Dublin, 2003).

43. Hore, *Wexford*, v, p. 104; *Cal, i. p. m.*, vi, p. 327.

44. J. A. Watt, 'The Anglo-Irish colony under strain' in *N. H. I.*, ii, pp 374–6.

45. P. Connolly, 'The financing of English expeditions to Ireland 1361–76' in J. Lydon (ed.), *England and Ireland in the later middle ages* (Dublin, 1981), pp 104–21.

46. Hore, *Wexford*, vi, pp 13–4.

47. *Cal. of pipe rolls*, 39 Ed. III, N. A. I., 999/184/18.

48. *Statutes and Ordinances and Acts of Parliament of Ireland, King John to Henry V*, H. F. Berry (ed.) (Dublin, 1907), pp 330–69.

49. *Cal. pat. and cl. rolls*, p. 99, nos. 275, 277; p. 137, no. 215.

50. *Cal. pat. and cl. rolls*, p.10, nos. 31–2; p. 105, nos. 92, 104; p. 117, no. 51; p. 131, no. 42.

51. The town of Castledermot, for example, bought him off with a tribute of 84 marks (Otway-Ruthven, *Med. Ire.*, p. 324); For a general discussion, see Frame, 'Two kings', pp 168–75.

52. Hore, *Wexford*, v, p. 123; Otway-Ruthven, *Med. Ire.*, p. 316.

53. Hore, *Wexford*, v, p. 419.

54. J. Lydon, 'Richard II's expedition to Ireland' in *R. S. A. I. Jn.*, xciii (1963), pp 139–41.

55. *A. F. M.*, iv, p. 731.

56. Lydon, 'Richard II's expedition', p. 146.

57. *Cal. pat. and cl. rolls*, p. 152; *Pat. rolls Jas. I*, p. 401. The grant was made up of most of the land of the manors of Fernegenel, Offelimy, Schyrmal, Shillelagh, Gorey, Deeps and Lymalagoughe (perhaps Kilmakilloge).

58. Nicholls, 'Anglo-French Ireland', p. 395; Goff, 'Scarawalsh 1540–1640', pp 122–49.

59. *Cal. pat. and cl. rolls*, p. 169, no. 30, p. 193, no. 158.

60. Curtis, *Med. Ire.*, p. 293.

61. R. Roche, 'Forth and Bargy: a place apart' in Whelan (ed.), *Wexford*, p. 114; D. Ó Muirithe and T. Dolan, 'Poole's glossary' in *The Past*, xiii (1979), pp 1–69.

62. M. Stokes, 'Funeral custom in the baronies of Bargy and Forth in county Wexford' in *R. S. A. I. Jn.*, iv (1894), p. 384.

63. T. Jones-Hughes, 'Town and baile in Irish place-names' in N. Stephens and R. Glasscock (eds.), *Irish geographical studies in honour of E. Estyn Evans* (Belfast, 1970), p 247; Smyth, 'Society and settlement', p. 61.

64. The word 'pill', meaning a tidal river estuary, was borrowed from the Bristol Channel area.

SOCIAL TURMOIL

1. H. F. Hore and J. Graves, *The social state of the southern and eastern counties of Ireland in the sixteenth century* (Dublin, 1870).

2. Hore, *Wexford*, v, p. 139.

3. Nicholls, *Gaelic and Gaelicised Ireland*, pp 166–69.

4. H. F. Berry (ed.), *Statute Rolls of the parliament of Ireland reign of Henry VI* (Dublin, 1910), p. 361.

5. Hore and Graves, *Social state*, pp 3–7.

6. D. Edwards, *The Ormond Lordship in county Kilkenny 1515–1642* (Dublin, 2003), pp 58–60.

7. Hore, *Wexford*, iv, p. 324.

8. P. J. Duffy, 'The nature of the medieval frontier in Ireland' in *Studia Hib.*, 22–3 (1982–3), pp 21–38.

9. Hore, *Wexford*, vi, p. 210.

10. J. B. Sheppard (ed.), *Letter Book of Christ Church, Canterbury* (London, 1887–1889), iii, p. 12.

11. Coulson, *Castles in medieval society*, p. 74.

12. Murtagh, *Fethard Castle*; Waterman, 'Somerset and other foreign building stone', p. 73.

13. Hore, *Wexford*, vi, p. 213.

14. Hore, *Wexford*, vi, p. 352.

15. Lydon, 'Bruce invasion', pp 279–80.

16. B. Colfer, 'Medieval Enniscorthy: urban origins' in C. Tóibín and C. Rafferty (eds.), *Enniscorthy: a history* (Wexford, 2010), pp 83–100.

17. Hore, *Wexford*, vi, pp 358–9.

18. Hore, *Wexford*, vi, p. 359.

19. Hore and Graves, *Social state*, pp 43, 77, 139.

20. C. Ó Crualaoich, 'Some evidence in Tudor Fiants, Calendar of Patent Rolls and Inquisitions for Irish among families of Anglo-Norman descent in county Wexford between 1540 and 1640' in *The Past*, xxvi (2005), pp 80–102.

21. G. Griffiths, *Chronicles of the county Wexford to 1877* (Enniscorthy, 1877), p. 454.

22. C. Ó Crualaoich, *Place-names of County Wexford* (forthcoming).

23. Jones-Hughes, 'Town and baile', pp 244–58.

24. R. Stanihurst, *De rebus in Hibernia gestis* (Antwerp, 1584).

25. [H. Collier?] *Dialogue of Silvynne and Peregrynne* (1590s), ucc.ie/celt/published/E590001, pp 120–1.

26. Thomas Fleming, Catholic Archbishop of Dublin, to Cardinal Ludovisi 1626 in *Collectanea Hib.* (1967), p. 17.

27. Lydon, 'Richard II's expedition to Ireland', pp 135–49.

28. P. Slattery, 'Woodland management, timber and wood production and trade in Anglo-Norman Ireland' in *R. S. A. I. Jn.*, cxxxix (2009) pp 63–79.

29. Hore and Graves, *Social state*, p. 22.

30. H. Shields, 'The walling of New Ross: a thirteenth-century poem in French' in *Long Room*, xi–xvi (1976), pp 24–33.

31. For an account of medieval Ross, see Colfer, *Arrogant trespass*, pp 171–82.

32. Hore, *Wexford*, i, p. 210.

33. Hore and Graves, *Social state*, p. 32.

34. *Cal. pat. and cl. rolls*, p. 169.

35. Hore and Graves, *Social state*, pp 35–6, 44–6.

36. Hore and Graves, *Social state*, pp 37, 47.

37. Hore, *Wexford*, iv, pp 322–3.

38. J. P. Prendergast, 'Letter of Queen Elizabeth on the murder of Robert Browne of Mulrankin, 1572' in *Kilkenny and S. E. of Ireland Arch. Soc. Jn.*, x (1868), pp 16–7.

39. P. H. Hore, 'Barony of Forth' in *The Past*, i, (1920), pp 77–8.

40. Hore, *Wexford*, iii, p. 139.

41. G. A. Hayes-McCoy, 'The Tudor conquest' in Moody and Martin (eds.), *Course of Irish history*, pp 174–82.

42. Hore, *Wexford*, ii, pp 72–3.

43. G. Parker, *The military revolution: military innovation and the rise of the west 1500–1800* (Cambridge, 1996), pp 16–7.

44. Hore, *Wexford*, ii, pp 85, ff.

45. A. Lynch, *Tintern Abbey, Co. Wexford: Cistercian and Colcloughs. Excavations 1982–2007* (Dublin, 2010), pp 23–7; D. Brown and M. Baillie, 'Notes on the dating of the Tintern timbers' in *ibid.* pp 235–6.

46. Hore, *Wexford*, iii, pp 131–4. An account of the Etchingham and Chichester families is given in S. Pierce, *Dunbrody Abbey county Wexford: monastery and monument* (Arthurstown, 1994), pp 18–23.

47. Moore, *Arch. inventory*, no. 1622.

48. Hore, *Wexford*, iv, p. 293.

49. Information on the Loftus family is taken from A. P. W. Malcomson, 'A house divided: the Loftus family, earls and marquesses of Ely, c. 1600–1900' in D. Dickson and C. Ó Grada (eds.), *Refiguring Ireland: essays in honour of L. M. Cullen* (Dublin, 2003); J. Lodge, *The peerage of Ireland*, vii (London, 1789), pp 246–70; B. Burke, *Peerage and baronetage* (1906), pp 590–91.

50. Lodge, *Peerage*, p. 264.

51. Hore, *Wexford*, i, pp 97, 130; Edwards, *Ormond Lordship*, pp 100–1, 178.

52. Goff, 'Scarawalsh', p 127–8.

53. D. Edwards, 'The Butler revolt of 1569' in *I. H. S.*, xviii, no. 111 (1993), p. 250; Hore, *Wexford*, vi, pp 372–5.

54. Hore, *Wexford*, vi, pp 372, 411.

55. Hore, *Wexford*, vi, pp 365–70, 408.

56. Hore, *Wexford*, vi, pp 404–7.

57. Information on Wallop is based on Hore, *Wexford*, vi, pp 397–474; K. Whelan, 'Enniscorthy' in J. H. Andrews and A. Simms (eds.), *Irish Country Towns* (Cork, 1994), pp 123–34.

58. Hore, *Wexford*, vi, p. 402.

59. Hore, *Wexford*, vi, pp 598–9; P. Kerrigan, *Castles and fortifications in Ireland 1185–1945* (Cork, 1995), pp 102–3.

60. Hore, *Wexford*, v, pp 201–2.

61. Hore, *Wexford*, vi, p. 445.

62. Hore, *Wexford*, vi, p. 401.

63. G. Cavanaugh, Caomhánach Internecine Warfare (unpublished paper).

64. Goff, 'Scarawalsh' p. 135.

DEFENDING THE COLONY

1. Hore, *Wexford*, v, p. 419.

2. *38th Rep. D. K. I.*, p. 70; *Cal. just. rolls*, ii, p. 13. For a discussion on fortalices, see T. Barry, 'The last frontier: defence and settlement in medieval Ireland' in T. Barry, R. Frame and K. Simms (eds.), *Colony and settlement in medieval Ireland: essays presented to J. F. Lydon* (London, 1995), pp 224–5.

3. Coulson, *Castles in medieval society*, p. 59.

4. Hore, *Wexford*, v, p. 147; Jeffrey, *Castles*, p. 93; *Extents of Irish monastic possessions 1540–41*, N. B. White (ed.), (Dublin, 1943), p. 100.

5. Barry, 'The last frontier', p. 217.

6. N. A. I., RC 8/32, pp 90–1.

7. McCullough and Mulvin, *A lost tradition*, pp 37–41.

8. G. Perbellini, 'The polysemic meaning of the tower: from defence to symbol' in *Europa Nostra: towers and smaller castles* (The Hague, 2009), pp 7–18; D. Nicolle, *Crusader castles in the Holy Land: an illustrated history of the Crusader fortifications of the Middle East and Mediterranean* (New York, 2008), pp 150–4.

9. Barry, 'The last frontier', p. 221.

10. T. O'Keeffe, *Medieval Ireland: an archaeology* (Stroud, 2000), pp 51–3.

11. G. Stell, 'The Scottishness of Scottish towers' in *Towers and smaller castles*, pp 57–68.

12. Sweetman, 'The tower house in Ireland', p. 267; O'Keeffe, *Medieval Ireland*, p. 52.

13. D. Sweetman, 'The hall-house in Ireland' in Kenyon and O'Conor (eds.), *Medieval castle*, p. 131.

14. K. Simms: 'Native sources for Gaelic settlement' in P. J. Duffy, D. Edwards and E. FitzPatrick (eds.), *Gaelic Ireland: land, lordship and settlement* (Dublin, 2001), pp 246–67; R. Loeber, 'An architectural history of Gaelic castles and settlements 1370–1600' in Duffy, Edwards and FitzPatrick (eds.), *Gaelic Ireland*, pp 271–314.

15. J. Bradley and B. Murtagh, 'Brady's Castle, Thomastown, Co. Kilkenny: a fourteenth-century fortified town house' in Kenyon and O'Conor (eds.), *Medieval castle*, p. 215.

16. Hore, *Wexford*, v, pp 426–7.

17. Coulson, *Castles in medieval society*, pp 29, 68.

18. Leask, *Irish churches and monastic buildings*, iii, pp 19–21.

19. B. Murtagh, 'Kilmurry castle and other related sites in Slieverue parish' in J. Walsh (ed.), *Sliabh Rua: a history of its people and places* (Naas, 2001), pp 59–87.

20. Moore, *Arch. inventory*, nos. 1257, 1283, 1302, 1430, 1431, 1481.

21. Hore and Graves, *Social state*, p. 26.

22. Leask, *Irish castles*, p. 76.

23. Leask, *Irish castles*, pp 76–7.

24. Bradley and Murtagh, 'Brady's castle', pp 213–6.

25. Murphy and Potterton, *Dublin region*, pp 267–8.

26. Hore, *Wexford*, v, p. 412.

27. Referred to as the English Pale in 1552 (Hore and Graves, *Social state*, p. 25).

28. Hore, *Wexford*, v, pp 412–3.

29. Hore and Graves, *Social state*, p. 26.

30. H. F. Hore (ed.), 'Particulars relative to Wexford and the barony of Forth: by Colonel Solomon Richards, 1682' in *Kilkenny and S. E. of Ireland Arch. Soc. Jn.*, iv (1862), p. 86.

31. K. Whelan, 'An underground gentry? Catholic middlemen in eighteenth-century Ireland' in *Eighteenth-century Ireland/Iris an dá chultúr*, x (1995), pp 7–68.

32. C. Murphy, '"Immensity confined": Luke Waddinge, bishop of Ferns' in *Wex. Hist. Soc. Jn.'*, xii (1988–9), p. 7.

33. Attestation of Noblesse, A. O'Callaghan, bishop of Ferns, to the daughters of Sir Peter Redmond (1732), Windsor Palace, Stuart papers, v. clii, f. 126.

34. James Edward Devereux, *Address to the People of the County of Wexford on the Repeal of the Union* (Dublin, 1830), pp 4–5.

35. Hore and Graves, *Social state*, pp 39, 45.

36. Simington (ed.), *Civil Survey*; *Down Survey* maps; First edition Ordnance Survey maps (1841); Moore, *Arch. inventory*, pp 167–87; Jeffrey, *Castles of county Wexford*.

37. Hore, 'Forth', i, p. 73.

38. Colfer, *Hook peninsula*, pp 47–50; 55–61.

39. G. O'C. Redmond, History and pedigree of the Redmond family of Hook, County Wexford (1903), N. L. I., Microfilm pos. 9505, p. 139.

40. Moore, *Arch. inventory*, nos. 970, 1577; *Civil Survey*, p. 47.

41. T. Barry, 'The defensive nature of Irish moated sites' in Kenyon and O'Conor (eds.), *The medieval castle*, p. 190; Moore, *Arch. inventory*, no. 1084.

42. Ben Murtagh, conservation archaeologist, pers. comm.

43. 1641 Depositions, T. C. D. Ms 819, fol. 270r–272r.

FORTIFIED CHURCHES

1. H. Fabini, 'Documentary survey on the church castles, the fortified churches, and the peasant fortresses of the Saxons in Transilvania' in *Towers and smaller castles*, pp 157–60.

2. Leask, *Irish churches and monastic buildings*, iii (Dundalk, 1978), pp 19–40.

3. Moore, *Arch. inventory*, no. 1481.

4. D. M. Waterman, 'Somerset and other foreign building stone in medieval Ireland c. 1175–1400' in *U. J. A.*, xxxiii (1970), p. 73.

5. Colfer, *Wexford*, pp 176–7.

6. Moore, *Arch. inventory*, no. 1480; Colfer, *Wexford*, pp 52–7; 67–71.

7. Moore, *Arch. inventory*, p. no. 1430. For an account of Clonmines and Bannow, see Colfer, *Arrogant trespass*, pp 155–6.

8. Waterman, 'Somerset and other foreign building stone', p. 73; Bradley and Murtagh, 'Brady's Castle, Thomastown', p. 210.

9. Hore, *Wexford*, ii, p. 200.

10. Moore, *Arch. inventory*, no. 1431.

11. G. V. Du Noyer, 'Notes on some peculiarities in ancient and medieval Irish ecclesiastical architecture' in *Kilkenny and S.-E. of Ireland Arch. Soc. Jn.*, v, 1 (1864), pp 35-40.

12. Leask, *Irish churches and monastic building*, iii, p. 180.

13. P. A. Doyle, 'Given, in the church of St Nicholas, Clonmines' in *The Past*, iii (1925), pp 67–75.

14. Moore, *Arch. inventory*, no. 1424.

15. Leask, *Irish churches and monastic buildings*, ii, p. 146.

16. Du Noyer, 'Notes', pp 32–5.

17. Hore, *Wexford*, i, p. 77.

18. Moore, *Arch. inventory*, no. 1257.

19. Moore, *Arch. inventory*, no. 1302; Colfer, *Hook peninsula*, pp 47–50, 55–61.

TOWER-HOUSE ECONOMY

1. Barry, 'Defence and settlement in late medieval Ireland', pp 222–8.

2. McCullough and Mulvin, *A lost tradition*, p. 37.

3. Sweetman, 'Tower-house in Ireland', pp 269–76.

4. B. Colfer, 'The Redmonds of the Hall' in B. Browne (ed.), *The Wexford man: essays in honour of Nicky Furlong* (Dublin, 2007), p. 151.

5. Prendergast, 'Letter of Queen Elizabeth', p. 16.

6. Hore, *Wexford*, vi, pp 103–8.

7. Hore, *Wexford*, v, p. 412.

8. Loeber, 'An architectural history of Gaelic castles', p. 272.

9. J. Otway-Ruthven, 'The organisation of Anglo-Irish agriculture in the Middle Ages' in *R. S. A. I. Jn.*, v. viii, no. i (1951), p. 3.

10. Colfer, *Hook peninsula*, pp 130, 135, 149.

11. A. T. Lucas, 'Furze: a survey and history of its uses in Ireland' in *Béaloideas*, 23 (1958), pp 50–2.

12. Otway-Ruthven, 'Anglo-Irish agriculture', p. 3.

13. H. Jager, 'Land use in medieval Ireland: a review of the documentary sources' in *Ir. Econ. Soc. Hist.* x (1983), p. 64.

14. Murphy and Potterton, *Dublin region*, pp 287–320.

15. K. Down, 'Colonial society and economy' in *N. H. I.*, ii (Oxford, 1993), pp 484–9.

16. H. F. Hore (ed.), 'An account of the barony of Forth, in the county of Wexford, written at the close of the seventeenth century' in *Kilkenny and S.E. of Ireland Arch. Soc. Jn.*, iv (1862) p. 86. The 1682 account refers to seaweed as 'oure'; the same word (woar) is still used on the south Wexford coast.

17. J. Mills, 'Accounts of the earl of Norfolk's estates in Ireland 1279–94' in *R. S. A. I. Jn.*, xxii (1892), p. 56.

18. Hore (ed.), 'The barony of Forth', p. 60.

19. The distribution map of mills is compiled from: Simington, *Civil survey of county Wexford*; Down Survey parish maps; cartographic sources.

20. Colfer, *Wexford*, pp 80–2.

21. *38th Rep. D. K. I.*, p. 41.

22. Down, 'Colonial society and economy', pp 487–8.

23. Hore, *Wexford*, iv, pp 6–24.

24. C. Breen, *The Gaelic lordship of the O'Sullivan Beare: a landscape cultural history* (Dublin, 2005), pp 113–5; T. O'Neill, *Merchants and mariners in medieval Ireland* (Dublin, 1987), pp 30–43.

25. Murphy and Potterton, *Dublin region*, p. 397.

26. Hore, 'Forth', iii, p. 37.

27. Hore, 'Forth', i, p. 91.

28. A. Went, 'Sprat or white-fish weirs in Waterford Harbour' in *R. S. A. I. Jn.*, lxxxvii (1959), pp 91–108; *Irish monastic possessions*, ii, Dunbrody, pp 353–7.

29. *Extents of Irish monastic possessions*, p. 355.

30. T. Fanning, J. G. Hurst and J. M. Lewis, 'A mid seventeenth-century pottery group and other objects from Ballyhack Castle, Co. Wexford' in *R. I. A. Proc.*, 75 C (1975), pp 103–18.

31. G. Mac Niocaill, *Na buirgéisí* (Baile Átha Cliath, 1964), ii, p. 528.

32. Colfer, *Hook peninsula*, pp 150–7.

33. H. Leask, 'Slade castle, Co. Wexford' in *R. S. A. I. Jn.*, lxxxi (1951), pp 198–202.

34. Hore (ed.), 'Chorographic account', pp 454–61.

35. Colfer, *Hook peninsula*, pp 150–53.

36. Sweetman, 'Tower-house in Ireland', pp 269–76.

37. J. P. Prendergast, 'Three valuable documents' in *Kilkenny and S. E. of Ireland Arch. Soc. Jn*, x (1868), pp 15–16.

38. A. Empey, 'The Augustinian Priory of Kells' in M. Clyne (ed.), *Kells Priory, Co. Kilkenny: archaeological excavations* (Dublin, 2007), p. 6.

Box Page 140. O'Glynn Note Book, written Sept 7 A.D. 1585 (N. L. I., Ms 792 F. L.).

TOWER-HOUSE LANDSCAPES

1. C. Manning, 'Irish tower houses' in *Europa Nostra: Towers and smaller castles* (The Hague, 2009), pp 19–30.

2. R. Sherlock, 'The evolution of the tower house as a domestic space' in *R. I. A. Proc.*, 111C (2010), p. 119.

3. Sherlock, 'Evolution of the Irish tower house', p. 126.

4. Jeffrey, *Castles of Co. Wexford*; Simington (ed.), *Civil survey*; *Down Survey*, maps and notes; O. S., first edition (1841); Hore, *Wexford*, i–vi; Hore, 'Forth', i–iii; Hore and Graves, *Social state*; Moore, *Arch. inventory*, pp 165–87.

5. Due to insufficient evidence, tentative tower-house sites in the following townlands are not included: Ballyharty, Ballykelly, Ballynastraw, Borris, Buncarrig, Castlehayestown, Castlemoyle, Doonooney, Fannystown, St Margaret's, Yolegrew. There is no evidence for a tower house at Ballykeerogemore, which is described as a courtyard castle.

6. 'Extensive': most of four walls and internal features surviving; 'Substantial': walls and internal features partially surviving (sometimes incorporated in a later building); 'Fragmentary': any identifiable surviving part of a tower house (sometimes incorporated in a later

building).

7. Survey of the lands of the Duke of Albemarle, 1669, Huntington Library, HAM, Box 78.

8. Edwards estate map, N. A. I., 1082/3, 1/22 x.

9. Lewis, *Topog. Dict.*, ii, p. 332.

10. W. Wilde, *Beauties of the Boyne and Blackwater* (Dublin, 1849), p. 107.

11. L. Gernon, 'A discourse of Ireland, anno 1620', www.ucc.ie/celt/published/E630001/

12. Colfer, *Arrogant trespass*, pp 131–5 and appendix 3.

13. Stanihurst, *De rebus in Hibernia gestis*, pp 32–4.

14. Colfer, *Arrogant trespass*, pp 135–82 and appendix 4.

15. Hore, *Wexford*, i, pp 150–60.

16. Hore (ed.), 'Chorographic account', pp 453–4.

17. Colfer, *Hook peninsula*, pp 42–65.

18. Colfer, *Hook peninsula*, p. 56.

19. *Irish monastic possessions*, ii, pp 100–3, 209, 353–63.

20. G. Mac Niocaill, *Na Mánaigh Liath in Éirinn 1142, c. 1600* (Baile Átha Cliath, 1959), pp 45–8.

21. Fr. Colmcille, *The story of Mellifont* (Dublin, 1958), pp xxiv–xxxiv; Stalley, *Cistercians*, p. 20.

22. Sweetman, *Medieval castles of Ireland*, pp 95–6; Sweetman, 'The hall-house in Ireland' in Kenyon and O'Conor (eds.), *Medieval castle*, p. 128.

23. Hore, *Wexford*, iv, pp 275–7.

24. *Irish monastic possessions*, ii, Dunbrody, pp 358–63; Tintern, pp 358–63; Kilcloggan, pp 100–3.

25. J. Burtchaell, 'The south Kilkenny farm villages' in Smyth and Whelan (eds.), *Common ground*, pp 110–23.

26. Hore, *Wexford*, iii, p. 106; Moore, *Arch. inventory*, no. 1583.

27. Moore, *Arch. inventory*, nos. 1503, 1539.

28. Moore, *Arch. inventory*, pp 170–83; nos. 1512, 1553, 1554, 1572; Jeffrey, *Castles*, pp 166–7.

29. *Irish monastic possessions*, pp 100–3.

30. Colfer, 'The Redmonds', p. 149.

31. Colfer, *Hook peninsula*, pp 118–20.

32. A. Gwynn and R. N. Hadcock, *Medieval religious houses Ireland* (Dublin, 1970), p. 199.

33 Hore (ed.), 'Particulars relative to Wexford and the barony of Forth' , pp 87–8.

34. Hore (ed.), 'An account of the barony of Forth', p. 62.

TOWER-HOUSE ARCHITECTURE AND TYPOLOGY

1. D. Sweetman, 'The tower houses of county Louth' in *Towers and smaller castles*, p. 31.

2. O'Keeffe, *Medieval Ireland*, p. 44; McNeill, *Castles in Ireland*, pp 173–4.

3. Sweetman, *Medieval castles*, p. 137; 'Origin and development of the tower house' in *Medieval Ireland: the Barrystown lectures*, p. 269.

4. R. Sherlock, 'The evolution of the tower house as a domestic space' in *R. I. A. Proc.*, 111C (2010), pp 119–31.

5. J. O'Callaghan, 'The castle of the Deeps' in *Old Wex. Soc. Jn.*, ii (1969), pp 26–38; Moore, *Arch. inventory*, no. 1522.

6. Leask, *Irish castles*, p. 82.

7. Sweetman, 'Origin and development of the tower house', p. 273.

8. Leask, *Irish castles*, p. 86.

9. M. E. McKenna, 'Evidence for the use of timber in medieval tower houses: a regional study in Lecale and Tipperary' in *U. J. A.*, xlvii (1984), p. 172.

10. Sweetman, *Medieval castles*, p. 142.

11. Hore, *Wexford*, iii, p. 242.

12. Sweetman, *Medieval castles*, pp 158–9.

13. Sweetman, *Medieval castles*, pp 137, 149.

14. Parker, *The military revolution*, pp 16–7; 160.

15. Hore, *Wexford*, vi, pp 18–21.

16. P. Kerrigan, *Castles and fortifications in Ireland* (Cork, 1995), pp 1, 18.

17. F. Moryson, *Containing his ten years of travel through the twelve dominions of Germany, Bohmerland, Switzerland, Netherland, Denmark, Poland, Italy, Turky, France, England, Scotland and Ireland* (London, 1617), iii, bk. 2, p. 74.

18. Stanihurst, *De rebus in Hibernia gestis*, pp 32–3.

19. Du Noyer collection, R. I. A.

20. Wakeman collection, R. I. A.

21. Moore, *Arch. inventory*, no. 1546.

22. Albemarle papers, quoted in R. Loeber, 'New light on Co. Wexford architecture and estates in the seventeenth century' in *Wex. Hist. Soc. Jn.* xii (1988–89), pp 66–71.

23. Hore (ed.), 'Account of the barony of Forth', p. 72.

24. Simington, *Civil survey*; Down survey notes; Hore, 'Forth', iii, p. 46; Jeffrey, *Castles*.

25. Edwards estate maps, Ballyhire, county Wexford; N. A. I. 1082/3, 1/22 x.

26. Fortunately, the tower at Lingstown was recorded before its collapse. J. O'Callaghan, 'Fortified houses of the sixteenth century in south Wexford' in *Wex. Hist. Soc. Jn.*, viii (1980–1), p. 6.

27. Moore, *Arch. inventory*, no. 1501.

28. K. A. Browne, 'Sixteenth-century stone at Ballyconnor, Co. Wexford' in *R. S. A. I. Jn.*, vii, 2 (1937), pp 298–9.

29. Moore, *Arch. inventory*, nos. 1549, 1564; Leask, 'Slade castle', pp 198–201.

30. Sweetman, *Medieval castles*, p. 183.

31. O'Callaghan, 'Fortified houses', p. 11.

32. Moore, *Arch. inventory*, nos 1530, 1542.

33. Moore, *Arch. inventory*, no. 1553.

34. Barry, *Archaeology of medieval Ireland*, p. 186.

35. Stanihurst, *De rebus in Hibernia gestis*, pp 32–3.

36. McCullough and Mulvin, *Lost tradition*, p. 40.

37. Moore, *Arch. inventory*, nos. 1434, 1501, 1520, 1535, 1548, 1553, 1556.

38. Hore (ed.), 'Account of the barony of Forth', p. 62.

39. Moore, *Arch. inventory*, no. 1506.

40. Loeber, 'New light on Co. Wexford architecture', p. 68.

41. Moore, *Arch. inventory*, nos. 1508, 1530, 1542.

FORTIFIED HALL-HOUSES

1. Sweetman, 'The hall-house in Ireland', p. 129; O'Callaghan, 'Fortified houses', p. 1.

2. McCullough and Mulvin, *Lost tradition*, p. 41.

3. O'Callaghan, 'Fortified houses', p. 25.

4. Moore, *Arch. inventory*, nos 1560, 1558, 1562, 1561.

5. J. M. F. French, 'Proceedings and papers' in *R. S. A. I. Jn.*, ix, no. 79 (1889), pp 83–6; Moore, *Arch. inventory*, no. 1496; Lewis, *Topog. dict.*, i, p. 8.

6. Moore, *Arch. inventory*, no. 1560; O'Callaghan, 'Fortified houses', pp 26–32.

7. Moore, *Arch. inventory*, no. 1558; O'Callaghan, 'Fortified houses', pp 35–9.

8. Moore, *Arch. inventory*, no. 1561; O'Callaghan, 'Fortified houses', pp 22–6.

9. Wakeman collection, R. I. A.; Du Noyer collection, R. S. A. I.

10. Moore, *Arch. inventory*, no. 1562; O'Callaghan, 'Fortified houses', pp 33–4.

11. Du Noyer collection, R. I. A.

12. Moore, *Arch. inventory*, no. 1619.

ENDGAME

1. Sweetman, *Medieval castles*, pp 150–65.

2. Kerrigan, *Castles and fortifications*, pp 3–6.

3. Colfer, *Wexford*, p. 91; Colfer, *Hook peninsula* pp 106–13.

4. G. A. Hayes-McCoy, 'The Tudor conquest' in Moody and Martin (eds.), *The course of Irish history*, pp 183–7.

5. G. A. Hayes-McCoy, 'Tudor conquest and counter-reformation 1571–1603' in *N. H. I.*, iii (Oxford, 1976), pp 115–37.

6. Hore, *Wexford*, vi, pp 445–9; H. Goff, 'English conquest of an Irish barony', pp 133–5.

7. W. Brereton, *Travels of Sir William Brereton in Ireland, 1635*, ucc.ie/celt/published/E630001, pp 388–9.

8. A. Clarke, 'Pacification, plantation, and the Catholic question 1603–23' in *N. H. I.*, iii, pp 187–242.

9. Moore, *Arch. inventory*, nos 1435, 1623, 1630.

10. Clarke, 'Pacification, plantation and the Catholic question', pp 187–203.

11. For details of the Wexford plantation, see Goff, 'English conquest of an Irish barony', pp 136–49.

12. R. Loeber and M. Stouthamer, 'The lost architecture of the Wexford plantation' in Whelan (ed.), *Wexford*, pp 173–200; Moore, *Arch. inventory*, pp 188–90.

13. Moore, *Arch. inventory*, no. 1622.

14. W. J. Smyth, *Map-making, landscapes and memory: a geography of colonial and early modern Ireland* (Cork, 2006), pp 421–50.

15. J. Mannion, 'Colonial beginnings: Lord Baltimore's Irish experience' in *Wex. Hist. Soc. Jn.*, xx (2004–5), pp 1–44.

16. Goff, 'English conquest of an Irish barony', pp 122–49.

17. P. Lenihan, *Confederate Catholics at war* (Cork, 2001); J. Lydon, *The making of Ireland* (London, 1998), pp 163–96.

18. M. Ó Siochrú, *Confederate Ireland 1642–1649: a constitutional and political analysis* (Dublin, 1999).

19. Smyth, *Map-making, landscapes and memory*, p. 458; Lenihan, *Confederate Catholics*, p. 49.

20. J. Ohlmeyer, 'The Dunkirk of Ireland': Wexford privateers during the 1640s' in *Wex. Hist. Soc. Jn.*, xii (1988–89), pp 23–49; N. Furlong, 'Life in Wexford port 1600-1800' in Whelan (ed.), *Wexford*, pp 150–72.

21. Griffiths, *Chronicles*, pp 29–30; Petty's map, 1685; the fort was still in existence in 1795 (Hore, *Wexford*, v, p. 54.

22. Hore, *Wexford*, pp 254–7.

23. For a comprehensive account of the 1641 Rebellion in county Wexford, see J. McHugh, "For our owne defence': Catholic insurrection in Wexford 1641–2' in B. Mac Cuarta (ed.), *Reshaping Ireland 1550–1700: colonization and its consequences* (Dublin, 2011), pp 214–40. For a list of the tower house gentry who played a prominent part in the Rebellion, see K. Whelan, 'A list of those from County Wexford implicated in the 1641 Rebellion' in *The Past*, xvii (1990), pp 15-42.

24. Colfer, *Hook peninsula*, pp 92–101. A detailed analysis of the Confederate siege of Duncannon Fort is given in Lenihan, *Confederate Catholics*, pp 40–4; 178–89.

25. An account of the attack on Tintern is given in Hore, *Wexford*, ii, pp 133–44.

26. J. Ohlmeyer, 'A failed revolution' in J. Ohlmeyer (ed.), *Ireland from independence to occupation* (Cambridge, 1995), p. 1; See also Lenihan, *Confederate Catholics*, pp 221–9.

27. N. Canny, 'Early modern Ireland c. 1500–1700' in R. Foster (ed.), *The Oxford illustrated history of Ireland* (Oxford, 1989), p. 146.

28. Ohlmeyer, 'The Dunkirk of Ireland', p. 29.

29. Hore, *Wexford*, vi, pp 122, 491, 495.

30. Hore, *Wexford*, v, pp 285–7.

31. Hore, *Wexford*, v, p. 291.

32. Colfer, *Wexford*, pp 95–9.

33. Hore, *Wexford*, i, pp 319–27.

34. Smyth, *Map-making, landscapes and memory*, pp 103–165.

35. Simington, *Civil Survey*; Down Survey maps (1655), N. L. I., Ms. 725.

36. Hore, 'An account of the barony of Forth', p. 72.

37. For an analysis of eighteenth-century Ireland, see K. Whelan, *The tree of liberty* (Cork, 1996). The dispersal of Wexford families is mapped in K. Whelan, *Fellowship of freedom* (Cork, 1998), p. 18.

38. J. Duffy (ed.) *The historical works of the Right Rev. Nicholas French, D.D., Bishop of Ferns*, 2 v. (Dublin, 1846).

39. E. Hay, *History of the insurrection in county Wexford A.D. 1798* (Dublin, 1803), pp ii–iii.

40. E. Bowen, *Bowen's Court* and *Seven winters: memories of a Dublin childhood* (Dublin, 1984), p. xvi.

41. Maps of the lordships and manors of Loftus Hall in the county of Wexford, 1771, N.L.I., Ms., 4153, p. 6.

42. McCullough, *Palimpsest*, p. 55.

43. D. Rowe and E. Scallan, *Houses of Wexford* (Whitegate, 2004), nos. 337, 450.

44. Valuation survey of the Ely estate in county Wexford, 1872, N. L. I., Ms 4170.

LEGACY

1. J. C. Scott, *The art of not being governed: an anarchist history of upland south-east Asia* (Yale, 2010).

2. T. B. Barry, 'The archaeology of the tower house in late medieval Ireland' in H. Anderson and J. Weinberg (eds.), *The study of medieval archaeology* (Stockholm, 1993), pp 211–17.

3. L. M. Cullen, *The emergence of modern Ireland* (Dublin, 1983), pp 26–9.

4. J. Andrews, 'Landmarks in early Wexford cartography' in Whelan (ed.), *Wexford*, p. 453.

5. Rowe and Scallan, *Houses of Wexford*, nos 337, 615, 547, 450.

6. Hore (ed.), 'Account of the barony of Forth', p. 54.

7. Davis, *Normans and their myth*, pp 131–2.

8. M.-T. Flanagan, 'Strategies of distinction: defining nations in medieval Ireland' in H. Tsurushima (ed.), *Nations in medieval Britain* (Donington, 2010), p. 116.

9. *Expugnatio*, p. 80

10. Hore, *Wexford*, iii, p. 64.

11. E. St John Brooks, 'An unpublished charter of Raymond le Gros' in *R. S. A. I. Jn.*, lxix (1939), pp 167–9.

12. Flanagan, 'Defining nations' p. 116.

13. Flanagan, 'Defining nations', pp 113–4.

14. Flanagan, 'Defining nations', pp 104–5.

15. P. Connolly, 'The enactments of the 1297 parliament' in Lydon (ed.), *Law and disorder*, pp 158–60.

16. J. A. Watt, 'The Anglo-Irish colony under strain' in *N. H. I.*, ii, pp 386–90.

17. Hore and Graves, *Social state*, pp 5, 24–7; Hore (ed.), 'Account of the barony of Forth', p. 59.

18. G. Keating, *The history of Ireland* (1634). http://www.exclassics.com

19. B. Cunningham, 'Geoffrey Keating' in *Dictionary of Irish biography* (Cambridge, 2009), p. 7.

20. E. Malins and P. Bowe, *Irish gardens and demesnes from 1830* (London, 1980).

21. J. Williams, *Companion Guide to architecture in Ireland 1837–1921* (Dublin, 1994).

22. R. Foster, *W. B. Yeats: a life, II, the arch-poet, 1915–1939* (Oxford, 2003), pp 84–5.

23. *W. B. Yeats: the poems*, D. Albright (ed.), (London, 1992), p. 633.

24. Flanagan, 'Defining nations', pp 116–7.

25. E. Curtis, *A history of medieval Ireland* (London, 1923).

26. Hore and Graves, *Social state*, p. 3.

FIGURE SOURCES AND ATTRIBUTIONS
Unless specifically attributed, all maps and diagrams in this volume are by the author.

Fig. 6, p. 5 After E. Culleton, *Celtic and Early Christian Ireland* (Dublin, 1999), p. 23.

Fig. 7, p. 5 After E. Culleton, *Celtic and Early Christian Ireland* (Dublin, 1999), p. 24.

Fig. 3, p. 10 From F. Aalen, K. Whelan and M. Stout (eds.), *Atlas of the Irish rural landscape*, second edition, (Cork, 2011), p. 35.

Fig. 6, p. 12 From Aalen, Whelan and Stout (eds.), *Atlas*, p. 44.

Fig. 8, p. 12 After Aalen, Whelan and Stout (eds.), *Atlas*, p. 51; Culleton, *Celtic and Early Christian Ireland*, pp 203–19.

Fig. 12, p. 14 After E. Roesdhal, *The Vikings* (London, 1987), pp xx–xxi.

Fig. 14, p. 22 After A. Simms, 'Core and periphery in medieval Europe: the Irish experience in a wider context' in W. Smyth and K. Whelan (eds.), *Common ground* (Cork, 1986), p. 23.

Fig. 3, p. 38 After I. Bennett, 'Preliminary archaeological excavations at Ferrycarrig ringwork, Newtown td., Co. Wexford' in *Wex. Hist. Soc. Jn.*, x (1985), p. 34.

Fig. 28F, p. 57 After O'Callaghan, 'Fortified houses', p. 4.

Fig. 8, p. 63 From D. Sweetman, *Medieval castles* (Cork, 1999), p. 78.

Fig. 3, p. 71 After C. Corlett and M. Potterton (eds.), *Rural settlement in medieval Ireland* (Dublin, 2009), p. 182.

Fig. 8, p. 76 After Black Death website www.insecta-inspecta.com/fleas/bdeath/Black

Fig. 16, p. 81 After W. Smyth, 'Society and settlement in seventeenth-century Ireland: the evidence of the 1659 'census' in Smyth and Whelan (eds.), *Common ground*, p. 61.

Fig. 17, p. 81 From Aalen, Whelan and Stout (eds.), *Atlas*, p. 57.

Fig. 4, p. 86 After Aalen, Whelan and Stout (eds.), *Atlas*, p. 60.

Figs. 8 and 9 p. 90 Based on C. Ó Crualaoich, 'Some evidence in Tudor *Fiants, Calendar of Patent Rolls and Inquisitions*, for Irish among families of Anglo-Norman descent in county Wexford between 1540 and 1640' in *The Past*, xxvi (2005), pp 80–102.

Fig. 14, p. 95 After Andrews, *Shapes of Ireland*, p. 34.

Fig. 2, p. 106 From D. Nicolle, *Crusader castles in the Holy Land* (Oxford, 2008), p. 153.

Fig. 2, p. 119 From Colfer, *Wexford*, p. 55.

Fig. 4C, p. 119 After G. V. Du Noyer, 'Notes on some peculiarities in ancient and medieval Irish ecclesiastical architecture' in *Kilkenny and S. E. Ire. Arch. Soc. Jn.*, v (1864), p. 37.

Fig. 7, p. 121 After Du Noyer in R. I. A. collection.

Fig. 10, p. 131 Based on Simington, *Civil Survey*.

Fig. 15H, p. 135 After Phelim Manning for OPW.

Fig. 17, p. 137 After W. Went, 'Sprat or white-fish weirs in Waterford Harbour' in *R. S. A. I. Jn.*, lxxxvii (1959), pp 91–108.

Fig. 2, p. 142 From Aalen, Whelan and Stout (eds.), *Atlas*. p. 60.

(Sections) Fig. 3, p. 143 Ballyhack after Phelim Manning for DEHLG; Burnchurch and Clara after Leask, *Irish castles*, pp 89, 83; Rathmacknee after Leask, 'Rathmacknee castle' p. 41; Slade after Leask, 'Slade castle', p. 200; Ballymalis, Bourchier's Castle, Fiddaun after Sweetman, *Medieval castles of Ireland*, pp 170, 142, 163; Pallas after Salter, *Castles and stronghouses*, p. 39. Ballyportry, Loughmoe, Mooghane, Shallee after McCullough and Mulvin, *Lost tradition*, p. 38; Roodstown after Sherlock, 'Evolution of the Irish tower house', p. 120.

Fig. 14, p. 151 Based on J. Andrews, 'Landmarks in early Wexford cartography' in Whelan (ed.), *Wexford*, p. 453.

(Plans) Fig. 9, p. 169 Rathmacknee after Leask, 'Rathmacknee Castle', p. 40; Slade after Leask, 'Slade Castle' p. 199; Barrystown, Clonmines, Killiane after Salter, *Castles and stronghouses*, pp 49, 78, 66; Ballyhack after Phelim Manning for OPW; Ferrycarrig after Hore, *Wexford*, v, p. 25; Danescastle after Du Noyer in R. I. A. collection; Adamstown after O'Callaghan, 'Fortified houses', p. 32; Deeps after O'Callaghan, 'Castle of the Deeps', p. 35.

Fig. 20, p. 174, After Leask, 'Slade Castle', p. 198.

(Bawns) Fig. 43, p. 185 Killiane after Salter, *Castles and stronghouses*, p. 66; Rathmacknee after Leask 'Rathmacknee Castle', p. 39.

(Fortified Houses) Fig. 20, p. 195 Coolhull after R. Stapleton, OPW; Bargy after O'Callaghan 'Fortified houses', p. 37; Dungulph after O'Callaghan, 'Fortified houses'.

Fig. 12, p. 205 Based on R. Loeber and M. Stouthamer-Loeber, 'The lost architecture of the Wexford plantation' in Whelan (ed.), *Wexford*, pp 173–200.

Fig. 26, p. 211 From K. Whelan, *Fellowship of freedom* (Cork, 1998), p. 18. (with additions).

Fig. 3, p. 217 From Aalen, Whelan and Stout (eds), *Atlas*, p. 260.

Fig. 8, p. 221 From Aalen, Whelan and Stout (eds), *Atlas*. p. 310.

Fig, 13, p. 223 After D. Miller, 'Mass attendance in Ireland in 1834' in S. Brown and D. Miller (eds.), *Piety and power in Ireland 1760–1960* (Notre Dame, 2000), p. 173.

BIBLIOGRAPHY

Manuscript sources

Attestation of Noblesse, A. O'Callaghan, bishop of Ferns, to the daughters of Sir Peter Redmond (1732), Windsor Palace, Stuart papers, v. clii, f. 126.

1641 Depositions, T. C. D., Ms 819, fol. 270r–272r (1641.tcd.ie).

Down Survey maps (1655), N. L. I. Ms. 725.

Du Noyer collection, R. S. A. I.

Du Noyer collection, R. I. A.

Dunbrody Estate Maps, 1803, N. L. I. 21.F.20.

Edwards estate maps, Ballyhire, county Wexford (1727); N. A. I. 1082/3, 1/22 x.

First edition Ordnance Survey maps (1841).

Jobson's map of Waterford Harbour, 1591, T. C. D. Ms. 1209, no. 64.

Redmond, G. O'C., History and pedigree of the Redmond family of Hook, Co. Wexford (1903), N. L. I., microfilm Pos 9505.

Survey of the lands of the Duke of Albemarle, 1669, HAM Box 78, Huntington Library, San Marino, California.

Valuation survey of the Ely estate in County Wexford, 1872, N. L. I., Ms 4170.

Wakeman collection, R. I. A.

Printed Primary Sources

'Accounts of the earl of Norfolk's estates in Ireland 1279–94', J. Mills (ed.) in *R. S. A. I. Jn.*, xxii (1892), pp 50–62.

Annals of Ireland by Friar John Clyn and Thady Dowling, R. Butler (ed.), (Dublin, 1849).

Annals of the kingdom of Ireland by the four masters, J. O'Donovan (ed.), 7 v. (Dublin, 1848–51).

Annals of Ulster, W. M. Hennessy and B. MacCarthy (eds.), 4 v. (Dublin, 1887–1901).

Brereton, W., *Travels of Sir William Brereton in Ireland, 1635*, www.ucc.ie/celt/published/E630001.

Brooks, E. St. John (ed.), *Knights' fees in counties Wexford, Carlow and Kilkenny* (Dublin, 1950).

Calendar of the justiciary rolls, Ireland, vols. i (1295–1303); ii (1305–7), (ed.) J. Mills (Dublin, 1905-14); iii (1308-14), (ed.) M. C. Griffith (Dublin, 1956).

Calendar of ancient deeds and muniments preserved in the Pembroke Estate Office, Dublin (Dublin, 1891).

Calendar of documents relating to Ireland, H. S. Sweetman (ed.), 5 v. (London, 1875–86).

Calendar of Inquisitions post mortem (London, 1904-74).

Calendar of Ormond deeds 1172–1350, E. Curtis (ed.), 6 v. (Dublin, 1932–1943).

Calendar of patent and close rolls, E. Tresham (ed.), (Dublin, 1828).

Chartularies of St Mary's Abbey, Dublin, J. T. Gilbert (ed.), 2 v. (London, 1884).

Chronica Roger de Hoveden, W. Stubbs (ed.), 4 v. (London, 1868–1871).

The Civil Survey of the county of Wexford, R. C. Simington (ed.), (Dublin, 1953).

Devereux, J. E., *Address to the people of the County of Wexford on the repeal of the Union* (Dublin, 1830).

Dictionary of Irish biography (Cambridge, 2009).

Expugnatio Hibernica, the conquest of Ireland, by Gerald de Barry, A. B. Scott and F. X. Martin (eds.), (Dublin, 1978).

Extents of Irish monastic possessions, N. B. White (ed.), (Dublin, 1943).

Flanagan, M.-T., 'An early Anglo-Norman charter of Hervey de Montmorency' in M. Meek (ed.), *The modern traveller to our past: festscrift in honour of Ann Hamlin* (Dublin, 2006), pp 232–42.

French, N., *The historical works of the Right Rev. Nicholas French, D.D., Bishop of Ferns*, J. Duffy (ed.), 2 v. (Dublin, 1846).

Gerald of Wales, *The history and topography of Ireland* (Harmondsworth, 1982).

Gernon, L., *A discourse of Ireland, anno 1620*. www.ucc.ie/celt/published/E62000.1.

Griffiths, G., *Chronicles of the county Wexford to 1877* (Enniscorthy, 1877).

Gwynn, A. and R. N. Hadcock, *Medieval religious houses Ireland* (Dublin, 1970).

Hanmer, M., *The chronicle of Ireland* (Dublin, 1571).

Hay, E., *History of the insurrection in county Wexford A.D. 1798* (Dublin, 1803).

Hogan, E., *Description of Ireland in 1598* (Dublin, 1878).

Hore, H. F. and J. Graves (eds.), *The social state of the southern and eastern counties of Ireland in the sixteenth century* (Dublin, 1870).

Hore, H. F. (ed.), 'Particulars relative to Wexford and the barony of Forth: by Colonel Solomon Richards, 1682' in *Kilkenny and S. E. of Ireland Arch. Soc. Jn.*, iv (1862), pp 84–92.

Hore, H. F. (ed.), 'An account of the barony of Forth, in the county of Wexford, written at the close of the seventeenth century' in *Kilkenny and S. E. of Ireland Arch. Soc. Jn.*, iv (1862), pp 53–84.

Hore, H. F. (ed.), 'A chorographic account of the southern part of the county of Wexford, written anno 1684: by Robert Leigh, esq., of Rosegarland, in that county' in *R. S. A. I. Jn.*, v (1858–1859), pp 451–67.

Hore, P. H., *History of the town and county of Wexford*, 6 v. (London, 1900–1911).

Hore, P. H., 'The barony of Forth' in *The Past*, i (1920), pp 62–106; ii (1921), pp 38–99; iii (1925), pp 9–40; iv (1949), pp 13–59.

Keating, Geoffrey (Céitinn, Seathrún), *Foras feasa ar Éirinn* (1634).

Lewis, S., *A topographical dictionary of Ireland*, 2 v. (London, 1837).

Meadows, H., *Alphabetical index to the townlands and towns of the county of Wexford* (Dublin, 1861).

Moryson, F., *A history of Ireland from the year 1599 to 1603* (Dublin, 1735), www.ucc.ie/celt..

Nicholls, K., The O'Dorans and the Kavanaghs (unpublished lecture).

Ó Crualaoich, C., 'Some evidence in Tudor Fiants, Calendar of Patent Rolls and Inquisitions for Irish among families of Anglo-Norman descent in county Wexford between 1540 and 1640' in *The Past*, xxvi (2005), pp 80–102.

Ó Dubhagáin, S. and G. Ó hUidrín, *Topographical poems*, J. O'Donovan (ed.), (Dublin, 1962).

Letter books of Christ Church, Canterbury, J. B. Sheppard (ed.), 3 v. (London, 1887–1889).

Letters containing information relative to the antiquities of the county of Wexford collected during the progress of the Ordnance Survey in 1840, M. O'Flanagan (compiler), 2 v. (Bray, 1933).

Orpen, G. (ed.), 'Charters of earl Richard Marshal of the forests of Ross and Taghmon' in *R. S. A. I. Jn.*, lxiv (1934), pp 54–63.

Prendergast, J. P., 'Three valuable documents' in *Kilkenny and S. E. of Ireland Arch. Soc. Jn.*, x (1868), pp 15–16.

Prendergast, J. P., 'Letter of Queen Elizabeth on the murder of Robert Browne of Mulrankin, 1572' in *Kilkenny and S. E. of Ireland Arch. Soc. Jn.*, x (1868), pp 16–17.

Register of the hospital of St John the Baptist, Dublin, E. St. John Brooks (ed.), (Dublin, 1936).

Registrum de Kilmainham, 1326–50, C. McNeill (ed.), (Dublin, 1932).

Sites and monument record, county Wexford (S. M. R.), G. Stout, *et al.* (Dublin, 1987).

Shields, H., 'The walling of New Ross: a thirteenth-century poem in French' in *Long Room*, xi–xvi (1976), pp 24–33.

Song of Dermot and the earl, G. Orpen (ed.), (Oxford, 1892).

Stanihurst, R., *De rebus in Hibernia gestis* (Antwerp, 1584).

Statute Rolls of the parliament of Ireland reign of Henry VI, H. F. Berry (ed.), (Dublin, 1910).

'Unpublished charters relating to Ireland 1177–82, from the archives of the city of Exeter', E. St. John Brooks (ed.) in *R. I. A. Proc.*, xxxxiii, C (1935-7), pp 313–66.

Wilson, D. M., *The Bayeux tapestry* (London, 2004).

Secondary works

Aalen, F. H. A., K. Whelan and M. Stout (eds.), *Atlas of the Irish rural landscape*, second edition (Cork, 2011).

Anderson, W., *Castles of Europe* (London, 1980).

Andrews, J., 'The Irish surveys of Robert Lythe' in *Imago Mundi*, xix (1965), pp 22–31.

Andrews, J., 'Landmarks in early Wexford cartography' in Whelan (ed.), *Wexford*, pp 447–66.

Andrews, J. *Shapes of Ireland: maps and their makers 1564–1839* (Dublin, 1997).

Avent, R., 'William Marshal's building works at Chepstow Castle' in Kenyon and O'Conor (eds.), *Medieval castle*, pp 50–71.

Barry, T., *Medieval moated sites of south-east Ireland* (Oxford, 1977).

Barry, T., 'Medieval moated sites of county Wexford' in *Wex. Hist. Soc. Jn.*, vi (1976–1977), pp 5–17.

Barry, T, 'The people of the country...dwell scattered': the pattern of rural settlement in Ireland in the later middle ages' in J. Bradley (ed.), *Settlement and society in medieval Ireland* (Kilkenny, 1988), pp 345–60.

Barry, T., 'The archaeology of the tower house in late medieval Ireland' in

H. Anderson and J. Weinberg (eds.), *The study of medieval archaeology* (Stockholm, 1993), pp 211–17.

Barry, T., R. Frame and K. Simms (eds.), *Colony and settlement in medieval Ireland: essays presented to J. F. Lydon* (London, 1995)

Barry, T., 'The last frontier: defence and settlement in medieval Ireland' in Barry, Frame and Simms (eds.), *Colony and frontier in medieval Ireland*, pp 217–28.

Barry, T., 'The defensive nature of Irish moated sites' in Kenyon and O'Conor (eds.), *Medieval castle*, pp 182–93.

Barry, T., 'The study of medieval Irish castles: a bibliographic survey' in *R. I. A. Proc.*, cviii (2008), pp 115–36.

Bartlett, R., *The making of Europe: conquest, colonisation and cultural change 950–1350* (Princeton, 1994).

Bartlett, R., *England under the Norman and Angevin kings* (Oxford, 2000).

Bennett, I., 'Preliminary archaeological excavations at Ferrycarrig ringwork, Newtown Td., Co. Wexford' in *Wex. Hist. Soc. Jn.*, x (1985), pp 25–43.

Bloch, M., *Feudal society*, 2 v. (London and New York, 1989).

Bowen, E., *Bowen's Court and Seven Winters: memories of a Dublin childhood* (Dublin, 1984).

Bradley, J. and B. Murtagh, 'Brady's Castle, Thomastown, Co. Kilkenny: a fourteenth-century fortified town house' in Kenyon and O'Conor (eds), *Medieval castle*, pp 194–216.

Breen, C., 'An eroding earthwork castle [Glascarrrig] in Wexford' in Manning (ed.), *From ringforts to fortified houses*, pp 65–74.

Breen, C., *The Gaelic lordship of the O'Sullivan Beare: a landscape cultural history* (Dublin, 2005).

Browne, B. (ed.), *The Wexford man: essays in honour of Nicky Furlong* (Dublin, 2007).

Browne, K. A., 'Heraldry: its history and its laws. With rubbing of the Whitty monument in the ruined church of Kilmore, Co. Wexford' in *The Past*, iii (1925), pp 79–85.

Browne, K. A., 'Sixteenth-century stone, commemorative of the Stafford family, at Ballyconnor, co. Wexford' in *R. S. A. I. Jn.*, vii (1937), pp 298–9.

Brown D. and M. Baillie, 'Notes on the dating of the Tintern timbers' in Lynch, *Tintern Abbey*, pp 235–6.

Burke, B., *Peerage and baronetage* (London, 1906), pp 590–91.

Burtchaell, J., 'The south Kilkenny farm villages' in Smyth and Whelan (eds.), *Common ground*, pp 110–23.

Butler, W. F. 'Confiscation in Irish history: the Plantation of Wexford' in *Studies*, iv (1915), pp 411–27.

Byrne, F. J., 'The trembling sod: Ireland in 1169' in *N. H. I.*, ii (Oxford, 1993), pp 1–42.

Cairns, C. T., *Irish tower houses: a county Tipperary case study* (Athlone, 1987).

Canny, N., 'Early modern Ireland c. 1500–1700' in R. Foster (ed.), *The Oxford illustrated history of Ireland* (Oxford, 1989), pp 104–60.

Cardini, F., 'The warrior and the knight' in J. Le Goff (ed.), *The medieval world* (London, 1990), pp 75–112.

Chibnell, M., *The Normans* (Oxford, 2000).

Clarke, A., 'Pacification, plantation and the Catholic question 1603–23' in *N. H. I.*, iii (Oxford, 1976), pp 187–242.

Colfer, B., 'In search of the barricade and ditch of Ballyconnor, county Wexford' in *Arch. Ire.*, xxxvi (1996), pp 16–19.

Colfer, B., *Arrogant trespass: Anglo-Norman Wexford 1169–1400* (Enniscorthy, 2002).

Colfer, B., *The Hook peninsula* (Cork, 2004).

Colfer, B., 'The Redmonds of the Hall' in Browne (ed.), *The Wexford man*, pp 147–58.

Colfer, B., *Wexford: a town and its landscape* (Cork, 2008).

Colfer, B., 'Medieval Enniscorthy: urban origins' in C. Tóibín and C. Rafferty (eds.), *Enniscorthy: a history* (Wexford, 2010), pp 83–100.

Colmcille, Fr., *The story of Mellifont* (Dublin, 1958).

Connolly, P., 'The financing of English expeditions to Ireland 1361–76' in J. Lydon (ed.), *England and Ireland in the later middle ages* (Dublin, 1981), pp 104–21.

Corlett, C. and M. Potterton (eds.), *Rural settlement in medieval Ireland* (Dublin, 2009).

Coulson, C., *Castles in medieval society* (Oxford, 2003).

Craig, M., *The architecture of Ireland from the earliest times to 1880* (Dublin, 1982).

Crouch, D., *William Marshal: court, career and chivalry in the Angevin empire 1147–1219* (London, 1990).

Cullen, L. M., *The emergence of modern Ireland 1600–1900* (Dublin, 1983).

Culleton, E. and W. Colfer, 'The Norman motte at Old Ross: method of construction' in *Old Wex. Soc. Jn.*, v (1975), pp 22–25.

Culleton, E., *The south Wexford landscape* (Dublin, 1980).

Culleton, E., *Early man in county Wexford 5000BC–300BC* (Dublin, 1984).

Culleton, E. (ed.), *Treasures of the landscape: County Wexford's rural heritage* (Wexford, 1994).

Culleton, E., *Celtic and Early Christian Wexford* (Dublin, 1999).

Curtis, E., 'Some further medieval seals out of the Ormond archives, including that of Donal Reagh MacMurrough Kavanagh, king of Leinster' in *R. S. A. I. Jn.*, vii (1937), pp 72–6.

Davis, R., *The Normans and their myth* (London, 1997).

Dehaene, G., 'Medieval rural settlement beside Duncormick motte, Co. Wexford' in Corlett and Potterton (eds.), *Rural settlement*, pp 59–66.

De Meulemeester, J. and K. O'Conor, 'Fortifications' in J. Graham-Campbell and M. Valor (eds.), *The archaeology of medieval Europe: eighth to twelfth centuries AD* (Aarhus, 2007), pp 316–41.

Ó Duinnín, P., *Foclóir Gaeilge agus Béarla* (Baile Átha Cliath, 1927).

Donnelly, C. J., 'A typological study of the tower houses of county Limerick' in *R. S. A. I. Jn.*, cxxix (1999), pp 19–39.

Doran L., 'Defending the sacred: from Crac de Chevalier to Aghavillier, a common thread' in *Hist. Ire.*, xv (2007), pp 15–19.

Down, K., 'Colonial society and economy' in *N. H. I.*, ii (Oxford, 1993), pp 484–9.

Doyle, P. A., 'Given, in the church of St Nicholas, Clonmines' in *The Past*, iii (1925), pp 67–75.

Duffy, P. J., 'The nature of the medieval frontier in Ireland' in *Studia Hib.*, xxii/xxiii (1983), pp 21–38.

Duffy, P. J., D. Edwards and E. FitzPatrick (eds.), *Gaelic Ireland: land, lordship and settlement* (Dublin, 2001).

Duffy, S., *Ireland in the Middle Ages* (Dublin, 1997).

Dunne, T. (ed.), *New Ross, Rossponte, Ros Mhic Treoin: an anthology celebrating 800 years* (Wexford, 2009).

Du Meulemeester, J. and K. O'Conor, 'Fortifications' in J. Graham-Campbell and M. Valor (eds.), *The archaeology of medieval Europe: eighth to twelfth centuries* (Aarhus, 2007), pp 316–41.

Du Noyer, G. V., 'Notes on some peculiarities in ancient and medieval Irish ecclesiastical architecture' in *Kilkenny and S. E. Ire. Arch. Soc. Jn.*, v (1864), pp 35–40.

Edwards, D., 'The Butler revolt of 1569' in *I. H. S.*, xviii, (1993), pp 228–55.

Edwards, D., *The Ormond Lordship in county Kilkenny 1515–1642: the rise and fall of Butler feudal power* (Dublin, 2003).

Empey, A., 'The Norman period' in W. Nolan (ed.), *Tipperary: history and society* (Dublin, 1985), pp 71–91.

Empey, A., 'The Augustinian Priory of Kells' in T. Fanning and M. Clyne (eds.), *Kells Priory, Co. Kilkenny: archaeological excavations* (Dublin, 2007), pp 1–12.

Fabini, H., 'Documentary survey on the church castles, the fortified churches, and the peasant fortresses of the Saxons in Transilvania' in *Europa Nostra: Towers and smaller castles* (The Hague, 2009), pp 157–60.

Fanning, T., J. G. Hurst and J. M. Lewis, 'A mid seventeenth-century pottery group and other objects from Ballyhack Castle, Co. Wexford' in *R. I. A. Proc.*, 75 C (1975), pp 103–18.

Fegan, G., 'Discovery and excavation of a medieval moated site at Coolamurry, Co. Wexford' in Corlett and Potterton (eds.), *Rural settlement*, pp 91–108.

Flanagan, M.-T., 'Mac Dalbaig, a Leinster chieftain' in *R. S. A. I. Jn.*, cxi (1981), pp 5–13.

Flanagan, M.-T., *Irish society, Anglo-Norman settlers, Angevin kingship* (Oxford, 1989).

Flanagan, M.-T., 'Strategies of lordship in pre-Norman and post-Norman Leinster' in *Anglo-Norman Studies*, xx (1998), p. 107–27.

Flanagan, M.-T., 'Defining nation in medieval Ireland' in H. Tsurushima (ed.), *Nations in medieval Britain* (Donington, 2010), pp 104-20.

Foley, T., 'Carnew Castle' in T. Condit and C. Corlett (eds.), *Above and beyond: essays in memory of Leo Swan* (Dublin, 2005), pp 423–34.

Frame, R., 'The Bruces in Ireland, 1315–8' in *I. H. S.*, xix (1974), pp 3–37.

French, J. M. F., 'Proceedings and papers' in *R. S. A. I. Jn.*, ix, (1889), pp 84–5.

Furlong, N., 'Life in Wexford port 1600-1800' in Whelan (ed.), *Wexford*, pp 150–72.

Furlong, N., *Diarmait: king of Leinster* (Cork, 2006).

Gardiner, M. and P. Ryan, *Soils of Co. Wexford* (Dublin, 1964).

Gillingham, J., 'The beginnings of English imperialism' in *Journal of Historical Sociology*, v (1992), pp 392–409.

Gillingham, J., 'Conquering the barbarians: war and chivalry in twelfth-century Britain' in *Haskins society journal: studies in medieval history*, iv (1993), pp 67–84.

Glasscock, R. and T. McNeill, 'Mottes in Ireland: a draft list' in *G. S. I .H. S. Bulletin*, iii (1972), 27–51.

Glasscock, R., 'Mottes in Ireland' in *Chateau-Gaillard*, vii (1975), pp 95–110.

Goff, H., 'English conquest of an Irish barony: the changing patterns of land ownership in the barony of Scarawalsh 1540–1640' in Whelan (ed.), *Wexford*, pp 122–49.

Goff, J. Le, (ed.), *The medieval world* (London, 1990).

Gwynn, A., 'The Black Death in Ireland' in *Studies*, xxiv (1935), pp 25–42.

Hayes-McCoy, G. A., 'The early history of guns in Ireland' in *Galway Arch. & Hist. Soc. Jn.*, xviii (1938), pp 43–65.

Hayes-McCoy, G. A., 'The Tudor conquest' in Moody and Martin (eds.), *Course of Irish history*, pp 174–88.

Hayes-McCoy, G. A., 'Tudor conquest and counter-reformation 1571–1603' in *N. H. I.*, iii (Oxford, 1976), pp 115–37.

Hogan, J., 'The trícha cét and related land measures', *R. I. A. Proc.*, xxxviii, C (1928–9), pp 148–235.

Hughes, K., 'The golden age of Early Christian Ireland' in Moody and Martin (eds.), *Course of Irish history*, pp 76–90.

Jager, H., 'Land use in medieval Ireland: a review of the documentary sources' in *Ir. Econ. Soc. Hist.* x (1983), pp 51–65.

Jeffrey, W., *The castles of county Wexford*, E. Culleton (ed.), (Wexford, 1979).

Jones-Hughes, T., 'Town and baile in Irish placenames' in N. Stephens and R. Glasscock (eds.), *Irish geographical studies in honour of E. Estyn Evans* (Belfast, 1970), pp 244–58.

Jordan, A., 'Date, chronology and evolution of the county Wexford tower house' in *Wex. Hist. Soc. Jn.*, xiii (1991), pp 30–82.

Kavanagh, A., *The Kavanagh kings of Leinster* (Dublin, 2003).

Kenyon, J. and K. O'Conor (eds.), *The medieval castle in Ireland and Wales* (Dublin, 2003).

Kerrigan, P., *Castles and fortifications in Ireland 1485–1945* (Cork, 1995).

Kinahan, G. H., 'Sepulchral and other prehistoric relics, counties Wexford and Wicklow' in *R. I. A. Proc.*, xvi (1879–82), pp 152–60.

Leask, H. G., 'Clara castle, county Kilkenny' in *R. S. A. I. Jn.*, lxvii (1937), pp 284–9.

Leask, H., *Irish castles and castellated houses* (Dundalk, 1977).

Leask, H., *Irish churches and monastic buildings*, 3 v. (Dundalk, 1977–8).

Leask, H., 'Slade castle, Co. Wexford' in *R. S. A. I. Jn.*, lxxxi (1951), pp 198–202.

Leask, H., 'Rathmacknee Castle, Co. Wexford' in *R. S. A. I. Jn.*, lxxxiii (1953), pp 37–45.

Lenihan, P., *Confederate Catholics at war* (Cork, 2001).

Lodge, J., *The peerage of Ireland* (London, 1789).

Loeber, R. and M. Stouthamer-Loeber, 'The lost architecture of the Wexford plantation' in Whelan (ed.), *Wexford*, pp 173–200.

Loeber, R., 'New light on Co. Wexford architecture and estates in the seventeenth century' in *Wex. Hist. Soc. Jn.* xii (1989), pp 66–71.

Loeber, R., *The geography and practice of English colonisation in Ireland from 1534 to 1609* (Athlone, 1991).

Loeber, R., 'An architectural history of Gaelic castles and settlement 1370–1600' in Duffy, Edwards and FitzPatrick (eds.), *Gaelic Ireland*, pp 271–314.

Lucas, A. T., 'Furze: a survey and history of its uses in Ireland' in *Béaloideas*, xxiii (1958), pp 1–204.

Lydon, J.,'The hobelar: an Irish contribution to medieval warfare' in *Irish Sword*, v (1954), pp 12–16.

Lydon, J., 'An Irish army in Scotland, 1296' in *Irish Sword*, v (1961–1962), pp 184–90.

Lydon, J., 'Richard II's expedition to Ireland' in *R. S. A. I. Jn.*, xciii (1963), pp 135–49.

Lydon, J., *The lordship of Ireland in the Middle Ages* (Dublin, 1972).

Lydon, J., 'Ireland in 1297: 'at peace after its manner' in J. Lydon (ed.), *Law and disorder in thirteenth-century Ireland: the Dublin parliament of 1297* (Dublin, 1997), pp 22–4.

Lydon, J., 'The impact of the Bruce invasion' in *N. H. I.*, ii, pp 275–302.

Lydon, J., *The making of Ireland* (London, 1998).

Lynch, A., *Tintern Abbey, Co. Wexford: Cistercian and Colcloughs. Excavations 1982–2007* (Dublin, 2010).

Lyttleton, J., Archaeological testing and excavation at Clohamon Castle, Castlequarter, Co. Wexford (Unpublished report, 2010).

Mac Niocaill, G., *Na Mánaigh Liath in Éirinn 1142–c.1600* (Baile Átha Cliath, 1959).

Mac Niocaill, G. *Na buirgéisí* (Baile Átha Cliath, 1964).

Malcomsom, A. P. W., 'A house divided: the Loftus family, earls and marquesses of Ely, *c.* 1600–1900' in D. Dickson and C. Ó Gráda (eds.), *Refiguring Ireland: essays in honour of L. M. Cullen* (Dublin, 2003), pp 184–224.

Manning, C. (ed.), *From ringforts to fortified houses: studies on castles and other monuments in honour of David Sweetman* (Bray, 2007).

Manning, C., 'Irish tower houses' in *Europa Nostra: Towers and smaller castles* (The Hague, 2009), pp 27–9.

Mannion, J., 'Colonial beginnings; Lord Baltimore's Irish experience' in P. Duffy and W. Nolan (eds.), *At the anvil; essays in honour of William J. Smyth* (Dublin, 2012), pp 151–85.

Martin, F. X., 'Diarmait Mac Murchada and the coming of the Anglo-Normans' in *N. H. I.*, ii, pp 43–66.

McCullough, N. and V. Mulvin, *A lost tradition: the nature of architecture in Ireland* (Dublin, 1987).

McCullough, N., *Palimpsest: change in Irish building traditions* (Dublin, 1994).

McHugh, J., 'The Kavanagh family of Clonmullen: a Gaelic Irish family' in *The Past*, xxiv (2003), pp 3–27.

McHugh, J., '"For our owne defence': Catholic insurrection in Wexford 1641–2' in B. Mac Cuarta (ed.), *Reshaping Ireland 1550–1700: colonization and consequences* (Dublin, 2011), pp 214–40.

McKenna, M. E., 'Evidence for the use of timber in medieval tower houses: a regional study in Lecale and Tipperary' in *U. J. A.*, 47 (1984), pp 171–4.

McNeill, T., *Castles in Ireland* (London, 1997).

McNeill, T., 'Squaring circles: flooring round towers in Wales and Ireland' in Kenyon and O'Conor (eds.), *Medieval castle*, pp 96–106.

Moody, T. W. and F. X. Martin (eds.), *The course of Irish history* (Cork, 1967).

Moore, M., *Archaeological inventory of county Wexford* (Dublin, 1996).

Mitchell, F. and M. Ryan, *Reading the Irish landscape* (Dublin, 1997).

Murphy, H., *Families of county Wexford* (Dublin, 1986).

Murtagh, B., *Fethard Castle, Co. Wexford: an architectural and archaeological report* (Fethard, 1993).

Murtagh, B., 'Kilmurry castle and other related sites in Slieverue parish' in J. Walsh (ed.), *Sliabh Rua: a history of its people and places* (Naas, 2001), pp 59–87.

Murtagh, B., 'The medieval castle of Enniscorthy' in C. Tóibín and C. Rafferty (eds.), *Enniscorthy: a history* (Wexford, 2010), pp 101–110.

Nicholls, K., 'Anglo-French Ireland and after' in *Peritia*, i (1982), pp 370–403.

Nicholls, K., *Gaelic and Gaelicised Ireland in the Middle Ages* (Dublin, 1983).

Nicholls, K., 'The land of the Leinstermen' in *Peritia*, iii (1984), pp 535–58.

Nicolle, D., *Crusader castles in the Holy Land: an illustrated history of the Crusader fortifications of the Middle East and Mediterranean* (New York, 2008).

Ní Dhonnchadha, M., 'Inis Teimle, between Uí Chennselaig and the Déissi' in *Peritia*, xvi (2002), pp 451–58.

O'Brien, R., P. Quinney and I. Russell, 'Preliminary report on the archaeological excavation and finds retrieval strategy of the Hiberno-Scandinavian site of Woodstown 6, County Waterford' in *Decies*, lxi (2005), pp 13–122.

O'Callaghan, J., 'The castle of the Deeps' in *Old Wex. Soc. Jn.*, ii (1969), pp 26–38.

O'Callaghan, J., 'Fortified houses of the sixteenth century in south Wexford' in *Wex. Hist. Soc. Jn.*, viii (1981), pp 1–51.

O'Conor, K., 'The origins of Carlow castle' in *Arch. Ire.*, xli (Autumn, 1997), pp 13–16.

O'Conor, K., *The archaeology of medieval rural settlement in Ireland* (Dublin, 1998).

O'Conor, K., 'A reinterpretation of the earthworks at Baginbun' in Kenyon and O'Conor (eds.), *Medieval castle*, pp 17–31.

Ó Corráin, D., *Ireland before the Normans* (Dublin, 1972).

Ó Corráin, D., 'Nationality and kingship in pre-Norman Ireland' in T. W. Moody (ed.), *Nationality and the pursuit of national independence* (Belfast, 1978), pp 1–35.

Ó Cróinín, D., *Early medieval Ireland* (Harlow, 1995).

Ó Crualaoich, C., *Logainmneacha na hÉireann iv: Contae Loch Garman/County Wexford* (forthcoming).

Ó Fiach, T., 'The beginnings of Christianity' in Moody and Martin (eds.), *Course of Irish history*, pp 61–75.

Ohlmeyer, J., 'The Dunkirk of Ireland': Wexford privateers during the

1640s' in *Wex. Hist. Soc. Jn.*, xii (1988–89), pp 23–49.

Ohlmeyer, J., 'A failed revolution' in J. Ohlmeyer (ed.), *Ireland from independence to occupation 1641–1660* (Cambridge, 1995), pp 1–23.

O'Keeffe, T., *Medieval Ireland: an archaeology* (Stroud, 2000).

O'Keeffe, T. and M. Coughlan, 'The chronology and formal affinities of the Ferns donjon, Co. Wexford' in Kenyon and O'Conor (eds.), *Medieval castle*, pp 133–48.

O'Keeffe, T., 'Barryscourt castle and the Irish tower house' in *Medieval Ireland: the Barrystown lectures* (Carrigtwohill, 2004), pp 3–31.

Ó Muirithe, D. and T. Dolan, 'Poole's glossary' in *The Past*, xiii (1979), pp 1–69.

O'Neill, T., *Merchants and mariners in medieval Ireland* (Dublin, 1987).

Orpen, G., 'Motes and Norman castles in Ireland' in *R. S. A. I. Jn.*, xxxvii (1907), pp 123–52.

Orpen, G., *Ireland under the Normans*, 4 v. (Oxford, 1911–1920).

Ó Siochrú, M., *Confederate Ireland 1642–1649: a constitutional and political analysis* (Dublin, 1999).

O'Sullivan, M. and L. Downey, 'Tower-houses and associated farming systems' in *Arch. Ire.*, xxiii, 2 (2009), pp 15–9.

Otway-Ruthven, J., 'The organisation of Anglo-Irish agriculture in the Middle Ages' in *R. S. A. I. Jn.*, lxxxi, no. 1 (1951), pp 1–13.

Otway-Ruthven, J., 'Parochial development in the rural deanery of Skreen' in *R. S. A. I. Jn.*, xciv (1964), pp 111–22.

Otway-Ruthven, J., *A history of medieval Ireland* (London, 1980).

Parker, G., *The military revolution: military innovation and the rise of the west 1500–1800* (Cambridge, 1996).

Perbellini, G. (ed.), *Europa Nostra bulletin 63: towers and smaller castles* (The Hague, 2009).

Perbellini, G., 'The polysemic meaning of the tower: from defence to symbol' in *Towers and smaller castles*, pp 7–18.

Perron, A., 'The face of the 'Pagan': portraits of religious deviance on the medieval periphery' in *Hist. Soc. Jn.*, ix, 4 (2009), pp 467–92.

Pierce, S., *Dunbrody Abbey, county Wexford: monastery and monument* (Arthurstown, 1994).

Murphy, C., ''Immensity confined': Luke Waddinge, bishop of Ferns' in *Wex. Hist. Soc. Jn.*, xii (1988–9), pp 5–22.

Raftery, B., 'The medieval settlement at Rathgall, County Wicklow' in Manning (ed.), *From ringforts to fortified houses*, pp 95–106.

Redmond, G. O'C., 'On a unique memorial slab to Sir Nicholas Devereux, knight, of Balmagir, Co. Wexford, and his wife, Dame Catherine Power of Coroghmore' in *R. S. A. I. Jn.*, viii (1888), pp 408–13.

Roche, R., *The Norman invasion of Ireland* (Tralee, 1970).

Roche, R., 'Forth and Bargy: a place apart' in Whelan (ed.), *Wexford*, pp 102–21.

Roesdahl, E., *The Vikings* (London, 1991).

Rowe, D. and E. Scallan, *Houses of Wexford* (Whitegate, 2004).

Rynne, C. and J. Lyttleton (eds.), *Plantation Ireland: settlement and material culture 1500–1700* (Dublin, 2009).

Salter, M., *Castles and stronghouses of Ireland* (Malvern, 1993).

Schweitzer, H. and C. McCutcheon, 'A medieval farmstead at Moneycross Upper, Co. Wexford' in Corlett and Potterton (eds.), *Rural settlement*, pp 175–88.

Scott, J. C., *The art of not being governed: an anarchist history of upland south-east Asia* (Yale, 2010).

Sherlock, R., 'Cross-cultural occurrences of mutations in tower-house architecture: evidence for cultural homogeneity in medieval Ireland' in *Jn. Ir. Arch.*, xv (2006), pp 73–92.

Sherlock, R., 'The evolution of the tower house as a domestic space' in *R. I. A. Proc.*, cxi C (2010), pp 115–40.

Simms, A., 'Core and periphery in medieval Europe: the Irish experience in a wider context' in Smyth and Whelan (eds.), *Common ground*, pp 22–40.

Simms, K., 'Native sources for Gaelic settlement: the house poems' in Duffy, Edwards and FitzPatrick (eds.), *Gaelic Ireland*, pp 246–67.

Simms. K., 'References to landscape and economy in Irish bardic poetry' in H. B. Clarke, J. Prunty and M. Hennessy (eds.), *Surveying Ireland's past:*

multidisciplinary essays in honour of Anngret Simms (Dublin, 2004), pp 145–68.

Slattery, P., 'Woodland management, timber and wood production and trade in Anglo-Norman Ireland *c.* 1170–*c.* 1350' in *R. S. A. I., Jn.*, cxxxix (2009), pp 63–79.

Smyth, W. and K. Whelan (eds.), *Common ground: essays on the historical geography of Ireland presented to T. Jones Hughes* (Cork, 1988).

Smyth, W., 'Society and settlement in seventeenth-century Ireland: the evidence of the 1659 'census'' in Smyth and Whelan (eds.), *Common ground*, pp 55–83.

Smyth, W. J., *Map-making, landscapes and memory: a geography of colonial and early modern Ireland* (Cork, 2006).

Stalley, R., *The Cistercian monasteries of Ireland* (Yale, 1987).

Stell, G., 'The Scottishness of Scottish towers' in *Towers and smaller castles*, pp 57–68.

Stokes, M., 'Funeral custom in the baronies of Bargy and Forth, county Wexford' in *R. S. A. I. Jn.*, iv (1894), pp 380–85.

Stout, M., *The Irish ringfort* (Dublin, 1997).

Stout, G. and M. Stout, 'Early landscapes: from pre-history to plantation' in Aalen, Whelan and Stout (eds.), *Atlas*, second edition, pp 31–65.

Stout, G. and M. Stout, *Newgrange* (Cork, 2008).

Sweetman, D., 'Archaeological excavations at Ferns castle, county Wexford' in *R. I. A. Proc.*, C, lxxix (1979), pp 217–45.

Sweetman, D., *The medieval castles of Ireland* (Cork, 1999).

Sweetman, D., 'The hall-house in Ireland' in Kenyon and O'Conor (eds.), *Medieval castle*, pp 121–32.

Sweetman, D., 'Origin and development of the tower house' in *Medieval Ireland: the Barrystown lectures* (Carrigtwohill, 2004), pp 257–88.

Sweetman, D., 'The tower houses of county Louth' in *Towers and smaller castles*, pp 31–4.

Tierney, M., 'Excavating feudalism? A medieval moated site at Carrowreagh, Co. Wexford' in Corlett and Potterton (eds.), *Rural settlement*, pp 189–200.

Toy, S., *Castles: their construction and history* (New York, 1985).

Twohig, D., 'Norman ringwork castles' in *Bull. G. S. I. H. S.*, v (1978), pp 7–9.

Wakeman, W. F., 'The castle of Adamstown and the Devereux monument. With a report by Rev J. F. M. French' in *Jn. Hist. and Arch. Assoc. Ire.*, ix (1889), pp 83–6.

Ward, J. C., 'Fashions in monastic endowment: the foundations of the Clare family' in *Jn. Eccles. Hist.*, xxxii (1981), pp 445–6.

Waterman, D. M., 'Somerset and other foreign building stone in medieval Ireland *c.* 1175–1400' in *U. J. A.*, xxxiii (1970), pp 63–75.

Watt, J. A., 'The Anglo-Irish colony under strain' in *N. H. I.*, ii, pp 374–6.

Went, A.,'Sprat or white-fish weirs in Waterford Harbour' in *R. S. A. I. Jn.*, lxxxvii (1959), pp 91–108.

Westropp, T., 'Five large earthworks in the barony of Shelburne, Co. Wexford' in *R. S. A. I. Jn.*, xlviii (1918), pp 1–18.

Westropp, T., 'On Irish motes and early Norman castles' in *R. S. A. I. Jn.*, xxxiv (1907), pp 1–18.

Whelan, K. (ed.), *Wexford: history and society* (Dublin, 1987).

Whelan, K., 'A list of those from County Wexford implicated in the 1641 Rebellion' in *The Past*, xvii (1990), pp 15–42.

Whelan, K., 'Enniscorthy' in J. H. Andrews and A. Simms (eds.) *Irish country towns* (Cork, 1994), pp 123–34.

Whelan, K., 'An underground gentry? Catholic middlemen in eighteenth-century Ireland' in *Eighteenth-century Ireland/Iris an dá chultúr*, x (1995), pp 7–68.

Whelan, K., *The tree of liberty* (Cork, 1996).

Whelan, K., *Fellowship of freedom* (Cork, 1998).

Wilde, W., *The beauties of the Boyne and Blackwater* (Dublin, 1849).

INDEX